CONSTRUCTIVE DISCONTENT IN EXECUTION

Creative Approaches to Technology and Management

CONSTRUCTIVE DISCONTENT IN EXECUTION

Creative Approaches to Technology and Management

Edited by

Sanjeev Bansal

Anita Venaik

Swati Upveja

Saritha S.

AAP | APPLE ACADEMIC PRESS

First edition published 2024

Apple Academic Press Inc.
1265 Goldenrod Circle, NE,
Palm Bay, FL 32905 USA

760 Laurentian Drive, Unit 19,
Burlington, ON L7N 0A4, CANADA

CRC Press
6000 Broken Sound Parkway NW,
Suite 300, Boca Raton, FL 33487-2742 USA

4 Park Square, Milton Park,
Abingdon, Oxon, OX14 4RN UK

Apple Academic Press exclusively co-publishes with CRC Press, an imprint of Taylor & Francis Group, LLC

Library and Archives Canada Cataloguing in Publication

Title: Constructive discontent in execution : creative approaches to technology and management / edited by Sanjeev Bansal, Anita Venaik, Swati Upveja, Saritha S.
Names: Bansal, Sanjeev, 1967- editor. | Venaik, Anita, editor. | Upveja, Swati, editor. | S., Saritha, editor.
Description: First edition. | Includes bibliographical references and index.
Identifiers: Canadiana (print) 2023018975X | Canadiana (ebook) 20230189873 | ISBN 9781774911754 (hardcover) | ISBN 9781774911761 (softcover) | ISBN 9781003314837 (ebook)
Subjects: LCSH: Technological innovations. | LCSH: Industrial management. | LCSH: Creative ability in business. | LCSH: Entrepreneurship.
Classification: LCC HD45 .C66 2023 | DDC 658.4/063—dc23

Library of Congress Cataloging-in-Publication Data

CIP data on file with US Library of Congress

ISBN: 978-1-77491-175-4 (hbk)
ISBN: 978-1-77491-176-1 (pbk)
ISBN: 978-1-00331-483-7 (ebk)

About the Editors

Prof. Sanjeev Bansal, PhD
Professor, Dean FMS and Director Amity Business School, Amity University, Noida, UP, India

Dr. Sanjeev Bansal is Dean of FMS & Director of Amity Business School, the first school of higher education of Amity University, established in 1995. In an acclaimed career spread over 31 years in teaching, research, and consultancy, he has been invited to be a part of several prestigious academic/ professional bodies. He has published 211 research papers, 44 books, and successfully guided 27 research scholars to produce works of immense educational impact. He is on boards of many national and international journals and has been honored with many awards. He has spearheaded numerous initiatives in the interest of his students, who are very close to his heart. With the help of his exceptional people skills, he has created a network of the corporate, alumni, students, and faculty members to work in synergy to take Amity Business School to unprecedented heights.

Prof. Anita Venaik, PhD, MSc (Comp. Sci.), MBA, PGDIM, PGDCA
Professor Information Technology, Head of General Management Department, ABS, Amity University, Noida, UP, India

Dr. Anita Venaik has over 25 years of work experience in industry and academia. She has worked in the corporate world at PCL and Coca Cola and joined academia in 1999. She is affiliated with the Amity Business School where she currently heads the General Management Department, where she been working as a teacher, trainer, and mentor to the students at various levels. She holds nine copyrights accepted by the Government of India and one patent that she filed during COVID-19 on "Internet of Things Based Ebola Virus Detection Among Masses." She has 10 national and two international book publications as an editor to her credit. Dr. Venaik has published papers in the top leading journals and publishing houses with 20 international and 15 national research papers to her credit as well as 12 case studies published with the Case Centre, UK. She is the content writer of MHRD E-Pathshala Project. She is the editor of biannual *Amity Journal of Energy and Environment Studies*.

Dr. Swati Upveja, PhD
Assistant Professor, ABS, Amity University, Noida, UP, India

Dr. Swati Upveja has over eight years of work experience in teaching and research and is currently Assistant Professor at Amity Business School, Amity University, India. Her areas of interest include macroeconomics, monetary economics, and quantitative techniques. She has been certified in the software package SPSS Statistics. She has presented papers at national conferences and attended various faculty development programs. She is a recipient of the Gargi Award given by the State Government of Rajasthan. Dr. Upveja completed her PhD in Development Economics under the research topic "Human Capital and Economic Growth in India: An Empirical Evidence." She was a silver medalist for her MA in Economics from Banasthali University.

Saritha S. MBA
Department of Management, Nehru Gram Bharati (Deemed to be University), Prayagraj, UP, India

Saritha S. has more than five years of teaching and seven years of research experiences at various institutes in India. She is currently affiliated with the Department of Management, Nehru Gram Bharati (Deemed to be University), Prayagraj, UP. India. She has supervised more than 30 postgraduate students for their final semester dissertation work. She is a member of many academic communities and has attended various seminars, webinars, and faculty development programs. She has received an Express of Gratitude from the United Institute of Technology, Prayagraj, for successfully organizing the 1st Young Manager Award, entitled "Inter-College PowerPoint Completion: Shifting Paradigm in Management: Issues and Challenges in the Global Era," 2010. Her research fields of interest are human resource management, employee welfare, and blockchain technology. She earned her BCom and MBA degrees from Kakatiya University, Warangal, Telangana, India.

Contents

Contributors

Sathiya Priya A.
Department of Computer Science, CMS College of Science & Commerce, Coimbatore, Tamil Nadu, India; E-mail: sathiyapriya1327@gmail.com

Sunmathi B.
Department of Computer Science, CMS College of Science & Commerce, Coimbatore, Tamil Nadu, India

Mubashir Majid Baba
Department of Management Studies, University of Kashmir, Jammu and Kashmir, India

Himank Bajpai
Assistant Key Account Manager, Easyrewardz IT Solutions, India; E-mail: bajpaihimank@gmail.com

Sanjeev Bansal
Amity Business School, Amity University, Noida, Uttar Pradesh, India

Ashok Chopra
Management and Commerce, Amity University, Dubai; E-mail: achopra@amityuniversity.ae

Ritesh Dwivedi
Amity Business School, Amity University, Noida, India

Harminder Kaur Gujral
Amity Business School, Amity University, Noida, Uttar Pradesh, India

Md. Ibrahim
School of Management Science, Apeejay Stya University, Sohna, Gurgaon, Haryana, India; E-mail: ibrahim.sbc123@gmail

Priyanka Kapoor Tandon
Department of Commerce, Avadh Girls' Degree College, Lucknow 226010, India

Shikha Kapoor
Amity International Business School, Amity University, Noida 201313, India

Inakshi Kapur
Amity College of Commerce and Finance, Amity University, Uttar Pradesh, India; E-mail: inakshik@gmail.com

Ramakrishna Karanth
Kimoha Entrepreneurs Ltd., JAFZA, Dubai, UAE

Yashaswini Karanth
Department of Materials Science and Engineering, Arizona State University, Tempe, Arizona, USA

Jaideep Kaur
Amity Business School Amity University, Noida, Uttar Pradesh, India; E-mail: jkaur@amity.edu

Chitra Krishnan
Amity International Business School, Amity University, Noida; E-mail: ckrishnan@amity.edu

Lawan Amdan Lawan
Department of Marketing, Ramat Polytechnic Maiduguri, Borno State, Nigeria;
E-mail: lawanamdan@gmail.com

Tawheed Nabi
Mittal School of Business (ACBSP, USA), Jalandhar, Punjab, India

Swati Nayak
Amity institute of Competitive Intelligence and Strategic Management, Amity University, Noida, India;
E-mail: swati.non@gmail.com

Abhishekh Negi
Amity Business School, Amity University, Noida 201301, Uttar Pradesh, India;
E-mail: abhishek.negi24@gmail.com

Sudir Padroo
Meril Endo-Surgery Pvt. Ltd, Mumbai, India

Aswin Sambhu PR
Amity Business School, Amity University Noida 201301, Uttar Pradesh, India

Sunil Kumar Roy
School of Management Science, Apeejay Stya University, Sohna, Gurgaon, and Haryana, India

Saritha S.
Department of Management, Nehru Gram Bharati (Deemed to be University), Prayagraj, Uttar Pradesh, India

Snehi Shahi
Amity Business School, Amity University, Noida, India

Kumar Shalender
Chitkara Business School, Chitkara University, Punjab, India;
E-mail:kshalender@gmail.com, kumar.shalender@chitkara.edu.in

Shiv Shanker
Amity Business School, Amity University, Noida, India

Bhawna Sharma
Amity Business School, Amity University Maharashtra, Mumbai, India;
E-mail: bhawnasharma22@gmail.com

Shalini Sharma
GNIOT Institute of Management Studies, Greater Noida, Uttar Pradesh, India;
E-mail: shalinish0506@gmail.com

Swaty Sharma
Mittal School of Business Lovely Professional University, Phagwara, Punjab, India;
E-mail: swaty.sharma@rediffmail.com

Shobhit
Department of Management and Social Sciences, Amity University, Tashkent 100028, Uzbekistan

Vidhushi Shrivastava
Amity International Business School, Amity University, Noida 201313, India;
E-mail:vidushishrivastava2@gmail.com

Anjani Kumar Singh
Amity Business School, Amity University, Uttar Pradesh, India

Swati Upveja
Amity Business School, Amity University, Noida, Uttar Pradesh, India;
E-mail: upveja.swati@gmail.com

Anita Venaik
General Management Department, ABS, Amity University, Noida, Uttar Pradesh, India
Department of IT, Amity Business School, Noida, India

Abbreviations

ABV	average basket value
ADF	Augmented Dickey-Fuller Test
AHP	analytical hierarchy process
AMOS	analysis of moment structures
AR	augmented reality
ATE	attitude toward entrepreneurship
ATGL	Above the Green Line
ATV	average transaction value
AVE	average variance extracted
B.C.	before Christ
B2C	business to consumer
B2G	business to government
B2B	business to business
BTGL	Below the Green Line
CEO	chief executive officer
CFI	comparative fit index
CRM	customer relationship management
DMC	Dairy Margin Coverage
DV	dependent variable
EDP	electronic data processing
EE	entrepreneurship education
EF	entrepreneurial failure
EI	entrepreneurial intention
ELC	endoscopic linear cutter
EM	entrepreneurial mindset
EO	entrepreneurial orientation
ERP	enterprise resource planning
ES	entrepreneurial success
ETL	extract-transform-load
EU	European Union
FTA	free trade areas
GEM	Global Entrepreneurship Monitor
GDP	gross domestic product
GeM	Government e-Marketplace

HYV	high yielding variety
H2H	head to head trial
ICT	information and communication technologies
IDRA	Insurance Development and Regulatory Authority, Bangladesh
IEO	individual entrepreneurial orientation
IFI	incremental fit index
IND	India
IRDA	Insurance Regulatory and Development Authority, India
IT	information technology
ITeS	information technology-enabled services
IV	independent variable
KPMG	Klynveld Peat Marwick and Goerdeler
KRA	key results area
LAP	Learning Action Performance
LAP	laparoscopic
LR	literature review
MSH	multispecialty hospital
MSME	micro, small, and medium enterprises
nAch	need for achievement
NCR	National Capital Region
NPD	new product development
NPS	Net Promoter Score
OBC	other backward caste
OFT	on farm trial
OPM	Option Performance Matrix
PF	psychological factors
PPC	pay-per-click
QFD	quality function deployment
QSR	quick service restaurant
RCEP	Regional Comprehensive Economic Partnership
RMSEA	root mean square error of approximation
ROI	return of investment
RVV	real value vector
SAP	Situation Actors Processes
SBC	Shadaran Bima Corporation
SC	scheduled caste
SCM	supply chain management
SE	success of entrepreneur
SEM	search engine marketing

SEO	search engine optimization
SHG	self help group
SME	small and medium enterprises
SMM	search media marketing
SN	subjective norm
SMO	search media optimization
SPSS	Statistical Package for Social Science
ST	scheduled tribe
STARS	Special Thanks and Recognition System
STRV	stress tolerant rice variety
TEA	total early age
TLI	Trucker Lewis index
TPB	theory of planned behavior
TRA	theory of reasoned action
US	United States
USD	United States Dollar
USSC	United States Surgical Corporation
VECM	Vector Error Correction Model
VFM	value for money
VOC	voice of consumer
VR	virtual reality
VUCA	Volatile, Uncertain, Complex, and Ambiguous
Y-o-Y	year on year

Foreword

It is a matter of great pride to compile a book with various thoughts by different intellectuals.

We need to remain competitive and innovative in our approach. This volume (title), focuses on how sustainable competitive advantage (SCA) can lead to business excellence (BE). It provides an insight on the entrepreneurial mindset to help gain agility, sustainability, and lead to growth in this competitive environment.

The book focuses on the various challenges that we are facing, such as development in technologies, unforeseen eventualities, and how to be resilient and handle the unforeseen situation. In the post-pandemic, the demand for IT innovation and output capacity is at the highest levels. Organizations are under greater pressure to digitize services quickly at scale to meet rising customer demands, to scale innovation, and to create new revenue channels. The need for IT innovation takes on a new urgency in the post-pandemic world, as the pandemic created a tipping point for IT.

This effort is to provide an insight on how different organizations operate, think, innovate, and cultivate culture for continuous growth to foster learning environment. It also gives insight about the concept that innovation doesn't lead only to success but surely gives path to a new process, leaving behind footprints for others to follow. This book is a cumulative effort by corporate practitioners, academicians, entrepreneurs, technologies, and management practitioners to understand how data collected from varied sources can be effectively used to gain knowledge and understand its position in the market. The chapters in the book are an effort to help organizations lead, innovate, and create a value for their customers.

I congratulate the editors for bringing together experts from various fields and all authors for their excellent contributions.

Professor J. K. Sharma
Ex-Professor, Faculty of Management Studies, University of Delhi, India
Professor, Amity Business School, Amity University, Noida. India

Preface

Innovation is the secret of survival and the source of sustainability in this volatile environment.

A desire to improve upon existing artifacts is an aspect of the constructive discontent displayed by creative individuals or visionary strategists. Innovation typically arises from personal need or direct experience of the individual inventor. In the global economic restructuring, creative economy is in the latest developmental stage. Organizations who are open to ideas are adopting change with agility in their approach to welcome creativity. Organizations are looking for people with innovative ideas and flexible mindsets, and they are open to tolerate and accept mistakes while innovating to foster entrepreneurial culture in the team.

This book is a collection of thoughts by independent thinkers, researchers, and corporate practitioners to show how innovative ways can help boost economy and bring agility in various functional areas of business. This book includes 18 chapters containing information about the advanced technologies used in industry to cope up with the unforeseen.

Chapter 1 by Sathiya Priya A and Sunmathi B focuses on the ever-growing and very important topic of image processing. This trend is a focused application system to develop and implement real-time applications. The applications are interesting and exciting in this field. Wheelchairs assist people to become mobile and independent without any human assistance. Innovation is used in developing advanced features of a wheelchair for special people. A variety of algorithms have been arrived to develop the wheelchair with the help of human body parts and their actions. The objective is to develop the wheelchair by extracting the movement of eye pupil and sclera by dividing it into three different sectors and the indicated movement in different directions or to stop. The system that works on the detection of the pupil using a webcam, which is continuously staring at special people's eyes, results in the movement of the wheelchair in the required directions needed for a seamless flow in commuting.

Chapter 2 by Kapur and Singh aims to design, evaluate, and find a validated measurement scale for an alternate multidimensional model of individual entrepreneurial orientation (IEO), adding an emerging dimension of resilience to the original entrepreneurial orientation dimensions of innovativeness and proactiveness. Though entrepreneurial resilience is a well-researched area, no studies exist that explore resilience as a dimension of individual entrepreneurial orientation.

Chapter 3 by Priyanka Kapoor and Dr. Shobhit explores the extent of digital penetration and adoption among small businesses. Growth and inclusive development in contemporary times cannot be achieved without a fertile digital ecosystem. Thus the chapter outlines the key factors that can help in the effective implementation of information system among these enterprises. The chapter also attempts to discern a conceptual framework for ascertaining the likelihood of digital adoption among the respondent enterprises. The findings of the study can be particularly beneficial in a plausible reconstruction of an agile digital landscape within SMEs.

Chapter 4 by Chitra Krishnan, Tawheed Nabi, and Mubashir Majid Baba deals with trade welfare effects due to COVID-19 shock. This pandemic has forced to take the decision of lockdown and quarantine because of which every sector's labor force is quarantined. In terms of international trade, most of the economies are affected by COVID-19 shock. This chapter discusses the threats faced by globalization and will help in learning the supply chain from China and various strategies undertaken by many nations.

Chapter 5 by Snehi Shahi and Dr. Jaideep Kaur focuses on the impact of films and how it has affected the tourism industry. It has been seen in the recent times that the entertainment industry has been exploring new destinations to shoot various films, songs and promotional material. Undoubtedly, film tourism has impacted the cultural tourism for locations that have become famous in films and television. It is found that various other factors also had a positive impact on the tourists for visiting a film destination. The results indicate that status has the highest impact, followed by celebrity presence, image, and success in choosing the tourist destination.

Chapter 6 demonstrates that people play the vital role in creating such culture of innovation, and that Below the Green Line (BTGL) factors play a crucial role. Success of innovation can be measured through several output-related Above the Green Line (ATGL) factors like outputs, sales, and number of successes. A number of possible measurement techniques are discussed in the chapter. Recommendations for promoting and sustaining a culture of innovation are listed as ATGL or BTGL. These recommendations include systems, structures, activities, and ways of communicating.

Chapter 7 advocates and stresses about important dimensions of innovation cultures across numerous business segments and industries which are further adapted to develop an evaluative framework for the organizations on their culture of innovation. Taking evidences from the passenger vehicle segment of the Indian automobile industry, this chapter contributes to a conceptual framework and specific measures which may help organizations in building and sustaining innovation culture in their organizations. The study is unique in the sense that it draws on both literature and real-world corporate examples to offer model on innovation culture and has important implications for both scholars and practitioners.

Chapter 8 by Dr. Shalini Sharma and Dr. Harminder Kaur Gujral attempts to analyze the role of competency approach in determining the success of entrepreneurs. This chapter evaluates the role of the psychological factor risk taking and its counterpart behavioral factor uncertainty avoidance in stimulating the success of an enterprise leading to the success of entrepreneur. The chapter entails the study on the IT sector entrepreneurs, considering the current turbulence in the businesses. In the present scenario, the relevance and importance of risk taking becomes imperative to study in the context of startups.

Chapter 9 by Swaty Sharma attempts to examine co-integration, causality, and volatility spillover among Indian copper and US copper market via using various econometric tools. This chapter helps to study about how Indian copper market grabs volatility from the US copper market and the United States as well and how the US copper market shocks Indian copper market. It also describes what type of tools should be used in any situation.

Chapter 10 by Bajpai and Venaik focuses on loyalty programs, its technical implementation aspects, and e-commerce business market structure across the globe. This literature will help end users understand and devise a 5x ROI model for the reward programs. The ROI model talks about different business verticals and its earn/burn values for reward points earned by the user. The readers would be able to develop business acumen from the knowledge jot down in the chapter and how businesses plan the campaigns using SMS/email mode of communication. Some of the strategies adopted by well-known apparel brands would help us understand best practices from the uncertain COVID scenarios as well.

Chapter 11 by Swati Nayak and Ritesh Dwivedi focuses on how farmer field-based varietal evaluations are more contextual and reliable method to advance, position, and scale right varieties in right market. These farm trials are based on robust research design to provide scientific data on varietal performance (of new varieties) against the older farmer grown varieties. The study shows the impact of these as an effective extension approach that may be streamlined under national systems to measure, realize the genetic gain potentials of new varieties under farmer managed condition. A contextual comparative trial can provide more reliable, experiential, and visual season long learnings for farmers and community to take the adoption decision simultaneously.

Chapter 12 by Md. Ibrahim and Dr. Sunil Kumar Roy attempts to focus on the advancement of nonlife insurance in both public and private area in Bangladesh. This chapter analyzes growth rate market share, penetration rate, and density rate to evaluate the advancement of nonlife insurance. This chapter reveals that the penetration rate, density rate, growth rate, and market share of public area is lower than that of private sector. The average penetration rate of public sector is .06% and .15% for private sector. The average density rate of public sector is Tk.40.83 and Tk. 98.55 for private area. The average growth rate of public sector is 8.58% and 16.43% for private sector. The average market share of public sector is 29.90% whereas, 70.09% captured by private sector business. The penetration rate of nonlife insurance (both public and private) of Bangladesh was 0.17% in 2008 and it was 0.18% in 2014, and 0.15% in 2017. The nonlife insurance density rate (both public and private) of Bangladesh was 1.40 (USD) in 2008 and it was 2.10 (USD) in 2017 in order to improve the advancement of nonlife insurance.

Chapter 13 focuses on predictive capability of the Theory of Planned Behavior (TPB). The TPB presuppose that those human behaviors are a function of behavioral, which focuses on normative and control beliefs. The model has been proved in different context across several disciples as capable of predicting the occurrence of a behavior provided. The aim of this chapter is to provide readers the understanding of efficacy of the TPB model in predicting the intention to find new business in Nigerian context.

Chapter 14 by Vidhushi Shrivastava and Dr. Shikha Kapoor looks at the future which has lot of surprises productivity and employee engagement have risen to the top of the priority list as businesses strive to ensure their employees' well-being during these troubled times. This chapter focuses on how the global epidemic will impact the future of work and how people and organizations can prepare to adapt to the technological changes that will be widely visible after the outbreak.

Chapter 15 by Dr. Swati Upveja and Aswin Sambhu PR is an attempt to explore the impact of cold chain on effective food supply chain management. An interactive approach has been followed with an ice-cream-consuming sample of people to better understand their perception of ice cream as a product and analyzing how the existing brands can effectively handle the ever-increasing consumer requirements in this sector and what they can offer from within their capacities, using quality function deployment (QFD). Also, the chapter aims to find the best brand of ice cream, based on the consumer inputs, from three brands of ice cream which are available in India, using the Analytical Hierarchy Process (AHP) is utilized.

Chapter 16 identifies the challenges and issues in RCEP from Indian dairy perspective using the SAP-LAP technique. India is a leading manufacturer and processor of milk and milk products. This case highlights crucial observations about the RCEP agreement on Indian dairy sector. The most important observation is that due to RCEP implementation in India, there would be surge in the production costs of milk and milk products and downward trends in earning of dairy farmers in turn bring dairy farmers into dire straits. This agreement have severely impacted dairy farmers, dairy cooperatives, milk and milk processing units' employee, fertilizer companies, business associates, government, freight forwarding agencies, NGOs, RCEP nations, foreign investors.

Chapter 17 by Dr. Bhawna Sharma and Sudir Padroo explores the technological advances of surgical devices. The new devices are studied with respect to the amendments and modifications. This chapter elaborates and provides insights to understand new surgical stapling advancements.

Chapter 18 by Negi and Upveja attempts to explore how augmented reality (AR) and virtual reality (VR) can be used as a sales and marketing strategy. Further, this chapter discusses the potential of AR and VR used as a retail marketing strategy across multiple channels, to see if implementing it properly will enhance experiences rather than only to solve problems.

The book is a cumulative effort by corporate practitioners, academicians, entrepreneurs and technologies, and management practitioners to understand how data collected will help to gain knowledge and understand its position in the market. The chapters in the book are an effort to help organizations to lead, innovate, and create a value for their customers.

CHAPTER 1

Virtual Automatic Wheelchairs for Special People

SATHIYA PRIYA A.* and SUNMATHI B.

Department of Computer Science, CMS College of Science & Commerce, Coimbatore, Tamil Nadu, India

**Corresponding author. E-mail: sathiyapriya1327@gmail.com*

ABSTRACT

Wheelchairs assist people to become mobile and independent without human assistance. Innovation in wheelchairs ultimately increase their specialization or helps to develop advanced features on automactic wheelchairs for special people. Wheelchairs create an innovative lifetime to the disabled persons in simpler manner and eliminate the human assistance required for them. In this, a variety of algorithms have been arrived to develop the wheelchair with the help of human body parts movements. The objective of this paper is to progress the wheelchair movement through the features extracted from the movement of eye iris and sclera by dividing it into the following four different sectors: To move left, right, and forward; and then to stop. In this method, the features are extracted from the pre-processed images; the threshold value predicts the iris location which is easier to propose a novel algorithm to inflate the accuracy of the iris position. The future outcome of the proposed work is to enrich with the Viola–Jones Hough algorithm that outperforms the existing techniques.

Constructive Discontent in Execution: Creative Approaches to Technology and Management.
Sanjeev Bansal, Anita Venaik, Swati Upveja, and Saritha S. (Eds.)

1.1 INTRODUCTION

In the last few decades, there is an increase in the number of persons who are paralyzed or suffering from quadriplegia due to some diseases or illnesses, and therefore they are dependent on other people. Making them self-reliant and independent from others to moving in and around for a long distance in reinstating their self-confidence. Most of the paralyses are constant; however, there are other forms also exist such as periodic paralysis (caused by either genetic diseases or by other factors). The image processing field has been massively growing in the past few years (Sahu, 2016). Image processing is everything in trends and it is a specialized application system to develop and to implement real-time applications. The purpose of this project is to develop a wheelchair that will be fully controlled by the eye movements of the person seated in the wheelchair. Eye movement-controlled wheelchair is an aid for completely paralyzed patient and helps the elderly people to make their life more attainable. People who are unable to walk are using wheelchair employ great amount of energy using physical strength to move the wheels Sonali et al. (2017). The applications are varied and attending their challenges through innovation are more interesting and exciting in this field. The advanced level of image processing with built-in library function is used for the face and eye detection. In addition, several applications and algorithms are used to find out the accurate pupil location by detection and tracking. One of them is Haar cascade feature detection algorithm which is used to detecting the exact eye pupil and its mid-point is ultimate goal of this system. It automatically finds pupil of the eye and starts tracking through computer vision libraries functions. In this, human eye is detected and process through several stages such as object and edge detection, motion detection, image color conversion, pattern matching, etc. For eye pupil tracking, there are several numbers of techniques available. However, a person with different form of paralysis uses different body parts for movement, that is, head movement-based system, which has its limitations, where the user cannot be able to access the system physically. The proposed work is about the automation of the wheelchair using eye gaze movement, tracking the iris movement to operate the wheelchair. The iris has a black circular region called the pupil and the white region is called the sclera. The human eye is divided into three different sectors as follows: If the eyeball lies in sector 1, it is denoted as "left"; if the eyeball lies in sector 2, it is denoted as "straight"; the eyeball lies in sector 3, it is denoted as "right"; and if the eye is closed, it is denoted as "to stop the wheelchair" (Kurrey and Gedam, 2017). The eyeball is extracted using various morphological processes such as edge detection, image to binary conversion, complement of image, erosion, dilation, noise removal, image enhancement, and image segmentation. The Viola–Jones Hough method is a very accurate method to detect human eyes' movements. However, it works best when an existing database of the eye is used but in real-world applications, it takes delay in processing; accuracy is best in detecting iris. Additionally, it works best on circular objects, that is, when the person is looking straight or any other direction, the accuracy of detecting the iris increases rapidly. Based on iris location, the wheelchair automatically moves.

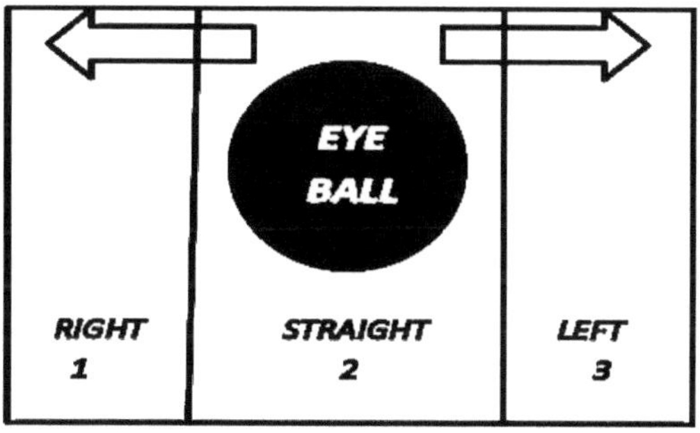

FIGURE 1.1 Predicting the location of eyeball.

From Fig. 1, it is noted that the iris movement is predicted if pupil lies in any of the three sectors; it is named as right, left, or straight. If the face of the user is not detected any of the three sectors, then it is concluded as sector 4.

1. Sector 1: Right—When the iris moves to the right, the wheelchair automatically moves to the person's right side.
2. Sector 2: Straight—When the iris is in the center of the eye, the wheelchair automatically moves forward.
3. Sector 3: Left—When the iris moves to the left, the wheelchair automatically moves to the person's left side.
4. Sector 4: Stop—When the eye is closed, the wheelchair automatically stops its action.

The paper is organized as follows: Section 1.1 explains the literature study of eyeball detection. Section 1.2 discusses about the research work. Section 1.3 describes the proposed work. Section 1.4 comprises the results and analysis. Section 1.5 concludes with suggestions to the future work.

1.2 HISTORICAL PERSPECTIVE

There were many proposed works on electronic wheelchairs. A few of their ideas are considered in our research work.

The study by Kokaje et al. (2019) discusses on the detection of pupil continuously starring at patient's eye by processing the images. It is for the paralyzed or handicapped people in which the combination of the hardware and software makes their life self-dependent.

Rajesh and Mantur (2017) studied on computationally efficient system for controlling the direction of a wheelchair based on eye movements. It helps the people who need assistance for controlling their wheelchairs. Images are captured and the gaze direction was classified using a deep learning algorithm. The outcome of the work is to build the automatic wheelchair which performs and analyzes.

Chetan and Chandak (2017) present an innovation in wheelchair by adding motor, which is easier and simpler to handle for a physically disabled and paralyzed person by using eye motion tracking. The aim of this system is contributed to the society, this minor technical system could make better the lives of millions of people across the world. This innovation has a new add-on to use it as home automation wheelchair where a disabled person can turn on/off home appliances without getting up from wheelchair.

Ashwini et al. (2016) studied about enhancing the wheelchair technology by providing mobility to the physically handicapped people with the help of their iris movements by capturing the eye images and performing different operations to perform optimized output. The users can move the wheelchair on different directions wherever they need to go, and as an additional feature, the obstacle detection is attached. Using the image-processing techniques and different algorithm, we achieve a better performance compared to all existing techniques.

Cigliano et al. (2015) proposed a new method to control and motorize the wheelchair using EOG signals. The method allows the user to look around freely and, simultaneously, the wheelchair navigates automatically to the desired goal point. The navigation of the wheelchair is controlled by the robot, which means that the electric wheelchair is dedicated to severely disabled persons. The design of this wheelchair and its equipment is of low cost for using only eye movements and gaze direction.

Rascanu and Solea (2011) developed a wheelchair with iris recognition is by describing key local variations. The basic idea is that limited the sharpen difference points is denote by appearing the image or vanishing the important of the image structure. They are utilized to represent the characteristics of the iris. Using the ideas listed in the survey can help to develop a wheelchair for paralyzed persons based on eyeball detection technology.

1.3 PROPOSED WORK

1.3.1 VIOLA–JONES ALGORITHM

The Viola Jones algorithm deals with detection of faces as an image. The researcher has made advancement in detecting faces. It is easy for humans to detect faces but computer uses only binary language; so, feeding instructions and commands to computer is necessary. To make the task easier to perform Viola–Jones algorithm requires full view frontal view faces. The basic starts with using the camera in which the person's pair of eyes are captured. The person should look forward toward camera to capture the image but if they move any other sides, then the output may not be as desired, and it leads to wrong interpretation by the software as detection of eyes is often followed by recognition. Viola–Jones algorithm deals with face detection so it can also easily detect the eyes of the people. This algorithm is based on Haar-like features. The Haar features possess similarity with Haar wavelets (Kusuma et al., 2018). Haar-like features exhibit rectangular structure – sum of the pixels from the white portion are subtracted from the ones present in the gray portion. Algorithms such as Viola–Jones and template matching have been used for the tracking and detection processes. Algorithms work according to the procedure discussed in Section 1.3.2.

1.3.2 SYSTEM APPROACH

MATLAB 2013 Image Processing Toolbox is discussed in this section for the software design. The web camera in the computer is used on which the MATLAB script is running. The continuous video signals on MATLAB from the web camera using the video processing toolbox is activated. The function "imaqhwinfo" is to recognize all video signals which are captured using the adaptors. The video signals of the eyeball movement perform different minor actions in each and every frame. It is practically impossible to do processing and to store all frames basis. So, we decided that if there are movements in sclera, they are automatically converted to frames and stored. The raw frame is not able to process; so, they are converted to images. The input image is in the form of RGB, and they are converted to a grayscale image to detect eye feature points. The conversion enhances the eyeball detecting capability of the Viola–Jones Hough algorithm. The image adjustment command is used to contrast the stretch in the image to make darker sections still darker for enhancing the eye feature points visible for the operations. This pre-processing of the image makes the image easier to process and extract the features of the pair of eyes. After the pre-processing techniques, the eye detection is made using the built-in command as computer vision object detection technique. The novel algorithm is enhancing the detection of the face by threshold value that is equal to the sum of pixels in a rectangular area. The large rectangle cutdown into many such smaller rectangles and their feature points in the human face. The cascade object detector function in MATLAB is used to utilize the algorithm to extract and detect the features of the pair of eyes from persons. They detected the features of eye by plotting the rectangle at the appropriate location of the iris.

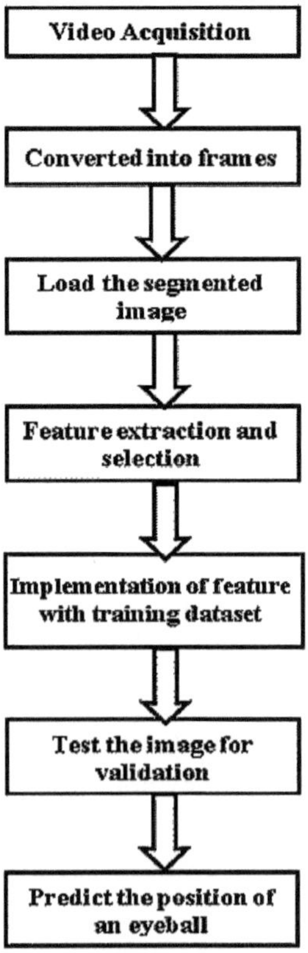

FIGURE 1.2 Workflow of the automatic wheelchair.

To increase the detection accuracy, the height and length of the iris was calculated (Figure 1.1). After repeated testing, we decided the length and height of a valid eye and set a range for the threshold and rejected if it was out of the range we set. The flag is set each and every time to validate the sclera by indicating a blink. The feature is extracted for both left and right eyes and saved it. To analyze, the difference in pixels of the left eye position and the right eye position in the current snapshots from the previous snapshots are compared. The threshold for the minimum movement of the eye required to be qualified as a valid attempt. In each snapshot, the difference is evaluated, and in some cases, the difference of the threshold value is higher than the wheelchair moves, and in such cases, the wheelchair automatically moves on the direction in which the flag indicates if it is left movement or right movement. If the difference is below the threshold, the flag indicates no movement on the eyeball. The optimization of the algorithm undergoes a series of processing to attain the steps. Figure 1.2 shows the workflow of the automatic wheelchair. The Viola–Jones Hough algorithm is applied to detect the location of the eyeball. The single eye is cropped from the detection and shown on the screen. To stop the wheelchair, the person must close his eyes for 1 s. This detection was carried out by finding the local maximum peaks in the image. An open eye will have a larger number of maximum peaks as compared to a closed eye. A closed eye will have its peaks spread; so, lesser number of peaks are found. With the help of image processing, we design the automatic wheelchair by enhancing the eye movement. If the eye is determined to be open, it indicates that the wheelchair needs to be moved in a specific direction. The main aim is to obtain the iris region to determine in which direction the eye is facing, and the wheelchair will move accordingly.

1.3.3 WORKING PRINCIPLE

The procedure mentioned in the following describes Figure 1.2 with consecutive steps that have been followed for image classification process:

- *Step 1*: Input video is converted into frames, gray scale image $I(u, v)$ for the classification process.
- *Step 2:* Pre-process a set of features such as bounding box, center, distance, radii, and metrics of the eye have been selected with the aim to analyze and extract the hidden useful knowledge from it (Rawarkar and Chandak, 2017).

- *Step 3:* The features are extracted from iris of the eye and have been applied for selection process.
- *Step 4:* Selection of the iris a flag is set based on their height and length
- *Step 5:* To identify the iris movement based on the threshold range either left or right.
- *Step 6:* Training the dataset, compare iris of both eyes on threshold range.
- *Step 7:* Validation based on the eye based on the threshold value.
- *Step 8:* Predict the eyeball position as a result.

1.3.4 PROCEDURE

The "procedure" describes the proposed system eyeball prediction and feature extraction calculation:

- *Step 1:* Initialization flag with threshold value for detecting the iris movement using Viola–Jones Hough algorithm.
- *Step 2:* Creating the bounding box for face and check if the eyes are available for extracting features.

  if ~ isempty(bbox) // If face exist with iris

  biggest_box=1;

  if ~ isempty(bboxeyes) // pair of eyes are available

  biggest_box_eyes =1;

- *Step 3:* Extract the single eye from the face by calculating the center, radii, and metric using Hough transform.
- *Step 4:* If the pupil, in middle its center when the iris moves from center to left edge its left, iris from center to right edge its right (Fig. 1.3)

  if ~isempty(centers)

  pupil_x = centers (1);

  disL=abs(0-pupil_x); //distance from left edge to center point

  disR=abs(3-pupil_x); //distance from right edge to center point

- *Step 5:* If the iris, in middle its straight when the iris is not found its no face that means to stop.

```
if
image(straight);
else
image(noface);
end
```

1.4 RESULTS AND ANALYSIS

The video is taken as input; covert them into frames. First, from each frame, the eyeball movement is detected. If there is no movement of the eye, the frame is not detected, and it goes to another frame. If the eyeball movement is detected on the pair of eyes, then the face is highlighted as yellow box. When the eyes are detected, the eyeballs are highlighted with a blue box. Then the eyes are compared with the threshold value and set a flag which is used the algorithm to validate left or right eye for processing. After the selection of the eyes, if the eyes are open, then based on the iris location on either left, right, or straight, the wheelchair moves according to the direction and pop up with a message on the screen. If the eyes are close for more than or equal to 2 s, then the wheelchair stops and displays a message on the screen. If the eyes are located just closer, and if the eyes are opened, it will work in this, and the eyeball movement is captured and their location is detected, accordingly the system works to the user's need and the algorithm works efficiently to prove the result.

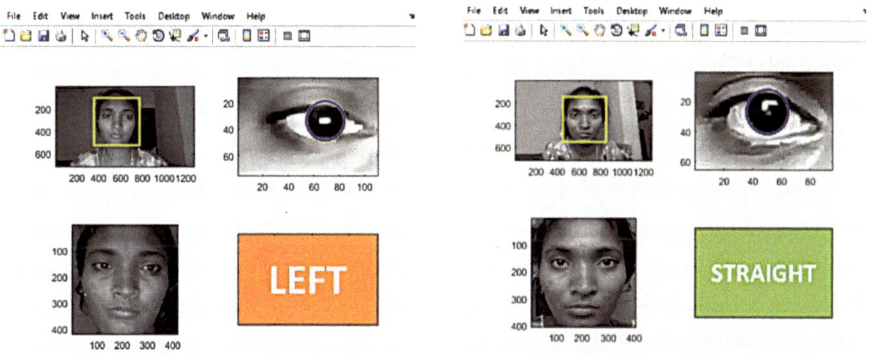

(a) Left (b) Straight

FIGURE 1.3 Position of the eyeball.

The proposed work was implemented in MATLAB using real-time video recorded and converted into frames that are pre-processed and the features are extracted based on the algorithm. The iris and pupil of the eye will be detected and produced result using Viola–Jones Hough algorithm that proposed on vision cascade face detection by its tools; the result of the location of the eyeball is show in the Table 1.1. As per the iris movement on left, right, and straight based on direction the wheelchair moves. The technique is evaluated and the effectiveness of optimization technique has evidence that Viola–Jones Hough algorithm had significantly improved the learning efficiency in yielding the fittest results in classification accuracy. It is tested and trained the system for different people and the result were calculated on classification accuracy of the proposed algorithm (Srimathi et al., 2015). To design an innovative technique to control the wheelchair with low cost, to solve the problem, and to overcome; as of now, we developed virtual wheelchair on compact GUI based model, which helps the user for easily capturing the eye images and control the direction of wheelchair by themselves.

TABLE 1.1 Classification accuracy of algorithm

Location	Accuracy
Right	97.37
Left	99.89
Straight	98.99
No face (Stop)	95.96

1.5 CONCLUSION

Viola–Jones algorithm as a proposed method to use to detect many faces and area of interested features like eyes, nose, mouth, etc. This research work is based on finding out a technique for controlling wheelchair system using eye gaze movement which helps the restricted patient to move their wheelchair independently on their own respected direction. This system works on the detection of pupil using web camera which is constantly starring at special person's eyes. Aim is to develop an automatic wheelchair system which enables the people to move their wheelchair independently on their own without human assistance (Gautam et al., 2014). The eyeball detection is optimized by the Viola–Jones Hough algorithm in which the accurate detection of features increases rapidly when a camera of high specifications is used and attain the average accuracy of 98%. The wheelchair operation may take some delay in time due to the reason that the dark light affects the performance is difficult to track the eye pupil in that situation. To make the system more interactive with people must add some additional sensors. Delay in time will been reduced and video-based processing is done in the future work. The automatic wheelchair moves in all required directions with good response and thereby we believe through it that a great justice to the idea is done, and accomplished by getting more than satisfying result on the accuracy.

KEYWORDS

- **pupil**
- **sclera**
- **eye movement**
- **wheelchair**
- **video acquisition**
- **Viola-Jones Hough algorithm**
- **eyeball detection**

REFERENCES

Arai, K.; Mardiyanto, R. Eyes Based Eletric Wheelchair Control System—I (Eye) Can Control Electric Wheelchair. *Int. J. Adv. Comp. Sci. Appl.* **2011**, 98.

Cigliano, P.; Lippiello, V.; Ruggiero, F. Robotic Ball Catching with an Eye-in-Hand Single-Camera System, *IEEE Trans. Cont. Syst. Technol.* **2015,** *23* (5), 1657–1671.

Gautam, G.; Sumanth, G.; Karthikeyan K. C.;Sundar, S.; Venkataraman, D. Eye Movement Based Electronic Wheel Chair for Physically Challenged Persons. *Int. J. Sci. Technol. Res.* **2014,** *3*, 206–212.

Kokaje, P.; Rane, N.; Shelar, P.; Tarave, O.; Chavan, V. Review Paper on Wheelchair Control Using Eye Movement. *IJSART* **2019,** *5* (1), 140.

Kurrey, D.; Gedam, R. A Review on EyeBall Detection Based Wheelchair Control Using Matlab and Arduino Platform for a Physically Disabled Persons. *J. Emerg. Technol. Innov. Res.* **2017**.

Lin, Y.-H.; Lin, H. W. In *Face Detection Based on the Use of Eyes Tracking*, International Computer Symposium (ICS), 2016; pp. 402–405.

Nashte, A. A.; Savkare, S. S.; Kole, S. G. Automation of Wheelchair Using Iris Movement. *Int. J. Comput. Eng. Res.* **2016**.

Plesnick, S.; Repice, D.; Loughnane, P. In *Eye-Controlled Wheelchair*, IEEE Canada International Humanitarian Technology Conference—(IHTC), 2014.

Rajesh, A.; Mantur, M. In *Eyeball Gesture Controlled Automatic Wheelchair Using Deep Learning*, IEEE Region 10 Humanitarian Technology Conference (R10-HTC), 2017.

Rascanu, G. C.; Solea, R. In Electric Wheel Chair Control for People with Loco Motor Disabilities Using Eye Movements, *15th International Conference on System Theory, Control and Computing*, 2011; pp. 1–5.

Rawarkar, C. W.; Chandak, D. S. Computerization of Wheel Chair Using Patient Iris and Arduino Board. *Int. J. Adv. Res. Innov. Ideas Educ.* **2017,** *3*, 462–467.

Sahin, B.; Lamory, B.; Levecq, X.; Harms, F.; Dainty, C. Adaptive Optics with Pupil Tracking for High-Resolution Retinal Imaging. *Biomed. Opt. Exp.* **2012,** *3* (2), 225–239.

Sahu, D. Automatic Camera Based Eye Controlled Wheelchair System Using Raspberry Pi. *Int. J. Sci. Eng. Technol. Res.* **2016**.

Sonali, P.; Isha, P.; Manish, J.; Ravi, D.; Lade, N. Advance Eye Controlled Wheelchair for Disabled Person. *Int. J. Eng. Res. Technol.* **2017**.

Sri, M. K.; Divya, P. N.; Vyshnavi, J.; Tejaswini, B. Detection of Drowsy Eyes Using Viola Jones Face Detection Algorithm. *Int. J. Curr. Eng. Sci. Res.* **2018**.

Srimathi, P.; Kanthini, B.; Sen, K. K. Wheelchair Control Using an Eye Tracking System for Assisted Mobility. *Int. J. Res. Appl. Sci. Eng. Technol.* **2015,** *110*.

Xiong, J.; Xu, W.; Liao, W.; Wang, Q.; Liu, J.; Liang, Q. Eye Control System Base on Ameliorated Hough Transform Algorithm. *IEEE Sens. J.* **2013,** 3421–3429.

CHAPTER 2

Resilience as a Dimension of Individual Entrepreneurial Orientation

INAKSHI KAPUR[1*] and ANJANI KUMAR SINGH[2]

[1]*Amity College of Commerce and Finance, Amity University Noida, Uttar Pradesh 201301, India*

[2]*Amity Business School, Amity University Noida, Uttar Pradesh 201301, India*

[*]*Corresponding author. E-mail: inakshik@gmail.com*

ABSTRACT

This study aims to develop, test, and validate a measurement scale for an alternate multidimensional model of individual entrepreneurial orientation (IEO), adding an emerging dimension of resilience to the original entrepreneurial orientation dimensions of innovativeness and proactiveness. Although the entrepreneurial resilience is a well-researched area, no studies which explore resilience as a dimension of individual entrepreneurial orientation exist. The study is based on a sample of 242 management students from the Delhi NCR region of India. The data were analyzed using exploratory factor analysis (EFA) and confirmatory factor analysis. The results show that resilience, innovativeness, and proactiveness explain a significant percentage of variance in individual entrepreneurial orientation. Resilience is depicted in being optimistic, adaptable, perseverant, and having an internal locus of control. The study's findings contribute to research by offering an alternative conceptualization of the IEO construct based on the evolving business context and requirements. Entrepreneurial organizations actively seek employees who have an entrepreneurial orientation (EO). To enhance the career readiness of

Constructive Discontent in Execution: Creative Approaches to Technology and Management.
Sanjeev Bansal, Anita Venaik, Swati Upveja, and Saritha S. (Eds.)

young management graduates, being resilient is vital in addition to traditional EO traits. There are no studies available exploring resilience as a dimension of individual entrepreneurial orientation.

2.1 INTRODUCTION

Entrepreneurship has long been an area of interest of researchers, policy-makers, business practitioners, and economists. It positively influences a nation's economic and social growth by encouraging opportunity-seeking behaviors and an innovative mindset (Goktan and Gupta, 2015). Entrepreneurs operate in an environment that is competitive and everchanging; being resilient is a critical factor for their entrepreneurial success (Ayala and Manzano, 2014). As the world still reels from the upheaval caused by the COVID-19 pandemic, the organization's resilience is being tested. In the business context, Williams et al. (2017) integrated two research streams of crisis management and resilience, and defined resilience as an iterative learning process from responding to significant disturbances, adjusting and creating durability capabilities (Williams et al., 2017). The need to be innovative and proactive, which was earlier meant as "to stay competitive," is critical for the survival. Thus, the present focus is on making organizations more resilient. Organizational resilience is influenced by various factors at the employee and organization levels (Gittell et al., 2006).

Entrepreneurial orientation as a concept was first introduced by Miller in 1983 and later operationalized by Covin and Sloan (1991) and Lumpkin and Dess (1996). Entrepreneurial orientation refers to "*processes, practices and decision-making activities that lead to a new entry. It involves the intentions and actions of key players functioning in a dynamic generative process aimed at new venture creation.*" (Lumpkin and Dess, 1996). Therefore, EO has been characterized by the following dimensions: *Innovativeness, proactiveness, risk-Taking, proactiveness, and competitive aggressiveness* (Covin and Slevin, 1991; Lumpkin and Dess, 1996). The majority of the extant research has studied EO at the firm level. As the individual is at the heart of the entrepreneurial process and is the major driving force of innovation at the firm level, studying EO at the individual level is needed. Kollmann et al. (2007) transferred the dimensions of the firm-level EO to the individual level to understand the mainspring behind individuals becoming entrepreneurs, which came to be known as IEO. Bolton and Lane modified the original firm-level EO scale to measure the EO at the individual level (Bolton and Lane, 2012).

Although entrepreneurial resilience has received the attention of many researchers (Ayala and Manzano, 2014; Bulmash, 2016; Calvo and García, 2010; Hedneret al., 2011; Jacelon, 1997; Korber and McNaughton, 2018; Mills et al., 2018; Pooley and Cohen, 2010), there is lack research which integrates resilience as a dimension of the multidimensional construct of individual entrepreneurial orientation. The present study proposes developing, testing, and validating a measurement scale based on the IEO dimensions of innovativeness, proactiveness, and the emerging dimension of resilience. The study was conducted on a sample of management students. Resilience is vital for students as it helps manage academic demands and prepares them to cope with the future stresses of study, work, and life (Caruana et al., 2011).

The research paper is structured as follows: In the first section, the topic will be introduced along with the focus of the study. In the second section, the theoretical understanding for EO, IEO, its dimension, innovativeness and proactiveness, and the new dimension of resilience will be discussed. The third section focuses on the methodology. The fourth and the fifth sections will present the results of the investigation and their discussion, respectively. The conclusion, implications, and suggestions for further research will be shown in the final section.

2.2 LITERATURE REVIEW

Over the past decades, the concept of EO has evolved to an important topic of interest in strategic entrepreneurship research. (Miller, 1983) inspired the idea of EO as an approach to strategic decision making, suggesting that for a firm to be characterized as entrepreneurial, it has to be innovative and not risk-averse when pursuing new opportunities. The work of Miller (1983) was later conceptualized by the authors Covin and Slevin (1991); Lumpkin and Dess (1996). Subsequently, the interest in EO grew drastically. Covin and Slevin (1989) explored a unidimensional perspective of Miller's (1983) work, stating that for a firm to be considered entrepreneurial, the presence of all three characteristics of innovativeness, proactiveness, and risk-taking was essential. Following this, Lumpkin and Dess, 1996 introduced the multidimensional perspective of the EO construct. Defining EO as the processes, practices, and decision-making activities that lead to new venture creation, Lumpkin and Dess (1996) model included the following five dimensions: Innovative, proactive, risk-taking, autonomy, and competitive aggressiveness. From a multidimensional view, the dimensions were not considered holistic. For a firm to be entrepreneurial could mean any or all of the EO characteristics are present (Hughes and Morgan, 2007). This is how the foundation of the EO construct was laid over the years. Entrepreneurial orientation has since been widely recognized as a firm-level construct that affects a firm's performance (Gupta and Gupta, 2015; Lumpkin and Dess, 1996; Rauch et al., 2009)

Further studies have explored the influence of EO on a firm's business performance within different contexts. For example, Anderson and Eshima (2013), in their study of Japanese SMEs, found that a firm's age and intangible resource advantage positively affect the EO–growth relationship. Covin and Miller (2014) have summarized the various themes of the growing research interest in international entrepreneurial orientation. The most recent development in EO is realizing the need for a global new multidimensional version of the construct to take it beyond its foundations of a firm-level unidimensional construct (Lumpkin and Pidduck, 2021).

Before EO gaining popularity as a firm-level construct, the prime focus of entrepreneurial research was on the individual entrepreneur. Post (Miller, 1983) seminal work, on the characteristics of entrepreneurial firms and the later its conceptualization (Covin and Slevin, 1991; Lumpkin and Dess, 1996), EO was subjected to firm-level analysis. A study (Kollmann et al., 2007) suggested shifting the focus back to the individual or the entrepreneur, who is the heart of the entrepreneurial process. The authors further adapted the firm-level dimensions of EO to individual-level analysis to study the effect of environmental factors on the determination of individual entrepreneurial orientation. The need for further individual-level analysis of the EO construct was proposed (Covin and Miller, 2014; Kollmann et al., 2007; Wales et al., 2011). One of the most important works in developing and validating the IEO measurement scale was by Bolton and Lane (2012). The authors modified the EO scales as proposed by Lumpkin and Dess (1996), and three sub-dimensions, namely, innovativeness, proactiveness, and risk-taking, emerged as the core elements of the IEO scale. The other two sub-dimensions of autonomy and competitive aggressiveness were not considered at the individual level due to low consistency. The multidimensionality of the EO construct considered for the IEO scale was congruent to the views of (Gartner, 1985) who suggested that to understand the complex process of new venture creation, multidimensional thinking is imperative. The implications of Bolton and Lane (2012) scale enabled researchers to study IEO from different perspectives. Individual entrepreneurial orientation positively impacts entrepreneurial intention (Koe, 2016; Kumar et al., 2020; Kurniawan et al., 2019; Taatila and Down, 2012). Many studies have reported gender differences in IEO (Fellnhofer et al., 2016; Goktan and Gupta, 2015; Júnior and Gimenez, 2012). Understanding IEO is valuable to students for forming better project teams and for the future business owners, incubators, and investors to evaluate business proposals. Knowledge of IEO would assist faculty in making entrepreneurship instruction and assessment more effective (Bolton and Lane, 2012). Based on the multidimensional EO construct, Satar and Natasha (2019) developed and validated an individual social entrepreneurial orientation scale, adding social passion as an additional dimension with innovativeness, proactiveness, and risk-taking.

From the research, Covin and Lumpkin (2011; Ferreira et al. (2017; and Wales et al. (2013) have suggested further theorizing the EO construct to include more meaningful sub-dimensions to be considered components to an alternative EO composite construct. Research has been conducted to test the validity for additional sub-dimensions in addition to the EO constructs (Covin and Slevin, 1991; Lumpkin and Dess, 1996). Santos et al. (2020) proposed and validated a scale for passion and perseverance as two new dimensions to the individual orientation scale in addition to the subdimensions of innovativeness, proactiveness, and risk-taking. A study by Taatila and Down (2012) has identified and validated networking as a new sub-dimension of the EO construct. Furthering the exploration of new sub-dimensions of the individual orientation construct, this study proposes developing, validating, and testing a measurement scale with resilience, innovativeness, and proactiveness as dimensions of IEO. Resilience has been recognized as an important behavior or trait of entrepreneurs (Bernard and Dubard Barbosa, 2016; Korber and McNaughton, 2018).

Resilience is the ability to adapt when facing tragedy, trauma, and adversity (Bonanno, 2004). It is an asset or strength, a desirable trait, process or characteristic that positively impacts an individual's performance, achievement, and wellbeing (Bartley et al., 2010). Entrepreneurs operate in a highly competitive and uncertain environment, and success is achieved only by those who are resilient during ambiguity, adapt quickly to change and persevere (Ayala and Manzano, 2014). According to a systematic literature review study (Korber and McNaughton, 2018), the construct of resilience is relevant to entrepreneurial research because studies have identified certain behavioral and cognitive traits such as hardiness, perseverance, or self-efficacy to explain why some resilient entrepreneurs or firms perform better than their non-resilient counterparts.

As seen in most of the definitions, resilience is manifested when adversity or challenge arises. The inherent ability or skill of overcoming these challenges and bouncing back is what can be defined as being resilient. Studies (Ayala and Manzano, 2014; Jacelon, 1997) resilience is a dynamic process that equips entrepreneurs with the skills and abilities to face an uncertain future and environmental stimuli with confidence and optimism. It can be seen as a real growth strategy. Resilience is a constellation of traits (Jacelon, 1997) or unification of a range of personal and behavioral qualities rather than a specific characteristic(Ayala and Manzano, 2014; Korber and McNaughton, 2018). Resilience is a fractal phenomenon which can be conceptualized at various spatial scales as follws: Micro (entrepreneur), meso (venture/team), macro (society), and cross scale (socio–ecological) (Bergström and Dekker, 2014). A multidisciplinary systematic literature review of 144 articles categorized into six scholarly conversations (Korber and McNaughton, 2018) found that most of the contributions to entrepreneurship resilience literature attempted to identify the factors that improve the inherent resilience of entrepreneurial firms and individuals. Entrepreneurial resilience in this context is *ex ante* conditions, which are inherent characteristics of individuals that enable them to manage adversity better. Individual resilience contributes to the overall organizational resilience (Hmieleski et al., 2015) could be considered a factor for entrepreneurial success (Ayala and Manzano, 2014; Calvo and García, 2010; Hayward et al., 2010).

Building on resilience as a multidimensional construct, it is an amalgamation of various behavioral qualities (Ayala and Manzano, 2014; Korber and McNaughton, 2018) that make an individual resilient. The distinct factors of individual resilience identified from the extant studies are as follows: Optimism, coping abilities, internal locus of control, adaptability, perseverance, social connectedness, and possessing a sense of humor (Baruah and Ward, 2014; Benight and Bandura, 2004; Fisher et al., 2016; Korber and McNaughton, 2018; Owens et al., 2013; Ratten, 2020; Richardson et al., 1990; Ungar et al., 2007). Optimism is the capacity of an entrepreneur to remain positive when facing adverse situations and see the challenges as an opportunity to learn rather than an impediment (Schneider, 2001). Unless people believe that they can produce desired effects from their actions, they are not motivated to take action or persevere in the face of difficulties (Bandura, 2010). The coping abilities of individuals differ from each other. It is the belief in their inherent coping efficacy that influences preparedness toward potential challenges and how they are perceived and cognitively processed (Benight and Bandura, 2004). Another sub-construct of resilience is the locus of control. According to Bulmash (2016), locus of control is the perception of having personal control and not being at the mercy of external factors. People with an internal locus of control tend to be more focused while responding to challenges and see their actions as the source of their success (Kirkcaldy et al., 2002). Adaptability is the ability, skill, or disposition of an individual to learn and change to fit to the evolving tasks, social or environmental features (Ployhart and Bliese, 2006). Perseverance is being able to focus on set goals with continued enthusiasm irrespective of adversity(Baum and Locke, 2004). Resilient entrepreneurs maintain meaningful social relationships within their families and beyond. Support from the social circles enables individuals to change perceptions of adversity, attempt innovative problem solving and reduce the adverse effects of challenges (Fine, 1991). Having a good sense of humor alleviates stress (Richardson et al., 1990). The literature review of the sub constructs of resilience have been iterated in Table 2.1.

TABLE 2.1 Literature Review of Findings For Sub-Constructs of Resilience.

Construct	Sub-construct	Source
Resilience	Optimism	Abiola and Udofia, 2011; Ayala and Manzano, 2014; Fisher and Maritz, 2016; Jacelon, 1997; Owens et al., 2013; Polk, 1997; Ratten, 2020; Rutter, 1985
	Coping ability	Abiola and Udofia, 2011; Benight and Bandura, 2004; Hamill, 2003; Polk, 1997; Ratten, 2020; Richardson et al., 1990
	Locus of control	Bulmash, 2016; Hamill, 2003; Hedner et al., 2011; Owens et al., 2013; Rauch and Frese, 2007; Richardson et al., 1990
	Adaptability	Abiola and Udofia, 2011; Korber and McNaughton, 2018; Polk, 1997; Richardson et al., 1990
	Perseverance	Fisher and Maritz, 2016; Hamill, 2003; Manzano-García and Ayala Calvo, 2013; Polk, 1997; Ratten, 2020; Santos et al., 2020
	Social connectedness	Abiola and Udofia, 2011; Denz-Penhey and Campbell Murdoch, 2008; Fine, 1991; Jacelon, 1997; Richardson et al., 1990; Ungar et al., 2007
	Sense of humor	Fisher and Maritz, 2016; Richardson et al., 1990

Through literature, a gap was identified that studies had not analyzed resilience as a construct of individual entrepreneurial orientation. This paper aims to examine individual-level resilience as a dimension of the individual entrepreneurial orientation. The study by Koe (2016) on undergraduate students' entrepreneurial intentions revealed that as students do not possess the necessary resources for becoming entrepreneurs, risk-taking did not affect their entrepreneurial drive(Koe, 2016). Therefore, in addition to resilience, dimensions of innovativeness and proactiveness (Covin and Slevin, 1991; Lumpkin and Dess, 1996) had been considered.

2.3 METHODOLOGY

2.3.1 SAMPLE

The measurement instrument used was a questionnaire distributed among the 350 management students in India's Delhi NCR region. After the responses were received, unengaged respondents were eliminated based on the responses with zero standard deviation and missing data. The final sample size was 242, comprised of females (47%) and males (53%). The majority of the sample was in the age group of 18–25 years (75%).

2.3.2 ITEM SELECTION

The literature review provided the basis for proposing a new IEO scale, consolidating various skills and behavioral traits that make an individual resilient. Out of the original dimensions of the Covin and Slevin (1991); Lumpkin and Dess (1996); and Miller (1983) models, innovativeness and proactiveness have been considered in this study as the sample comprises management students. The IEO scale, which has modified the firm-based scale for individual-level analysis (Bolton and Lane, 2012) has been adapted for innovativeness and proactiveness. The resilience construct has been divided into various sub-constructs based on the literature review and questions framed for its measurement. Responses for the items were reported on a 5-point Likert scale; 1 being "strongly disagree" and 5 being "strongly agree."

2.4 RESULTS

Exploratory factor analysis and confirmatory factor analysis were carried out using IBM SPSS 26 and IBM AMOS 23 software packages. First, the validity and reliability of the survey questionnaire were tested. The internal reliability was measured by the Cronbach's α (Cronbach, 1951). All the standardized scales adapted had a Cronbach's α of above 0.70, and the consolidated scale used in this study reported a value of 0.875, which is above the cut-off (>0.70) (Khine, 2013). Then, (EFA) was performed to reduce the dimensions. The Kaiser–Meyer–Olkin's measure result was 0.76 (>0.50), denoting sampling adequacy and the Bartlett's test for sphericity was significant at $p = 0.000$ (Field, 2009). This was followed by another parameter of measurement, the one based on the eigenvalue of each factor. For a group of items to be considered a factor, each factor's eigenvalue must be equal or more than 1 (Field, 2009). The factor loading of each item of each construct must have a value equal to or above 0.50 (Hair et al., 2006). Finally, based on the factor loading, eigenvalues, and cross-loadings, six components were extracted, including 14 items, explaining 69% of the variance. The resulting final model was a multidimensional instrument with six distinct factors; four relating to resilience. The original measurement instrument comprising 33 items of various subconstructs of resilience, innovativeness and proactiveness was adjusted and 19 items were removed. Based on the individual sampling adequacy of above 0.50 (Kaiser, 1974), suppressing factor loadings of below 0.05 and making adjustments for high cross-loadings, the final scale was reduced to 14 items (Hair et al., 2006). The items selected are shown in Table 2.2. The original individual orientation scale is shown in Annexure 2.1.

The factor's construct reliability (CR) was good. For perseverance (0.75), internal locus of control (0.74), adaptability (0.77), optimism (0.77), proactivity (0.72), and innovativeness (0.83). The Cronbach's α for all items in the final scale was above 0.775 (>0.70); hence, showing the adequacy of construct validity (CR) (Cronbach, 1951). The factor's convergent validity, indicated by average variance extracted (AVE), was adequate with all values equal to or above 0.50. For perseverance, 0.50; internal locus of control, 0.590; adaptability, 0.54; optimism, 0.62; proactivity, 0.56; and innovativeness, 0.71. The standardized factor loadings (SFL), CR, Cronbach's α, and AVE for the final model are presented in Table 2.2.

TABLE 2.2 Standardized Factor Loadings, Construct Reliability (CR), Average Variance Explained (AVE), Cronbach's alpha (α) For the Final Model.

Factor	Item	SFL	CR	AVE	α
Optimism	RE1	0.74	0.77	0.62	0.68
	RE3	0.69			
Locus of control	RE12	0.62	0.74	0.59	0.63
	RE7	0.77			
Adaptability	RE17	0.76	0.77	0.54	0.64
	RE19	0.60			
	RE18	0.53			
Perseverance	RE23	0.83	0.75	0.50	0.75
	RE24	0.62			
	RE22	0.73			
Proactiveness	PRO2	0.74	0.72	0.56	0.68
	PRO1	0.71			
Innovativeness	INN1	0.70	0.83	0.71	0.72
	INN2	0.84			

The discriminant validity was confirmed using the Fornell and Larcker Criterion (Fornell and Larcker, 1981), a test wherein each construct's AVE is compared to its squared correlations with other constructs in the model. The factor's (AVE) should be more than the square of correlation. The results show that the discriminant validity has been proved, and this is depicted in Table 2.3, indicating that the AVE for the factors is higher than the squared correlations.

TABLE 2.3 Discriminant Validity.

	PER	ILOC	OPT	ADAPT	PRO	INN
PER	0.50*					
LOC	0.34	0.59*				
OPT	0.13	0.10	**0.62***			
ADAPT	0.03	0.02	0.09	**0.54***		
PRO	0.31	0.10	0.28	0.14	**0.56***	
INN	0.14	0.06	0.13	0.15	0.15	0.71*

**Average values*

The overall goodness of fit (GIF) was reported by two model fit values; the absolute fit indices and the comparative fit index (CFI). Under absolute fit indices, the Chi-squared/Df was 1.167, well within the desired value (1–3). The root mean square error of approximation (RMSEA) was 0.041 (<0.05) and GFI was 0.908 (>0.90). All these values indicate a good fit. Additionally, the CFI results were elucidated by the incremental fit index (IFI) = 0.968, Trucker Lewis index (TLI) = 0.950 and CFI = 0.965. The results show a good model fit (Sivo et al., 2006; Hair et al., 2009). Table 2.4 shows the model fit indices values. Figure 2.1 shows the confirmatory factor analysis results.

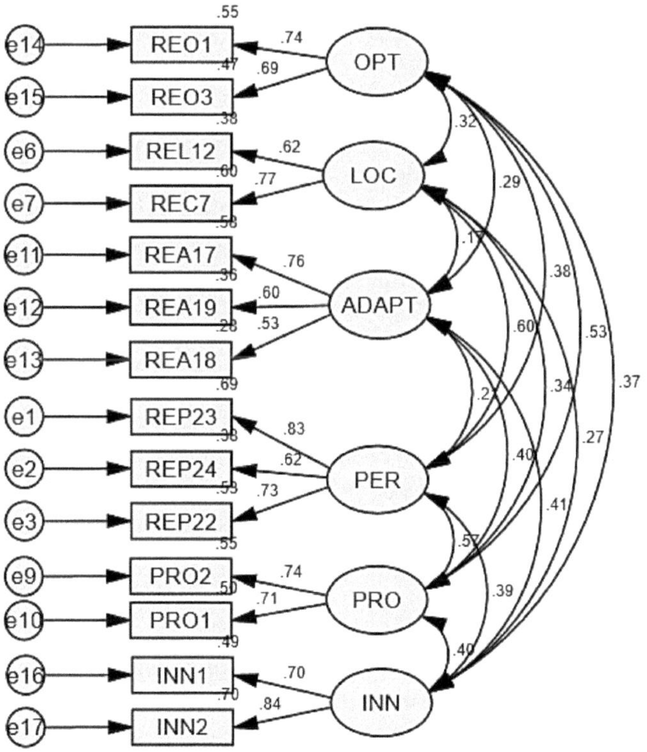

FIGURE 2.1 confirmatory factor analysis results (standardized factor loadings, correlation).

TABLE 2.4 Model Fit Indices Result.

	CMIN	RMSEA	GFI	IFI	TLI	CFI
Result	1.171	0.042	0.909	0.969	0.952	0.967

2.5 DISCUSSION

Individual entrepreneurial orientation is more effective as a multidimensional construct, and new dimensions or indicators are encouraged (Anderson et al., 2015). Researchers are now exploring different conceptualizations of the IEO construct. (Santos et al., 2020) developed and validated a scale with passion and perseverance as new dimensions of IEO. Drawing from Korber and McNaughton (2018 suggestions of incorporating psychological traits, behavioral patterns, and organizational characteristics that entrepreneurs use to prepare and respond to challenges; the present study proposed developing an IEO scale with the dimensions of resilience, innovativeness, and proactiveness. According to this study results, for an individual to be resilient, perseverance, an internal locus of control, optimism, and adaptability are vital. The items of the perseverance sub-construct reflect the unwavering desire for achieving set goals and objectives when facing challenges. How one reacts to a challenge ultimately guides how one handles it, making the internal locus of control key for being resilient. Entrepreneurs operate in an unpredictable environment. In such situations, having self-belief and an optimistic perception propels individuals to keep adapting and evolving according to cues of the external environment. Being proactive and innovative are cornerstones of IEO. Preparedness and acting in anticipation of future challenges are marks of an individual who is proactive and resilient.

The overall entrepreneurial orientation is depicted by resilience, proactiveness, and innovativeness. The findings are corroborated with the extant research on the various cognitive and behavioral traits and skills that empower individuals to be prepared; face, learn, and bounce back in the face of adversity (Ayala and Manzano, 2014; Bulmash, 2016; Fisher et al., 2016; Korber and McNaughton, 2018; Manzano–García and Ayala Calvo, 2013; Owens et al., 2013; Ratten, 2020; Santos et al., 2020). According to Santos et al. (2020), IEO being a reflexive construct, increasing the dimensions or first-order constructs, deepens our understanding of IEO, the second-order construct. The proposed model is structurally sound, and IEO is reflected in the various first-order constructs of resilience, innovativeness, and proactiveness. The findings suggest that in an alternative conceptualization of IEO, resilience can be an essential part. Entrepreneurial training and education will benefit from identifying and measuring the various dimensions or behavioral facets that reinforce EO among its youth. Understanding which education approaches are relevant keeping the local environment into consideration is vital for its efficacy (Paul Dana 2001).

2.6 CONCLUSIONS AND IMPLICATIONS

As the world reels with the destruction caused by the COVID-19 pandemic and organizations prepares for the new normal, it has widely been recognized that being resilient, be it at the individual or organizational level, is a characteristic that has empowered a successful fight-back. The undying human desire to rise from adversity stronger encapsulates what being resilient is. Entrepreneurs operate in unpredictable environments, and being resilient differentiates between those who are entrepreneurial and those who are not. The measurement instruments for individual-level analysis of EO are scarce. The majority of the extant research has been based on the dimensions defined decades back. Entrepreneurship is a dynamic process, and lately, the need to explore new dimensions of EO has been expressed, calling for reimagining its dimensions. Thus, this study proposed that resilience is an important trait that should be a part of an alternative multidimensional IEO construct. Resilience makes an individual less vulnerable to adversities and challenges and adds to the overall success and growth of the organization.

For practical and research implications, this study could be of interest to researchers to explore and evaluate resilience as a dimension of IEO, to deepen the understanding of the behavioral and cognitive processes that affect IEO. Academicians, faculty members, and career managers could understand how to harness students' inherent resilience skills or develop it as a resource. The development of resilience skills is not part of the learning outcomes of most management courses. To enhance the employability of the future generation of managers, in addition to being innovative and proactive, resilience is vital. The study is an important guide for current managers to understand the role resilience plays in ensuring sustained levels of growth and enhancement of the organization and its human capital.

Although the study opens doors to various research possibilities, it has limitations that provide further investigation possibilities. The sample could be increased further with wider geographical coverage to make the study more robust. A longitudinal study could be conducted to analyze how IEO tends to change owing to the external environmental factors. Gender differences in response to adversity can also be explored.

KEYWORDS

- **resilience**
- **individual entrepreneurial orientation**
- **entrepreneurial orientation**
- **management students**

REFERENCES

Anderson, B. S.; Eshima, Y. The Influence of Firm Age and Intangible Resources on the Relationship Between Entrepreneurial Orientation and Firm Growth Among Japanese Smes. *J. Bus. Ventur.* **2013,** *28* (*3*), 413–429.

Anderson, B. S.; Kreiser, P. M.; Kuratko, D. F.; Hornsby, J. S.; Eshima, Y. Reconceptualising Entrepreneurial Orientation. *Strat. Manag. J.* **2015,** *36* (10), 1579–1596.

Ayala, J. C.; Manzano, G. The Resilience of the Entrepreneur. Influence on the Success of the Business. A Longitudinal Analysis. *J. Econ. Psychol.* **2014,** *42*, 126–135.

Bandura, A. Self-Efficacy. In the *Corsini Encyclopedia of Psychology*; John Wiley & Sons, Inc.; Hoboken, NJ, USA, 2010.

Bartley, M.; Schoon, I.; Mitchell, R.; Blane, D. Resilience As an Asset for Healthy Development. In *Health Assets in a Global Context*; Springer New York, New York, 2010.

Baruah, B.; Ward, A. Metamorphosis of Intrapreneurship As an Effective Organizational Strategy. *Int. Entrep. Manag. J.* **2014,** *11* (4), 811–822.

Baum, J. R.; Locke, E. A. The Relationship of Entrepreneurial Traits, Skill, and Motivation to Subsequent Venture Growth. *J. Appl. Psychol.* **2004,** *89* (4), 587–598.

Benight, C. C.; Bandura, A. Social Cognitive Theory of Posttraumatic Recovery: The Role of Perceived Self-Efficacy. *Behav. Res. Ther.* **2004,** *42* (10), 1129–1148.

Bergström, J.; Dekker, S. W. A. Bridging the Macro and the Micro by Considering the Meso: Reflections on the Fractal Nature of Resilience. *Ecol. Soc.* **2014,** *19* (4).

Bernard, M.-J.; Barbosa, S. D. Resilience and Entrepreneurship: A Dynamic and Biographical Approach to the Entrepreneurial Act. *M@N@Gement* **2016,** *19* (2), 89–123.

Bolton, D. L.; Lane, M. D. Individual Entrepreneurial Orientation: Development of A Measurement Instrument. *Educ. Train.* **2012,** *54* (2–3), 219–233.

Bonanno, G. A. Loss, Trauma, and Human Resilience: Have We Underestimated the Human Capacity to Thrive After Extremely Aversive Events? *Am. Psychol.* **2004,** *59* (1), 20–8.

Bulmash, B. Entrepreneurial Resilience: Locus of Control and Well-Being of Entrepreneurs. *J. Entrep. Organ. Manag.* **2016,** *05* (1).

Calvo, J. C. A.; García, G. M. Established Business Owners' Success: Influencing Factors. *J. Dev. Entrep.* **2010,** *15* (*3*), 263–286.

Caruana, V.; Clegg, S.; Ploner, J.; Stevenson, J.; Wood, R. Promoting Students' "Resilient Thinking". In *Diverse Higher Education Learning Environments: Twelve Voices of Diversity, Challenge and Resilience Project Lead*: Viv Caruana Project Team. 2011.

Covin, J. G.; Lumpkin, G. T. Entrepreneurial Orientation Theory and Research: Reflections on A Needed Construct. *Entrep. Theory Pract.* **2011,** *35* (5), 855–872.

Covin, J. G.; Miller, D. International Entrepreneurial Orientation: Conceptual Considerations, Research Themes, Measurement Issues, and Future Research Directions. *Entrep. Theo. Pract.* **2014,** *38* (1), 11–44.

Covin, J. G.; Slevin, D. P. Strategic Management of Small Firms in Hostile and Benign Environments. *Strat. Manag. J.* **1989,** *10* (1), 75–87.

Covin, J. G.; Slevin, D. P. A Conceptual Model of Entrepreneurship As Firm Behavior. *Entrep. Theor. Pract.* **1991,** *16* (1), 7–26.

Cronbach, L. J. Coefficient Alpha and the Internal Structure of Tests. *Psychometrika* **1951,** 16, 297–334.

Fellnhofer, K.; Puumalainen, K.; Sjögrén, H. Entrepreneurial Orientation and Performance—Are Sexes Equal? *Int. J. Entrep. Behav. Res.* **2016,** *22* (3), 346–374.

Ferreira, F. A. F.; Jalali, M. S.; Bento, P.; Marques, C. S. E.; Ferreira, J. J. M. Enhancing Individual Entrepreneurial Orientation Measurement Using a Metacognitive Decision Making-Based Framework. *Int. Entrep. Manag. J.* **2017,** *13* (2), 327–346.

Field, A. P. *Discovering Statistics Using Spss (And Sex and Drugs and Rock'N'Roll)*, 3rd ed.; Sage: London. 2009.

Fine, S. B. Resilience and Human Adaptability: Who Rises above Adversity? 1990 Eleanor Clarke Slagle Lecture. *Am. J. Occup. Ther.* **1991,** *45* (6), 493–503.

Fisher, R.; Maritz, A. Does Individual Resilience Influence Entrepreneurial Success Pro-Environmental Behaviour in Emerging Markets: A Study of Vietnamese Consumer Purchase of Energy Efficient Appliances. *Acad. Entrep. J.* **2016,** *22* (2).

Fornell, C.; Larcker, D. F. Structural Equation Models with Unobservable Variables and Measurement Error: Algebra and Statistics. *J. Mark. Res.* **1981,** *18* (3), 382–388.

Gartner, W. B. A Conceptual Framework For Describing the Phenomenon of New Venture Creation. *Acad. Manag. Rev.* **1985,** *10* (4), 696–706.

Gittell, J. H.; Cameron, K.; Lim, S.; Rivas, V. Relationships, Layoffs, and Organizational Resilience: Airline Industry Responses to September 11. *J. Appl. Behav. Sci.* **2006,** *42* (3), 300–329.

Goktan, A. B.; Gupta, V. K. Sex, Gender, and Individual Entrepreneurial Orientation: Evidence From Four Countries. *Int. Entrep. Manag. J.* **2015,** *11* (1), 95–112.

Gupta, V.; Gupta, A. The Concept of Entrepreneurial Orientation. *Found. Trends Entrep.* **2015,** *11* (2), 55–137.

Hair, J. F.; Black, W. C.; Babin, B. J.; Anderson, R. E. *Multivariate Data Analysis*, 7th ed.; Prentice Hall: Englewood Cliffs, NJ. 2009.

Hair, J. F.; Black, W. C.; Babin, B. J.; Anderson, E. R.; et al. *Multivariate Data Analysis*, 6th ed.; Pearson-Prentice Hall: New Jersey, 2006.

Hedner, T.; Abouzeedan, A.; Klofsten, M. Entrepreneurial Resilience. *Ann. Innov. Entrep.* **2011,** *2* (1), 79–86.

Hmieleski, K. M.; Carr, J. C.; Baron, R. A. Integrating Discovery and Creation Perspectives of Entrepreneurial Action: The Relative Roles of Founding Ceo Human Capital, Social Capital, and Psychological Capital in Contexts of Risk Versus Uncertainty. *Strat. Entrep. J.* **2015,** *9* (4), 289–312.

Hughes, M.; Morgan, R. E. Deconstructing the Relationship Between Entrepreneurial Orientation and Business Performance at the Embryonic Stage of Firm Growth. *Indus. Mark. Manag.* **2007,** *36* (5), 651–661.

Jacelon, C. S. The Trait and Process of Resilience. *J. Adv. Nurs.* **1997,** *25*, 123–129.

Júnior, E.; Gimenez, F. An Investigation of the Reliablity and Validity of an Entrepreneurial Orientation Index in Brazil. *Acad. Entrep. J.* **2012,** *18*, 41–56.

Kaiser, H. F. An Index of Factorial Simplicity. *Psychometrika* **1974,** *39* (1), 31–36.

Khine, M. *Application of Structural Equation Modeling in Educational Research and Practice*; Sense Publishers. 2013.

Kirkcaldy, B.; Shephard, R.; Furnham, A. The Influence of Type A Behavior and Locus of Control Upon Job Satisfaction and Occupational Health. *Pers. Individ. Differ.* **2002,** *33*, 1361–1371.

Koe, W.-L. The Relationship between Individual Entrepreneurial Orientation (IEO) and Entrepreneurial Intention. *J. Glob. Entrep. Res.* **2016,** *6*, 13.

Kollmann, T.; Christofor, J.; Kuckertz, A. Explaining Individual Entrepreneurial Orientation: Conceptualization of a Cross-Cultural Research Framework. *Int. J. Entrep. Small Bus.* **2007,** *4*, 325–340.

Korber, S.; McNaughton, R. B. Resilience and Entrepreneurship: A Systematic Literature Review. *Int. J. Entrep. Behav. Res.* **2018,** *24* (4).

Kumar, S.; Paray, Z. A.; Dwivedi, A. K. Student's Entrepreneurial Orientation and Intentions. In *Higher Education. Skills and Work-Based Learning*; Emerald, 2020**.**

Kurniawan, J. E.; Setiawan, J. L.; Sanjaya, E. L.; Wardhani, F. P. I.; Virlia, S.; Dewi, K.; Kasim, A.; et al. Developing A Measurement Instrument for High School Students' Entrepreneurial Orientation. *Cogent Educ.* **2019,** *6* (1).

Lumpkin, G. T.; Dess, G. G. Clarifying the Entrepreneurial Orientation Construct and Linking it to Performance, *Acad. Manag. Rev.* **1996,** *21*, 135–172.

Manzano-García, G.; Ayala Calvo, J. C. Psychometric Properties of Connor-Davidson Resilience Scale in a Spanish Sample of Entrepreneurs. *Psicothema* **2013,** *25* (2), 245–251.

Miller, D. The Correlates of Entrepreneurship in Three Types of Firms. *Manag. Sci.* **1983,** *29* (7), 70–791.

Mills, A.; Davis, P.; Mclaughlin, P. In *Building Resilience in Construction Management Students*, 54TH Asc Annual International Conference Proceeding, 2018.

Owens, K. S.; Kirwan, J. R.; Lounsbury, J. W.; Levy, J. J.; Gibson, L. W. Personality Correlates of Self-Employed Small Business Owners' Success. *Work* **2013,** *45* (1), 73–85.

Paul Dana, L. The Education and Training of Entrepreneurs in Asia. *Educ. Train.* **2001,** *43* (8/9), 405–416.

Ployhart, R. E.; Bliese, P. D. Individual Adaptability (I-Adapt) Theory: Conceptualizing the Antecedents, Consequences, and Measurement of Individual Differences in Adaptability. *Adv. Hum. Perform. Cogn. Eng. Res.* **2006,** 6, 3–39.

Pooley, J.; Cohen, L. Resilience: A Definition in Context. *Aust. Commun. Psychol.* **2010,** 22, 30–37.

Ratten, V. Coronavirus (Covid-19) and Entrepreneurship: Cultural, Lifestyle and Societal Changes. *J. Entrep. Emer. Econ.* 2020.

Rauch, A.; Wiklund, J.; Lumpkin, G. T.; Frese, M. Entrepreneurial Orientation and Business Performance: An Assessment of Past Research and Suggestions For the Future. *Entrep. Theor. Pract.* **2009,** *33* (3), 761–787.

Richardson, G. E.; Neiger, B. L.; Jensen, S.; Kumpfer, K. L. The Resiliency Model. *Health Educ.* **1990,** *21* (6), 33–39.

Santos, G.; Marques, C. S.; Ferreira, J. J. M. Passion and Perseverance as Two New Dimensions of An Individual Entrepreneurial Orientation Scale. *J. Bus. Res.* **2020,** *112*, 190–199.

Schneider, S. L. In Search of Realistic Optimism: Meaning, Knowledge, and Warm Fuzziness. *Am. Psychol.* **2001,** *56* (3) 250–263.
Shahid Satar, M.; Natasha, S. Individual Social Entrepreneurship Orientation: Towards Development of A Measurement Scale Measurement Scale 49. *Asia Pacific J. Innov. Entrep.* **2019,** *13* (1), 49–72.
Sivo, S. A.; Xitao, F. A. N.; Witta, E. L.; Willse, J. T. The Search For 'Optimal' Cutoff Properties: Fit Index Criteria In Structural Equation Modeling. *J. Exp. Educ.* **2006,** *74* (3), 267–288.
Taatila, V.; Down, S. Measuring Entrepreneurial Orientation of University Students. *Educ. Train.* **2012,** *54* (8), 744–760.
Ungar, M.; Brown, M.; Liebenberg, L.; Othman, R.; Kwong, W. M.; Armstrong, M.; Gilgun, J. Unique Pathways To Resilience Across Cultures. *Adolescence* **2007,** *42* (166), 287–310.
Wales, W.; Monsen, E.; Mckelvie, A. The Organizational Pervasiveness of Entrepreneurial Orientation. *Entrep. Theor. Pract.* **2011,** *35* (5), 895–923.
Wales, W. J.; Gupta, V. K.; Mousa, F. T. Empirical Research on Entrepreneurial Orientation: An Assessment and Suggestions For Future Research. *Int. Small Bus. J.* **2013,** *31* (4), 357–383.
Williams, T. A.; Gruber, D. A.; Sutcliffe, K. M.; Shepherd, D. A.; Zhao, E. Y. Organizational Response to Adversity: Fusing Crisis Management and Resilience Research Streams. *Acad. Manag. Ann.* **2017,** *11* (2), 733–769.

ANNEXURE 2.1 Questionnaire (Individual Orientation Scale).

Construct	Sub-construct	Item code	Item
Resilience	Optimism	RE1	In challenging situations, I will find a way
		RE2	I am facing my future in an optimistic way
		RE3	I can master difficulties
		RE4	I worry about my future
		RE5	Thanks to my resourcefulness, I know how to handle unforeseen situations
	Coping Abilities	RE6	I look for ways to change tough situations creatively
		RE7	Regardless of what happens to me, I believe I can control my reaction to it
		RE8	By dealing with difficult situations, I can grow in positive ways
		RE9	I seek out ways to replace losses I face in life
	Locus of Control	RE10	When I make plans, I am almost positive I can make them work
		RE11	To get people to do what is right depends upon capability; luck has nothing to do with it
		RE12	I am responsible for what happens to me
		RE13	Often, I feel that I have little influence over the things that happen to me

ANNEXURE 2.1 *(Continued)*

Construct	Sub-construct	Item code	Item
	Social Connectedness	RE14	In times of difficulties, I have people to rely on
		RE15	In times of difficulties, people can rely on me
	Sense of Humour	RE16	I can often see the humorous side of situations
	Adaptability	RE17	Unpredictability does not frustrate me
		RE18	In case of unanticipated events, I actively readjust in response
		RE19	I believe I am capable of handling stress
		RE20	Stable environments are where I perform best
		RE21	I can easily respond to changing conditions
	Perseverance	RE22	I have achieved my goals irrespective of how much time it took.
		RE23	Setbacks have not deterred me in meeting major challenges
		RE24	If I start something, I finish it
		RE25	I do not get disheartened by setbacks
		RE26	In difficult situations, despite seeing others cede, I follow through in the pursuit of achieving my goals.
		INN1	I often like to try unexplored and unique activities
Innovativeness		INN2	In general, instead of tried and tested approaches, I emphasize on innovative approaches
		INN3	If I learn something new, I would instead try to do it my unique way than imitating others
		INN4	Instead of using existing problem-solving techniques, I prefer trying out new approaches
		PRO 1	I usually act in expectation of future challenges, needs or change
Proactiveness		PRO2	I tend to plan projects beforehand
		PRO3	I prefer to take the initiative and to get projects going rather than waiting for someone else to do it

CHAPTER 3

Mapping the Digital Entrepreneurial Landscape of SMEs

PRIYANKA KAPOOR TANDON[1*] and SHOBHIT[2]

[1]*Department of Commerce, Avadh Girls' Degree College, Lucknow 226010, India*

[2]*Department of Management and Social Sciences, Amity University,Tashkent 100028, Uzbekistan*

Corresponding author. E-mail: priyak13_tandon@yahoo.co.in

ABSTRACT

Small and medium enterprises (SMEs) are globally recognized as the stimulator for economic development. They serve as breeding grounds for innovative entrepreneurship. The importance of this sector has been highly recognized by the policy makers. Growth and inclusive development in the present milieu cannot be achieved without a fertile digital ecosystem. A strong collaborated digital ecosystem can be mutually beneficial to various stakeholders. Growth and success in this digital era necessitates investments in technology, knowledge, and skill development. In the given context, this research paper explores the extent of digital penetration and adoption among small businesses prevalent in India and outlines the key factors that can help in the effective implementation of information system among these enterprises. The study also attempts to discern a conceptual framework for ascertaining the likelihood of digital adoption among the respondent enterprises. For the purpose of the study, a survey method using structured questionnaires from the incumbent

Constructive Discontent in Execution: Creative Approaches to Technology and Management.
Sanjeev Bansal, Anita Venaik, Swati Upveja, and Saritha S. (Eds.)

executives and owner-managers of the firms operational in central Uttar Pradesh and NCR region was employed. The findings of the research can be particularly beneficial in a plausible reconstruction of an agile "digital landscape" within SMEs.

3.1 INTRODUCTION

Technology and human existence and advances have a concurrent bearing on each other. They have mutually coexisted and acclimatized apiece since times immemorial. The Activity Theory stands at the fulcrum of this tenacious interaction. It deals with the asymmetrical relationship of people and things and the role of artifacts in everyday life (Nardi, 1996). This super dynamic theory reiterates the kinetic business transformation with the advent of technology to enhance business practices. When businesses and the way they operate shift from their traditional mode of operations and management to the modern and technology-oriented ways of operation, the transition is referred to as digital transformation or disruption (Rashid, 2017). Digital transformation is not only about espousing new technology but also about reconstituting organizational construct and adroitness leading to value creation through innovative and transformational business practices. Digitalization has been highly influential in fostering a paradigm shift in the ways we do business today. We stand with our feet well established into the fourth industrial revolution: A digitally smart revolution, a revolution of Internet of Things (Sommer, 2015). The new age has forced us to rethink the way we perceive the traditional definitions of economy, wealth creation, business organizations, and other institutional structures (Tapscott, 1996). From achieving profitability through economies of scale (by way of large-scale production) where the producer and end customer were indirectly linked through a barrage of middlemen marketers to the prime focus shifting to customers and their needs, modern technology has been highly instrumental in shifting the spotlight on the customer. It has enabled the study of customer needs and preferences and mass customization (Rogers, 2016). Digital platforms have enabled uninterrupted customer interface. Customers can virtually verify the make and kind of the required product before ordering. Today, equipped with graphics and designing tools on the one hand and web and social networking platforms on the other, collective innovation and digitalization have led to yawning landscapes for existing and new players in the business arena demolishing geographical boundaries. Digital transformation has ordained the turf for contemporary business modeling. Indian business arena has gradually exhibited the diffusion of technology in business operations in order to remain both domestically and globally competitive. In the current Indian context, ICT adoption is inevitable but insufficient. It is laced with immense heterogeneity. Its role is limited to apprehending data rather than interpreting (Ponelis and Britz, 2011). Digital penetration has escalated the opportunity businesses possess by virtue of changing times.

3.2 REVIEW OF LITERATURE

In the current scenario, no firm, irrespective of size, can remain completely detached from digitalization. Though requirements, level of acceptance, and challenges in digital adoption vary significantly between firms. Firm size and nature of work are primary determining factors of digital adoption condition. Likewise, small businesses have needs and scope unique and significantly different from their larger counterparts (Müller et al., 2017). Small businesses can make efficient use of technology to establish its presence in newer horizons and gain competitive advantage (Hamad et al., 2018; Lee and Falahat, 2019; Mogos, 2015; Whiteley, 1998). In order to achieve this competitive edge, firms are bound to adapt transformational technologies for innovative business procedures and practices fundamentally driven on agile digital platforms. Past researches have proved that firms that enroute operational business modeling through digital gateways fair better than their competitors (Bouwman et al., 2019; Joensuu-Salo et al., 2018; Koch and Windsperger, 2017). It is therefore important and, in contemporary times, advisable for firms to have a focused digital transformation strategy in place (Bouncken et al., 2019). To put the most effective strategic foot forward, a firm needs to have a clear picture of its prevalent digital resources and its usage. Expansive literature on theoretical models of technology adoption at both individual and firm level is available within the academic domain. An extensive study of the same was conducted in order to funnel down a construct which resonate the objectives set to infer. Table 3.1 illustrates some of the firm/individual technology adoption models taken up for the review of literature.

3.3 OBJECTIVES OF STUDY

The body of literature available with respect to the implementation and adoption of digital platforms majorly relate to larger firms. Smaller firms have shown to exhibit distinct digital requirements and adoption pattern (Cragg and King, 1993). Thus, there evidently was a need to examine the level of digital acceptance of small businesses, through a scholarly approach. The purpose of this study is thus to examine the awareness, readiness, and existing usage of technology in the business operations of small businesses (especially SMEs) to meet the challenges of digitalization taking into account the special role these incumbent firms play in the economic development of the nation. The study proposes to understand and identify the inhibitors and facilitators for these firms in being digitally abreast with contemporary business practices, the level of adoption of ICT platforms, and the congeniality of the business ecosystem toward digital ingestion with respect to the demographic profile of the firms. The study further attempts to discern a conceptual framework for ascertaining the likelihood of digital adoption among the respondent enterprises. Several studies in the past have brought forward the theories focusing on the factors influencing acceptance of technology and models to analyze the level of adoption. This study moves one step ahead and investigates through an empirical approach, technology adoption and exploitation at firm level, thereby entailing application of the theory to practice.

TABLE 3.1 Theoretical Models of Technology Adoption.

Model	Variables/constructs	Literature
Diffusion of innovation (DOI)	• Time • Communication channel • Innovation • Social system	Rogers (2003)
Technology adoption model (TAM)	• Perceived usefulness (PU) • Perceived ease-of-use (PEOU)	Davis (1989)
Technology-organization-environment (TOE)	• Technology • Organization • Environment	Tonatzky and Fleischer (1990)

TABLE 3.1 *(Continued)*

Model	Variables/constructs	Literature
Unified theory of acceptance and use of technology (UTAUT)	• Performance expectancy • Effort expectancy • Social influence • Facilitating conditions	Venkatesh et al. (2003)
The integrated acceptance and sustainability assessment model (IASAM)	• Management • Quality of technology • Technology acceptance • Domain development	Aizstrauta et al. (2013)

An SME/small business is a mirror reflection of the capabilities of its owner. Small businesses are synonymous to the strengths, weaknesses, attitude, and vision of its owner-manager. Thus, the generic characteristic, knowledge, attitude, and innovativeness of the entrepreneur are strongly reflected in the organizational digital adoption scale too (Tagliavini et al., 2001). The owner's organizational decision-making with respect to digital adoption is also influenced by the available technology and the existing environment. Thus, this paper has based its interrogative structural construct on the basis of technology, and organizational and environmental factors as significant determinants of enterprise digital adoption as laid by Tonatzky and Fleischer (1990) in his book *The Processes of Technological Innovation*. The various attributes of technology, organization, and environment have been thoroughly reviewed and thoughtfully included to suffice contemporary business practices (see Fig. 3.1; Table 3.2).

TOE framework has proved to be a holistic model of technology adoption study. Various researches in the past have used the TOE framework to illustrate the factors, level, and pattern of enterprise technical adoption (Almoawi and Mahmood, 2011; Awa and Ojiabo, 2016; Gangwar et al., 2015; Ramdani et al., 2013).

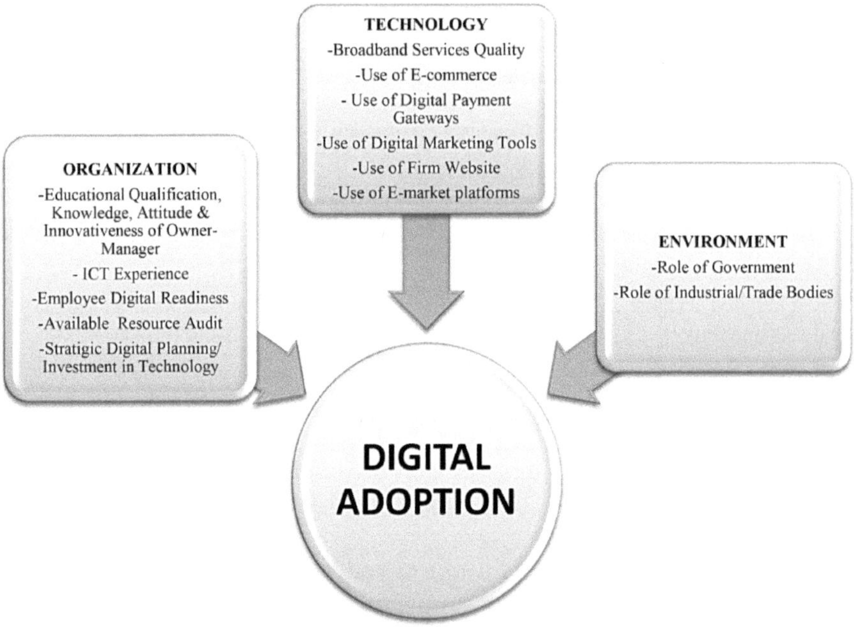

FIGURE 3.1 An overview of digital adoption model along with its attributes.

3.4 RESEARCH METHODOLOGY

The research design is based on an empirical study of the status of digital adoption among small businesses, especially small and medium enterprises, in the state of Uttar Pradesh and NCR region. For the purpose of data collection, four cities of Uttar Pradesh and NCR region namely Lucknow, Barabanki, Raebareli, and Noida were considered. Multistage sampling was deployed for the purpose, keeping strict vigilance on fair representation of all categories. A thorough review of the available literature along with industry expert opinions was considered in order to formulate the instrument for measurement of the level of digital acceptance. Based on the digital adoption model considered for the study, a survey instrument was constructed and dispensed to 52 small business owners. Only 35 enterprises provided completed responses. The collected data was pilot tested and henceforth tested for reliability and were found to have satisfactory levels of Cronbach's alpha, all being above 0.7 (Nunnally, 1978). The questionnaire was developed to assess

TABLE 3.2 Factors Influencing Digital Adoption among Small Businesses.

Factor influencing adoption	Variables	Related literature
Organization	Owner/CEO characteristic, Knowledge/Awareness, Zeal	MacGregor et al. (1996); Tagliavini et al. (2001); Sabherwal et al. (2006); Arendt, L. (2008); Ramdani et al. (2013)
	ICT experience	
	Employee digital readiness	Nasution et al. (2018); Ahmed et al. (2019)
	Available resource audit	
Technology	Use of e-commerce	Raymond et al. (2005); Salwani et al. (2009); Kurnia et al. (2009)
	Use of digital payment gateways	
	Use of digital marketing tools	
	Use of firm website	
	Use of e-market platforms	
Environment	Role of government	Yap et al. (1994); Locke (2004) Martin et al. (2012)
	Role of industrial/trade bodies	

three parameters—the internal factors like nature and digital requirement of the firms, strategic planning, and enthusiasm and knowledge of the owner-manager.

The final questionnaire was divided into two sections. The first part dealt with the demographic profile of the enterprise deemed necessary for the purpose of study like age, location, nature of work, and qualification of owner-manager. The second part sought to comprehend and examine the perception of the owner-manager toward digital adoption at firm level, adaptability toward IT platforms, knowledge and eagerness of owner, along with availability of technically skilled manpower. This section also inquired about the quality of technical infrastructure present in the area of operation based on the level of satisfaction derived from the broadband provider in terms of connectivity, speed, and rates. The second section also makes an enquiry into the internal and external inhibiting factors for these firms. This part also examines government participation and benefits availed by these entrepreneurs from the administration.

The data collected was henceforth tabulated, coded, processed, and analyzed using the statistical package SPSS 20.0. Independent *t*-test was used to calculate the level of satisfaction derived by user firms from the broadband service provider based on connectivity, speed, and rates. Toward the denouement, a conceptual framework was designed to determine the likelihood of digital adoption by using the Logistics Regression model. For the development of the model, a set of important TOE predictors have been chosen (see Table 3.2), the selection of these have been made on the basis of expert interviews conducted with the owner-managers of the respondent firms. The sample of 35 firms was split into two subsets—one training set of 20 firms and the other holdout set of testing data comprising 15 firms.

3.5 RESULTS AND DISCUSSION

TABLE 3.3 Sample Characteristics.

Characteristics	Sample composition
Nature of business	
Manufacturing	28
Trading	08
Service	08
*05 Enterprises were found to be both manufacturers and service providers	
*04 Enterprises were found to be both traders and service providers	
Age of firm	
Less than 10 years	13
10–30 years	13
Above 30 years	09
Average number of employees	
1–20	09
20–40	25
More than 40	01
First-generation entrepreneur	
Yes	20
No	15

TABLE 3.3 *(Continued)*

Characteristics	Sample composition
Qualification of owner-manager	
Under graduate	07
Post graduate	19
Professional degree	09
Age of respondent	
18–30 years	03
31–50 years	24
51–70 years	08
Above 70 years	Nil
Website ownership	
Have a website	20
Do not have a website	15
Broadband connectivity	
Have connectivity	35
Do not have connectivity	Nil

3.5.1 DEMOGRAPHIC CHARACTERISTICS

Survey instruments were administered to 52 owners of small business. Despite repeated follow up, complete responses were received from 35 enterprises only. Sample characteristics have been illustrated in Table 3.3. About 37% of these respondent firms were less than 10 years old; another 37% were between 10 and 30 years and the rest 26% were operational for more than 30 years. Out of the total responding firms, 57.1% comprised of first-generation entrepreneurs. Thus, the data was a proportional embodiment of fair representation of old and relatively new firms. Majority of the owner-manager were tricenerian and quadragenerian (composite figure—69.4%) (see Fig. 3.2). Most firm owners were post graduates (54.3%), followed by professional degree holders (25.7%) and undergraduates (20%). Responses were majorly received from Lucknow, Barabanki, Noida, and Raebareli regions of Uttar Pradesh and NCR (see Fig. 3.3)

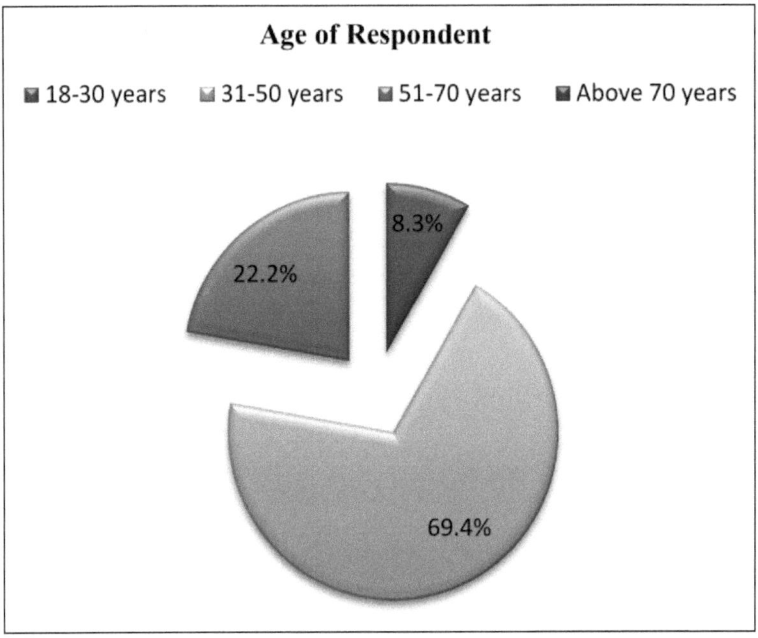

FIGURE 3.2 Age of respondents.

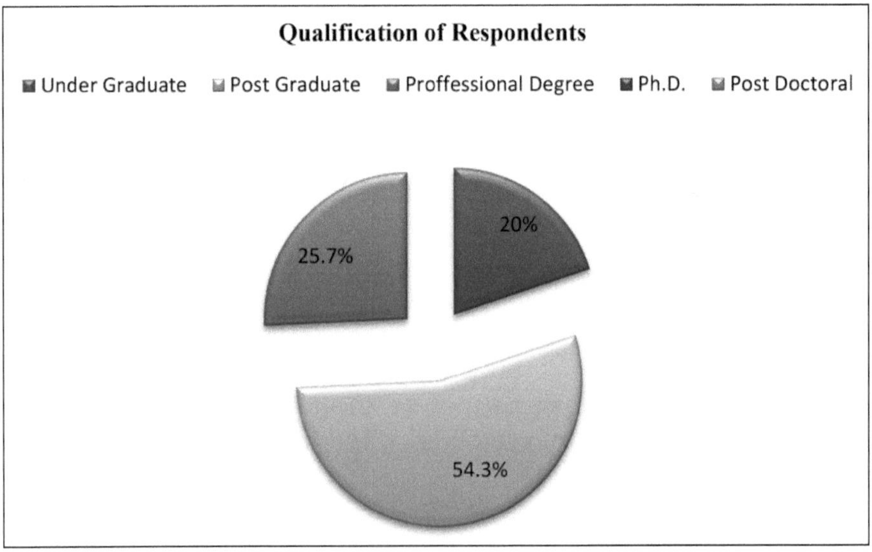

FIGURE 3.3 Qualification of respondents.

A very interesting observation derived from the responses showed majority of manufacturing firms being less than 15 years of age which was reconfirmed by the fact that 66.7% of the manufacturing enterprises were being run by first-generation entrepreneurs. Similarly, among the service providers, a strong 72.7% were first-generation entrepreneurs. Contrary to the aforementioned situation, trading firms were being run by only 16.7% first-generation entrepreneurs. Most enterprises were found to be business-to-consumer (B2C) e-commerce users (58.3%), closely followed by business-to-business (B2B) e-commerce users (47.2%) and business-to-government (B2G) (25%) e-commerce users. About 13.9% of the respondent did not resort to any e-commerce interface (see Fig. 3.4).

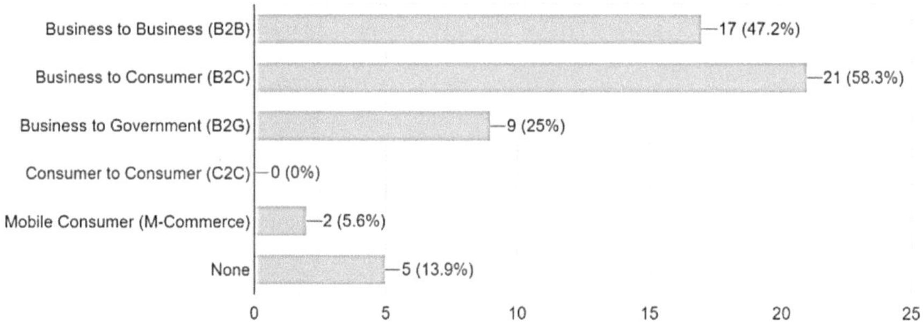

FIGURE 3.4 Type of e-commerce interface used by the enterprise.

3.5.2 ENTREPRENEUR PERCEPTION OF DIGITALIZATION

About 58.3% of the respondents found technical adoption an arduous exercise on being enquired whether they found digitalization a challenge. A deeper exploration revealed that nonavailability of technically skilled manpower (52.8%) was the biggest inhibiter, closely followed by investments in technology (50%). It resurfaced that entrepreneurs also faced a lack of knowledge of key digital technology (38.9%) and a major vacuum in the prevalent ecosystem for cyber security (30.6%). On further examination, it was found that 14 out of the 20 first-generation owner found digitalization a challenge, but at the same time, 85% of them were optimistic that if these roadblocks were worked upon, it would definitely help in their firms' growth. A cross-sectional study revealed that digitalization was viewed as a necessary hurdle across all geographical areas of the study. It was also observed that older firms did not find digitalization an obstacle to firm growth. This can also be correlated to the fact that older firms are relatively in a better financial position than their newer counterpart, thus investment in technology would not surface as a major hurdle for them, also the fact that most older firms deal in trading and resort to traditional ways of doing business (see Table 3.4).

TABLE 3.4 Cross Tabulation of Assessment of First-Generation Entrepreneur and Their Perception about their Firm's Growth if the Road Block/s Were Reduced/Eliminated.

First-generation entrepreneur		Perception about their firm's growth if the road block/s were reduced/eliminated		
		Positive	**Not sure**	**Total**
Yes	Number of respondents/firms	17	3	20
	Percentage of respondents/firms	85%	15%	100%
No	Number of respondents/firms	8	7	15
	Percentage of respondents/firms	53.3%	46.7%	100%
Total	Aggregate number of respondents/firms	25	10	35
	Aggregate percentage of respondents/firms	71.4%	28.6%	100%

H_{01}: *The first-generation entrepreneurs exhibit greater affirmation to the thought that improving on the road block/s would reflect on their firm's growth in the positive direction.*

The statistical analysis shows that Pearson's Chi-square statistic for this contingency table is 4.212 with 1 df and p-value of 0.047 which is significant at 5% level of significance. Therefore, the corresponding null hypothesis that affirmation to the aforesaid thought does not vary across first-generation and other generation of entrepreneur is rejected and it is concluded that "*the first-generation entrepreneurs exhibit greater affirmation to the thought that improving on the road block/s would reflect on their firm's growth in the positive direction.*"

3.5.3 ORGANIZATIONAL DIGITAL ADOPTION PLATFORMS

Figure 3.5 clearly demonstrates that all firms had their footing onto some or the other digital terrain. Depending on the nature of work of these firms, various platforms were used by them. Manufacturing firms are observed to have judiciously used all digital platforms. These firms make use of digital banking, as can be inferred by their use of internet banking and digital signatures. They also resort to own/third-party website and enlistment in online directories to reach out to existing or prospective customers. Service providers are the biggest user of enlistment in online directories and enterprise website for marketing their products. Trading firms resort to internet banking the most. Business management systems like Enterprise Resource Planning (ERP), was the least adopted digital platform across all forms of enterprise. E-market platforms like Government e-Marketplace (GeM) too were not used extensively by any of these enterprises.

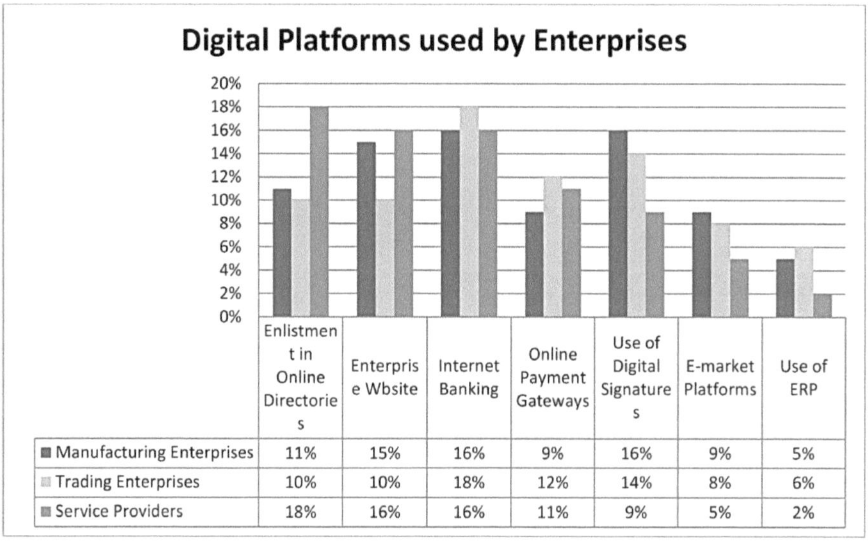

	Enlistment in Online Directories	Enterprise Wbsite	Internet Banking	Online Payment Gateways	Use of Digital Signatures	E-market Platforms	Use of ERP
Manufacturing Enterprises	11%	15%	16%	9%	16%	9%	5%
Trading Enterprises	10%	10%	18%	12%	14%	8%	6%
Service Providers	18%	16%	16%	11%	9%	5%	2%

FIGURE 3.5 Digital platforms used by organizations.

About 55.6% of the respondent firms had a website (see to Fig. 3.6). It was observed that a few of these firms did have a website since 2000 but rampant awareness/usage can only be noticed post the year 2010. Also, 70% of the firms that have their own website have outsourced its designing and maintenance. The responses indicate that 47.2% of these firms do not allow customers to order goods and services and pay directly through their own website (see Fig. 3.7). Thus, firms majorly use their website for promotional activities (69.4%) and as a medium for customer interface (41.7%) (see Fig. 3.8).

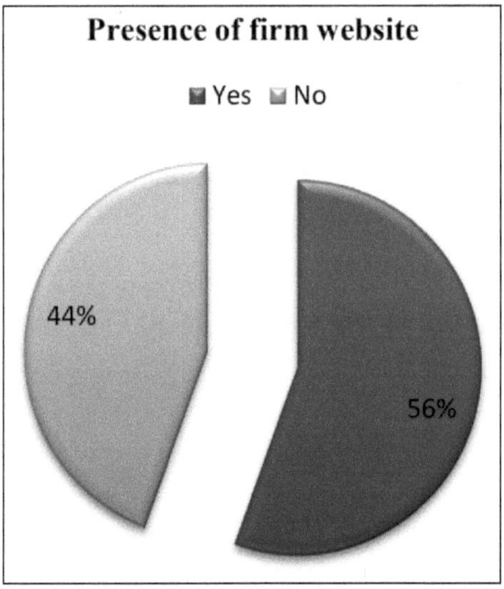

FIGURE 3.6 Presence of firm website.

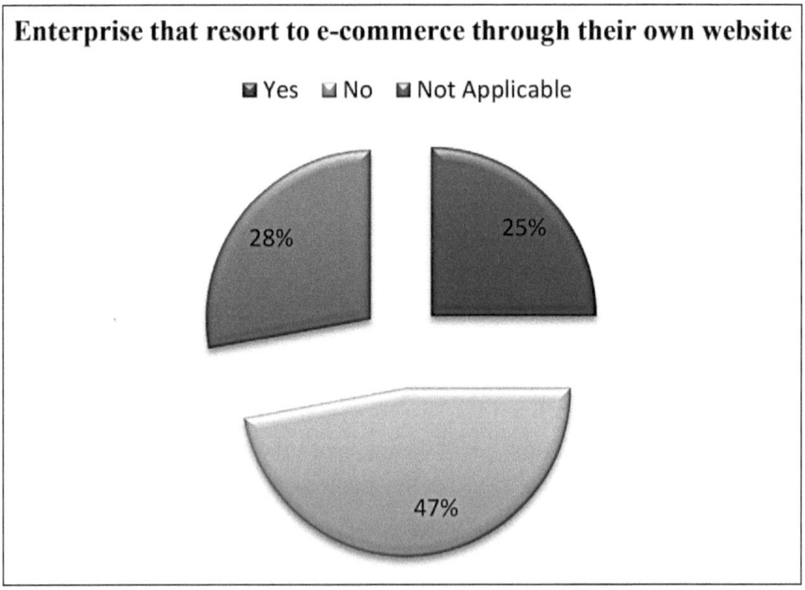

FIGURE 3.7 Enterprise that resort to e-commerce through their own website allowing customers to order goods and services and pay directly.

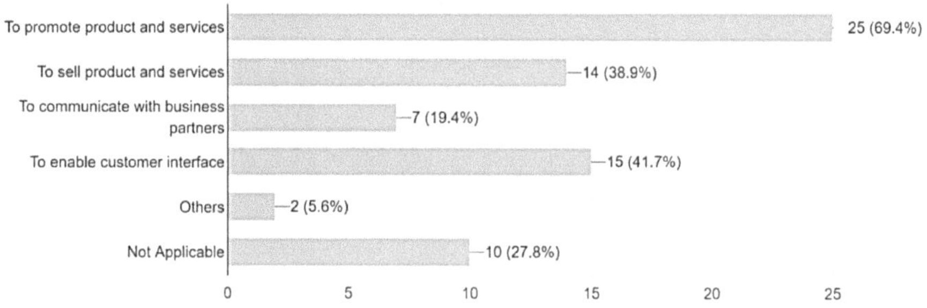

FIGURE 3.8 Usage of enterprise website.

3.5.4 ANALYSIS OF BROADBAND SERVICE QUALITY BASED ON SATISFACTION LEVEL

Digital adroitness strongly depends on robust internet connectivity. In order to understand the quality of broadband/internet service prevalent in the area of business operation, respondents were asked to enlist the name of the service provider and their satisfaction level on a five-point Likert scale based on three parameters—connectivity, speed, and rate ranging from very good/high to very poor/low. Henceforth, to perform a comparative analysis between two regions, independent sample *t*-test was applied for Lucknow-Noida in the western region and Lucknow-Barabanki in the eastern region.

Airtel seemed to have the market controlled with 75% of the respondent usage, followed by JioNet (27.8%) and local broadband provider (16.7%) across all geographical areas. Table 3.5 clearly exhibits that with standard deviation of 0.859 (connectivity), 0.863 (speed), and 0.812 (rate), Airtel dominates the market (Reliance Communication has been excluded for consideration as it has weak representation with just one user). Connectivity and speed of the local broadband provider are also satisfactory but its relative cost is high.

3.5.5 COMPARATIVE ANALYSIS OF BROADBAND SERVICE QUALITY

3.5.5.1 COMPARATIVE ANALYSIS OF BROADBAND SERVICE QUALITY BETWEEN LUCKNOW AND NOIDA

Tables 3.6 and 3.7 indicate the group statistics and independent sample *t*-test for Lucknow and Noida. The p-value is 0.049 (observed level of

TABLE 3.5 Satisfaction Derived from the Broadband Service Provider on the Basis of Connectivity, Speed, and Rates.

Broadband service provider		Satisfaction derived from broadband service provider on the basis of		
		Connectivity	Speed	Rates
BSNL	Mean	3.50	3.50	3.50
	Std. Deviation	2.121	2.121	2.121
AIRTEL	Mean	2.26	2.23	2.50
	Std. Deviation	.859	.863	.812
JIO NET	Mean	2.30	2.40	2.60
	Std. Deviation	1.160	1.075	.966
RELIANCE COMMUNICATION	Mean	2.00	2.00	2.00
	Std. Deviation	-	-	-
LOCAL BROADBAND PROVIDER	Mean	2.40	2.40	2.00
	Std. Deviation	.548	.548	1.000
OTHERS	Mean	2.00	2.00	2.00
	Std. Deviation	-	-	-

significance), which is less than 0.050. Therefore, it is evident that there exists a significant difference in the connectivity between Lucknow and Noida. With mean (connectivity) of 1.50 for Noida and 2.19 for Lucknow, it is evident that Noida enjoys better broadband connectivity than Lucknow. Similarly, p-value is $0.033 < 0.050$. Therefore, it is evident that there also exists a significant difference in speed between Lucknow and Noida. With mean (speed) of 1.50 for Noida and 2.20 for Lucknow, it is evident that Noida enjoys better broadband speed than Lucknow. In case of rates, p-value $0.501 > 0.050$, thus there is no significant difference in entrepreneur sentiments toward broadband rates between the two places.

TABLE 3.6 Group Statistics of Satisfaction derived from broadband service across Lucknow and Noida on the basis of Connectivity, Speed, and Rates.

Basis of satisfaction derived from the broadband service provider	City (Location)	N	Mean	Std. deviation	Std. error mean
Connectivity	Lucknow	26	2.19	.634	.124
	Noida	4	1.50	.577	.289
Speed	Lucknow	25	2.20	.577	.115
	Noida	4	1.50	.577	.289
Rates	Lucknow	25	2.24	.723	.145
	Noida	4	2.50	.577	.289

TABLE 3.7 Independent Samples Test.

		Levene's test for equality of variances		t-Test for equality of means						
Basis of satisfaction derived from the broad band service provider		**F**	**Sig**	**t**	**df**	**Sig (2-tailed)**	**Mean difference**	**Std. error difference**	**95% Confidence interval of the difference**	
									Upper	**Lower**
Connectivity	Equal variances assumed	.000	.988	2.053	28	.049	.692	.337	.002	1.383
Speed	Equal variances assumed	.084	.774	2.251	27	.033	.700	.311	.062	1.338
Rates	Equal variances assumed	.327	.572	-.681	27	.501	-.260	.382	-1.043	.523

3.5.5.2 COMPARATIVE ANALYSIS OF BROADBAND SERVICE QUALITY BETWEEN LUCKNOW AND BARABANKI

Tables 3.8 and 3.9 indicate the group statistics and independent sample *t*-test for Lucknow and Barabanki. The p-value is 0.011 (observed level of significance), which is less than 0.050. Therefore, it is evident that there exists a significant difference in the connectivity between the two places. With mean (connectivity) of 3.25 for Barabanki and 2.19 for Lucknow, it is evident that entrepreneurs in Lucknow enjoy better broadband connectivity than their Barabanki counterparts. Similarly, p-value = 0.009 < 0.050. Therefore, it is evident that there also exists a significant difference in speed between Lucknow and Barabanki. With mean (speed) of 3.25 for Barabanki and 2.20 for Lucknow, it is evident that Lucknow entrepreneurs enjoy better broadband speed than Barabanki. In case of rates, p-value 0.027 < 0.050, thus there is a significant difference in perception among the entrepreneurs in both places with respect to rates. With a mean of 3.25 against 2.24 for Lucknow, entrepreneurs in Barabanki find broadband connectivity costlier.

3.5.6 ENTREPRENEUR DIGITAL AWARENESS

The last segment of the structured questionnaire assessed entrepreneurs about their awareness of functional and transformational digital platforms and techniques and the ways they resort to keep themselves abreast with the ever-changing paradigm of digitalization. It was found that 55.6% of the respondents had never been part of any digital courses, seminars, conferences, workshops, or awareness initiative/camp conducted by either any private organizations or the government bodies. Out of the 44.4% who had undertaken some digital training, only a mere 5.6% had touched the issue of cyber security. This holistically provides a very grim picture of the level of awareness of the functional digital techniques among entrepreneurs. Most of these entrepreneurs neither possessed digital knowledge themselves nor did they hire employees who possess technical acumen. Only 27.8% of these firms had employees who had technical knowledge to tap the resources of firm optimally. 72.2% of the respondent did not provide any form of IT training/EDP to their work-force either. A vacuum could also be observed between the government initiatives and the business owners' cognizance of the government schemes. 63.9% of the respondents did not find the government making any efforts toward improving digital literacy and a major

TABLE 3.8 Group Statistics of Satisfaction Derived from Broadband Service across Lucknow and Barabanki on the Basis of Connectivity, Speed, and Rates.

Basis of satisfaction derived from the broadband service provider	City (location)	N	Mean	Std. deviation	Std. error mean
Connectivity	Lucknow	26	2.19	.634	.124
	Barabanki	4	3.25	1.258	.629
Speed	Lucknow	25	2.20	.577	.115
	Barabanki	4	3.25	1.258	.629
Rates	Lucknow	25	2.24	.723	.145
	Barabanki	4	3.25	1.258	.629

TABLE 3.9 Independent Samples Test.

		Levene's test for equality of variances		t-Test for equality of means						
Basis of satisfaction derived from the broad band service provider		F	Sig	t	df	Sig (2-tailed)	Mean difference	Std. error difference	95% confidence interval of the difference: Upper	Lower
Connectivity	Equal variances assumed	2.615	.117	−2.710	28	.011	1.058	.390	−1.857	−.258
Speed	Equal variances assumed	3.635	.067	−2.837	27	.009	1.050	.370	−1.809	−.291
Rates	Equal variances assumed	1.326	.260	−2.342	27	.027	1.010	.431	−1.895	−.125

80.6% of the respondents were not aware of any government schemes being run to uplift and improve digital absorption among these firms. Also, 94.4% had never benefited from any such schemes. Indeed, only 54.3% of these firms were in the practice of allocating funds for digital maintenance and upgradation. All in all, the groundwork for digital absorption seems to be amiss.

3.5.7 *LIKELIHOOD OF DIGITAL ADOPTION*

The study based on the enumeration of digital adoption among the sample of 35 attempted to evaluate the likelihood of digital adoption among the respondents/firm using logistic regression model. The different characteristics related to the organization, that is, firm, technology, and environment (government support and role of trade bodies) were considered as the variables that influence this likelihood (see Table 3.10).

The model utilizes the cases that furnished complete information on both the predictors set and the response variable (likelihood of digital adoption). The model uses maximum likelihood estimation technique to determine the conditional mean value of natural logarithm of the odds of digital adoption.

The classification table (Table 3.10) clearly shows that 90% cases are correctly classified by the current logistic regression model, implying that our model is good enough.

TABLE 3.10 Classification Table.[a]

Observed			Predicted		
			Digital adoption		Percentage correct
			Likely	Not likely	
Step 1	Digital adoption	Likely	10	1	90.9
		not likely	1	8	88.9
	Overall percentage				90.0

[a]*The cut value is .500.*

The classification table (see Table 3.10) shows that the present logistic regression model does an excellent job of correctly classifying respondents into two groups—digital adaptors and nonadaptors. It correctly classifies 90% cases overall based on employee digital readiness, strategic digital planning/investment in technology, use of e-commerce, use of firm website, role of industrial/trade bodies, and role of government.

3.5.8 STATISTICAL SIGNIFICANCE OF OVERALL MODEL

Cox and Snell's R-square, Nagelkerke's R-square, and Hosmer and Lemeshow goodness-of-fit test were used to test the model reliability (Malhotra et al., 2017). To adjudge the reliability of this model, it is seen that -2 log likelihood measure (that measures that how likely this present model can predict the values of Y as observed) is 10.687 (see Table 3.11). This coefficient can take values between 0 and infinity. The results exhibit that Cox and Snell R square value is 0.569 and the Nagelkerke R square value is 0.761. The values of these coefficients lie between 0 and 1. The result of employing Hosmer and Lemeshow goodness-of-fit test (chi-square test) shows that the statistic is statistically insignificant with p-value of 0.989. The lack of significance on this test is implicative of the fact that the values predicted on the basis of this model will have no significant difference from the observed values.

3.5.9 SIGNIFICANCE OF INDIVIDUAL PREDICTORS

The examination of the individual predictors from the variables in the equation table (see Table 3.12) exhibit that the predictors namely strategic digital planning/investment in technology, use of firm website, and role of government show up as significant predictors at 5% level of significance. Since employee digital readiness, use of e-commerce, and role of industrial/trade bodies are not significant predictors, an attempt was made to run the regression model without them and it was found that it diminishes the prediction accuracy. Since the sample size is small, an attempt was made to run the regression model without these variables and examine the prediction accuracy of the resulting model. For a small sample size, it cannot be concluded that these variables are statistically insignificant and should be ignored as Wald's test is best suited for large samples.

TABLE 3.11 Model Summary.

Step	-2 log likelihood	Cox and Snell R square	Nagelkerke R square
1	10.687[a]	.569	.761

[a]*Estimation terminated at iteration number 7 because parameter estimates changed by less than .001.*

TABLE 3.12 Variables in the Equation.

		B	S.E.	Wald	df	Sig.	Exp(B)
Step 1[a]	Employee digital readiness	.193	.125	2.392	1	.122	1.213
	Strategic digital planning/investment in technology	.010	.000	3.578	1	.049	1.000
	Use of e-commerce	.030	.467	.004	1	.948	1.031
	Use of firm website	.460	.657	1.641	2	.040	1.584
	Role of industrial/trade bodies	.885	2.299	.148	1	.700	2.423
	Role of government.	3.200	2.585	1.533	1	.021	24.527
	Constant	-13.694	6.473	4.476	1	.034	.000

[a]*Variable(s) entered on step 1*: Employee Digital Readiness, Strategic Digital Planning/Investment in Technology, Use of E-commerce, Use of Firm Website, Role of Industrial/Trade Bodies, and Role of Government.

Prediction Equation

Log (odds of digital adoption) = –13.694 + .193 (employee digital readiness) + .010 (strategic digital planning/investment in technology) + .46 (use of e-commerce) + .885 (use of firm website) + 0.885 (role of industrial/trade bodies) + 3.200 (role of government).

Each of the coefficients is positive implying that all the predictors namely employee digital readiness, strategic digital planning/investment in technology), use of e-commerce, use of firm website, role of industrial/trade bodies, and role of government are contributing in increasing the likelihood of digital adoption among the respondent firms.

3.6 FINDINGS AND LIMITATIONS

The review clearly illustrates that there exists widespread awareness among the small business owners about the importance and need to embrace digital business transformations and sync them with their firm's operational mechanism. None the less, not many entrepreneurs have taken any strategic measures toward this end. Majority of them find digitalization a major challenge, especially the first-generation entrepreneurs. Although the adoption of various e-commerce and other digital platforms among relatively new enterprises clearly exhibit that these firms do not shy away from adopting technology but they definitely lack strategic planning to remove operational constraints. The readiness and the competence to meet the digital transformation exist in parts, strongly reflecting dependence on the size and nature of work of the enterprise. Detailed investigations make it imperative that there exists a major knowledge gap between the functional technology providers and the end users. Apparently, existence of firm website, but fractured use of the same, strongly reflects absence of strategic planning in adoption. Removal of information asymmetry and strategizing the use of existing investment in digital platforms would enable firms to not only improve their customer reach but also make optimal use of available resources. The government should work as the facilitator for the process of mass digital adoption enrooting its outreach through trade and industrial bodies. These industrial organizations are an embodiment of the business community and have the advantage of understanding their comprehensive needs and sentiments. Thus, the government can work as the initiator and these industrial bodies can serve as its agile limbs for dissemination of information and advancing the pursuit further. Accelerating digital awareness; providing subsidies for equipment purchase; standardizing broadband connectivity; and plugging the divide in service quality between urban, semi-urban, and rural areas should be a priority for the government. It should also work toward the promotion of direct e-selling platforms like GeM, which can enable small enterprises to market their products to a larger audience without incurring any excess cost. Digital adoption can be encouraged by conducting adoption and awareness programs, organizing informative sessions, marshaling enterprise bootcamps, promoting digital-health checks, and floating customized schemes to suit enterprise requirements. Smaller the firm, higher would be its chances of becoming a victim to this technological revolution. Thus, needs and interest of SMEs should be prioritized by the government. A coordinated and strategized effort by all stakeholders can definitely pay results in the times to come. Digital and technical platforms can serve as catalyst for product development, innovative process modeling, product and brand marketing, constructing value chain, enhancing competitiveness, building customer loyalty, etc. But all of these would stand as a distant dream if a robust internet framework invigorated with contemporary digital security was not put in place. Mammoth Indian central government schemes like GST, aadhaar, and demonitization too require expeditious digital upheaval in order to plug technological aperture and thereby reduce human interface. Digitalization can no longer be viewed as a threat; rather it should be treated as the biggest imperative to strategic business modeling.

Nevertheless, the findings are subject to a number of caveats. Primarily, the enterprise survey covers only the formal sector, excluding the informal firms. Hence, the results do not take into account unregistered enterprises. Also, data on micro enterprises have not been considered in the sample. Data collection too was hindered due to paucity of physical interaction. Since the area of research (digital adoption) is highly dynamic in nature, it is likely that some attributes might become obsolete in near future; likewise, some attributes might find inclusion in future researches. The research has tried to include as many attributes that seemed applicable in the current context as possible.

3.7 CONCLUSION

Globalization has transmuted business borderless thereby turning many local businesses global. Enterprises, irrespective of size, nature, and location, are expected to stay ahead of their respective antagonists by enhancing customer experiences and minimizing operational costs simultaneously. Enterprises in all industries are striving to provide services and products as needs arise, even before customers become aware of them. Rather than occasional or episodic interactions, firms can be continuously connected to their customers digitally. A great digital business experience for all stakeholder backed by cost-effectiveness is the mainstay of business practices homogeneously. Digital adroitness is core to creation of contemporary business practices irrespective of firm size. This digital dexterity requires agility in planning and adoption of malleable business applications. Business enterprises are required to maintain a steady flow of fully-integrated, actionable information about all key business domains, including human resource, production, marketing, sales and customer service (B Liautaud, Hammond, 2000). Integrated information technology backup is essential to work hand-in-hand to meet the business requirements, plug the digital divide, drive innovation, and march toward continuous and holistic improvement.

A more fertile, unique, and cohesive digitally integrated entrepreneurial ecosystem needs to be undertaken. Firms are expected to be active players of the internet-driven world. There is an urgent need for organizations in India to address the change in business scenarios, dynamic business demands, and innovate ways to quickly cater to these changing demands. SME needs are peculiar and different from their larger counterparts, thus their resolve should also be customized to suit their needs. These measures require a collaborative effort by all stakeholders—enterprise, government organizations, sectoral representatives, and industrial bodies. Enterprises need to conduct a resource and talent audit to identify skill gaps and evaluate the stage of digitization in their workplaces in order to be up breast with modifying business practices. The government definitely needs to work on enhancing the cyberspace infrastructure and thus work toward providing a well-ordered digital terrain for enterprises to work and progress. The organizational /industrial bodies need to conduct awareness and skill-enhancement workshops to enable a skill-based digital ecosystem. Among the new business models is a common thread: "technology," which enables firms to fundamentally change the craft of conducting business.

KEYWORDS

- **small and medium enterprises (SMEs)**
- **digital India**
- **digital adoption**
- **organizational adoption**
- **digital divide**
- **digital awareness**
- **information and communication technologies (ICTs)**
- **barriers to digital advancement**

REFERENCES

Ahmed, F.; Qin, Y. J.; Martínez, L. Sustainable Change Management through Employee Readiness: Decision Support System Adoption in Technology-Intensive British E-Businesses. *Sustainability* **2019**, *11* (11), 2998.

Almoawi, A. R. N. A.; Mahmood, R. Applying the OTE Model in Determining the E-Commerce Adoption on SMEs in Saudi Arabia. *Asian J. Bus.Manag. Sci.* **2011,** *1* (7), 12–24.

Arendt, L. Barriers to ICT Adoption in SMEs: How to Bridge the Digital Divide? *J. Syst. Inf. Technol.* **2008**, *10* (2), 93–108.

Awa, H. O.; Ojiabo, O. U. A Model of Adoption Determinants of ERP within T-O-E Framework. *Inf. Technol. People*. **2016,** *9* (4), 30.

Aizstrauta, D.; Celmina, A.; Ginters, E.; Mazza, R. Validation of Integrated Acceptance and Sustainability Assessment Methodology. *Procedia Comput. Sci.* **2013,** *26*, 33–40.

Bouncken, R. B.; Kraus, S.; Roig-Tierno, N. Knowledge-and Innovation-Based Business Models for Future Growth: Digitalized Business Models and Portfolio Considerations. *Rev. Manag. Sci.* **2021,** *15*, 1–14.

Bouwman, H.; Nikou, S.; de Reuver, M. Digitalization, Business Models, and SMEs: How Do Business Model Innovation Practices Improve Performance of Digitalizing SMEs? *Telecomm Policy* **2019,** *43* (9), 101828.

Cragg, P. B.; King, M. Small-Firm Computing: Motivators and Inhibitors. *MIS Q.* **1993,** *17*, 47–60.

Davis, F. D. Perceived Usefulness, Perceived Ease of Use, and User Acceptance of Information Technology. *MIS Q.* **1989,** 319–339.

Elbeltagi, I.; Al Sharji, Y.; Hardaker, G.; Elsetouhi, A. The Role of the Owner-Manager in SMEs' Adoption of Information and Communication Technology in the United Arab Emirates. *J. Glob. Inf. Manag.* **2013,** *21* (2), 23–50.

Gangwar, H.; Date, H.; Ramaswamy, R. Understanding Determinants of Cloud Computing Adoption Using an Integrated TAM-TOE Model. *J. Ent. Inf. Manag.* **2015,** *28*, 107–130.

Hamad, H.; Elbeltagi, I.; El-Gohary, H. An Empirical Investigation of Business-to-Business E-Commerce Adoption and Its Impact on SMEs Competitive Advantage: The Case of Egyptian manufacturing SMEs. *Strateg. Change* **2018,** *27* (3), 209–229.

Joensuu-Salo, S.; Sorama, K.; Viljamaa, A.; Varamäki, E. Firm Performance Among Internationalized SMEs: The Interplay of Market Orientation, Marketing Capability and Digitalization. *Adm. Sci.* **2018,** *8* (3), 31.

Kurnia, S.; Alzougool, B.; Ali, M.; Alhashmi, S. M. In *Adoption of Electronic Commerce Technologies by SMEs in Malaysia*, Proceedings of the 42nd Annual Hawaii International Conference on System Sciences, HICSS, 2009; pp. 1–10.

Koch, T.; Windsperger, J. Seeing Through the Network: Competitive Advantage in the Digital Economy. *J. Organ. Des.* **2017,** *6* (1), 6.

Lee, Y. Y.; Falahat, M. The Impact of Digitalization and Resources on Gaining Competitive Advantage in International Markets: Mediating Role of Marketing, Innovation and Learning Capabilities. *Technol. Innov. Manag. Rev.* **2019,** *9* (11), 26–38.

Locke, S. ICT Adoption and SME Growth in New Zealand. Available at SSRN 3284905, 2004.

MacGregor, R. C.; Waugh, P.; Bunker, D. *Attitudes of Small Business to the Implementation and Use of IT: Are we Basing EDI Design Initiatives for Small Business on Myths?* 9th International Conference on EDI-IOS, 1996; pp. 377–388.

Malhotra, N. K.; Nunan, D.; Birks, D. F. *Marketing Research: An Applied Approach*; Pearson Education Limited, 2017.

Martin, F.; Cristescu, M.; Ciovica, L.; Ciovica, L. E-Readiness of Romanian SMEs. *Anale. Seria Stiinte Economice. Timisoara.* **2012,** *18*, 150.

Mogos, R. I. Digital Marketing for Identifying Customers' Preferences—A Solution for SMEs in Obtaining Competitive Advantages. *Int. J. Econom. Pract. Theor.* **2015,** *5* (3), 240–247.

Müller, J.; Maier, L.; Veile, J.; Voigt, K. I. Cooperation Strategies among SMEs for Implementing Industry 4.0. In *Digitalization in Supply Chain Management and Logistics: Smart and Digital Solutions for an Industry 4.0 Environment*, Proceedings of the Hamburg International Conference of Logistics (HICL), Vol. 23. epubli GmbH: Berlin, 2017; pp. 301–318.

Mirchandani, D. A.; Motwani, J. Understanding Small Business Electronic Commerce Adoption: An empirical Analysis. *J. Comput. Inf. Syst.* **2001,** *41* (3), 70–73.

Nardi, B. A. (Ed.). *Context and Consciousness: Activity Theory and Human-Computer Interaction.* MIT Press, 1996.

Nasution, R. A.; Rusnandi, L. S. L.; Qodariah, E.; Arnita, D.; Windasari, N. A. The Evaluation of Digital Readiness Concept: Existing Models and Future Directions. *Asian J. Technol. Manag.* **2018,** *11* (2), 94–117.

Nunnally, J. C. An Overview of Psychological Measurement. In *Clinical Diagnosis of Mental Disorders*; Wolman, B.B., Eds.; Springer: Boston, MA, 1978**;** pp. 97–146.

Ponelis, S. R.; Britz, J. J. An Exploratory Study of Business Intelligence in Knowledge Based South African SMEs. In GlobDev 2011 Pre-AMCIS Workshop: ICT in Global Development, August 2011.

Ramdani, B.; Chevers, D.; Williams, D. A. SMEs' Adoption of Enterprise Applications: A Technology-Organisation-Environment Model. *J. Small Bus. Enterp. Dev.* **2013,** *20* (4), 735–753.

Rashid, B. Digital Transformation and Innovation in Today's Business World. Forbes [Online] June 13, 2017. https://www.forbes.com/sites/brianrashid/2017/06/13/

digital-transformation-and-innovation-in-todays-business-world/#5963469c4905 (accessed Nov 23, 2018).

Raymond, L.; Bergeron, F.; Blili, S. The Assimilation of E-Business in Manufacturing SMEs: Determinants and Effects on Growth and Internationalization. *Electron. Mark.* **2005,** *15* (2), 106–118.

Rogers, D. L. *The Digital Transformation Playbook: Rethink Your Business for the Digital Age*. Columbia University Press: New York, 2016.

Rogers, E. M. *Diffusion of Innovations. A Division of Simon & Schuster*; New York, 2003.

Sabherwal, R.; Jeyaraj, A.; Chowa, C. Information System Success: Individual and Organizational Determinants. *Manag. Sci.* **2006,** *52* (12), 1849–1864.

Salwani, M. I.; Marthandan, G.; Norzaidi, M. D.; Chong, S. C. E-Commerce Usage and Business Performance in the Malaysian Tourism Sector: Empirical Analysis. *Inform. Manag. Comput. Sec.* **2009,** *17* (2), 166–185.

Sommer, L. Industrial Revolution-Industry 4.0: Are German Manufacturing SMEs the First Victims of this Revolution? *J. Ind. Eng. Manag.* **2015,** *8* (5), 1512–1532.

Tagliavini, M.; Ravarini, A.; Antonelli, A. An Evaluation Model for Electronic Commerce Activities within SMEs. *Inf. Technol. Manag.* **2001,** *2* (2), 211–230.

Tapscott, D. *The Digital Economy: Promise and Peril in the Age of Networked Intelligence*, Vol. 1; McGraw-Hill: New York, 1996.

Tornatzky, L.; Fleischer, M. *The Process of Technology Innovation*; Lexington Books: Lexington, MA, 1990; p. 165.

Venkatesh, V.; Morris, M. G.; Davis, G. B.; Davis, F. D. User Acceptance of Information Technology: Toward a Unified View. *MIS Q.* **2003,** *17*, 425-478.

Whiteley, D. In *Merging Electronic Commerce Technologies for Competitive Advantage*, AMCIS 1998 Proceedings, 1998; p. 127.

Yap, C. S.; Thong, J. Y.; Raman, K. S. Effect of Government Incentives on Computerisation in Small Business. *Eur. J. Inf. Syst.* **1994,** *3* (3), 191–206.

CHAPTER 4

COVID-19 Shock: Flip Side of Globalization

CHITRA KRISHNAN[1*], TAWHEED NABI[2], and MUBASHIR MAJID BABA[3]

[1]*Amity International Business School, Amity University, Noida 201313, India*

[2]*Mittal School of Business (ACBSP, USA), Jalandhar 144402, Punjab, India*

[3]*Department of Management Studies, University of Kashmir 190001, J&K, India*

Corresponding author. E-mail: ckrishnan@amity.edu

ABSTRACT

COVID-19 has given a shock to every economy, which has hampered all the sectors of economy. This pandemic has forced to take the decision of lockdown and quarantine because of which every sector's labor force is quarantined. Countries are connected with each other in terms of global production network. In terms of international trade, most of the economies are affected by the COVID-19 shock. In this paper, we have analyzed the effects of the COVID-19 shock upon trade welfare. It discusses the threats faced by globalization due to the pandemic. Data related to GDP of various countries and growth of import/export during the COVID-19 pandemic has been analyzed. Various nations' industries, like pharmaceutical, electrical gadgets, and automobiles, are dependent on China for input. This study has analyzed the problems faced by nations who had cut their supply chain from China. Various strategies have also been discussed according to decisions taken by many nations.

Constructive Discontent in Execution: Creative Approaches to Technology and Management.
Sanjeev Bansal, Anita Venaik, Swati Upveja, and Saritha S. (Eds.)

4.1 INTRODUCTION

COVID-19 is an infectious disease caused by the SARS-CoV-2 virus disease that started in China and which spread all over the world and become a pandemic. It has disrupted economic production in all sectors including input and output of tradable and nontradable goods and services. COVID-19 has become the reason for the biggest production disruption in world history. It has been observed by researchers that COVID-19 is the largest pandemic ever experienced in the world's history. As per the latest update, the total corona virus cases in the world are 28,659,615 and has resulted in around 919,715 deaths. In India, there are 4,659,984 total cases at present and total deaths are 77,506. This is a totally different noneconomic shock ever experienced, which has turned into a global shock. This huge loss to the world forced all economies to take the decision of lockdown, shutdown all the production houses, and quarantine human resources in countries affected by COVID-19. Because industries were not making new products, the cost of existing goods and services increased in domestic as well as foreign market. The demand for pharmaceutical products increased. Medicines, ventilators, masks, sanitizers, etc., are the products which are demanded by every economy affected by the coronavirus.

Till April 2020, it has been measured that COVID-19 has affected 210 countries and territories all over the world. Around 3 million people are found to be positive of this disease (coronavirus), out of which around 0.2 million people have died. This virus had spread in most of the countries like wild fire and the economies found unable to control it as there was no vaccine discovered till the date. The only preservation measure that had been taken by most of the economies which were affected from it was "lockdown." All the economies made the strategy of isolation at all levels, whether it is local, regional, national, or international.

The devastating effect of this was observed in employment loss and decrease in real income of economies affected by this pandemic. The world lost nearly 400 million full-time jobs in second quarter (April–June 2020) due to COVID-19 pandemic, as was observed by the International Labor Organization. Approximately 4% drop was observed in real income in the world. According to the World Bank, "there is 5.2% contraction in global GDP in 2020." It was observed that per capita income decreased because of which most countries faced the situation of recession. Almost 8% global growth had shrinked in this downfall scenario.

Globalization allows countries to interact with each other in terms of trade relations, political relations, and their economic dependency on each other. Countries are connected with each other through global value chain in which firms are sourcing intermediate input and sell their final products in various countries. COVID-19 pandemic has brought loss of global production. Understanding its impact on global production or production disruption is very complex because it is related to disruption in most of the major sectors of economy. Education, healthcare, financial institutions, food production, textiles, automobiles, etc., are the examples of some intermediate goods and services having sectoral linkages. When the quarantine of labor force was imposed in all sectors of the economy, it turned into production barrier because of which cost of the production has increased not only in the domestic market but in the foreign market also. In this study, the major impacted economies have been analyzed by comparison of GDP. Sectorwise import and export growth have been analyzed to understand the impact of COVID-19 pandemic. India's GDP is the lowest among the strong economies which witnessed the de-growth of India. The recovery is dependent on the huge investment and new government policies in which government expenditure should be increased in major affected sectors of the economy. Investment in digitalization and healthcare system can be beneficial to cope up with future uncertainties.

Sforza and Steiniger (2020) studied the importance of trade in transitional inputs and global value chains. They thoroughly analyzed the Ricardian trade model and tried to understand the link between tradable and nontradable sectors. The study discusses the production barriers occurring during the spread of the SARS coronavirus (COVID-19) and the bad effects of natural disasters and epidemics. COVID-19 gave a direct shock to the cost of each input and had indirect effects upon sectorwise linkages. The study results show that COVID-19 shock reduced the real income of all countries.

Baldwin and di Mauro (2020) studied the COVID-19 pandemic from the perspective of supply and demand shock, which impacted the international trade of goods and services. They analyzed the situation of six hard-hit nations during March 2020 which accounts for 55% world's supply and demand, 60% world's manufacturing, and 50% world's manufacturing exports which resulted into bad global consequences. The concluding remarks of this paper suggests that overdependence of countries upon China for import purpose inculcate welfare redundant consequences which should be removed by technology enhancement and appropriate use of global sourcing.

Barua (2020) examines the impact of COVID-19 on macroeconomic level and analyzed what kind of impacts have to be faced by economies from this pandemic. The nature of impacts like demand and supply shock, trade, investment, price level, financial stability and risk, and international cooperation, all these sectors are affected by COVID-19. This paper suggests some policy change responses which the government need to consider while framing fiscal policy. The suggestions are given on the basis of AD–AS model's likely impacts at the macro-economic level. Wide-ranging and revealing overview has been given on the impacts of COVID-19 by predicting short- and long-run impacts.

Jackson (2020) studied the negative impact of COVID-19 on the global value chain network as many countries are dependent on China for trade. China is the only country which accounts for high percentage of global supply and demand. But now, the scenario has changed as USA and China trade war is going on. Not only USA but many other countries have cut their import dependency. India is the witness in this case as the Indian government has banned various Chinese applications in the country. The concluding remarks suggests that real investment should be spend on human resources so that they should invent some new strategies to pull resources and to stabilize the world's economy.

Gossling et al. (2020) studies the impact of COVID-19 pandemic with other epidemics which have impacted globally. COVID-19 pandemic is measured as one of the biggest epidemics that has affected globally. It is predicted that this epidemic is likely to impact the 2030 sustainable development goals which could be more difficult to achieve after this pandemic, and would be even more difficult for underdeveloped countries.

Ilyas (2020) analyzed the changes occurring in globalization in geopolitical perspective due to spread of COVID-19. This study discusses the economic choices in the pandemic situation of COVID-19. The countries are pondering upon three main problems, i.e., the distribution and allocation of resources in the situation of pandemic, how to reduce the impact of this dangerous disease on the common people, and what measures governments should take to recover the situation after the pandemic to stabilize the economy. Allocation of funds (government expenditure) by different countries on public health measures have been discussed to prevent the spread of coronavirus.

4.2 OBJECTIVES

- To discuss the threats faced by globalization due to COVID-19 pandemic
- To understand the problems faced by nations due to cut of the supply chain with China

- To analyze the adverse impacts of COVID-19 pandemic on international trade and GDP of different nations
- To make strategies to maintain the economies of scale for any nation

4.3 METHODOLOGY

Qualitative as well as quantitative methodology have been used for this study. The information presented in this study were collected from various articles, journals, and newspapers. Current data of COVID-19 has been taken from official national and international agencies. GDP and international trade data have been taken from official websites like World bank and Statista. Data have been analyzed by various statistical techniques using MS Excel. Some good research papers and journals available on JSTORE related with impact of COVID-19 on globalization have been referred.

4.4.1 IMPACT OF COVID-19 ON GLOBALIZATION

COVID-19 had started spreading from China, mainly in Wuhan City, and it spread in many developed and underdeveloped nations like India, USA, Italy, Dubai, England, etc. No one could think that this virus could spread so wide globally like it has wings to pass all the territories and boundaries. In a very less time, it turned to be a pandemic. The World Health Organization named it "COVID-19." The world is connected with each other by globalization. All nations are dependent on each other by trade relations, commerce, and tourism. The cities and nations which are well developed and known as the nerve centers of trade like New York in USA, London, Paris, Italy, England, etc., are also hugely affected. Many countries lost their natives at a high rate. All nations which are affected by coronavirus are connected with China in terms of trade. They have import–export relations. The Wuhan city of China is the main hub of technology from which all countries are importing digital goods and services. Because of the spread of COVID-19, trading from this city is closed. The "global value chain" is therefore destroyed.

On the other hand, there are some countries which are not much globally connected, those countries are less affected by COVID-19. Many countries in the African continent are less affected. Similarly, if we see at the regional level, the states which are not much globally connected by trade or any other means, they are least affected states. For example, the North-Eastern states of India like Assam, Arunachal Pradesh, Manipur, Meghalaya, Mizoram,

Tripura, and Nagaland are observed as the least affected states of India. States like these could prepare themselves before the virus reached their state. They could make strategies to prevent from coronavirus. For example, they could prepare areas for isolation wards, proper basic health facilities, availability of masks, sanitizers, ventilators, etc.

As of now, vaccine has not been invented till the time of the study. All the researchers and scientists are working toward it. If we see the time period, four to five months of lockdown are completed. Some relaxation is given, but all the industries, education institutions, and transportation are still restricted. The people have made their minds that they cannot wait for vaccine. They are now ready to put their foot out of the house with health care preventions. According to scientists, we cannot remove a virus completely at once, it takes time. So, people may prepare themselves to live with the virus. If all people take care of health, wear proper masks, use sanitizers, take care of environment, and follow social distancing, then it may be possible that the virus itself loses its vitality. Taking care of virus prevention measures will be good step toward gaining global connectivity and crossing natural barrier against infections.

To gain economic benefit, every nation has the agenda of producing goods and services at low cost and get the market place at global level through which they can sustain their production and continue with global value chain. However, after the outbreak of the COVID-19 pandemic, everything is going the opposite to what we expected. Economies of scale are going downfall, because production processes are postponed. All labor force is quarantined and we didn't achieve capitalized economies of scale. The global value chain is disconnected just to deal with the coronavirus by following the extenuation strategies. But we have to manage the loss by optimizing the economic gain which is subject to the least cost in terms of loss of the life of their native people facing out of epidemics such as the COVID-19.

4.4.2 DATA ANALYSIS AND INTERPRETATION

Today, we are living in globalized world where consumers have *n* number of choices from the different corners of the world. A consumer can import the products as per their choice. The reason behind preferring foreign goods over domestically produced goods is that imported goods were produced cheaper than the domestic goods, which helps manage their household budget. The international trade (import–export activities) can impact the GDP of an economy.

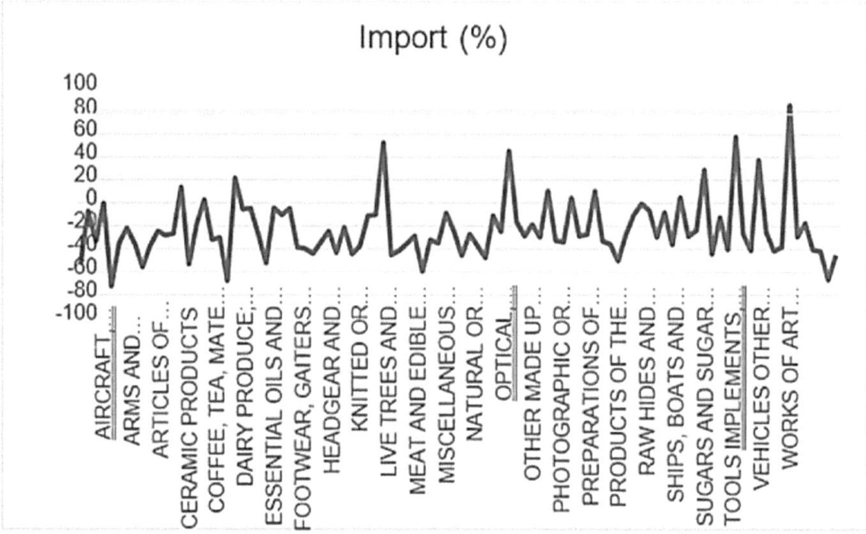

FIGURE 4.1 India's total import (% growth) as per commodity, January–August 2020. *Source*: Ministry of Commerce and Industry, Government of India.

Growing trade deficit or the increase in imports more than export can have negative effect. As we can see in Figure 4.1, the fluctuations in imports in the period of January to August 2020 can have negative impact on the GDP growth of a country. The study is showing commodity-wise imports from which we can analyze that there is negative percentage growth in imports of India. The reason is already clear and that is the COVID-19 pandemic has adversely affected international trade. People reduce their consumption because of which imports' growth fall negatively. Recent data show that the imports of India in September 2020 have declined to 19.6%, which led to $2.91 billion contraction in trade deficit as compared to the previous fiscal year.

A study by the Ministry of Commerce and Industry reveals that due to fall in exports from August 2020, trade deficit will go five months high. August is the month when the unlock phase had started, which gives hope of improvement in trade activities, but the inverse was observed. The reason is that COVID-19 cases had not improved as the positive cases were rising at the same speed. As we can see in Figure 4.2, India's percentage growth in exports as per commodity in the period of April to August 2020 had recorded a negative growth. If we compare the fall in export with the previous fiscal year (2019), it is 35% year-on-year. This fall is seen in almost every commodity group. Major export decline can be observed in textiles, engineering goods,

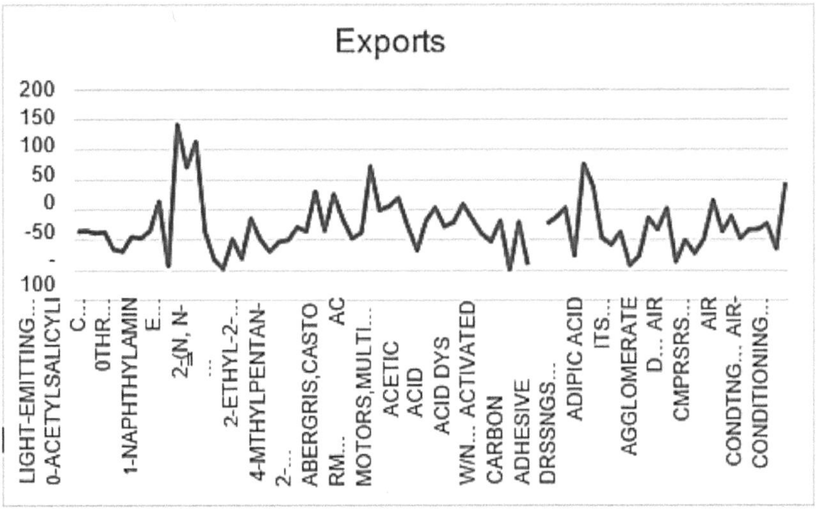

FIGURE 4.2 India's total export (% growth) as per commodity April–August 2020. *Source*: Department of Commerce, Ministry of Commerce and Industry, Government of India.

cereals, chemicals, and plastic during the COVID-19 pandemic. The imposition of national lockdown resulted in poor performance of exports of India.

TABLE 4.1 Quarterly GDP Growth (2012–2020).

Year	Q1	Q2	Q3	Q4	Total
2012–13	13.2	16.14	13.52	12.69	13.82
2013–14	10.9	13.97	14.62	12.31	12.97
2014–15	13.6	13.69	9.03	8.29	10.99
2015–16	12.22	11.87	11.46	11.55	11.76
2016–17	13.57	11.4	11.36	7.89	10.95
2017–18	10.1	11.13	11.64	11.4	11.09
2018–19	11.29	9.89	9.16	11.5	10.46
2019–20	8.06	5.87	7.39	7.53	7.21
2020–21	−22.57	..	..	..	−22.57

Source: World Bank.

COVID-19 pandemic has resulted in production shock, which affected all the economies of the world in terms of welfare. Negative effects can be seen on the sectoral level as well as aggregate level of different nations. The major reason behind considerable impact on many of the economies is that labor force is quarantined in homes. With the 60% share of quarantined labor force, real income is impacted to upto 14%. Table 4.1 shows quarterly data of GDP of India from 2012 to 2020. Increase or decrease of GDP was 2% or 3% in quarterly data of various years. In 2012–13, GDP in first quarter was 13.2 and in the end of year (in quarter 4), GDP was 12.69, which shows that it declined by 0.51 that did not affect too much. In 2013–14, quarter 1 shows GDP was 10.9 which increased in quarter 4, i.e., 12.31, it increased by 1.41 as a positive economic growth. Change of 1.29 can be seen in the quarter 1 of 2014–15 which declined by 5.1 in quarter 4 which is less appreciated as compared to previous years. If we consider recent years like 2017–18, GDP was 11.5 in quarter 4 which is sustained on 2018–19 also as it was 11.5 at that year. When it comes to the financial year 2019–20, the GDP was decreased by 3.97 as it was 7.53 in quarter 4 of 2019–20. COVID-19 has brought devastating effects on the economy as the GDP of India is going downward negatively, i.e., –22.57, which is a witness of de-growth of an economy.

TABLE 4.2 Impact on Exports.

Fuels	48.6	15.1
Chemicals	44.6	13.1
Stone and glass	43.1	13.4
Textiles and clothing	37.0	11.5
Mach and elec	32.2	10.0
Metals	26.6	8.3
Transport at ion	24.3	7.6
Vegetable	18.0	5.6
Plastic or rubber	11.0	3.4
Animals	10.6	3.3
Food products	6.8	2.1
Miscellaneous	6.4	2.0
Minerals	3.9	1.2
Hides and skin	3.3	1.0
Footwear	3.1	1.0
Wood	2.7	0.8

Moderate High Low

Source: World Bank WITS.

India is facing direct impact on exports due to COVID-19. In the total production of one fiscal year, 18% production was made for exports including sectors like transportation, textile, and clothing. As we can see in Table 4.2, the dark red color is showing the sectors with high potential impact. There is a moderate exposure in the top three exports of India that are listed in orange color—fuels, chemicals, stone, and glass and minerals. These sectors have share of 40% in India's exports. Other sectors have low impact and less share in Indian exports which are shown in light skin color. COVID-19 pandemic is responsible for shutdown of all economic activities and trade (import/export), which resulted has into negative contraction in GDP of India.

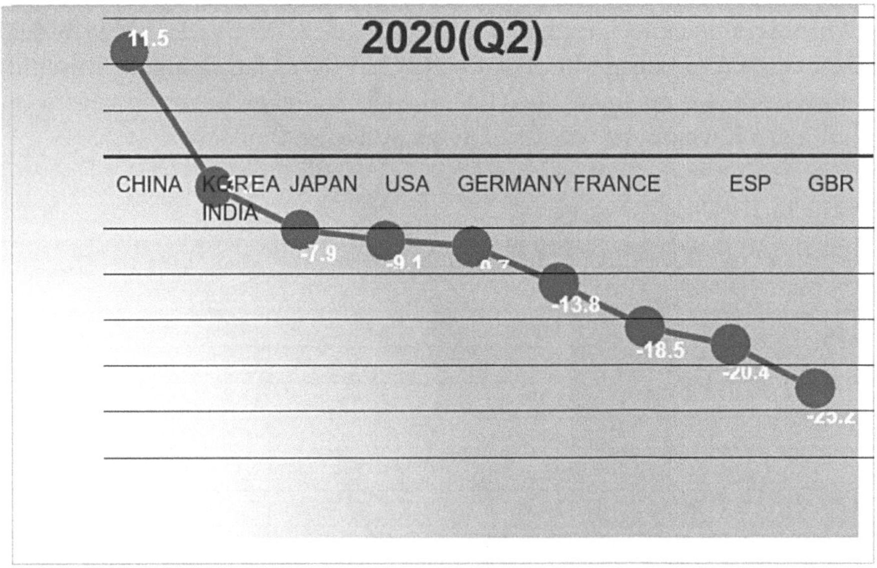

FIGURE 4.3 GDP contraction around the world.

Source: Statista.

We can see in the Figure 4.3 that COVID-19 spread all over the world and this has led to the decline of economic growth of developing as well as developed nations. Only China has positive GDP of 11.5; rest of the countries like Korea, Japan, USA, Germany, France, Spain, Great Britain, and India has negative GDP. A huge contraction of GDP in various economies show that COVID-19 pandemic is responsible for de-growth of various nations. India's GDP is less than all countries. As we can see in the figure, Korea has –3.2, Japan—7.9, USA—9.1, Germany—9.7, France—13.8, Spain—18.5, Great Britain—20.4, and India—25.2. The GDP of Spain and UK were worse than predicted in the lockdown. A huge decline in GDP shows that there is de-growth in major sectors of economy like import, export, employment, education, food productions, etc. Quarter 1 of fiscal year 2020–21 turned into lockdown because of which demand of individuals and private businesses fell. The existing demand of quarter 1 didn't even cover the cost of products. The goods and services produced in India have 24% absolute value which is less than the cost of goods and services. On the other side, evidences say that economies are recovering in the unlock phase of lockdown. All the countries, whether developing or developed, including India, are practicing measures of liquidity, transfers, and credits which will impact aggregate demand. The increase in demand and other recoveries is possible in the unlock phase. When it comes to India's GDP, we can see in the figure that India's GDP contraction is more than any of the major economies. This is the first time India is facing a huge decline in GDP (negative growth) in the past four decades. Although "exogenous factors" are witnessed, we cannot ignore the year-on-year quarterly decline in GDP of India.

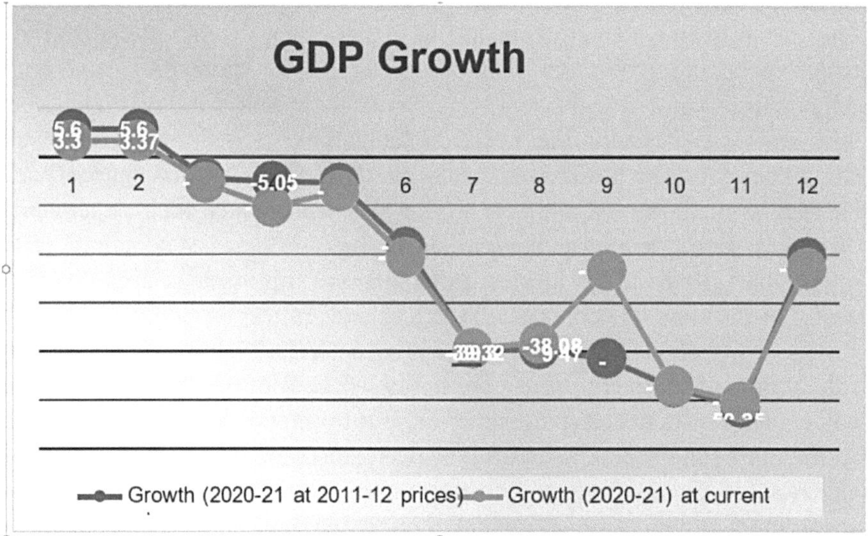

FIGURE 4.4 India's GDP (Fiscal year 2020–21).

Source: Statista.

The growth in GDP is measured negative at 2011–12 prices as well as at current prices. Even if we see the trend of past years, the growth in gross domestic product was slowest from the past year 2009–10. Due to

COVID-19 pandemic, India is facing problem of negative growth from the third month of fiscal year 2020–21. As we can see in Figure 4.4, in the first two months of 2020, the GDP was 5.69, i.e., positive, but after that lockdown has been imposed on labor force and all industries, which turned into less demand and investment. The growth of GDP will go down at negative level that shows devastating impacts of economy. Individually, this will impact to the employees in many forms. For example, many companies encourage their employees to work from home which will benefit to companies as they can make their employees to work for longer or more hours. With the contraction in GDP, it has been analyzed that consumption is also contracted by 26.7%, which will impact on the revenue from the production which further lead to less profit. Industries get back their decision of expansion plan. Overall understanding gives an idea that GDP contraction not only impacts directly on individuals but indirectly also.

4.4.3 STRATEGIES

The one strategy which could be useful in this time is "gated-globalization," which means all economies should be selective to whom they trade with. All countries created walls as a boundary of their nation and restricted open trade and travel. By adopting "gated-globalization," a particular nation could strengthen domestic production, promote self-sufficiency, and support local businesses of their own country, so that they can reduce their dependency on other nations. "Gated-globalization" is useful in times of economic crisis rather than unfettered market-led globalization. This strategy could be very useful at the time of economic crisis and pandemics, especially in today's situation, where each nation is affected by COVID-19 and is facing the flip side of globalization. To protect our nations from future economic crisis and epidemics, we should strengthen our nations by supporting local production. At the same time, it can be harmful also as it discourages global competition and flow of capital from one country to another. So, we have to manage accordingly and promote international trade, integration of different nations, and international investments at the time of sustained economic progress.

Many economies, whether developed or underdeveloped, had set their global value chain around China, mainly connected with Wuhan city from where coronavirus started. Global firms like automobile industries and technology-led industries are dependent on China for spare parts of vehicles and technological parts of digital devices. Industries which are producing pharmaceutical products, electrical goods, and automobiles in developing and developed nations had to face incredible lacks because they import inputs from China. At the time of national emergencies, all countries had to cut off relations with China. Countries like India, USA, Italy, etc., have shut their doors to China to protect their nation from dangerous outcomes of COVID-19 pandemic. Even developed nations like USA, UK, Italy, France, etc., have been stuck in very hard situation where they lack in basic medical apparatus and equipment like COVID-19 testing kits, personal protection equipment (PPE), ventilators, sanitizers, gloves, masks, disinfectants, amplifiers, stethoscope, thermal cameras, thermal guns, etc. COVID-19 pandemic attacks very hard and it infects people at a very huge level. Millions of people get infected from this disease. Hospitals face lack of beds, isolation wards, and ventilators to COVID-19 positive patients. China was the major producer of gloves, masks, and sanitizers, but all countries cut their trade relation in the situation of COVID-19, because air ways and other transportation were totally closed at that time.

From this situation, it has been observed that total dependence on other nations can cause dangerous outcomes at the time of emergencies and epidemics. It gives threats to all economies who are depending on single source country, that is, China. It not only downs the business but affects all spheres of life. The only solution which is realized is that all countries should have one alternative in situation of economic crisis so that their supply chain does not get affected. They should have other option so that if one way is closed, business can turn to another way and switch the dependency from one input place to another when required.

India has taken a very good step toward making alternative in case of emergency. The Prime Minister of India, Mr. Narendra Modi, has shared his vision to make India self--reliant and self-sufficient, so that the nation could manage situation of any economic crisis and epidemic spread. "Atmnirbhar Bharat" does not mean "self-containment" or "isolating away from the world," it is just a strategy which can be helpful in times of emergency like COVID-19 spread. Self-sufficiency can make bigger positive impact and very important part of global economy. Various decisions like boosting MSME companies by increasing private players participation, FDI increase in defense sector, and investment in solar manufacture sector would lead toward self-sufficiency. Defense Minister Mr. Rajnath Singh announced an initiative by imposing import restriction on 101 items. Other nations can also put changes to their public policies and strengthen their domestic production.

Global economy should relook into the financial strategies which should be innovative according to the present situation of pandemic. There should be proper agenda to control and manage the risk which can justify the steps taken in emergency situation. Health calamity is the major disaster which can destroy human resources. So, for saving global value chain of human beings and mobility of other resources and businesses, capitalist countries like USA, United Kingdom, Italy, etc., have to come forward and make serious innovation plans with the help of financial institutions to invest in the health sector.

KEYWORDS

- **globalization**
- **COVID-19 shock**
- **production**
- **welfare affect**

4.5 CONCLUSION

From all the pros and cons of globalization, it can be observed that economies can face crisis, emergency, and epidemic at any time. All countries should have proper public policy agenda to cope with any emergency situation. Although it takes time to make our nation self-sufficient, we should be able to manage the situation before it turns into massive devastating effects on economy. Although strengthening the international market of any economy is very important to make capitalized economies of scale, community of a country plays crucial role. If we cannot save the human resources, there is no benefit of technological development. "Gated-globalization" is a way forward to learn alternative uses of domestic production. More focus should be on research and development so that future uncertainties will be controlled and global economy can be sustained from the threats of health and economic instability. There should be universal access to healthcare. There should be extension in the existing foreign trade policy to improve exports of a country. The government should give push to domestic production through which well paid jobs can be created for skilled and semi-skilled laborers. According to the need of technology, there should be broadband connectivity all over the nation to ensure digital skills. COVID-19 gives us the lesson through which we realized that not only traditional economic policies are important for development of any nation but health economic policies should also be taken care of and revised time to time so that we have enough strategies to manage health uncertainty.

REFERENCES

Ilyas, A. Covid-19 Pandemic: Emergence of a New Geopolitical Perspective. Renewal A. ECA estimates billions worth of losses in Africa due to COVID-19 impact, 2020.

Baldwin, R.; Di Mauro, B. W. *Economics in the Time of COVID-19: A New eBook*; VOX CEPR Policy Portal, 2020; pp. 2–3.

Baldwin, R. E.; Weder, B., Eds. *Mitigating the COVID Economic Crisis: Act Fast and do Whatever it Takes*; CEPR press, 2020.

Barua, S. Understanding Coronanomics: The Economic Implications of the Coronavirus (COVID-19) Pandemic [Online] Apr 1, 2020. Available at SSRN 3566477.

Coyne, J.; Jennings, P., Eds. *After Covid-19: Australia and the World Rebuild*; Australian Strategic Policy Institute, 2020.

David, G.; Thomas, K.; Oliver, M.; Martin, S.; Adenauer Stiftung, K. Coronavirus Infects the Global Economy: The Economic Impact of an Unforeseeable Pandemic [Online] 2020. https://www.jstor.org/stable/resrep25284

Eichenbaum, M. S.; Rebelo, S.; Trabandt, M. M. The Macroeconomics of Epidemics. *Working paper 26882, National Bureau of Economic Research*; 2020.

Ruiz Estrada, M. A. Is Globalization Responsible of the Wuhan-COVID-19 Worldwide Crisis? [Online] 2020 Mar 10. SSRN 3551944.

Jackson, E. A. Emerging Innovative Thoughts on Globalization Amidst the Contageon of COVID-19. In *Industry, Innovation and Infrastructure*; Springer Nature, 2020; pp. 1–12.

Sforza, A.; Steininger, M. Globalization in the Time of COVID-19, CESifo Working Paper No. 8184; 2020.

Tardy, T. *COVID-19: Shaping Future Threats and Security Policies*; NATO in the Age of Pandemics, 2020; pp. 13–20.

Van de Pas, R. *Globalization Paradox and the Coronavirus Pandemic*; Clingendael Institute, 2020.

CHAPTER 5

The Study of Impact of Films on the Tourism Industry: An Analysis

SNEHI SHAHI and JAIDEEP KAUR*

Amity Business School, Amity University, Noida 201303, UP, India

**Corresponding author. jkaur@amity.edu*

ABSTRACT

It has been seen in the recent times that the entertainment industry has been exploring new destinations to shoot various films, songs, and promotional material. This has led to the emergence of a brand new avenue in the tourism sector. We tested to what extent Films are going to impact tourism. The 258 people were interviewed with the help of questionnaires. There is a positive relationship between film and tourism. Film tourism has impacted the branch of cultural tourism as it refers to the growing interest and rising demand for locations that have become popular due to their appearance in the films and television. It was found out that various other factors also have a positive impact on the tourists for visiting a film destination.

5.1 INTRODUCTION

Film tourism has been defined as a branch of cultural tourism and it refers to the growing interest and rising demand for locations that have become popular due to their appearance in the films and television series (Zimmermann et al., 2003). Tourism has been seen as a system, which includes places, territories, tourists, tourist networks, markets, laws, values, and practices, interactions between social institutions, and among others. Therefore, taking this into

Constructive Discontent in Execution: Creative Approaches to Technology and Management.
Sanjeev Bansal, Anita Venaik, Swati Upveja, and Saritha S. (Eds.)

account the perspective of tourism as a system, the economic conjuncture and tourism-related phenomena play a vital role in the world of globalization. Globalization has been attracting new clients and has established a positive position and this is equally important for countries and companies as well as for destinations that are famous for tourism (Cerviño, 2007). From the beginning, we have understood tourism as a sector that has constantly been changing and transforming, and therefore, there is equal competition between destinations and individual tourist products and destinations. There have been various tourist destinations that have been perceived subjectively in accordance to variety sociological and psychological conditions, along with motivational and cultural situations of the consumers themselves. The revolution in technologies and information meant that every individual who is a tourist has become more aware with the availability of information, and has therefore been demanding more. The markets not only have become more heterogeneous than customer's experience, instead of looking for and experience or a destination or a dream. These changes in the expectations and habits of tourists from the very start have meant that the tourism destinations should focus on designing a brand of their own and then they need to manage it in accordance with the strategic position (Blanco, 2015). Destinations have now been competing primarily on the basis the basis of their perceived image in relation to the image help by their competitors in the market Zimmermann has described Film tourism as a set of all forms of travel to destinations, which allow a connection with the film world (Zimmermann et al., 2003). According to various foreign scholars that have been studying films and tourism, this is important and is possible to increase awareness. Some researchers have also reported that awareness of various sites have increased due to their appearance in a film (Klug and Busby, 2001; Baker and Tooke, 1996; Riley, 1998). The main purpose of films is not generally to induce tourism but indirectly films do lead to a rise in awareness of certain locations that have been shown in the films (Buttler, 1990). It has been observed that postmodern and especially western tourism has been influenced strongly by the film industry. Various films and shows, such as Game of Thrones, Lord of the Rings, and even Harry Potter are prominent examples in terms of film-induced tourism. Schofield in the year 1996 stated that an organic image of various tourism locations is usually formed by a mediated consumption of television and films without any form of bias created by promotional material. This means that the stakeholder in the film industry can use films as a medium of promotion and creating awareness regarding various location that appear in the films without making the viewers realize that they are advertising a certain location.

Attitudes have proved to be a useful predictor of overall preferences, but their success in predicting behavior was less definitive (Aassael, 1984).

Destination imagery is an aspect which drives an individual to visit a destination or a place, an image becomes embedded in the minds of individuals. Fakeye and Crompton (1991), in their article, discuss how an image plays as a prerequisite for an individual tourist to travel to a particular destination.

Hunt (1975) argues that each place or a destination has a perceived image which might be positive, negative or mediocre. These perceived images can be changed or manipulated. According to Gunn (1988), the image of a destination can be divided into two: namely, organic and induced image. Organic image simply means that images which are formed without any conscious efforts and are natural in nature. Induced images, on the other hand, are images where marketers place special emphasis on pushing an idea of a destination to the prospect individual. With the growing importance of the subject, various definitions and frameworks have been formed. Due to human inputs of the subject, there has been constant criticism (Echtner and Ritchie, 1993; Fakeye and Crompton, 1991; Gartner, 1993).

Ko and Park (2000), in their article, analyzed that the researchers focus on certain aspects, that is, composite structure of the image, which form the sum of beliefs and impressions about a particular place or a destination. This image is formed from information received from various information sources over time (Aassael, 1984; Baloglu and McCleary, 1999; Crompton, 1979; Gartner, 1993) which is accepted generally.

Lawson and Baud-Bovy (1977) have defined the formation of a destination image as the culmination of impressions, imagination, and prejudice, emotional thoughts of an individual or a group. The definition is not concrete and other researchers have sought that destination image is formed with the overall impression from individual attributes which contain both cognition and emotion (Oxenfeldt, 1975. Dichter (1985) has placed importance on formation of image with objective evaluation which has gained further consensus from Mazursky and Jacoby (1986).

Mayo and Jarvis (1981) had discussed the positive correlation of perceived destination image with visiting a destination, that is, purchase decision when it comes to selecting a destination. Woodside and Lysonski (1989) also place affirmative nuance that the image of a place is an important selection factor.

There have been various definitions of how movies affect destination image, although movies have been classified under art and culture of local traditions, film tourism has become a part of cultural tourism (McKercher and Du Cros, 2002; Hudson and Ritchie, 2006). Movie tourism implies when a tourist visits a particular destination because they saw it in a movie or was featured on television.

Movies in popular culture are produced not to lure tourists to a specific destination but because those destinations play a crucial role to the story line in some way, movies have induced tourism in the recent years by showcasing scenic beauty and cultural festivals. Marketers have realized the true potential of movies in regard to tourism (Kim and Richardson, 2003; Riley and Van Doren, 1992).

According to Riley and Van Doren (1992), traditional means of tourism marketing do not reach the masses because of hefty financial requirements, whereas movies penetrate different market segments at the same time with very little investment solely done for promotion of a destination. Further, Dore and Crouch (2003) added that out of all the publicity tools for destination, marketing movies serve as the greater influencer of a destination. Film-induced tourism only becomes a reality when the movie is successful, such success in terms of tourism and for the movie has carious critical factors (Hudson and Ritchie, 2006). Generally, the success of film locations relies on the success of films. Some film locations are more successful than others in terms of the number of tourist arrivals. Further research is needed on the critical success of the film tourism and the psychological aspects of tourist behavior in visiting film locations (Hudson and Ritchie, 2006).

5.2 OBJECTIVES OF THE STUDY

1. To understand the role of movies on tourism in India.
2. To determine the factors that influence consumer's attitude of movies toward tourism.
3. To study the extent of impact of these factors of movies toward tourism.

5.3 METHODOLOGY

5.3.1 RESEARCH DESIGN

The descriptive research design was used in this study.

5.3.2 SAMPLING TECHNIQUE

The sampling technique used is convenience sampling.

5.3.3 DATA COLLECTION

This study, carried out through primary research with the help of a questionnaire, focuses on finding out the problem. Data were collected with the help of Google forms and 258 respondents were chosen from the Delhi NCR region.

5.3.4 STATISTICAL TOOLS USED

For efficient and effective analysis and to achieve the objectives of the study, correlation analysis was done and the tool used was IBM SPSS Statistics 25.

5.3.5 DATA ANALYSIS

5.3.5.1 DEMOGRAPHIC ANALYSIS

5.3.5.1.1 *Age*

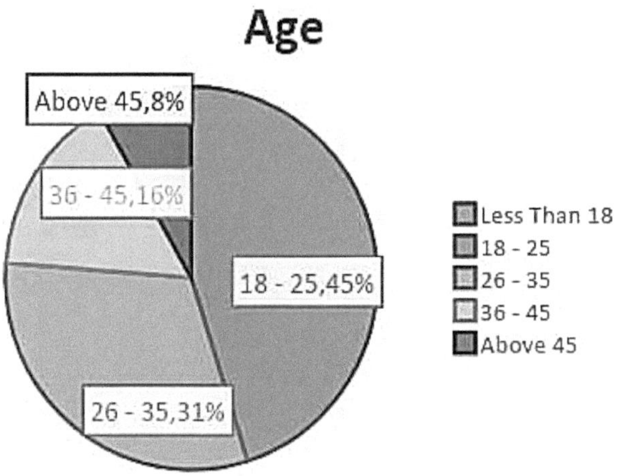

FIGURE 5.1 Age of the respondents.

TABLE 5.1 Percentage of Respondents in Different Age Groups.

Age	Respondents	Percentage
Less than 18 years	0	0
18–25 years	116	45
26–35 years	80	31
36–45 years	40	16
Above 45 years	7	3

Figure 5.1 depicts the age of the respondents as per the data shown in Table 5.1. There were no respondents from the age group of less than 18 years (0 respondents out of 258), 45% from 18 to 25 years (116 respondents out of 258), and 31% from 26 to 35.

Years (80 respondents out of 258), 16% from 36 to 45 years (40 respondents out of 258), and there were 8% respondents above the age of 45 (21 out of 258).

5.3.5.1.2 Income

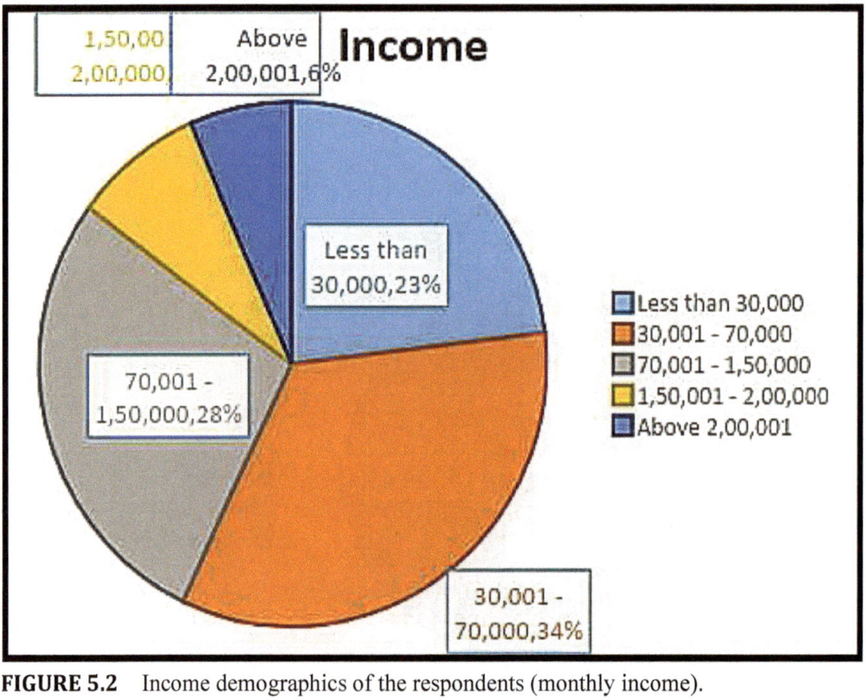

FIGURE 5.2 Income demographics of the respondents (monthly income).

Figure 5.2 depicts the Income demographics of the respondents. Out of 258 respondents, 23% where people whose income was less than Rs. 30,000, 34% where people whose income was between Rs. 30,001 and 70,000, then 28% where between Rs. 70,001 and 150,000, 8% where between Rs. 150,001 and 200,000 and 7% were above Rs. 200,001.

5.3.5.1.3 Gender

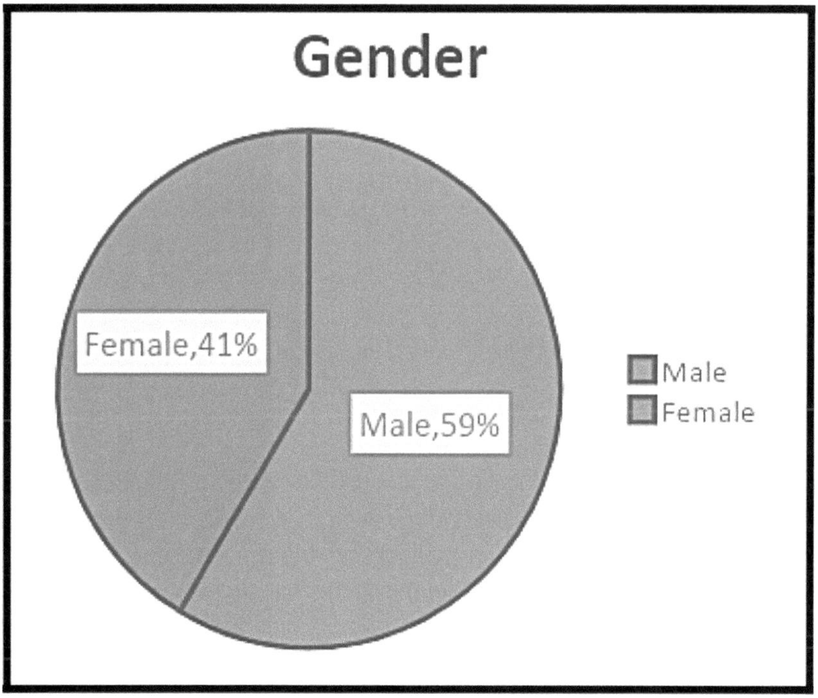

Out of 258 respondents 164 were male and 94 were females.

5.3.5.2 RELIABILITY

The data collected through the questionnaire were subjected to a reliability test using the SPSS software. The **Cronbach's alpha value** obtained from the test was 0.884. The value obtained is above 0.6 which indicates that the questionnaire is reliable.

5.3.5.3 *CORRELATION ANALYSIS*

Table 5.2 depicts the results of the correlation analysis. Correlation analysis was carried out between the other factors and the attitude of the consumer. The test was carried out on SPSS software.

TABLE 5.2 Correlations Table.

		Attitude	Status	Celebrity	Promotion	Success	Image
Attitude	Pearson Correlation	1	0.504**	0.238**	0.182**	0.298**	0.439**
	Sig. (2-tailed)		0.000	0.000	0.003	0.000	0.000
	N	258	258	258	258	258	258

From Table 5.2, it is observed that attitude has a positive correlation of 0.504 with status then followed by the image of the film, success of the film, celebrity endorsement of film, and the last promotions of the film. This indicates that there is an impact of films on the tourism industry, and the following factors were responsible for the enhancing the tourism industry.

5.3.6 *FINDINGS*

- 50% of attitude of the consumers' impacts the decision of travel toward tourism is based on status.
- 43% of attitude of the consumers' impacts the decision of travel toward tourism is based on the Image of the destination.
- 29% of attitude of the consumers' impacts the decision of travel toward tourism is based on the success of the movie.
- 23% of attitude of the consumers' impacts the decision of travel toward tourism is based on the celebrity presence in a movie.

5.4 CONCLUSION

It has been found out that status is one of the major factors on a tourist' attitude when comes to visiting a film destination. The results indicate that status has the highest impact, followed by celebrity presence, image, and success. The results also indicate that film promotion has no impact on a tourist' attitude when it comes to visiting a film destination. Although previous research had laid down the groundwork for film-induced tourism and studying the factor of image, under this study, it was found out that various other factors also have a positive impact on the tourists' attitude for visiting a film destination.

KEYWORDS

- **films**
- **tourism**
- **cultural tourism**
- **correlation**

REFERENCES

Aassael, H. *Consumer Behaviour and Marketing Action*; Kent Pub. Co.: Kent, 1984.

Baloglu, S.; McCleary, K. W. A Model of Destination Image Formation. *Ann. Tour. Res.* **1999,** *26* (4), 868–897.

Baloglu, S.; Mangaloglu, M. Tourism Destination Images of Turkey, Egypt, Greece, and Italy as Perceived by US-Based Tour Operators and Travel Agents. *Tour. Manage.* **2001,** *22* (1), 1–9.

Dichter, E. What's in an Image. *J. Consum. Mark.* **1985,** *2* (1), 75–81.

Dore, L.; Crouch, G. I. Promoting Destinations: An Exploratory Study of Publicity Programs Used by National Tourism Organizations. *J. Vac. Mark.* **2003,** *9* (2), 137–151.

Fakeye, P. C.; Crompton, J. L. Image Difference between Prospective, First-Time, and Repeat Visitors to the Lower Rio Grande Valley. *J. Travel Res.* **1991,** *30* (2), 10–16.

Gunn, C. A. *Tourism Planning*, 2nd ed.; Taylor & Francis: Milton Park, 1988.

Hunt, J. D. Image as a Factor in Tourism Development. *J. Travel Res.* **1975,** *13* (3), 1–7.

Hudson, S.; Ritchie, J. B. Promoting Destinations via Film Tourism: An Empirical Identification of Supporting Marketing Initiatives. *J. Travel Res.* **2006,** *44* (4), 387–396.

Ko, D. W.; Park, S. H. Five Aspects of Tourism Image: A Review. *Int. J. Tour. Sci.* **2000,** *1* (1), 79–92.

Kim, H.; Richardson, S. L. Motion Picture Impacts on Destination Images. *Ann. Tour. Res.* **2003,** *30* (1), 216–237.

Lawson, F.; Baud-Bovy, M. Tourism and Recreation Development. *A Handbook of Physical Planning*; Princeton Architectural Press: New York, NY, 1977.

Mayo, E. J.; Jarvis, L. P. The Psychology of Leisure Travel. *Effective Marketing and Selling of Travel Services*; CBI Public Company, Inc.: New York, NY, 1981.

Mazursky, D.; Jacoby, J. Exploring the Development of Store Images. *J. Retail.* **1986,** *62* (2), 145–165.

McKercher, B.; Du Cros, H. Cultural Tourism. *The Partnership between Tourism and Culture Heritage Management*; Routledge: Milton Park, 2002.

Riley, R. W.; Van Doren, C. S. Movies as Tourism Promotion. A 'Pull' Factor in a 'Push' Location. *Tour. Manage.* **1992,** *13* (3), 267–274.

Woodside, A. G.; Lysonski, S. A General Model of Traveler Destination Choice. *J. Travel Res.* **1989,** *27* (4), 8–14.

Zimmermann, C., Daigle, J.; Pol, J. *Tourism Business and Intelligent Transportation Systems*; Acadia National Park: Maine. *Transport. Res. Rec.: J. Transport. Res. Board,* 1895; pp 182–187.

CHAPTER 6

Innovation—A Strategic Imperative

RAMAKRISHNA KARANTH[1*], YASHASWINI KARANTH[2], and ASHOK CHOPRA[3]

[1]*Kimoha Entrepreneurs Ltd., JAFZA, Dubai, UAE*

[2]*Department of Materials Science and Engineering, Arizona State University, Tempe, AZ, USA*

[3]*Management and Commerce, Amity University, Dubai, UAE*

[*]*Corresponding author. E-mail: achopra@amityuniversity.ae*

ABSTRACT

"A slow sort of country" said the Red Queen. "Nowhere, you see, it takes all the running you can do to keep in the same place. If one wants to get somewhere else, one must run at least twice as fast as that!"

Lewis Caroll, Alice through the Looking Glass

In the volatile, uncertain, complex, and ambiguous (VUCA) world that we live in today, the global forces place more demands on businesses, which in turn demand more from their supply chain and operations. Technological evolution and easy liquidity have been helping to reduce entry barriers in many industries. Automation and artificial intelligence have gradually made redundant the human skill element in manufacturing industries, and the outcome is the wafer-thin difference in quality and efficiency of the best in class and the rest of them. With this backdrop, in today's fast-paced world, the differentiating factor that defines success is the ability of organizations to innovate and reinvent. Innovation has become a critical element in any company's strategic plans for success.

Constructive Discontent in Execution: Creative Approaches to Technology and Management.
Sanjeev Bansal, Anita Venaik, Swati Upveja, and Saritha S. (Eds.)

In order to become an innovative organization, the culture of the organization must be conducive to develop and support creativity. Organizations with a work atmosphere that promotes conceiving, nurturing, and developing abstract ideas into successfully implemented innovations are the ones that will grow continuously and will outshine the competition, and lead the way in the complex marketplace today.

Several case studies of innovations and innovative practices in manufacturing and service industries, when examined to identify the common threads, facilitated organizations to reap the benefits of innovation as a routine. Each case study amply demonstrates that people play a vital role in creating such a culture of innovation and that "Below the Green Line" (BTGL) factors play an essential role in determining organizational culture.

The success of innovation when measured through several outputs related to "Above the Green Line" (ATGL) factors, such as outputs, sales, and successes. Several possible measurement techniques, when discussed, found there is a clear need for standardization. Recommendations for promoting and sustaining a culture of innovation, the ATGL or BTGL, were most prominent. These recommendations include systems, structures, activities, and ways of communicating.

6.1 INTRODUCTION

6.1.1 THE CASE FOR INNOVATION

The primary goal of any business is to maximize stakeholder value, the stakeholders being the shareholders, the employees, the customers, and the communities in which the business operates. In order to achieve this goal continuously, business needs to have sustainable growth, favorable economic returns, and continuous value creation, thereby for the stakeholders.

Commoditization, excess production capacities, financial volatility, globalization, and ever-increasing customer and consumer expectations drive change at an unprecedented rate in today's business scenario. Global competition, corporate restructuring, and rapid technological progress are the norms of the day, and hence it is essential for organizations to continuously strive to identify new opportunities beyond their existing competencies and ensure continual growth.

A few of the commonly heard definitions of innovation are:

"Making changes, introducing new practices."

"Thinking out of the box."

"Finding new ways to do things better."

"The ability to do something impossible."

"Innovation = conception + invention + exploitation."

However, it is important to address the business case when we define innovation so that the innovation, in turn, helps in building and guiding the future course of businesses. The same brings us to the business case definition of innovation as:

"Adding value to the customer's product."

"Increasing the perceived customer value."

"Helping our customers sell more."

"Helping the Organization to become the low-cost producer."

Innovation means creating and implementing ideas that are novel and useful. It is a long process of conceiving a good idea, developing it as sound output, and carrying this good idea/output to a meaningful end through widespread and practical usage to generate value for the organization.

Today, the customer is flooded with information and has access to sources previously inaccessible. Inevitably, customers have become more sophisticated and more demanding. On the other end, globalization has removed entry barriers and has opened the gate to worldwide competition. Add to that the constant improvements in science and technology, and we have a setting where companies that cannot provide new value to customers will disappear. The same brings us to innovation, the mainspring of new value.

Today, high-end technology is available at an affordable price to every player in the industry. There is ample availability of an educated workforce to put this technology to practical use. Further, the continuous evolution in technology and automation is making human skills redundant day by day. With this, the gap between the leader and the follower is diminishing day by day. With the improved logistics network and innovative approach to warehousing and delivery, the locational advantage of local players has become redundant. Gone are the days of the solid monopolistic presence of many multinational players, and local homegrown players are capturing substantial market shares and are strengthening their positions in many developing nations. All this has paved the way to a significant price war and sought success in the marketplace by brand recognition and recall, high service levels, and positioning of innovative products.

In a nutshell, organizations need to realize, if the rate of change inside the organization is less than the rate of change outside, the end is in sight! Organizations need to recognize the importance of customers' demand for them to be innovative, just to be in business. Nevertheless, we cannot just stop here! Let us get it right; innovation extends a competitive advantage and is a strategic imperative for the survival and growth of the organization.

6.1.2 A CULTURE OF INNOVATION

Innovative organizations always operate at the edge of their competence, focusing more of their resources and attention on what they do not know than controlling what they already know. We need to imbibe this approach in our work lives to stay ahead of the competition, build a learning organization, and be successful in the marketplace. An organization's future will be secure when they differentiate themselves clearly from the competition and provide a clear value addition to their processes and the customer, and the work-life of individuals in the organization through an innovative approach.

Successful organizations of the 21st century are required to effectively use talents available both within their organization and with the extended family of suppliers, customers, and other like-minded organizations by networking with them, that is, partnership with firms that agree to extend innovative abilities by mutual benefit. It may become a mandatory requirement for survival shortly as nobody can afford to stand alone in this fast-paced world.

Culture refers to the organization's values, beliefs, and behaviors. Firms with solid culture achieve higher results because employees sustain focus on what to do and how to do it. Similarly, a culture of innovation is the organization's belief and drive towards achieving excellence in its sphere of activity through the continuous pursuit of innovation. Accepting and recognizing failures on the arduous path of innovation as a welcome possibility and encouraging people to innovate, recognize and reward the innovative people, and enable the people to have fun on the way to innovation help nurture and build innovation.

Establishing a culture of innovation is hard work. Top-driven sustained strenuous efforts are essential to establish a strong culture of innovation. Culture of Innovation stems from the zeal and attitude of continuous sustained growth, as the spirit of relentless growth keeps fresh ideas flowing and reinvigorates the organization.

An underutilized resource in today's economy is the knowledge available for innovation. Organizations need to devise a structured way of funneling the surplus of ideas that are being wasted and finding a home for them through "collaborative communities." By building collaborative communities, we can strive to achieve significant improvements in our innovative drives through the effective positioning of these surplus ideas. Though sharing such ideas across the organizations may sound somewhat utopian, it can be achieved through networking at the highest levels and building the required level of trust. Before building such "collaborative communities," it is essential for organizations to learn and imbibe the art of teamwork. Working in silos (with a fear that sharing an idea with another department might give them a competitive advantage) can be highly detrimental to creating a culture of innovation.

Further, all the employees need to see themselves as inventors rather than leaving the innovation to select few like R&D people and the Client servicing team. Next in the line is to agree that "customer knows the best," and paying attention to customers' needs can help drive innovative breakthroughs.

The Futures Triangle Model (Burke, 2005) illustrates the necessity to balance the forces of weight of history, push of the present, and the future to map and achieve a plausible future scenario. Organizations must learn from their history, work out a strategy for success while facing the current market forces, and imbibe a futuristic approach to pave the way for a better tomorrow by innovating to gain a competitive advantage and keep themselves relevant during the years ahead. Achieving a competitive advantage by effectively leveraging the cumulative knowledge, technical skills, and expertise available to innovate and create new products, processes, and services will help lead the organization in its march to the future.

Most organizations use only a fraction of their innovation potential (Miles et al., 2005). The collaborative relationship between a network of firms across the globe to pursue continuous innovation is likely to be the reality in the 21st century. This collaborative network can only succeed with a strong culture of trust and social responsibility. While the large firms will be keen on this collaborative network to maximize their results and reach, smaller firms' interest is due to lack of in-house resources and to build the culture of innovation.

The culture of an organization is what outsiders will often see. It is usually evident in the way people in the organization deal with each other and with customers and suppliers. Edgar Schein has described organizational culture as existing on three levels (Hatch, 1997):

On the surface are the artifacts Beneath those lie the values and norms. Furthermore, at the deepest level are the beliefs and assumptions.

Elements of the organization include artifacts and espoused values when considered to be ATGL in that they are management operations, that is, related to patterns, structures, and processes. Boas (2005) described these elements as being ATGL or BTGL. BTGL are the elements that determine the relationships, the information, and the passion and identity of the social relationships in the organization.

Schein described assumptions as being what members of the organization believe to be a reality, taken for granted. However, organizational culture is not a single belief or assumption but a combination of a number of them. Values are the social principles, goals, and standards that form the basis for decisions about right and wrong. On the other hand, norms are unwritten rules that allow members of the organization to know expected performance under different circumstances. The artifacts are the visible, tangible, and audible remains of the behaviors, and they can be physical objects, verbal, for example, legends and stories, rituals.

An innovative culture is one in which there is an environment where creative thinking is central to corporate assumptions and values, the evidence of which may be in the artifacts. Employees in an innovative culture seek new opportunities, accept risk, collaborate well with others, and align themselves with their goals. Therefore, these critical elements of an innovative culture are to be found by BTGL, that is, they require a sense of identity and self-worth.

So, what would an innovative organizational culture target? Birdi and Wall (2003) suggested that employees must get opportunities to explore, investigate, and experiment. Management should provide support through active encouragement of these types of behavior. The organization itself should have structures and processes that allow for a smooth transition from the appearance of new ideas to their implementation. The organization could then grow through the growth of its people.

Research conducted by the Institute of Work Psychology at Sheffield University highlighted how some of this culture can be grown (Birdi and Wall, 2003):

- Selecting, recruiting, and developing innovative employees.
- Training for creativity and innovation.
- Advocating and developing a learning culture.
- Empowering employees to be innovative.
- Setting up idea capture schemes.
- Developing managers to support the innovative ideas and works of others.
- Making creativity a requirement of the job.
- Improving employee participation in decision-making.
- Having an appropriate reward system for innovation.
- Allowing and encouraging constructive risk-taking as an acceptable work practice.

- Encouraging investment in research and development and working out a budget accordingly.
- Benchmarking.

In order to enable building such innovative culture, organizations need to make the work environment conducive and encouraging to build such culture. The same can sound easy when we track, measure, and reward innovations.

Chopra (2018) believed majority organizations would need to focus on balancing internal and external pressures and the evolution necessary for innovation in every aspect, including procurement so to reach a sophisticated equilibrium.

In order to have a sense of trust, teamwork must also recognize along with individual brilliance. Measuring the innovation with the count of innovations that have occurred with collaboration with the customers, suppliers, and other collaborative communities can help build an open culture conducive to innovative thinking and develop two-way communication outside the organization.

As per Chopra (2018), one can attribute many innovative ideas lead to why organizational practice is directly proportional to the probability of high success that an individual may venture into a new company.

Tidd et al. (2001) identify four phases that make up the innovation process. These are the following:

- Scan and search the environment (internal and external) to pick up and process signals about potential innovations.
- Strategically select from these triggers those things which the organization will commit resources to have.
- Resource the option.
- Implement the innovation by growing it from an idea through the stages of development to the final launch.
- Reflect on and review past successes and failures.
- A survey and analysis of various case studies on innovation across the globe in various industries like manufacturing (steel, automobile, and packaging), hospitality, and Information Technology reveal the underlying principle commonly seen across all of them. The reasons for the successes achieved by these groups can be summarized as follows:

- Working and performing together as teams, either purpose designed or cross-functional, is featured in almost all examples and represent an evident strength.
- We are meeting the customer's needs by listening to and engaging them in the innovation process. During the process, organizations deliver results way above the generally accepted expectation!
- The listening element can also mean obtaining a clear development brief from our customers.
- They use what we have in an innovative and new way to achieve more than we had thought possible.
- They are leveraging the global resources and locational advantages.
- Empowering the teams. Encouraging and promoting involvement.
- They are celebrating successes.

Becoming a true partner in our customer's innovation process is a very effective strategy to change perceptions and reduce the overall risk that generally comes with innovation.

6.2 MEASURING INNOVATION PERFORMANCE

Like every other key performance indicator, it is necessary to measure and monitor the progress in Innovation performance too. Several measures and indicators that can help the organizations track and review the innovation performance are as follows:

- Measures of specific innovation-related outputs, such as patents acquired and technology licenses lodged as indicators of successful innovation efforts, scientific papers presented as indicators of knowledge produced, or the number of new products introduced (and percentage of sales and profits derived from them) as indicators of product innovation success.
- A measure of the thinking process and speed and efficiency of ideation—number of new ideas generated on a periodical basis, failure rates, overruns on developmental costs and timelines, person-hours spent per completed innovation, time to market for new ideas and products.
- Investment in business intelligence—will show how an organization seeks data about its external environment as input into innovative activities.

- The number of research programs targeted with universities and external research centers can infuse brand new ideas and a fresh wave of thinking. Out-of-the-box solutions.
- In an innovative solution, several options are typically offered in collaboration with the suppliers, customers, and other like-minded partners. Interdepartmental workgroups have taken up several innovative projects.
- The number of innovative projects suggestions collected and the number of suggestions taken up for implementation are the basis of offering solutions.
- Output measures of operational or process elements—such as process improvements taken up and efficiency improvement, cost reduction, the improved quality achieved, customer satisfaction surveys to measure and track improvements in quality and service.
- Output measures can be compared across sectors or enterprises—for example, cost of the product, market share, quality performance.
- Output measures of strategic success—where the overall business performance is improved somehow and where at least some of the benefit can be attributed directly or indirectly to innovation. For example, revenue or market share growth, reduced raw material content, improved profitability, and higher value add manufacturing cost reduction.
- Continuous improvement efforts—number of small groups working on process improvement projects, number of successful projects, savings per project, cumulative savings, suggestions per employee, and savings accrued per employee.
- Quantum of machine-hours and person-hours spent working on innovative projects.
- In this, sales value is generated through the innovative product as a percentage of the total sale value.
- Feedback sought and obtained from the customers on the organization's contribution to meet the customer's need for innovative solutions.
- Defining a life period of innovation becomes an absolute necessity in today's situation where a newly introduced product is considered "high-value" forever-shortening periods. The product life-cycle graph of a "high-end" introduction would inevitably drop toward "almost commoditization" at a faster pace than before. In order to retain technical leadership and reasonable operating margins, it is critical to keep doing new things all the time and help our customers with

product differentiation in the marketplace. "Plan obsolescence," and simultaneously bring down the production cost of the product as it moved down the product life-cycle graph so that the volumes could be, at least, the "capacity fillers" that recover fixed costs.
- Setting up targets for the annual sales generated through innovative solutions as a percentage of total annual sales and recognizing the teams that have achieved set targets can help encourage teams to innovate continuously.

BTGL measurements of innovation success at an individual level are based on:

- absenteeism
- staff turnover
- measures of staff morale

The key is to have innovation as part of the business unit's deliverables and link this to incentives and rewards. The rewards and recognition are to be measured and granted based on the team results of a business unit and not just the functional department. It is important to remember and practice only what gets measured can be improved and rewarded. At the individual level, the contributions of each employee to the Innovation process could as part of the review process.

Creating an encouraging environment that promotes and recognizes innovative thinking by treating every innovative suggestion as big and giving them visibility in the organization, irrespective of however complicated or straightforward it is, similar to STARS—Special Thanks And Recognition System of Taj Group of Hotels, shall help harness the innovative power of every employee. Such initiative is offered through some instances of innovative suggestions that are ideally shared across the group.

Monitoring the quantum of person-hours and machine-hours spent on innovative activities and encouraging the operational teams to invest more in such activities shall help the team focus on innovation in greater detail. Including this as a part of the MIS submitted should help improve the team commitment toward such investment made in innovative activity.

Seeking feedback from the customers on the organization's contribution in meeting their need for an innovative solution and monitoring feedback regularly can help us understand where we stand in customers' viewpoint concerning innovation. This should also help us take corrective actions in-house and decide further courses of action to strengthen the innovative drive within the organization.

6.3 DISCUSSIONS AND RECOMMENDATIONS

Once a clear understanding has reached that building the culture of innovation is mandatory for the success and longevity of the organization, it is critical to assess the organization's current culture and innovation management capability. This is often a tedious and long-drawn process. Gaps are to be identified, and necessary HR intervention to improve the culture needs to be initiated.

The Green Line Model provides a framework for changing and transforming an organization into a more innovative culture. The structures, patterns, and processes used are considered the elements ATGL. An organization that concentrates only on ATGL elements has only power and control as management tools, as emphasized by Boas (2005). Having only these management tools is insufficient to promote the culture of innovation and is somewhat inconsistent with the need for an innovative culture.

Changing an organization's culture requires a multipronged approach covering the organization's fundamental ethos and human resources. The steps involved are:

- Improving the interpersonal relation and behavior of people in the organization.
- Changing the mental models, values, and belief systems.
- Revisiting and improving the vision of the organization.
- Promoting the culture of unlearning and learning at various levels.

These are BTGL elements.

Debackere (2003) outlined a process for integrated design capability and reviewed several methodologies to sustain information communication. These include:

- The use of flowchart-based decision and monitoring models of the new product development process.
- The use of creativity stimulating and idea-generating techniques like brainstorming and mind mapping.
- The design and use of grid methodologies and techniques to identify, define, and monitor innovation opportunities.
- The use of selection methodologies to filter and channel ideas into concepts.
- The use of project management techniques to follow up on new product development endeavors.

These represent elements ATGL.

6.3.1 RECOMMENDATIONS—ABOVE THE GREEN LINE (ATGL)

- Set a time in the business calendar for discussions around new product development (NPD). It should become a routine activity.
- To succeed in any change management efforts, the leaders must walk the talk. Senior management needs to contribute actively to New Product Development efforts and Innovation drive. It is necessary to set a time where anyone in the company can present NPD ideas to senior management during their planned visits to plant locations and business units.
- Senior management should talk about innovation in every review, formal gathering, and every possible opportunity. The leadership team needs to encourage and support formal systems and processes to track and drive innovation efforts. Further, the Leadership team needs to extend moral and financial support for Innovation drive.
- When appointed for culture-building, a Learning and Development Manager and his deliverables are well defined and communicated across the organization. Empowering him is of utmost importance for the success of the change management efforts. He needs to audit the business unit for the health of the work environment and relationships.
- A group to monitor the progress in building the culture and innovation management may be formed and entrusted with periodical reviews and reporting.
- Champions are to be appointed in every business unit and are tasked with maintaining the focus on innovation and promoting learnings from other business units.
- A knowledge management system is to be put in place. Effective use of magazines and journals and internal communication means are to be used for adequate dissemination of knowledge.
- The budget is to be planned and to be approved for innovation expenses. A suitable periodical reporting structure is to be enforced to report and review the money spent and the results of the efforts.
- NPD as part of the measurement in the key results areas (KRAs), appraisals, and incentives of the senior management team.

6.3.2 RECOMMENDATIONS—BELOW THE GREEN LINE (BTGL)

- Engage experts to have regular team-building activities to promote team spirit and creativity.
- Focus on people development to lead changes—this is crucial when the organization aims to change. Building a culture of innovation requires that people actively participate in doing things differently and questioning the routine in even the most minor things. Culture will be developed through spending adequate time and efforts after the necessary groundwork and planning, and not overnight.
- Leaders need to practice tolerance and patience to treat mistakes as learning experiences.
- Share and widely publicize success stories, celebrate every success, irrespective of whether small or big. Visual displays of progress and achievements will bring in excitement and improved involvement.
- Strengthen internal communications and review the organizational structure to allow more "freedom" in communication. Build an environment that promotes communications/ideas not only top-down but across the organization.
- Provide information to all employees about the company's performance relative to its competitors. Bring in transparency concerning MIS data on key performance indicators and operating performance.
- While it is easier to recognize and recognize tangible achievements recognizing, intangible achievements are mired by personal views and preferences. Line managers are to be trained and encouraged to take cognizance of this and are encouraged to recognize intangible achievements, as BTGL things are far more critical for long-term success and culture-building. Aiming for quick fixes is likely to prove counterproductive.

6.3.3 ASSESSING THE CURRENT INNOVATION CAPABILITY

- Scan and search the environment (internal and external) to pick up and process signals about potential innovations.
- Strategically select from these triggers those things to which the organization will commit resources.
- Resource the option.
- Implement the Innovation by growing it from an idea through the stages of development to final launch.
- Reflect on and review past successes and failures.

The same can be achieved by asking a series of critical questions to assess the current culture or "how we do things around here."

There are different tools to assess the current innovation capabilities; Tidd et al. (2001) and Harvard Manage Mentor Creativity Checklist (2000) describe a series of questions for an innovation management audit.

6.4 CONCLUSIONS

To foster innovation, organizations need to show clear commitment and focus on innovation, build a work environment that encourages innovation, and implement systems and structures that facilitate innovation.

Relatively flat organizational structures and personnel systems bring agility and promote involvement. A good framework for communication (MIS databases, transparency and data visibility, intranet, excellent cross-functional teams) always helps bring urgency in the innovation drive.

When the organization's vision and values show a commitment to innovation, both explicitly and by encouraging the underlying commitment to quality and partnerships with customers, the journey of innovation takes a quantum leap. Specific and measurable objectives are to be defined rather than generic statements. These objectives need to be aligned with the vision of the organization and strongly communicated.

Finally, there is a need to institutionalize behavior that allows innovation to flourish.

Disciplined and well-managed creativity breeds a thriving culture of innovation. Most companies are not short of new ideas, but they are short on assessing, screen, prioritizing, and executing those new ideas. Organizations have limited resources, funds, and time to give creative dreamers free rein to produce new ideas (Chopra, 2017) magically.

As strong focus on below green line elements is an absolute must to bring an innovation culture. The force of conformity, adoption to worldview, risk-averse "we have always done it this way" culture, frameworks that prevent us from thinking out of the box stifle the innovative approach of many creative people.

Few focused BTGL actions that can help build a culture of innovation are:

- Encourage people to move away from the monotony and celebrate the diversity of the thinking process. Encourage and reassure people to think, do, talk, and be different. Listen to the people with different ideas instead of just brushing them away. Understand that there are people in organizations who "need to be permitted to innovate."

- Talk innovation as often as possible. Encourage people to think of a new, cost-effective alternative method for everything that they do every day. Forums like monthly review meetings, weekly area, meets, and in-house periodicals can effectively bring about consciousness and a high degree of visibility to the organization's innovation drive.
- Create an encouraging environment that allows and recognizes innovative thinking by treating every innovative suggestion as big and sharing them. Across the organization, irrespective of however complicated or straightforward, it is similar to STARS (Special Thanks and Recognition System of Taj Group of Hotels). The same helps harness the innovative power of every employee.
- Promote the routine interaction of the operating team with customers, suppliers, industry peers, and technology partners. Discussions of the latest trends in the industry, changes in the customer's needs, learning from innovative ideas at the partner organizations discussed in such interaction helps improve awareness and promote innovative approach.

ATGL actions that help promote innovation drive are:

- In order to build an innovative culture, it is essential to make the work environment conducive and encouraging to build the culture. The same can be made only when we track, measure, and reward innovations. New projects in progress and ideas available for commercialization are tracked, monitored, and reported on an ongoing basis.
- Monitoring the quantum of person-hours and machine-hours spent on innovative activities and encouraging the operational teams to invest more in such activities helps the team focus on innovation in greater detail. Including this as a part of MIS submitted should help improve the team commitment toward such investment made in innovative activity (Chopra, 2017).
- Set innovation as a KRA in annual performance appraisals. Set both individual KRAs and team KRAs.
- Setting up targets for the annual sales generated through innovative solutions as a percentage of total annual sales and recognizing the teams that have achieved set targets can help encourage teams to innovate continuously.

- Measuring the innovation with the count of innovations that have occurred with collaboration with the customers, suppliers, and other collaborative communities can help build an open culture conducive to innovative thinking and develops two-way communication outside the organization.
- Seeking feedback from the customers on the organization's contribution in meeting their need for innovative solutions and monitoring such innovative solutions regularly can help understand where the organization stands in customers' viewpoint concerning innovation. This shall also help take up corrective actions in-house and decide further action to strengthen the organization's innovative drive.

In a nutshell, innovation keeps the organization strong in its march to the future by:

- Helping customers sell more—create value and help customers to meet their customers' needs.
- Future-proofing business, which means introducing changes today to survive in tomorrow's markets.
- Making the organization more effective and efficient than competitors—finding new ways to do things better (lower cost, better quality, service, better design, more user friendly).

We need to realize that the actual growth of the organization springs from innovation. A company cannot outgrow its competitors unless it can out-innovate them. Innovation is the fuel for growth. When a company runs out of innovation, it runs out of growth (Hamel and Getz, 2004).

KEYWORDS

- **strategy**
- **imperative**
- **innovation**
- **reinvent**
- **creativity**
- **culture of the organization**

REFERENCES

Birdi, K.; Wall, T. *Developing an Innovation Culture: Implications from Research.* Discussion Paper for Department of Trade and Industry Innovation Review, March 2003.

Boas, P. *The Green Line—A Model for Management and Leadership in Organizations Wanting Behavioral Culture Change*, 2005.

Chopra, A. *Garage to the Boardroom—A Myth or Reality*; November 17, 2017a. Available at SSRN: https://ssrn.com/abstract=3073471 or http://dx.doi.org/10.2139/ssrn.3073471.

Chopra, A. *Garage to the Boardroom—A Myth or Reality*, November 17, 2017b. Available at SSRN: https://ssrn.com/abstract=3073471 or http://dx.doi.org/10.2139/ssrn.307347105). We are exploring alternative societal and organizational futures.

Chopra, A. *International Conference on Automation and Computational Engineering (ICACE). Technology in Procurement and Supply as Prevalent Today and Scope for Future*, October 01, 2018, 2018; pp 216–223.

Debackere, K. *Managing Integrated Product Design in a Highly Competitive Harvard Manage Mentor®: Managing Creativity and Innovation* (2000); Harvard Business School Publishing: Boston, MA, 2003.

Hamel, G.; Getz, G. Funding Growth in an Age of Austerity. *Harvard Business Review*, July–August 2004, 2004.

Hatch, M. J. *Organization Theory: Modern, Symbolic, and Postmodern Perspectives*; Oxford Press: Oxford, 1997.

Leede, J.; Louise, J. Innovation and HRM: Towards an Integrated Framework. *Creativity and Innovation Management*; Blackwell Publishing Ltd.: Hoboken, NJ, 2005; Vol. 14, No. 2.

Meer, H. Open Innovation—The Dutch Treat Challenges in Thinking in Business Models. *Creativity and Innovation Management*; Blackwell Publishing Ltd., 2007; Vol. 16, No. 2.

Miles, R.; Miles, G.; Snow, C. *Collaborative Entrepreneurship*; Stanford Business Books: Stanford, CA, 2005.

Tidd, J., Bessant, J. and Pavitt, K. *Managing Innovation—Integrating Technological, Market, and Organizational Change*; John Wiley & Sons: Hoboken, NJ, 2001.

CHAPTER 7

Risk-Taking and Uncertainty Avoidance in Determining the Success of an Entrepreneur

SHALINI SHARMA[1*] and HARMINDER KAUR GUJRAL[2]

[1]*GNIOT Institute of Management Studies, Greater Noida 201307, Uttar Pradesh, India*

[2]*Amity Business School, Amity University, Noida 201306, Uttar Pradesh, India*

[*]*Corresponding author. E-mail: shalinish0506@gmail.com*

ABSTRACT

Entrepreneurship has always been the buzzword of research since past three decades. This has been especially relevant owing to recent developments in micro, small, and medium enterprises (MSMEs). There have been many studies conducted on entrepreneurial traits, entrepreneurial intent and entrepreneurship. Success of an entrepreneur/enterprise has also been studied by various scholars but in the parlance of social and economic factors. Very few studies are available in terms of entrepreneurial success and competency approach. This study intends to explore two such factors—risk taking and uncertainty avoidance and their impact on the success of the entrepreneur. The study was conducted in National Capital Region of Delhi on eighty nine IT companies' owners to find out the role of these two factors in their success. The data collected was subjected to multiple regression analysis which further proved the impact that these two factors had in making an entrepreneur successful. The study is relevant in terms of the current

Constructive Discontent in Execution: Creative Approaches to Technology and Management.
Sanjeev Bansal, Anita Venaik, Swati Upveja, and Saritha S. (Eds.)

entrepreneurial scenario where a lot of ventures are in quandary because of economic instability and despite that many are still striving to bounce back.

7.1 INTRODUCTION

Entrepreneurship is considered to be an important means of formation and growth of new firms, which act as an accelerator for the development of economy, alleviation of poverty and generator of employment by creating jobs and generating wealth (Choubey et al., 2013). The word is taken from French. It originally meant adventurer when first appeared in the middle of the 17th century. The new meaning of the word "Entrepreneurship" originally meaning an adventurer, infers it to be "*a step-by-step process to create a new business starting from something small and aiming for something bigger*" (Batzogianni, 2018). It was given to it in the beginning of the 20th century. The recent developments have laid emphasis on micro, small, and medium enterprises (MSME). The governments off late realized the significance of the MSMEs in the growth of the economy by generating employment, fostering equitable growth in the economy and enhancing the export potential. This sector reported an extraordinary success in relation to production scale, the quantum of investment, and overall involvement in the national gross development product (GDP) in recent years.

7.1.1 MSMEs AND STARTUPS IN ECONOMY DEVELOPMENT

MSMEs are the backbone of any economy. In the United States alone, approximately two-thirds of employment in the private sector is provided by 30 million SMEs in the recent many years. The small and medium enterprise (SMEs) in exports grew even faster thereby creating more employment opportunities and paying enhanced wages than similar businesses. As per the Annual Report on European SMEs 2017–2018, the SMEs provided around 52% of the gross employment in the European Union (EU) and also an enhancement of 47% in the value-added in the non-financial business sector marked from 2008. There also has been an increase of 4.1% in the value-added SMEs in overall 2018–2019 (Annual Report on European SMEs, 2018–2019). As per the Global Entrepreneurship Monitor (GEM), India Report 2019–2020, 11.9% of the Indian population is engaged in entrepreneurship. In India, the MSME sector contributes to 29% of its GDP. The growth of MSME has been on the upward trend in the year 2020 also despite the worldwide pandemic mayhem. The MSME sector witnessed an increase in a year-on-year (Y-o-Y) growth of 18.5% in the year 2020 to 2.5 million units as compared with 2.1 million units in 2019.

Creation of jobs has always been one of the biggest challenges faced in India. The country has a huge potential to create jobs via innovation and nurturing entrepreneurs as it has a unique demographic advantage. According to NASSCOM, the third-largest start-up base in the world is of India with a total of 8625 start-ups. As per the Report on Fourth Annual Employment & Unemployment Survey (2013–2014) issued by the Government of India's Ministry of Labour and Employment, Labour Bureau, the employment generated by the Proprietary and partnership enterprises together shares more than 50% of the total employment in India and the informal sector accounts for around 52% of the total employment generated in India[3]. Therefore, start-ups are the new buzzword in the country as they are more adaptable, flexible, and quick in responding to change in the market.

A start-up is the first stage of a company or any company at its inception, which is primarily funded by the entrepreneur himself/herself as he/she tries to exploit the market on the product or service offered by the company. Its acceptance in the market and the profit earned has the sole right of the proprietor of the business. The start-ups in India began with the dotcom wave in the 1980s. These dotcoms businesses had a lot of venture capitalists ready to invest in the business and gaining capital was quite easy in those times because of euphoria among investors to suppose on the arrival of those new business types. The government has been very supportive to encourage these start-ups and building a conducive environment through its ease of doing business initiatives and business friendly policies. As per the GEM India Report (2019–2020), that the entrepreneurial ecosystem in India has improved in terms of ease of business compared with the BRICS nations in 2019–2020 and India ranks thirteenth in total fifty countries in terms of increase in the total early-age (TEA) entrepreneurial ventures. The COVID-19 surge has disrupted not only the economy but also shattered the hopes of many entrepreneurs who were yet to start their journey for the whole year in 2020. Despite that there were many start-ups cropping up considering the needs of common man. The ventures in the technical area were found to be more successful with IT taking the front seat in the pandemic year. The National Association of Software and Services Companies (NASSCOM) report for 2019–2020 projects the reason for the technology-driven companies to be on having an edge and leading the path to progression and recovery is the dramatic acceleration in the need for digitization across the world (NASSCOM, 2020).

Entrepreneurship research suggests that small firm as compared with the bigger enterprises generate employment at a faster rate but on the contrary, it is eliminated at much faster rate because of an even faster rate of failure. The mortality rate of start-ups is 20–25% and it has risen over the years (KPMG, 2018). The reasons can be many. It could be the lack of particular infrastructure for the business, lack of apt workforce, money deficit, changes in the state or government policies, and many others. The reasons for failure could be enormous but the reason for not shutting down a set up will be more of a fighting spirit of an entrepreneur. The reasons for this fighting spirit could be enormous. The current study attempts to look for such factors in entrepreneurs.

7.1.2 ENTREPRENEURSHIP

Entrepreneurship as a subject has fascinated a lot of research and is termed to be multivariate as it is affected by various dimensions. It is mostly associated with the fields of administration, management economy. The patronage of entrepreneurship has been the prime factor for the economic progress of any country. The more entrepreneurial potential higher will be the industrial growth thereby furthering the country's economic growth. This could be possible by the efforts of the entrepreneurs in establishing their venture and pulling in foreign investment through foreign entrepreneurs. Foreign investment is one of the major factors behind the economic progress of the developing countries by contributing to the more purposeful allocation of the resources of the developing countries. The success of the entrepreneurial ventures marks the progress of any economy.

Entrepreneurship has primarily been associated with the risk-taking capability of a person in order to achieve a preconceived business or industrial goal. The risk-taking capability had to be substantiated with confidence and presence of mind as a result of making good decisions for the venture. Risk-taking capability is the most prominent requirement of modern entrepreneurship which aids in yielding profits by seizing market opportunities to sustain an organization in the market-oriented economy. Thus, in an enterprise, earning profits by means of goods production and their marketing to cater to the ever demanding and diversifying market needs and satisfying the customer is all the constituent of an entrepreneurial pursuit. Apart from risk-taking capability, innovation has been another major contributor to the success of an entrepreneur in the market. As rightly maintained by McClelland success in entrepreneurship is directly proportional to the economic development of any country. The need for achievement (nAch) level of the population of any country is the decisive factor in the entrepreneurial instinct of the citizens of that country. Higher the level of "nAch," the more energetic will be the entrepreneurs (McClelland, 1961).

7.1.3 ENTREPRENEURSHIP AND PSYCHOLOGY

Entrepreneurship was made a broader concept of study by psychology which evaluates the various concepts of this subject and thereby had given it the shape in which it is studied by the researchers now (Kalkan and Kaygusuz, 2012). The first psychologists to study entrepreneurship were McClelland, Atkinson, and Feather who discovered the motivational factors responsible for a person to undertake entrepreneurship. "NAch" is said to be one of the factors which was responsible for the entrepreneurial growth but in fact, it is the society's progressive perception as well. The study of entrepreneurship mainly has studied the small and medium-scale enterprises, as because of their volatile nature, the entrepreneurial traits are more visible in small ventures as compared with big and established businesses. Although entrepreneurship amalgamated psychology, anthropology, sociology, economics, regional sciences, and management, yet it gave psychologists the fodder to research in the perspective of the traits of the firm owners as a factor of company's economic success. Since psychology has always been associated with the comprehending people's perceptions, cognitions, motivation, emotions and behavior, therefore, if entrepreneurship is studied in terms of psychology, it will indeed provide the cognizance of decisive actions (behaviors), perceptions, and implementation of opportunities in terms of entrepreneurship. Organizational psychology has also initiated an interest in entrepreneurship (Frese, 1982).

Andrew Raine, an essayist at Friends Select School in Philadelphia, derived a model of entrepreneurship with three Cs—curiosity, creativity, and commitment (Fig. 7.1). His theory says that only commitment was not enough, it was grit which made an ordinary human being win over the circumstances. He further claimed the PF to the behavioral output stating that optimism leads to curiosity, innovativeness leads to creativity, and perseverance leads to commitment. Thus, psychology played a vital role in knowing the factors responsible for entrepreneurship and the success of enterprises.

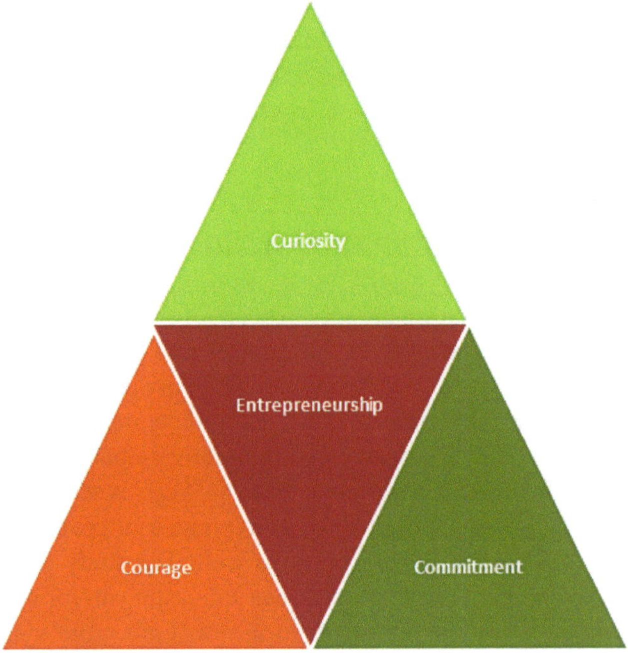

FIGURE 7.1 The three Cs of entrepreneurship. *Source*: Andrew Raine's Model of Entrepreneurship; A Research Project Builds the "Three C's Model of Entrepreneurial Success." Retrieved from https://kwhs.wharton.upenn.edu/2019/05/three-cs-model-entrepreneurial-success/

7.1.4 ENTREPRENEURIAL SUCCESS

Various researchers have defined the success of entrepreneurs differently. Zott and Amit (2000) and Perren (1999) have defined success of entrepreneurs in terms of tangible factors such as income, or the growth of a firm, profitability and increase in net worth, and sustainability. Another school of thought relates ES with relentless trading whereas entrepreneurial failure (EF) is related to ceased or unrewarding trading (Dafna, 2008). As per the psychological school of thought, the entrepreneurs are viewed as people with distinctive ethics, attitude, and need which drive them toward their goals. It also puts forward the difference between the people to become successful entrepreneurs (SEs). This new trend seeks psychological determinants of entrepreneurial success (ES) which brings down the focus to the personality variables (Harada, 2003). Moreover, their competencies are exhibited and observed through their behavior patterns, actions, motivation, and the abilities (Staniewski and Awruk, 2018). The outcomes or the performance is the result of different level of competencies (Man, 2006). The present study aims at finding out the role the factors risk-taking and its ally uncertainty avoidance play in the success of any entrepreneur.

The research based on entrepreneurship has primarily predicted a firm's success through some personal factors which did not find any relevance with the entrepreneurs. When examined at the individual level, entrepreneurial success (ES) involves the approach of identifying and investigating the importance of those factors to the entrepreneurs with common success criteria.

7.1.5 MEASURING ES

Entrepreneurial success cannot be measured in one standard way, because success is a very subjective term and every entrepreneur takes it differently. Some people measure it in terms of monetary benefits, some measure in terms of customer satisfaction, and some in terms of the sustenance of the company in the market. As propounded by Gazdecki (2018), the different schools of thoughts suggested ways to measure ES, which take a look at each different approach. One can involve to evaluate success and know what system of measurement to be used to trace one's progress toward achievement. The ways to measure success are given as under:

7.1.5.1 MONETARY GAIN

The easiest and the evident way to measure the success of any firm is through the profits earned by the company in a financial year through the account books, financial statements, balance sheets, and cash flow statements. This gives a clear idea of the growth of the organization in terms of revenue earned. Although money is a good quantifier which gives a clear picture of the revenue earned and capital invested yet assessing the growth of any organization in terms of money does not serve a long-term perspective.

7.1.5.2 CUSTOMER SATISFACTION

Another aspect of measuring the success of an enterprise is through the satisfaction of its target customers. This school of thought deduced the financial stability of any company from the high satisfaction level of the customers only. This could be a bit more tedious than profit calculation as the satisfaction level of customers is deduced through active surveys through survey questions shared via emails or personally, review sites, or social media.

7.1.5.3 COMPANY GROWTH

Another measure could be through the company's growth. This has a few parameters for it to be measured accurately. First comes the reach of brand/ products in the market, then the acquisition of the new customer base, followed by hiring of new employees and sustenance of the old workforce. Growth of the company has many tangents to it which signify the overall health of the company.

7.1.5.4 EMPLOYEE SATISFACTION

Employee satisfaction also sought as employee happiness is considered to be the measure of success by some entrepreneurs. The principle of employee satisfaction says that when the employee progresses and feels happy, they participate equally in the growth of the organization and thus the organization progresses.

7.1.5.5 MARKET POSITION

The fallacies of estimating a firm's success on the basis of financial gains are also that the market may or may not respond because of the slump or rise in the market. If the profits are not reaped in a particular quarter, it does not necessarily mean that the business is going down. There could be a possibility of a market slump. The correct approach should be to analyze the competitors' progress as well.

7.1.6 RATIONALE OF THE STUDY

The success of an entrepreneur is measured in terms of the success of his firm. Success is a very subjective term. As mentioned in the above section, some measure it in terms of profits and some in terms of provision of quality and service to the society. Success is a very subjective term and has various interpretations of it. Some measure success in the accomplishment of their tasks, some in achieving the desired outcome, some in disseminating the idea to the society and serving it solving its issues and some in earning profits. In business, economists measure entrepreneurial success (ES) by the number of years of a firm's sustenance and the profit earned percentage by the firm. There are several other measures to it as well. ES is equivalent to the success of an enterprise. In the case of start-ups, their success depends largely on their founders or owners as the hierarchy is not very tall. The characteristics, such as education, industry experience, managerial experience, and previous entrepreneurial experience have also been proven to be positively associated with the success of a venture (Unger et al., 2011). The owner him/herself has to look after the various management functions of planning, coordinating, directing, and controlling in the organization. Therefore, the final decision-making is his/her authority. The entrepreneur primarily deals with the uncertainties of the environment, evaluates the market conditions and then takes decisions for his firm which yields either success or failure for himself and the enterprise. The success parameters taken in this study are: (i) The firm is established for at least 5–7 years (a notch higher than the conservative 3-year graveyard norm) and continues to be in the market (Taormina et al., 2007; Dafna, 2008). (ii) The average profit percentage of the firm over the past 5 years should be at least 35%. (iii) Customer and Employee Satisfaction Index of the firm. Apart from the financial profit, satisfaction also should be taken as a criterion to adjudge success (Gorgievski et al., 2011).

Entrepreneurship is said to be the need to foster competitiveness in the recently building global economy (Verheul et al., 2006; O'Connor, 2013). Prior to entrepreneurship it is the intent/mindset which comes into the picture. Many recent studies have focused on entrepreneurial intention, intent or orientation. It is said to be "*the natural tendency, attitude of a person toward building his own venture, that is, entrepreneurship*" (Fayolle and DeGeorge, 2006). This concept of entrepreneurial mindset (EM) and entrepreneurial intent (EI) was considered equally important to understand the process of entrepreneurship. EM is the way of thinking, beliefs, and actions of an entrepreneur which help him to identify the opportunities and convert them into profits. It is the core of the process of entrepreneurship (Krueger and Carsrud, 1993). The EM for success addresses the challenges of coping with the complexities of the business and the methods of adapting to them with dynamism (Sharma et al., 2019). It is the intent of an individual which leads to the formation of an enterprise. EI is the precursor to the success or failure of any business (Irwin et al., 2018) and plays a very important role in conducting a business. The study of entrepreneurship has multiple facets and understanding the factors responsible for an individual to pursue entrepreneurship (which may be several in counts) are crucial to the study of entrepreneurship.

Entrepreneurship is a subject which is vividly studied by various researchers in psychological parlance also. The first psychologists to study entrepreneurship were McClelland (1965), Atkinson (1957), and Feather (1969) who discovered the motivational factors to be responsible for a person to undertake entrepreneurship.

7.1.7 OPPORTUNITY AND SUCCESS

As mentioned above, success is all about perceiving the opportunities. Entrepreneurs also succeed or fail based on their discerning any opportunity. Shane and Nicoloau (2015) proposed that individuals who are creative are more active in opportunity recognition. However, it does not conclude to be associated with the success of a firm. Various cognitive psychologists propagate that the entrepreneurs identify opportunities through some signals given by the environment that are filtered by them and transformed with the help of their intentions and they recognize the useful patterns in a multitude of cues and signals received. These patterns propose a potential opportunity. This points out toward Shapero's theory of "antennae." He proposed that everyone has his/her own antennae which are tuned to particular frequency patterns. Entrepreneurs differ from others in the direction of the frequencies they have set their antennas in. Jakson and Dutton (1989) classified these opportunities on the basis of perception of the individual. They tested a model on categorization of issue on the basis of strategic decision-making. They classified the perception of opportunity on the basis of positive and negative knowledge of an individual which are deemed as opportunity and threat respectively.

7.1.8 PERFORMANCE AND SUCCESS

The perception of ES has been multifarious by different scholars. Success is a specific aspect of performance (Brush and Vanderwerf, 1992). Since, success is a measure of certain elements of performance, therefore, researchers have found it tough to differentiate the theory of success from performance. According to Peters et al. (1980), Waldman and Spangler (1989), and Blumberg and Pringle (1982), as cited by Rogozińska-Pawełczyk (2021), performance is a function of motivation, ability, and opportunity.

The entrepreneurs who are always on a quest for profit-bearing opportunities and have the ability to be motivated despite several untoward circumstances, are the ones who achieve their targets (Aldrich and Martinez, 2001). As discussed in Section 7.1 of this study, failures are more than the triumphs in the case of entrepreneurship; therefore, it requires a lot of motivation, utilizing one's abilities and making full use of the opportunity available in order to stand in the brutal market.

As propounded by Aykan (2002), there are a total of five categories of personality traits for entrepreneurs, namely, socially accepted values, socially approved emotion, interpersonal skills, life skills, and a larger bracket of qualities, such as risk-taking, leadership, clear objectives (opportunity recognition), tolerance against uncertainty, and courage under which almost all other traits fall.

7.1.9 SUCCESS OF AN ENTREPRENEUR (SE) AND ENTREPRENEURIAL COMPETENCIES APPROACH

Personality variables are important in both the emergence and success of entrepreneurs. Some authors argue that personality becomes more critical for the emergence of entrepreneurs rather than for success (Utsch and Rauch, 2009). This decision is not the result of one personality trait but a blend of a gamut of personality factors responsible for the decision of laying the foundation of a firm. Davidkov and Yordanova's (2016), through one of their studies on SMEs found that the firms willing to be proactive take risks and act creatively, have more tendency to see, use and make to fullest of the entrepreneurial opportunities in external environment which eventually leads to their success.

The success of any firm is determined as the success of the founder of the firm (Morse and Wagner, 1978). According to Cheng et al. (2005), the performance or success of any individual is a multidimensional ensemble which includes inputs, process, outputs, and context of different components. But merely possessing these competencies may not suffice rather instead integrating them one's values, beliefs, and attitude is essential (Man, 2001). He also propagated that these competencies also must be exhibited through their behavior, actions, and activities conducted. There have been various competencies propagated by the researchers which play an important role in the success of an entrepreneur, namely, autonomy, risk-taking, innovativeness, locus of control, need for achievement, and self-efficacy (Antoncic et al., 2018; Chaterjee and Das, 2015; Barbosa, 2014; Lang and Manove, 2011; Carland et al., 2007; Bradley and Sundaram, 2003; Markman, et al., 2002, 2003; Carree and Thurik, 2002; Thompson, 1999). Sharma (2016) emphasized on the fact that the SEs exhibited the behavior of uncertainty avoidance and individualism. Apart from high individualism, low uncertainty avoidance is also a trait which distinguishes a SE from and lesser SE (Shane, 1993). These factors have although never been regular and in association with the other factors of entrepreneurship and survival of the business. Unlike risk-taking which is synonymous to entrepreneurship and expected to be more uncertainty, avoidance has an inverse relationship with it. So lower the uncertainty avoidance, higher the risk-taking propensity. This study attempts to explore the relationship of risk-taking and uncertainty avoidance between SE.

7.1.10 SE AND RISK-TAKING

Since the word "entrepreneur" is fore mostly associated with the risk-bearing capability of an individual, therefore, they are actively involved in taking the organization forward (Jain, 2019). It has been associated with the risk-taking capability of a person in order to achieve a preconceived business or industrial goal. The risk-taking capability had to be substantiated with confidence and presence of mind as a result of making good decisions for the venture. Risk-taking capability is the most prominent requirement of modern entrepreneurship which aids in yielding profits by seizing market opportunities to sustain an organization in the market-oriented economy. Thus, in an enterprise, earning profits by means of goods production and their marketing to cater to the ever demanding and diversifying market needs and satisfying the customer is all the constituent of an entrepreneurial pursuit. Apart from risk-taking capability, innovation has been another major contributor to the success of an entrepreneur in the market. Some scholars believed that entrepreneurship happens only when an idea is well-conceived in society, profit follows afterwards. In a developing economy like India, the species of entrepreneurs which is desirable is the innovation oriented and focusing on welfare and social justice rather than profit earning only. According to Dess and Lumpkin (2005), the successful entrepreneurs learn to manage the risks successfully by applying various techniques including reward system, biases, and personal experience. Highly innovative entrepreneurs encompass high level of risk in comparison to the followers or less-innovative entrepreneurs.

There are two schools of thoughts prevailing in the entrepreneurial literature on risk-taking propensity. The former strictly talks about risk attitude and the latter on cognitive factors. Risk-taking also differs according to gender diversity.

7.1.11 BASED ON RISK ATTITUDE

This school of thought propagates that there not necessarily any direct influence of risk-taking on the success of creation of a new venture. An entrepreneur is neither characterized by a higher risk propensity nor by a low risk aversion (Caliendo et al., 2010). On the contrary, several studies support the reverse phenomenon, for example, a study by Simon and Houghton (2003) in IT industry that higher risk propensity is associated with the launch of pioneering product innovations and lesser in the launch incremental innovations.

7.1.12 COGNITIVE FACTORS

The second school of thoughts highlight that the cognitive factors play a vital role in structuring the psychology of risk-taking. As cited by Zhao et al. (2005) and quoted by Sitkin and Pablo, problem framing is the process which germinates willingness toward risk-taking. As per Antoncic and Hisrich (2004); McCline et al. (2000), it is a culmination of attitude, cognition, and emotions and not only the risk attitude. Another study by Mullins and Forlani (2005) and Norton and Moore (2006) suggested the difference in established entrepreneurs and naïve entrepreneurs is the perception toward risk-taking. The established entrepreneurs see calculated risk-taking more positively and visualize favorable outcomes compared with nonentrepreneurs or beginners in the field, who perceive calculated risk-taking either negative or of no value (Mullins and Forlani, 2005). It was further enunciated in the same study that entrepreneurs with high risk-taking tendency more likely choose risky deals.

So it could be perceived that the risk-prone entrepreneurs see low risk in situations with high degree of loss. The risk-taking is supported by a systematic market research and knowledge of exploitation of resources. There have been various tests administered by some growing bodies of management and economics to assess risk-taking propensity in relation to the financial gains or losses. But their workability is not appropriate in testing non-financial risk propensity. Research proves that the female CEOs are low on risk-taking and more on risk aversion (Bernasek and Shwiff, 2001).

7.1.13 RISK-TAKING AND UNCERTAINTY AVOIDANCE

Schumpeter (1991) in his theory of innovation asserted that it is not only innovation, which is required for the production, marketing, and strategizing of the products but also risk-taking and superintendence in the demeanor which is highly required. Aykan (2002) propounded some 42 personality traits of SEs which were segregated into social skills, interpersonal skills, and life skills. Those 10 life skills also include risk-taking and avoidance toward uncertainty as the essential skills for ES.

Tolerances to uncertainty/ambiguity, autonomy, and independence (Rauch and Frese, 2000; Gibcus and Kemp, 2003) have been found associated with entrepreneur and factors leading to the survival of his firm. Bygrave and Hofer (1991) also associated risk-taking and tolerance to uncertainty as the trait having a significant role in the sustenance of a firm.

Risk-taking is the core of any business or entrepreneurial behavior (Barbosa and Fayolle, 2007; Barbosa, 2014) is associated with the entrepreneur depending on his/her skills. Thus, innovativeness is high in entrepreneurs with high self-efficacy and self-confidence and it is also an exploratory process, therefore, it is bound to be associated with risk-taking ability as well. Though entrepreneurs are not blind risk takers, as per Drucker (1985), they are calculative risk takers. The established entrepreneurs see calculated risk-taking more positively and visualize favorable outcomes compared with nonentrepreneurs or beginners in the field, who perceive calculated risk-taking either negative or of no value (Mullins and Forlani, 2005).

Uncertainty avoidance is the behavioral counterpart of the psychological factor risk-taking. Uncertainty is the condition without any assurance or insurance of the result. Entrepreneurial activities are always done under uncertain situations, so the question here will be how to deal with the uncertainties in the business. Miller (1988) defined three types of uncertainties, namely, what, when, and whether. Competency has a curvilinear relationship with uncertainties, that is, if the person has the competency to deal with uncertainty then the uncertainty seems to be low but if the competency is low then the uncertainty seems to be high (Frese, 2009).

Risk and uncertainty are complementary to each other. Each risk has an element of uncertainty with it and vice versa. Frank H. Knight, an economist from the United States of America, differentiated risk-taking (insurable) with uncertainty (non-insurable). Risk relates to the events which have occurred in the past and uncertainty applies to exclusive events whose probability is quite subjective to be assessed. The change of a customer's mindset is what uncertainty is and risk is what the insurance companies play in the case of term insurance.

Individuals who display high tolerance toward uncertainties reflect the command over dealing with the uncertain problems without any mental pressure despite unidentified situations and lack of information (Keller and Siegrist, 2006). In order to be successful, the Entrepreneurs not only perform in uncertain conditions but also look for new possibilities so that they can study and conquer uncertainty as they see it as an achievement (Fellner and Maciejovsky, 2007). Uncertainty avoidance works has an inverse relationship with risk-taking (Guiso et al., 2008). They proposed that more is the risk-taking propensity, lesser is the uncertainty avoidance and vice versa. So, more is the entrepreneur confident of the situation more is his uncertainty avoidance.

7.2 OBJECTIVES

Since the research objectives provide clarity and vision to the research, it is foremost for any research scholar to formulate the research objectives. They are categorized according to their target in the research. The research objective may be exploratory, descriptive, diagnostic, or hypothesis testing. The research which tends to have some novel opinions and aims for skillfulness will have exploratory research objectives, to find out characteristics of any condition, person or groups descriptive research objectives come into picture. Then the diagnostic research objectives are derived to establish a relationship between any phenomenon occurring. The most commonly used research objectives are the ones which are formulated to test the hypotheses of a reasonable link between different variables. Following are the research objectives of this study:

(a) To find out the impact of risk-taking on the success of an entrepreneur/firm.
(b) To find out the impact of uncertainty avoidance on the success of an entrepreneur/firm.

7.3 METHODOLOGY

The research is descriptive in nature as the concept of ES is well-established and has been explored in this study. The research gaps were identified during the literature review based on which the research methodology was designed. The target population chosen was of the entrepreneurs in the IT sector in Delhi-NCR. The profit index and the employee satisfaction index were either asked by the respondent directly or was accessed through the internet from the glassdoor.in, zaubatechnologies.in, and easyleads.com.

The research design was meta-inference/mixed-method research design. This involved both qualitative as well as quantitative.

7.3.1 *DESIGN OF THE RESEARCH*

It is a theoretical structure of conducting of research it comprises of the outline for collection, measurement, and analysis of the data. It includes the roadmap of what has to be done by the researcher right from hypothesis framing and its functional indicators to the final analysis of the data. The Research Design of this study can be conveniently categorized as:

Meta-Inference (Mixed-Method Research Design): Mixed-method research design is governed by different yardsticks, such as common sense, critical practicality, and changing—free and targeted approach to analyze the qualitative and the numerical data (Teddlie and Tashakkori, 2003). This proposes that meta-inference involves joining more than one method of research "in the same study" or a "research." This kind of design occurs across and that "mixing [methods] might occur through strongly associated studies." Johnson et al. (2007) gave the following definition to such study:

"The type of research in which the qualitative and the quantitative research approaches are combined together by the researcher for a bigger target of understanding the breadth and depth of the data."

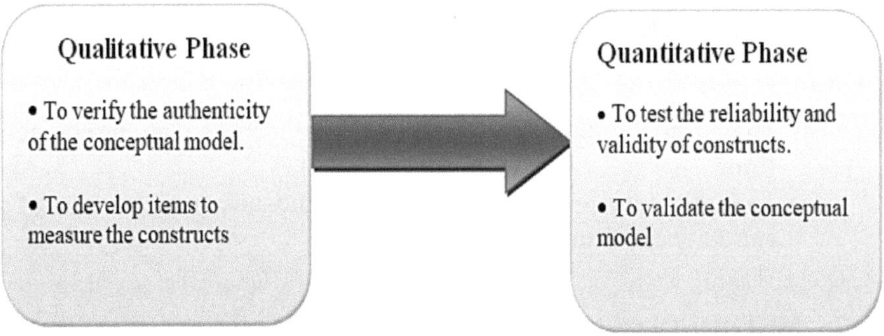

FIGURE 7.2 Aim of mixed-method research.

This study has employed the meta-inference design. Initially, qualitative study was conducted through content analysis on finalizing the variables to be considered in the study and then again after collecting the data through face-to-face interviews, the data were again sorted with the help of content analysis to pick-up the final set of variables for the research (Fig. 7.2). The quantitative study was conducted thereafter through questionnaires and the data collected were further analyzed to derive the results.

7.3.2 QUALITATIVE RESEARCH

Qualitative research was once viewed as theoretically contrasting research design with experimental research; it is now being accepted more and more in interventional studies. Initially applied in psychological studies, qualitative research, as researchers found it to be tedious to evaluate human behavior numerically, now it has been adopted in other research fields as well like clinical research, through which the data could be viewed more extensively. The qualitative part was the content analysis of the literature studied. The aim of the qualitative research is to discover, analyze and understand the role of the traits responsible for the success of an entrepreneur or a firm. The steps were as follows: (i) The literature review involved around 102 research papers. The main findings were tabulated and classified period wise. For example, 1911–1980, 1981–2000, 2001–2019. (ii) Further through content analysis, some factors which were found to be prominently propagated by the researchers were filtered. (iii) After the LR and the content analysis, some face-to-face interviews of 20 respondents from the given area were conducted using appreciative inquiry technique based on the questions framed on the basis of the factors identified through content analysis. (iv) With the help of these interviews, the factors which were emphasized upon by these entrepreneurs were selected and considered for further analysis. (v) A questionnaire was developed on the basis of these selected factors.

7.3.3 QUANTITATIVE RESEARCH

After formulating the research objective, and further literature review on the issue, hypotheses were generated for further analyzing the research objectives. A questionnaire of 20 items was designed for further collection of the data based on the factors finalized by the content analysis of the findings of various researchers studied A pilot study was conducted on the same set of respondents who were chosen for the appreciative enquiry. Based on the pilot study, the reliability of the questionnaire was evaluated. The Cronbach's alpha of the questionnaire was acceptable at combined $\alpha = 0.97$ and individual section $\alpha = 0.851$ and 0.728 both section A and B, respectively (Table 7.1).

TABLE 7.1 Cronbach's Alpha: Reliability Test Questionnaire.

	Cronbach's alpha	Cronbach's alpha based on standardized items	No. of items
Combined	0.97	0.98	20
Section—A	0.85	0.85	10
Section—B	0.72	0.75	10

The questionnaire is based on Likert Scale with choice ranging from 1 to 5 where 1 = Strongly Disagree to 5 = Strongly Agree. As the study aims to measure the impact of the independent variables (IVs) risk-taking and uncertainty avoidance on the dependent variables (DVs) profit percentage and age of the firm, therefore, it was decided to administer multiple regression analysis on the data. The following research hypotheses were formulated based on the test to be administered on the data. The research hypotheses were formulated based on the test to be administered on the data, as mentioned in Table 7.2.

TABLE 7.2 Null and Alternate Hypothesis.

H_{01}	There is no significant impact of risk-taking of entrepreneurs with respect to the age of a firm
H_1	There is a significant impact of risk-taking of entrepreneurs with respect to the age of a firm
H_{02}	There is no significant impact of uncertainty avoidance of entrepreneurs with respect to the age of a firm
H_2	There is a significant impact of uncertainty avoidance of entrepreneurs with respect to the age of a firm
H_{03}	There is no significant impact of risk-taking of entrepreneurs with respect to profit earned by a firm
H_3	There is a significant impact of risk-taking of entrepreneurs with respect to profit earned by a firm
H_{04}	There is no significant impact of uncertainty avoidance of entrepreneurs with respect to profit earned by a firm
H_4	There is a significant impact of uncertainty avoidance of entrepreneurs with respect to profit earned by a firm

7.4 DATA COLLECTION

The data collection was the next step. The study involved both primary and secondary sources of data collection. The secondary sources preceded the primary sources, as in this study, qualitative study preceded the quantitative study. The primary data were collected from the target population, that is, the IT/ITeS entrepreneurs in Delhi-NCR. The initial stage of data collection was done by content analysis of the secondary data collected through literature review and primary through Appreciative Interview Technique. Appropriate statistical tool was then used for data analysis and validation. The target population was of the entrepreneurs of IT companies in Delhi-NCR. Around 105 entrepreneurs were approached and out of them 94 respondents responded. The data collected did not have much outlier which were filtered by the Microsoft Excel (V. 2007). There were no missing responses. And the total responses came out to be 89 which were subjected to further analysis.

7.5 ANALYSIS

The current work is hypothesized on the concept that competencies, risk-taking, and uncertainty avoidance of the entrepreneur have a bearing on the success of an enterprise. This mainly involved testing the effect that the entrepreneurial competencies—risk-taking and uncertainty avoidance have on the success of an entrepreneur and the enterprise both. As this study involved multiple IVs and DVs, the researcher was interested in the degree of association among these. Therefore, this study relied on multivariate statistical techniques. The data were then filtered and tabulated and categorized in IBM SPSS (Statistical Package for Social Science) Statistics 20. The statistical tests applied on the data were conducted in IBM SPSS Statistics 20.

There were two independent variables considered for the study which were continuous with five answer choices. The two dependent variables used in the study were categorical. The demographic variables included were gender and age of the respondents/entrepreneurs. The respondent's gender variable had used nominal scale with two choices: (a) male and (b) female. In the respondent's age variable, the interval scale was applied having three choices, namely, (a) 26–35 years, (b) 36–45 years, and (c) Above 46 years.

The analysis of the demographic factors was done through mean. The details are as illustrated in Figures 7.3 and 7.4. Figure 7.3 gives the graphical representation of the percentage of male and female entrepreneurs among the respondents. The graph clearly depicts that the percentage of female entrepreneurs in IT sector in Delhi/NCR is quite low in comparison to males. Out of 89 respondents, the turn-up ratio of females was 16.85–83.14% of males. The female entrepreneurs were found quite less in the IT business in the geographical area of the research.

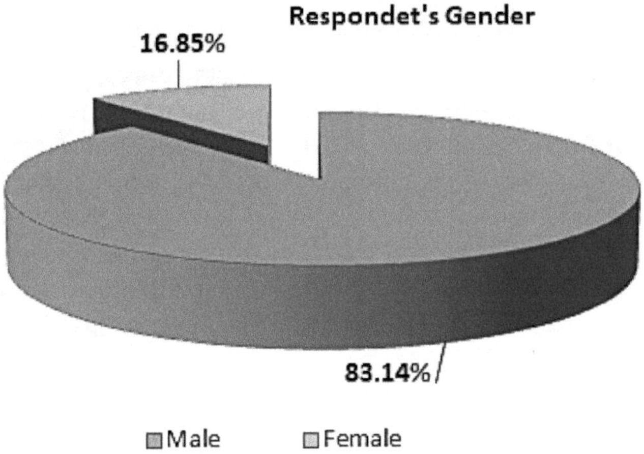

FIGURE 7.3 Demographic analysis: respondent's gender.

Figure 7.4 is the graphical representation of the percentage of respondent's age in each category. It revealed that most of the respondents (46.95%) fell in the age group of 36–45 years and slightly less with 44.34% are in the age group of 26–35 years.

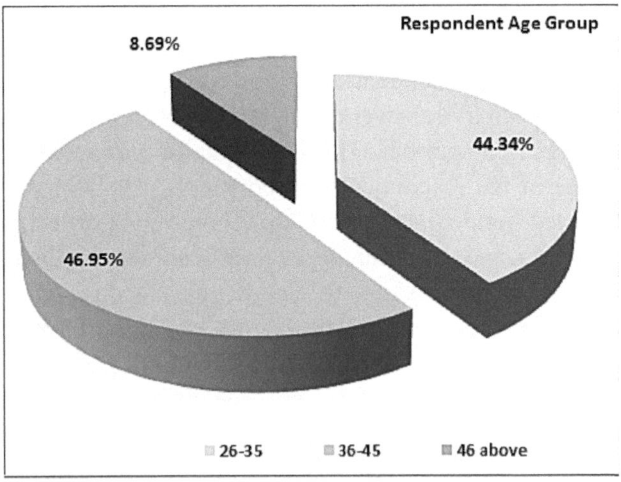

FIGURE 7.4 Demographic analysis: respondent's age.

Since the research instrument was based on Likert scale and the sample size was also not very large therefore, in order to test the normal distribution of the data Kolmogrov–Smirnov and Shapiro–Wilk test were conducted on the data. The result of the test is depicted in Table 7.3.

TABLE 7.3 Kolmogorov–Smirnov and Shapiro–Wilk Normality Test.

Factors	Kolmogorov–Smirnov			Shapiro–Wilk		
	Statistics	**Df**	**Sig.**	**Statistics**	**Df**	**Sig.**
Risk-taking	0.13	89	0	0.96	89	0
Uncertainty avoidance	0.12	89	0	0.95	89	0

Since the value of $\alpha \leq 0.05$, therefore we do not reject the H_0 (null hypothesis) and deduce that the variables of the data collected do not follow the normal distribution, and hence, nonparametric tests were conducted on the data for further analysis.

For further testing, the data were subjected to multiple regression analysis to test the impact of the IVs risk-taking and uncertainty avoidance on the DVs profit percentage and age of the firm. The results of the multiple regression analysis are depicted in Tables 7.4 and 7.5.

TABLE 7.4 Multiple Regression Analysis: Risk-Taking and Uncertainty Avoidance on Firm's Age.

Model	Unstandardized coefficients		Standardized coefficients	T	Sig.	R	R square	Adjusted R square	Std. error of the estimate
	B	**Std. error**	**Beta**						
Risk-taking	0.24	0.12	0.23	1.99	0.05	0.25	0.06	0.05	0.46
Uncertainty avoidance	0.18	0.11	0.27	1.7	0.05	0.40[a]	0.16	0.12	0.29

7.5.1 *INTERPRETATION*

(a) The obtained value of $p = 0.05$ (significant at the level of confidence 95%). Therefore, the null hypothesis H_{01} is rejected. Risk-taking of entrepreneurs has a significant influence w.r.t. firm's age. The value $\beta = 0.23$ shows the direct impact of risk-taking to firm's age. The value of $R^2 = 0.06$ shows 6% variation can be explained by firm's age in risk-taking.

(b) The obtained value of $p = 0.05$ (significant at a confidence level of 95%). Therefore, the null hypothesis H_{02} is rejected. Uncertainty avoidance of entrepreneurs has a significant influence w.r.t. firm's age. The value of β = 0.27 shows an impact of uncertainty avoidance to firm's age. The value of $R^2 = 0.16$ shows that 16% variation can be explained by firm's age in uncertainty avoidance.

TABLE 7.5 Multiple Regression Analysis: Risk-Taking and Uncertainty Avoidance on Profit Percentage of a Firm.

Model	Unstandardized coefficients		Standardized coefficients	t	Sig.	R	R square	Adjusted R square	Std. error of the estimate
	B	Std. error	Beta						
Risk-taking	−0.12	0.06	−0.22	−1.94	0.05	0.25	0.06	0.05	0.46
Uncertainty avoidance	0.22	0.06	0.41	3.34	0	0.40	0.16	0.12	0.29

7.5.2 *INTERPRETATION*

The above results reveal the following interpretations: (a) The obtained value of $p = 0.05$ (significant at the level of confidence of 95%). Therefore, the null hypothesis H_{03} is rejected. There is a significant impact of risk-taking of entrepreneurs with respect to profit percentage earned by a firm. The value β = −0.22 shows the inverse impact of risk-taking to profit percentage of a firm. The value $R^2 = 0.06$ shows that 6% variation can be explained by profit percentage earned by a firm in risk-taking. (b) The obtained value of $p = 0$ (significant at the level of confidence 95%). Therefore, the null hypothesis H_{04} is rejected. Uncertainty avoidance of entrepreneurs has a significant influence w.r.t. profit percentage earned by a firm. The value of β = 0.41 shows a fairly good impact of uncertainty avoidance to profit percentage. The value $R^2 = 0.16$ shows that 16% variation can be explained by firm's profit percentage in uncertainty avoidance.

7.6 CONCLUSION AND DISCUSSION

The data analysis reveals that risk-taking has a positive impact on the performance of a firm/success of an entrepreneur (SE) in terms of firm's age, whereas it impacts in reverse order to the performance of a firm/SE in terms of profit percentage. Uncertainty avoidance is a behavioral factor of risk-taking, since uncertainty avoidance has an impact on the success of an entrepreneur, therefore the same goes with risk-taking with respect to its impact on the success of an entrepreneur (SE). There are many studies which reveal that the psychological and behavioral factors are not affected by the gender of the entrepreneur. However, some scholars have argued that gender has an influence on risk-taking, optimism, and self-efficacy for the success of an entrepreneur. Bernasek and Shwiff (2001) argued that the female CEOs are more averse toward risk-taking and making decisions related to finances. Innovativeness and risk-taking propensity are found to have significant influence on women entrepreneurs. Sundheim (2013), in his article "Do Women take as Many Risks as Men," asserted that the males avoid risk-taking under stress, but the females take more risks under stress.

Risk-taking is a combination of attitude, cognition, and emotions. Different cognitive factors have been highlighted by the second school of thought to have a role in the perception of eagerness of taking risk and risk-taking, that is, of problem framing (Sitkin and Weingart, 1995). The propensity of risk-taking culminates as a combination of a bigger concept comprising emotions, cognition, and attitude (Antoncic and Hisrich, 2004; McCline et al., 2000) rather the risk attitude only. Entrepreneurs' achievement motivation influences their risk-taking propensity as well as new venture performance. The entrepreneurs see risk-taking more positively and with conducive results, namely, more strengths and possibilities rather frailty or challenges as perceived by nonentrepreneurs (Norton and Moore, 2006). Risk-taking is more predominant in those who are ambitious and aspire for greater success.

Researchers assert that to do so, the entrepreneurs may use the influence and legitimacy to reduce the discerned uncertainty by associating with well-regarded contacts (Gluckler and Armbruster, 2003). Age increases an individual's ability to exploit opportunities along with the increase in reluctance to bear risks because of increased opportunity costs (Rai, 2008). However, uncertainty avoidance is high as the age increases (Blanchflower et al., 2001). Therefore, it is concluded that risk-taking may be required when the firm has to be established but the entrepreneur may not exhibit this trait in order to grow his establishment as blind risk-taking may incur losses as well. A better understanding of a successful entrepreneurial type may be provided by a combined systematic analysis of all such values, traits, and behavioral tendencies.

The study reveals that the psychological and behavioral factors—risk-taking and uncertainty avoidance, considered in the study have an impact on achieving success in terms of earning profits. The maximum influence is of uncertainty avoidance which also plays an important role in the sustenance of a firm, whereas the factor risk-taking plays a lesser significant role. As discussed by the researchers, avoidance to uncertainty is low in increased creativity. Therefore, it plays the most prominent role in this research, so it can be concluded that the uncertainty avoidance comes into the picture where the entrepreneur has to earn profit and sustain his/her firm along with a combination of innovativeness and optimism. This shows that the entrepreneur must always look forward with a positive approach. There should not be any stagnation in the business.

The current scenario where the economy is at its ever time low, the businesses are not flourishing, uncertainty avoidance factor of any entrepreneur especially the start-ups is a key factor which may lead to the sustenance of an enterprise. This study becomes quite relevance in the parlance of current instability despite several boosts from the government to help the businesses pickup and thereby give a thrust to the economy.

This study focuses on the two factors in terms of entrepreneurial psychology. As propounded by many scholars, the study could be further extended in terms of studying the role of other factors, such as motivation achievement, creativeness, optimism, innovativeness, leadership, decision-making, and many more. The study could be further extended into studying the entrepreneurial failures considering risk-taking and uncertainty avoidance and the reasons thereof. The absence of certain traits or the presence of certain traits could be further explored in the future studies.

KEYWORDS

- **strategy**
- **imperative**
- **innovation**
- **reinvent**
- **creativity**
- **culture of the organization**

REFERENCES

Antoncic, B.; Hisrich, R. Corporate Entrepreneurship Contingencies and Organizational Wealth Creation. *J. Manage. Dev.* **2004,** *23* (6), 518–550.

Antoncic, J.; Antoncic, B.; Gantar, M.; Hisrich, R.; Marks, L.; Bachkirov, A.; et al. Risk-Taking Propensity and Entrepreneurship: The Role of Power Distance. *J. Enterp. Cult.* **2018,** *26*, 1–26. doi: 10.1142/S0218495818500012.

Annual Report on European SMEs. *Annual Report on European SMEs 2106/2017, Focus on Self-employment*, 2018–2019. Retrieved from https://ec.europa.eu/docsroom/documents/2653/attachments/1/translations/en/...../native.

Atkinson, J. Motivational Determinants of Risk-Taking Behavior. *Psychol. Rev.* **1957**, *64* (6, Pt. 1), 359–372. doi: 10.1037/h0043445.

Aykan, E. *Entrepreneurship and Leadership Behaviour of Enterpreneuers*. Unpublished Master Thesis, Erciyes University, Kayseri, Turkey, 2002.

Barbosa, S. Revisiting Entrepreneurship Research from a Decision Making Perspective. *Handbook of Research on Entrepreneurship*; Edward Elgar Publishing, 2014. doi: 10.4337/9780857936929.00025.

Bernasek, A.; Shwiff, S. Gender, Risk, and Retirement. *J. Econ. Issues* **2001,** *35*, 345–356.

Blanchflower, D.; Oswald A.; Stutzer, A. Latent Entrepreneurship across Nations. *Eur. Econ. Rev.* **2001,** *45* (4–6), 680–691.

Blumberg, M.; Pringle, C. The Missing Opportunity in Organizational Research: Some Implications for a Theory of Work Performance. *Acad. Manage. Rev.* **1982,** *7* (4), 560–569. doi: 10.2307/257222.

Brush, C.; Vanderwerf, P. A Comparison of Methods and Sources for Obtaining Estimates of New Venture Performance. *J. Bus. Ventur.* **1992,** *7* (2), 157–170. Retrieved from https://EconPapers.repec.org/RePEc:eee:jbvent:v:7:y:1992:i:2:p:157–170.

Caliendo, M.; Kritikos, A. Searching for the Entrepreneurial Personality: New Evidence and Avenues for Further Research. *J. Econ. Psychol.* **2011,** *33* (2), 319–324. Retrieved from http://nbn-resolving.de/urn:nbn:de:101:1-201106224706.

Carree, M.; Thurik, R. The Impact of Entrepreneurship on Economic Growth. In *International Handbook of Entrepreneurship Research*; Zoltan, A. C. S., Audretsch, D. B., Eds.; Kluwer Academic Publishers: Boston/Dordrecht, 2002.

Carland, J.; Hoy, F.; Boulton, W. Differentiating Entrepreneurs from Small Business Owners: A Conceptualization. *Entrepreneurship*. Springer: Berlin, Heidelberg, 2007. doi: 10.1007/978-3-540-48543-8_3.

Chatterjee, N.; Das, N. Key Psychological Factors as Predictors of Entrepreneurial Success: A Conceptual Framework. *Acad. Entrepr. J.* **2015,** *21* (1), 102–115.

Bradley, M.; Sundaram, A. The Emergence of Shareholder Value in the German Corporation, *SSRN Electron. J.* **2003**. doi:10.2139/ssrn.463840.

Bygrave, W.; Hofer, C. Theorizing about Entrepreneurship. *Entrepr.: Theor. Pract.* **1991,** *16* (2), 13–22.

Dafna, K. Managerial Performance and Business Success: Gender Differences in Canadian and Israeli Entrepreneurs. *J. Enterpris. Commun.: People Places Glob. Econ.* **2008,** *2* (4), 300–331. doi: 10.1108/17506200810913890.

Davidkov, T.; Yordanova, D. Exploring the Bulgarian Family SMEs' Reluctance to Internationalise. *Int. J. Bus. Global.* **2016,** *17* (1), 123–148.

Dess, G.; Lumpkin, G. Entrepreneurial Orientation as a Source of Innovative Strategy. In *Innovating Strategy Process*; Floyd, S. S. Roos, J., Jacobs, C. D., Kellermanns, F. W., Eds.; Blackwell Publishing: Oxford, 2005.

Fayolle, A.; DeGeorge, J. Attitudes, Intentions, and Behaviour: New Approaches to Evaluating Entrepreneurship Education. In *International Entrepreneurship Education: Issues and Newness*; Fayolle, A., Klandt, H., Eds.; Edward Elgar Publishing Ltd.: Cheltenham, 2006; pp 74–89.

Feather, N. Attribution of Responsibility and Valence of Success and Failure in Relation to Initial Confidence and Task Performance. *J. Pers. Soc. Psychol.* **1969,** *13*, 129–144.

Fellner, G.; Maciejovsky, B. Risk Attitude and Market Behavior: Evidence from Experimental Asset Markets. *J. Econ. Psychol.* **2007,** *28* (3), 338–350.

Frese, M. Occupational Socialization and Psychological Development: An Underemphasized Research Perspective in Industrial Psychology. *J. Occup. Psychol.* **1982,** *55*, 209–224. doi: 10.1111/j.2044-8325.1982.tb00095.x.

Frese, M. Towards a Psychology of Entrepreneurship—An Action Theory Perspective. *Found. Trends Entrepr.* **2009,** *5* (6), 437–496. doi: 10.1561/0300000028.

Fourth Annual Employment & Unemployment Survey Report. Labour Bureau Ministry of Labour and Employment, Government of India, Chandigarh, 2013–2014; pp 1–11.

Gazdecki, A. *How to Measure Entrepreneurial Success*, 2018. Retrieved from https://yourstory.com/mystory/d776ab694c-how-to-measure-entrepr.

Gibcus, P.; Kemp, R. Strategy and Small Firm Performance. *Research Report H200208*; EIM: Zoetermeer, January 2003.

Gluckler, J.; Armbruster, T. Bridging Uncertainty in Management Consulting: The Mechanisms of Trust and Networked Reputation. *Organ. Stud.* **2003,** *24*, 269–297.

Harada, N. Who Succeeds as an Entrepreneur? An Analysis of the Post-Entry Performance of New Firms in Japan. *Jpn. World Success Econ.* **2003,** *15* (2), 211–222.

Keller, C.; Siegrist, M. Investing in Stocks: The Influence of Financial Risk Attitude and Values-Related Money and Stock Market Attitudes. *J. Econ. Psychol.* **2006,** *27*, 285–303. doi: 10.1016/j.joep.2005.07.002.

Krueger, N. F.; Carsrud, A. L. Entrepreneurial Intentions: Applying the Theory of Planned Behaviour. *Entrepr. Region. Dev.* **1993,** 5 (4), 315–330.

KPMG. *Startup Ecosystem in India—Growing or Matured?* 2018. Retrieved from https://assets.kpmg/content/dam/kpmg/in/pdf/2019/01/startup-landscape-ecosystem-growing-mature.pdf.

Irwin, K.; Landay, K.; Aaron, J.; McDowell, W.; Marino, L.; Geho, P. Entrepreneurial Orientation (EO) and Human Resources Outsourcing (HRO): A Hero Combination for SME Performance. *J. Bus. Res.* **2018,** *90*, 134–140.

Jakson, S.; Dutton, J. Discerning Threats and Opportunities. *Admin. Sci. Q.* **1989,** *33*, 370–387.

Johnson, R.; Onwuegbuzie, A.; Turner, L. Toward a Definition of Mixed Methods Research. *J. Mixed Methods Res.* **2007,** *1* (2), 112–133.

Lang, K.; Manove, M. Education and Labor-Market Discrimination. *Am. Econ. Rev.* **2011,** *101* (4), 1467–1496. doi: 10.1257/aer.101.4.1467.

Man, T. Exploring the Behavioural Patterns of Entrepreneurial Learning. *Educ. Train.* **2006,** *48* (5), 309–321. doi: 10.1108/00400910610677027.

Markman, G.; Balkin, D.; Baron, R. Person–Entrepreneurship Fit: Why Some People Are More Successful as Entrepreneurs than Others. *Hum. Resour. Manage. Rev.* **2003,** *13* (2), 281–301. doi: 10.1016/S1053-4822(03)00018-4.

McClelland, D. *The Achieving Society*; The Free Press (The Macmillan Company): New York, 1961; pp 159–205.
McCline, R.; Bhat, S.; Baj, P. Opportunity Recognition: An Exploratory Investigation of a Component of the Entrepreneurial Process in the Context of the Health Care Industry. *Entrepr. Theor. Pract.* **2000,** *25* (2), 81–94. doi: 10.1177/104225870002500205.
Miller, D. Relating Porter's Business Strategies to Environmental Structure: Analysis and Performance Implications. *Acad. Manage. J.* **1988,** *32*, 280–308. doi: 10.2307/256549.
Morse, J.; Wagner, F. Measuring the Process of Managerial Effectiveness. *Acad. Manage. J.* **1978,** *21* (1), 23–35.
MSME Industry in India. April 2021. https://www.ibef.org/industry/msme.aspx.
Mullins, J.; Forlani, D. Missing the Boat or Sinking the Boat: A Study of New Venture Decision Making. *J. Bus. Ventur.* **2005,** *20* (1), 47–69.
NASSCOM. *Future of Technology Services: Navigating the New Normal*; Mckinsey and Company, 2020. Retrieved from https://nasscom.in/sites/default/files/secure-pdf/Future-of-technology-services-Navigating-the-New-Normal_Summary.pdf.
Norton, W.; Moore, W. The Influence of Entrepreneurial Risk Assessment on Venture Launch or Growth Decisions. *Small Bus. Econ.* **2006,** *26* (3), 215–226.
O'Connor, A. A Conceptual Framework for Entrepreneurship Education Policy: Meeting Government and Economic Purposes. *J. Bus. Ventur.* **2013,** *28* (1), 546–563.
Perren, L. Factors in the Growth of Micro-Enterprises (Part 1): Developing a Framework. *J. Small Bus. Enterpr. Dev.* **1999,** *6*, 366–385. doi: 10.1108/EUM0000000006691.
Peters, L.; O'Connor, E.; Rudolf, C. The Behavioral and Affective Consequences of Performance—Relevant Situational Variables. *Organ. Behav. Hum. Perform.* **1980,** *25* (1), 79–96. doi: 10.1016/0030-5073(80)90026-4.
Rai, S. K. Indian Entrepreneurs: An Empirical Investigation of Entrepreneur's Age and Firm Entry, Type of Ownership and Risk Behavior. *J. Serv. Res.* **2008,** *8* (1), 213–228. Retrieved from https://search.ebscohost.com/login.aspx?direct=true&db=bth&AN=32732753&site=ehost-live.
Rauch, A.; Frese, M. Psychological Approaches to Entrepreneurial Success. A General Model and an Overview of Findings. In *International Review of Industrial and Organizational Psychology*; Cooper, C. L., Robertson, I. T., Eds.; Wiley: Chichester, 2000; pp 101–142.
Rogozińska-Pawełczyk, A. The Effect of HR Practices and Psychological Contract on Employee Performance: The Polish Experience in Business Services Sector. *Euras. Bus. Econ. Perspect.* **2021,** *17*, 3–19. doi: 10.1007/978-3-030-65147-3_1.
Shane, S. Cultural Influences on National Rates of Innovation. *J. Bus. Ventur.* **1993,** 8, 59–73.
Shane, S.; Nicolaou, N. Creative Personality, Opportunity Recognition and the Tendency to Start Businesses: A Study of Their Genetic Predispositions. *J. Bus. Ventur.* **2015,** *30* (3), 407–419.
Sharma, S. *Entrepreneurship Development*; PHI Learning Pvt. Ltd.: New Delhi, 2016.
Sharma, S.; Bhardwaj, S.; Gujral, H. Entrepreneurial Mindset for Success: An Interview-Based Learning in Delhi NCR. *Int. J. Rec. Technol. Eng.* **2019,** *8* (3S2). ISSN: 2277-3878.
Simon, M.; Houghton, S. The Relationship between Overconfidence and the Introduction of Risky Products: Evidence from a Field Study. *Acad. Manage. J.* **2003,** *46* (2), 139–149.
Staniewski, M.; Awruk, K. Systems Approach to Entrepreneurial Success: The Theoretical Discussion on the Significance of Family Factors for Effective Entrepreneurship. *Inside Mind Entrepr.* **2018,** 163–174. doi: 10.1007/978-3-319-62455-6_12.

Sundheim, D. *Do Women Take as Many Risks as Men?* Feb 2013. Retrieved from https://hbr.org/2013/02/do-women-take-as-many-risks-as.

Thompson, J. The World of the Entrepreneur—A New Perspective. *J. Workplace Learn.: Employee counsel. Today* **1999,** *11* (6), 209–224.

Teddlie, C.; Tashakkori, A. Major Issues and Controversies in the Use of Mixed Methods in the Social and Behavioral Sciences. In *Handbook of Mixed Methods in Social and Behavioral Research,* 1st ed.; Tashakkori, A., Teddlie, C., Eds.; Sage: Thousand Oaks, CA, 2003; pp 3–50.

Unger, J.; Rauch, A.; Frese, M.; Rosenbusch, N. Human Capital and Entrepreneurial Success: A Meta-Analytical Review. *J. Bus. Ventur.* **2011,** *26* (3), 341–358. doi: 10.1016/j.jbusvent.2009.09.004.

Utsch, A.; Rauch, A. Innovativeness and Initiative as Mediators between Achievement Orientation and Venture Performance. *Eur. J. Work Organ. Psychol.* **2009,** *9* (1), 45–62. doi: 10.1080/135943200398058.

van Praag, C. *Determinants of SEship*; UvA: Amsterdam, 1997.

Verheul, I.; VanStel, A.; Thurik, R. Explaining Female and Male Entrepreneurship at the Country Level. *Entrepr. Reg. Dev.* **2006,** *18*, 151–183.

Waldman, D.; Spangler, W. Putting Together the Pieces: A Closer Look at the Determinants of Job Performance. *Hum. Perform.* **1989,** *2* (1), 29–59. doi: 10.1207/s15327043hup0201_2.

Zhao, H.; Seibert, S. E.; Hills, G. E. The Mediating Role of Self-Efficacy in the Development of Entrepreneurial Intentions. *J. Appl. Psychol.* **2005,** *90* (6), 1265–1272. doi: 10.1037/0021-9010.90.6.1265.

Zott, C.; Amit, R. Strategies for Value Creation in E-Commerce: Best Practice in Europe. *Eur. Manage. J.* **2000,** *18* (5), 463–475. doi: 10.1016/S0263-2373(00)00036-0.

CHAPTER 8

Building Innovation Culture for the Automobile Industry: Insights from the Indian Passenger Vehicle Market

KUMAR SHALENDER[1] and SHIV SHANKER[2]

[1]Chitkara Business School, Chitkara University, Punjab, Rajpura 140401, India

[2]Amity Business School, Amity University, Noida, India

**Corresponding author.*
E-mail: kshalender@gmail.com, kumar.shalender@chitkara.edu.in

ABSTRACT

This chapter develops indicators for building and sustaining innovation culture in organizations. Using the literature review, the chapter identifies important dimensions of innovation cultures from the extant studies across the business segments and industries. These dimensions are then used to develop an evaluative framework for assessing organizations on their culture of innovation. The framework analyzes four carmakers operating in the passenger vehicle segment of the Indian automobile industry on selected dimensions of innovation culture. This chapter then provides a conceptual framework and specific measures to help companies build and sustain innovation culture in their organizations. The study is unique in the sense that it draws on both literature and real-world corporate examples to offer model on innovation culture and has important implications for both scholars and practitioners.

Constructive Discontent in Execution: Creative Approaches to Technology and Management.
Sanjeev Bansal, Anita Venaik, Swati Upveja, and Saritha S. (Eds.)

8.1 INTRODUCTION

Companies which encourage creativity, exercise two-way communication, and explore collaborative opportunities are ranked higher on the innovation index (Kim and Wilemon, 2007; Kley et al., 2011; Pratt et al., 2013). Unsurprisingly, these organizations are also figured among the most preferred work places (Carlile, 2004; Jones et al., 2010; Bohnsack et al., 2013; Pratt et al., 2013). Now despite its popularity, innovation culture is hard to build—and even harder to implement and sustain with. Be it a business organization, government institution, or a nonprofit agency, the top leadership finds it difficult to build and sustain the culture of innovation (Gemünden et al., 2007; West and Bogers, 2013). This is indeed perplexing as to why the innovation practices which are highly admired universally are so hard to implement and get along with (Mueller, 2012; Shalender and Yadav, 2019). One plausible reason behind this difficulty is the approach that organizations adopt while building and practicing the culture of innovation (Aggeri et al., 2009; Chesbrough, 2010; Shalender and Singh, 2015). While we openly embrace desirable features of innovation, such as creative freedom, team work, and empowered decision-making, we fail to counterbalance these with disciplined working, strong leadership, and accountability (Wang et al., 2013; Pisano, 2019). In order to ingrain the culture of innovation, one has to counterbalance its cool behaviors with strict work practices. This is because only the interplay of these contrasting behaviors will help companies to achieve desirable results on building and sustaining culture of innovation in their working practices (Tushman and O'Reilly, 1997; Richter et al., 2012).

In the context of automobile industry, this chapter examines how carmakers competing in the Indian passenger vehicle market are embracing the culture of innovation for sustained profitability. The automobile market in India is intensely competitive and amidst changing preferences and tightening compliances, companies are finding it increasingly difficult to survive with conventional work practices (Kim and Wilemon, 2007; Shalender and Singh, 2015; Shalender and Yadav, 2019). Developing innovation culture in such a turbulent business environment has become more of a necessity than a matter of choice. The rest of the research is divided into five parts. Firstly, the extant literature review is done to identify the key dimensions and characteristics of the innovation culture. Secondly, based on the literature review, an evaluative framework for assessing the culture of innovation has been developed. Thirdly, four innovative projects of carmakers from the Indian passenger vehicle segments are selected and analyzed on the evaluative framework developed in the second step. Fourthly, based on the literature and framework analysis, a conceptual model and specific measures for building innovation culture in organizations are proposed. Fifthly and lastly, this study discusses the theoretical and practical implications in addition to mentioning the future course of action in conclusion.

8.2 INNOVATION CULTURE: THEORETICAL LINKAGES

The term innovation culture has been used widely in the literature. It has been investigated in different contexts and depending upon the scope of the investigation, the definition of the term keeps on changing. For example, some studies have defined the culture of innovation in a very generic manner, that is, referring to market leadership or creativity of employees (Prahalad and Hamel, 1990; Hitt et al., 1998; Senge and Carstedt, 2001; Hamel, 2002; Johnson et al., 2003; Dhar et al., 2015) while others have been very specific while elaborating in terms of specific roles, functional procedures, and operating mechanisms (Wang and Ahmed, 2004; Martins and Terblanche, 2003; Dobni, 2006; San Román et al., 2011; Richter et al., 2012; Rigby et al., 2018). In the context of this study, we define the innovation culture as a multidimensional concept that includes the focused freedom to explore, the disciplined approach to transformation, the honest employee feedback system, the mechanism to fix individual accountability, and the presence of a decentralized structure. One of the inherent characteristics of innovation cultures is their quest to explore the unknown. The journey of innovation is fraught with uncertainties, and hence, it is quite natural to encounter failures in the exploration process (Tukker, 2004; Sosna et al., 2010; Bouquet et al., 2018). However, an organization can easily minimize the chances of failure by adopting a focused approach to the exploration process. In fact, many past studies have emphasized (and some have proven) that organizations which use "focused exploration" are far more likely to imbibe innovative culture and retain it in the long term (Zott and Amit, 2011; Mueller, 2012; Pisano, 2019). The focused exploration helps companies streamline innovation and ensure that failures occur as a function of uncertainty rather than caused by vague ideas, imprecise research, or ambiguous analysis (Ragatz et al., 1997; Chesbrough, 2003; Kim and Wilemon, 2007).

8.3 DEVELOPMENT OF EVALUATIVE FRAMEWORK

The innovation culture has been explored by a number of researchers in the past (Chesbrough, 2003; Carlile, 2004; Gemünden et al., 2007; Gassmann et al., 2010; Winter and Lasch, 2016; Pisano, 2019). While these researches differ in the context of perspective, application, and industry, we find an uncanny similarity in dimensions emerging from findings of these studies. The key dimensions that come out to be common on majority of the innovation studies are: exploration, transformation, feedback, accountability, and control (refer Table 8.1 for details):

We have used these key dimensions of innovation culture for evaluating select car companies operating in the highly competitive Indian automobile industry. These real-world cases reflect on efforts of auto companies to build innovation into their DNAs while balancing out the likable and dislikable characteristics of the culture.

8.4 INNOVATION DIMENSIONS AND SELECTED CASES

8.4.1 MARUTI SUZUKI INDIA LIMITED: SMART HYBRID PROJECT

With nearly 50% market share, Maruti Suzuki India Limited (MSIL) is the market leader and a dominant force in Indian auto space. It has remained at the forefront of innovation, with every 2 out of 3 small cars sold in the country belong to the company's stable. The invention of smart hybrid technology of MSIL is the proper example of the company's innovation framework in action (Ghosh, 2020). The technology was invented to enhance the power and fuel efficiency of cars while reducing their net emissions at the same time. The objective was tricky especially the company wanted invention that will not feel heavy on customers' pockets. To accomplish that the team decided to apply the incremental "exploration." They took the existing vehicle architecture and "transformed" the system with an addition of lithium-ion battery, a starter motor, and a regenerative-braking system (Maruti Suzuki, 2020). The team aptly work on "feedback" of suppliers and partners though no consumer capsules were arranged to know customers' viewpoint. The whole development team was "accountable" for project and the hierarchical "structure" in team was kept at minimum—only one team leader leading the exploration process. The project was successfully completed and now, the Smart Hybrid technology is a part of the company's portfolio powering its new-gen of petrol cars. The best part of the technology

TABLE 8.1 Key Dimensions and Evaluative Framework.

Dimension	Authors	Implications	Evaluation	Rating (0–5)
Focused exploration	Ragatz et al. (1997), Chesbrough (2003), Kim and Wilemon (2007), Zott and Amit (2011), Mueller (2012), Pisano (2019)	Exploration can significantly impact rate of inventions while signaling a healthy culture of innovation	Whether company offers freedom to explore and create?	Absolute freedom (5)–No freedom (0)
Disciplined experimentation	Trott and Hartmann (2009), West and Bogers (2013), Wong et al. (2013), West et al. (2014), Rigby et al. (2018)	Successful transformation of inputs into output is what brings innovation to life	Whether company approach transformation in a disciplined manner?	Disciplines approach (5)–random process (0)
Honest feedback	McGrath (2001), Read (2002), Hatch (2004), Steward and Raman (2007), Takeuchi et al. (2008), San Román et al. (2011), Pisano (2019)	Honest feedback creates a conducive environment for innovation	Whether company has direct and honest channel for feedback?	Honest feedback (5)–diplomatic culture (0)
Individual accountability	Prahalad and Hamel (1990), Deshpande et al. (1993), Aggeri et al. (2009), Chesbrough (2010), Jones et al. (2010), Winter and Lasch (2016)	Holding people accountable can significantly boost disciplined innovation	Whether company has a system of fixing accountability?	Individual accountability (5)–collective responsibility (0)
Decentralized structure	Spencer and Grindley (1993), Jones et al. (2010), Visnjic and Neely (2011), Liu et al. (2012), Shalender and Yadav (2019)	Strong leadership is required to present a compelling vision in a flat work culture	Whether company has flat hierarchical structure?	Flat structure (5)–hierarchical structure (0)

is that cars fitted with smart hybrid is only marginally costlier than their standard counterparts.

8.4.2 TATA MOTORS: NANO HATCHBACK

Tata Nano has the distinction of being the most affordable car in the history of the automobile world. The car was launched in 2008 and came with a dealer price of $2000 (INR 1 lakh). The premise behind its innovation was deeply rooted in Ratan Tata's (the then chairman of the TATA Group) idea of making an affordable vehicle for a lower income class of India. Touted to be an impossible task, Tata constituted a small team of engineers from different disciplines to realize Nano's project. The team started "exploring" the possibilities of making a car that must not exceed the stringent cost constraint of $2000 set by the firm (Kripalani, 2008). A strict vigil was exercised and an ultradisciplined approach to cost-cutting was adopted to achieve successful "transformation." Each and every component was tested on its absolute necessity rather than the utility—questions were asked why this component is required, what purpose it serves, and more importantly, can we do away with this part? This pointed assessment made a score of parts that are used in making conventional cars deemed unnecessary. Further, Nano team added some clever engineering designs and tweaks (e.g., rear-mounted engine, three bolt pattern tire, single wiper blade) that helped the carmaker to achieve its price target (Fairs, 2009). At every stage, top management including Ratan Tata was in constant touch with the development team and seamless "feedback" made sure that every requirement of the team was met swiftly. The "accountability" of each member of the team is fixed and this was in addition to the "joint accountability" that team had for the development of Nano. The "structure" of the team was absolutely flat and the strong team spirit helped the Tata to develop Nano with world's lowest price tag.

8.4.3 TOYOTA KIRLOSKAR: 360-DEGREE FEEDBACK SYSTEM

An organization can save enormously on resources with a robust feedback and communication system (Fisher and Amabile, 2009; Schein, 2010; Gerhart and Fang, 2015). This has been very well exemplified by the Toyota Kirloskar Motor Private Limited (TKMPL), an Indian arm of Japanese car manufacturer Toyota Motor Corporation. The feedback system designed by company is comprehensive, well-thought out, and includes not only its internal departments but also integrates suppliers, channel partners, dealerships, and customers in the loop. TKMPL has designed a 360-degree feedback system and the beauty of the system lies in its ability to provide actionable information to improve the decision-making process at different levels (Toyota, 2020). At the heart of this successful system is the honest and candid "feedback" that all stakeholders are encouraged to share with the management. The "exploration" of this system was comprehensive and the team tasked with conceptualizing the system was carefully selected from across departments. In addition, external consultants were also involved in the "transformation" process and the management extended its full support for creating the system. The loop of feedback involved not only company's internal departments but also external partners including suppliers and partners. Every member involved in building the system had specifically designated role for which he/she was accounted for. The hierarchical system though existed in the team as executives and managers from different levels were part of the project (Toyota, 2020).

8.4.4 HYUNDAI MOTORS: EV PROJECT COLLABORATION

Hyundai Motors company has signed an agreement with the Canoo to co-develop the platform for their future electric vehicles (EVs) (Hyundai Motors, 2020). Canoo is a Los Angeles-based organization which will provide its fully-integrated "Skateboard Platform" to the Hyundai and its group company Kia for their future EVs. The company researched the fledgling market for EVs, and after a thorough "exploration" of options, the company decided to partner with Canoo. The "transformation" process from the agreement stage to execution stage between the partners is in progress and thanks to the disciplined approach, both companies are successfully meeting the deadlines of commensuration. An active system of "feedback" is deployed between companies and roles of each of the team along with their "accountability" are clearly identified. According to the agreement, Canoo will be responsible for supplying basic underpinnings of the EV platform while engineers at Hyundai will customize the platform to meet the different specifications and body-style requirements of vehicles (Boudway, 2020). The "structure" of Hyundai team is quite flat although it has representation of different departments.

8.5 ANALYSIS

8.5.1 INNOVATION CULTURE AT MSIL

From the analysis of MSIL's case, it is quite clear that the company scores high on the aspect of exploration and creativity. It had offered sufficient freedom for employees to explore though the team was directed to invent that should not result in price hike for consumers (4/5).

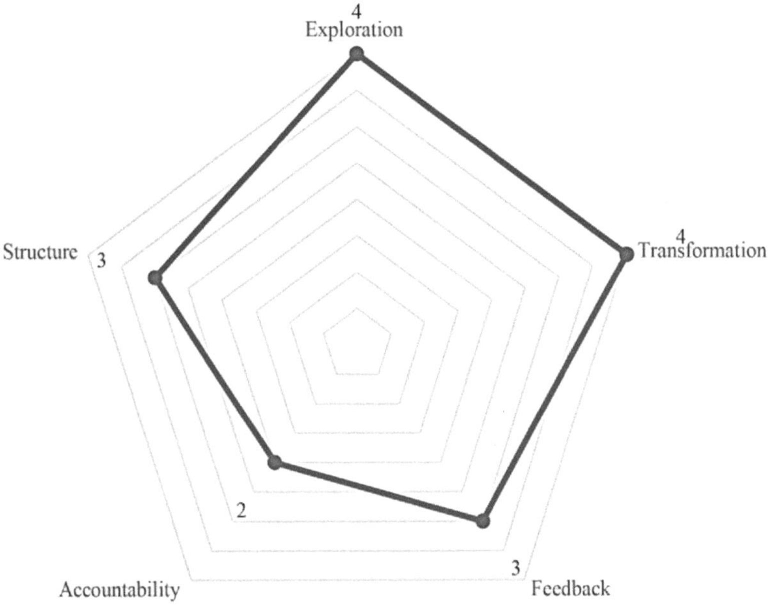

FIGURE 8.1 MSIL analysis.

The whole transformation was approached in a discipline approach (4/5) though the feedback system was just about average (3/5). The organization did not fix individual accountability on project as the responsibility was on the entire team to make the project successful (2/5). The company followed flat structure for the project though the company works through the hierarchical structure (3/5) (refer Fig. 8.1 for analysis).

8.5.2 INNOVATION CULTURE AT TATA MOTORS

Tata's approach toward the invention of Nano reveals high creative freedom to "explore" that company offers to its employees (4/5). The Nano project stands out in the "transformation" process as the ultra-disciplined approach made it possible for the company to price Nano at Rs 1 lakh price tag (5/5).

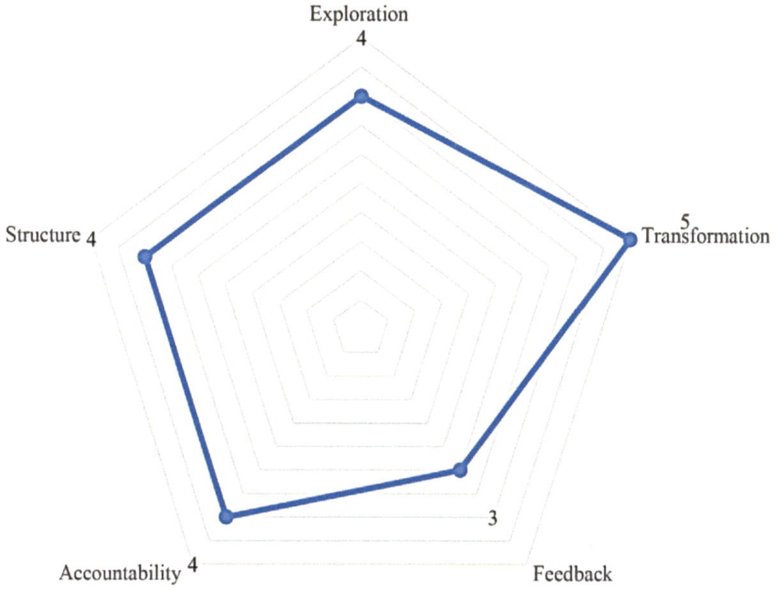

FIGURE 8.2 Tata Motors analysis.

The "feedback" system was also robust during the invention of Nano though it was operational only between the top management and the team rather than being across the company (3/5). Both individual and team "accountability" was fixed which is an ideal aspect for building the innovation culture in the company (4/5). The team worked in a completely flat structure with members from across disciplines worked in harmony to tap on each other's expertise for the innovation process (4/5) (Fig. 8.2).

8.5.3 INNOVATION CULTURE AT TOYOTA KIRLOSKAR

The team behind the invention of 360-degree feedback system explored comprehensively within the loosely defined directive of the organization. The fares quite well on the creative freedom in the "exploration" process (4/5). The "transformation" is disciplined and thanks to the involvement of the consultants, the process was disciplined and rooted in reality (3/5).

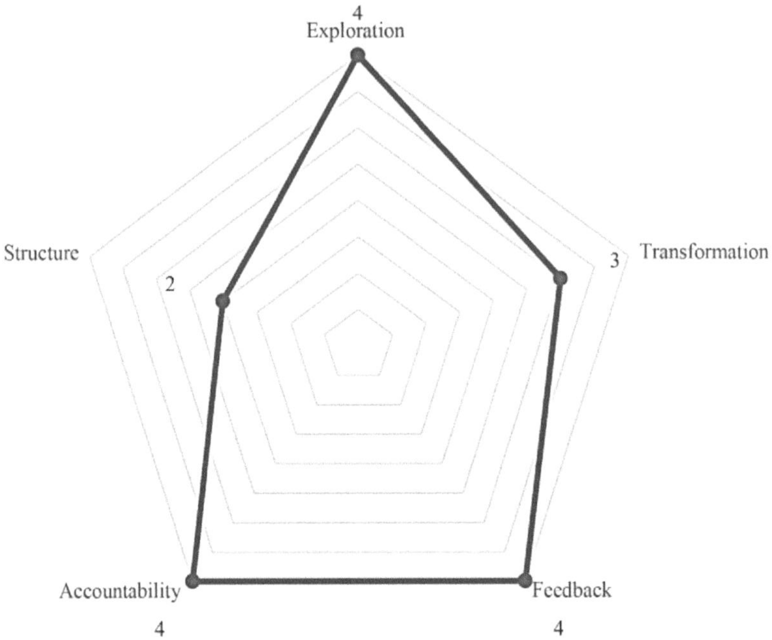

FIGURE 8.3 Toyota Kirloskar analysis.

The "feedback" system was active and involved all stakeholders to express their views to build a superior system of two-way communication (4/5). The accountability of both team and individuals were fixed (4/5) though the project features levels of hierarchy that reflected poor on the "structure" of the company (2/5) (refer Fig. 8.3 for analysis).

8.5.4 INNOVATION CULTURE AT HYUNDAI MOTORS

Hyundai Motors fares quite well on both exploration (4/5) and transformation (4/5). Its performance on the dimension of feedback is also good (4/5) and it has also successfully implemented its accountability procedure to make sure that teams and individuals know exactly "what they are expected to do" and "what they are exactly accountable for" (4/5). The team of the EV project has hierarchical structure which means the interaction between different levels are not as seamless as it should be (3/5) (refer Fig. 8.4 for analysis).

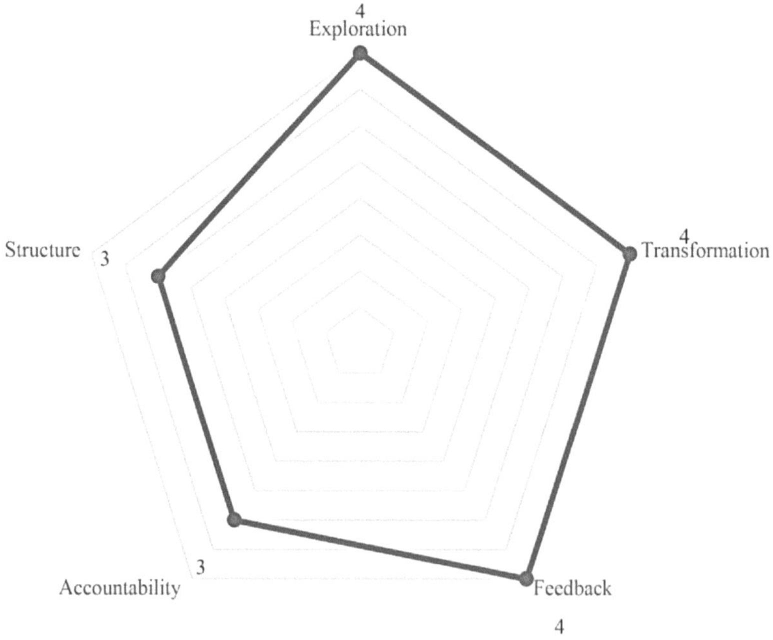

FIGURE 8.4 Hyundai Motors analysis.

8.6 DEVELOPMENT OF CONCEPTUAL FRAMEWORK AND SPECIFIC MEASURES

8.6.1 CONCEPTUAL FRAMEWORK

By combining insights from the literature and cases, this study has been able to identify three common themes which are indispensable to building a culture of innovation in organizations cutting across industries. These three elements are: (1) leadership support, (2) flat structure, and (3) two-way communication (refer Fig. 8.5). The support of the top leadership is absolutely essential for building the innovation culture in a company (Kark and Carmeli, 2009; Kley et al., 2011). People occupying top positions in organizations must imbibe the values, such as strategic vision, creativity, open communication, and constant learning among others. This will help send the message that the company is willing to promote innovation and wants its employees to invent new ways of accomplishing things. The commitment of top management also needs to manifest in making the financial resources available for building and sustaining innovation culture in the organization.

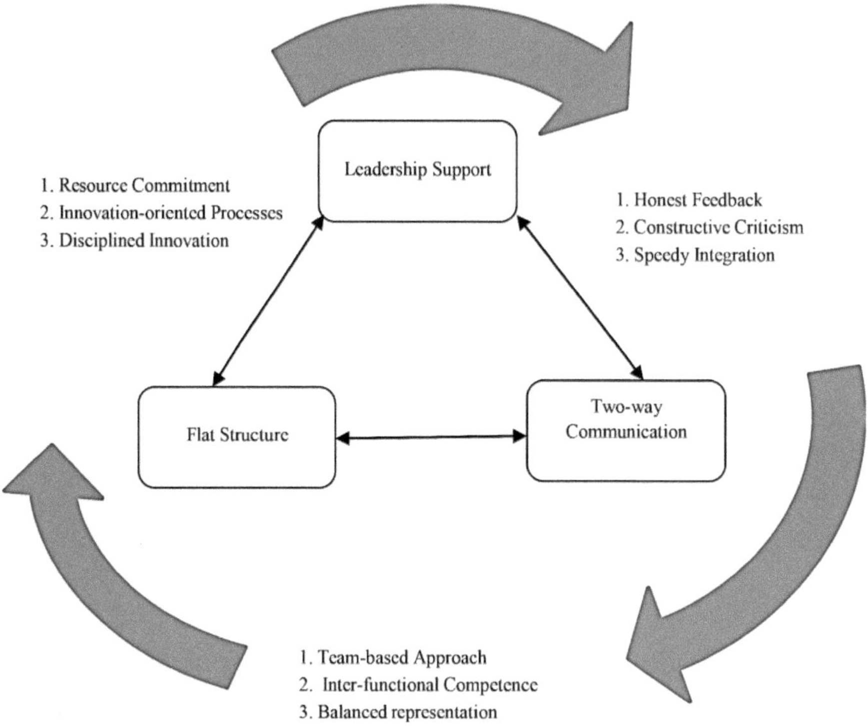

FIGURE 8.5 Conceptual framework.

In addition to finance, other important areas that might require considerable realignment include organizational culture, functional procedures, and operation mechanisms. The flat structure is another basic prerequisite for encouraging the culture of innovation. The literature states that decentralized approach helps people work effectively and use of inter-functional expertise makes sure that the given task is completed with desired efficiency and effectiveness (Tukker, 2004; Adner and Kapoor, 2010; West et al., 2014). Flat structure is also touted to be an effective tool to end red-tape and decrease the response time by cutting excessive flab in decision-making (Read, 2002; Rigby et al., 2018; Pisano, 2019).

While most of extant studies highlight the benefits of flat structure in accomplishing impressive feats, it is equally true that working in such a decentralized system is quite complex. This is because in the absence of a centralized command, employees working in the flat structure arrangement might lose focus. The personality issues might creep up and teams possibly start indulging in the backbiting and slandering. Here again, the role of top management becomes crucial. While constituting teams, leaders must pay close attention to individual team members and people complementing each other's strengths should be brought together as a team. This will help minimize likelihood of conflict in team members while working toward a common cause.

The third important element of building innovation culture is the two-way communication. Creating an atmosphere of respect and admiration where employees can express their views without any fear goes a long way in building and strengthening culture of innovation (Deshpande et al., 1993; Turrentine et al., 2007; Visnjic and Neely, 2011). As discussed above in cases, two-way communication helps to bridge the gaps between top management and functional teams. This, in turn, helps in better planning and speedy implementation of the workflow.

8.6.2 SPECIFIC MEASURES

- Taking a cue from extant literature and practical examples, it is recommended that automobile companies should apply stringent criteria of selection while hiring employees and staff. The performance standards must be set high and ideally, the selection committee should also have external experts as well. It is important to include both domain experts and industry experts in the committee so that the important traits of the candidate, such as risk-taking ability, creativity, and proactiveness can be accurately screened by interviewers. Competent employees will bring and apply creativity with finesse which helps to reduce chances of failure in the innovation process.
- While the culture of open feedback and constructive criticism has got its own share of merits, organizations need to be equally cautious of not letting the work environment become too harsh or severe for employees. This is specifically true in the case of new hires who might find the candid and honest feedback too intimidating to handle. The open feedback system can also drive a wedge between different teams, and hence, the procedure and protocols to implement it should be carried out under the supervision of experienced team of professionals—who are well-versed with social, cultural, and psychological aspects of employees' behavior.

- The tension between collaboration and accountability is subtle and might not surface until it reaches its crescendo. Holding people accountable for specific tasks might also render the feedback useless as the concerned person would try to stick to the proven methods of accomplishing jobs, thereby killing the very basic tenants of innovation. The challenge here is to select the right person who is willing to take accountability while remaining open to new ideas and methodologies to accomplish the task.
- It is essential to strike the right balance between strong visionary leadership and flat organizational structure. The top leadership of the company must articulate a compelling, overarching vision for the company though it has to be done without being excessively oriented toward procedural nitty-gritty or technical details. Employees, on the other hand, need to become more accountable while accomplishing the tasks assigned within a broader framework of empowerment.

8.7 CONCLUSION AND DISCUSSION

Building a culture of innovation is a complex process. It entails imbibing new values, adopting new systems, and ditching conventional procedures in favor of novel mechanisms. Even more difficult is to get rid of the older mindset as people thriving on the past processes are unlikely to change and will resist the new culture vehemently (Gasper and Clore, 2002; Hirst et al., 2009; Bouquet et al., 2018). The inherent contradictions in the nature of innovation culture—encouraging people to explore but then asking them to remain disciplined, giving employees more freedom but then demanding greater accountability, striving to create a harmonious environment but then stressing on providing candid feedback—makes it further difficult for companies to implement and sustain it successfully. The primary reason behind failure of organizations to pursue innovation culture is their inability to adopt a balanced approach and walked on it steadfastly. Most companies fall for either one or another extreme of the innovation continuum, leading to a totally chaotic situation and disastrous results. For example, some companies might choose to give employees full random creative freedom while others will quell any innovative idea by directing staff to stick to the time-tested methods of accomplishing things. Both these extreme positions are wrong and adopting a well-balanced position somewhere between these extreme ends will help to build and sustain culture of innovation. This research should motivate scholars to investigate further the process of building and sustaining innovation culture in companies cutting across industries. More cases of companies from other industries can be analyzed on the evaluative framework developed by the research. Further research can be done to expand the number of innovation dimensions and a separate list of dimensions relevant for specific industries can also be prepared as a repository for future research. The conceptual framework and measures developed by the study has significant implications for the automobile industry. Executives can use these cases to help understand the process of imbibing innovation while the framework and measures can be used to implement and sustain the culture for long. The conceptual framework proposed by the study is purely based on the theory and cases, and we propose to test these dimensions empirically in the future. We also intend to develop a scale on creating an innovation culture in corporate wherein these dimensions will be used as an initial set of items for starting the scale development process.

KEYWORDS

- **automobile**
- **culture**
- **indicators**
- **innovation**
- **structure**

REFERENCES

Aggeri, F.; Elmquist, M.; Pohl, H. Managing Learning in the Automotive Industry: The Innovation Race for Electric Vehicles. *Int. J. Autom. Technol. Manage.* **2009,** *9* (2), 123–147.

Adner, R.; Kapoor, R. Value Creation in Innovation Ecosystems: How the Structure of Technological Interdependence Affects Firm Performance in New Technology Generations. *Strat. Manage. J.* **2010,** *31* (3), 306–333.

Bohnsack, R.; Pinkse, J.; Kolk, A. Business Models for Sustainable Technologies: Exploring Business Model Evolution in the Case of Electric Vehicles. *Res. Pol.* **2013,** *43* (2), 284–300.

Boudway, I. *Hyundai Bets on Canoo to Supercharge Its Electric Vehicle Plans*, 2020. https://www.bloomberg.com/news/articles/2020-02-11/hyundai-bets-on-canoo-to-supercharge-its-electric-vehicle-plans (accessed March 15, 2020).

Bouquet, C.; Barsoux, J. L.; Wade, M. Bring Your Breakthrough Ideas to Life. *Harvard Bus. Rev.* **2018,** *96* (6), 102–113.

Carlile, P. R. Transferring, Translating, & Transforming: An Integrative Framework for Managing Knowledge across Boundaries. *Organ. Sci.* **2004,** *15* (5), 555–568.

Chesbrough, H. *Open Innovation: The New Imperative for Creating and Profiting from Technology*; Harvard Business School Press: Boston, MA, 2003.

Chesbrough, H. W. Business Model Innovation: Opportunities and Barriers. *Long Range Plann.* **2010,** *43* (2/3), 354–363.

Deshpande, R.; Farley, J. U.; Webster, F. E. Jr. Corporate Culture, Customer Orientation, and Innovativeness in Japanese Firms: A Quadrad Analysis. *J. Mark.* **1993,** *57* (1), 23–37.

Fairs, M. *Tata Nano by Tata Motors*, 2009. https://www.dezeen.com/2009/03/25/tata-nano-by-tata-motors/ (accessed March 6, 2020).

Fisher, C.; Amabile, T. M. Creativity, Improvisation, and Organizations. In *The Routledge Companion to Creativity*; Rickards, T., Runco, M. A., Moger, S., Eds.; Routledge: Oxford, 2009.

Gasper, K.; Clore, G. L. Attending to the Big Picture: Mood and Global Versus Local Processing of Visual Information. *Psychol. Sci.* **2002,** *13* (1), 34–40.

Gassmann, O.; Enkel, E.; Chesbrough, H. The Future of Open Innovation. *R&D Manage.* **2010,** *40* (3), 213–221.

Gemünden, H. G.; Salomo, S.; Hölzle, K. Role Models for Radical Innovations in Times of Open Innovation. *Creat. Innov. Manage.* **2007,** *16* (4), 408–421.

Gerhart, B.; Fang, M. Pay, Intrinsic Motivation, Extrinsic Motivation, Performance, and Creativity in the Workplace: Revisiting Long-Held Beliefs. *Annu. Rev. Organ. Psychol. Organ. Behav.* **2015,** *2* (1), 489–521.

Ghosh, R. *Network, Localisation, Pricing Keep Maruti Unchallenged. Amid Slowdown, Rivals Sit on the Fence*, 2020, https://prime.economictimes.indiatimes.com/news/74484003/transportation/network-localisation-pricing-keep-maruti-unchallenged-amid-slowdown-rivals-sit-on-the-fence (accessed March 5, 2020).

Hatch, M. *New Direction in the Study of Organizational Change and Innovation Processes*; Oxford University Press: New York, 2004.

Hirst, G.; Van Knippenberg, D.; Zhou, J. A Cross-Level Perspective on Employee Creativity: Goal Orientation, Team Learning Behaviour, and Individual Creativity. *Acad. Manage. J.* **2009,** *52* (2), 280–293.

Hyundai Motors. *Hyundai Motor Group, Canoo to Co-Develop All-Electric Platform for Future Electric Vehicles*, 2020. https://www.hyundai.com/worldwide/en/company/news/news-room/news/hyundai-motor-group%2C-canoo-to-co-develop-all-electric-platform-for-future-electric-vehicles-0000016402 (accessed January 25, 2020).

Jones, O.; Macpherson, A.; Thorpe, R. Learning in Owner-Managed Small Firms: Mediating Artefacts and Strategic Space. *Entrepr. Reg. Dev.* **2010,** *22* (7/8), 649–673.

Kark, R.; Carmeli, A. Alive and Creating: The Mediating Role of Vitality and Aliveness in the Relationship between Psychological Safety and Creative Work Involvement. *J. Organ. Behav.* **2009,** *30* (6), 785–804.

Kim, J.; Wilemon, D. The Learning Organization as Facilitator of Complex NPD Projects. *Creat. Innov. Manage.* **2007,** *16* (2), 176–191.

Kley, F.; Lerch, C.; Dallinger, D. New Business Models for Electric Cars—A Holistic Approach. *Energy Pol.* **2011,** *39* (6), 3392–3403.

Kripalani, M. *The story behind the Tata Nano*, 2008, https://www.rediff.com/money/2008/may/14tata.htm (accessed March 5, 2020).

Maruti Suzuki. *Smart Hybrid Technology*, 2020. Available at: https://www.marutisuzuki.com/corporate/technology/smart-hybrid (accessed February 24, 2020).

McGrath, R. G. Exploratory Learning, Innovative Capacity and Managerial Oversight. *Acad. Manage. J.* **2001,** *44* (1), 118–131.

Mueller, J. The Interactive Relationship of Corporate Culture and Knowledge Management: A Review. *Rev. Manage. Sci.* **2012,** *6* (2), 183–201.

Pisano, G. P. The Hard Truth about Innovative Cultures. *Harvard Bus. Rev.* **2019,** *97* (1), 62–71.

Prahalad, C. K.; Hamel, G. The Core Competence of the Corporation. *Harvard Bus. Rev.* **1990,** *68* (3), 79–91.

Pratt, M. G.; Pradies, C.; Lepisto, D. A. Doing Well, Doing Good, and Doing with: Organizational Practices for Effectively Cultivating Meaningful Work. In *Purpose and Meaning in the Workplace*; Dik, B., Byrne, Z., Steger, M., Eds.; American Psychological Association: Washington, DC, 2013.

Ragatz, G. L.; Handfield, R. B.; Scannell, T. V. Success Factors for Integrating Suppliers into New Product Development. *J. Prod. Innov. Manage.* **1997,** *14* (3), 190–202.

Read, A. Determinants of Successful Organizational Innovation: A Review of Current Research. *J. Manage. Pract.* **2002,** *3* (1), 95–119.

Richter, A.; Hirst, G.; van Knippenberg, D.; Baer, M. Creative Self-Efficacy and Individual Creativity in Team Contexts: Cross-Level Interactions with Team Informational Resources. *J. Appl. Psychol.* **2012,** *97* (6), 1282–1290.

Rigby, D. K.; Suther, J.; Noble, A. Agile at Scale. *Harvard Bus. Rev.* **2018,** *96* (3), 88–96.

San Román, T. G.; Momber, I.; Abbad, M. R.; Miralles, A. S. Regulatory Framework and Business Models for Charging Plug-In Electric Vehicles: Infrastructure, Agents, and Commercial Relationships. *Energy Pol.* **2011,** *39* (10), 6360–6375.

Schein, E. H. *Organizational Culture and Leadership*, 4th ed.; John Wiley and Sons: Hoboken, NJ, 2010.

Shalender, K.; Singh, N. Marketing Flexibility: Significance and Implications for Automobile Industry. *Glob. J. Flex. Syst. Manage.* **2015,** *16* (3), 251–262.

Shalender, K.; Yadav, R. K. Strategic Flexibility, Manager Personality, and Firm Performance: The Case of Indian Automobile Industry. *Glob. J. Flex. Syst. Manage.* **2019,** *20* (1), 77–90.

Spencer, W. J.; Grindley, P. SEMATECH after Five Years: High-Technology Consortia & US Competitiveness. *Calif. Manage. Rev.* **1993,** *35* (4), 9–32.

Steward, T. A.; Raman, A. P. Lessons from Toyota Long Way. *Harvard Bus. Rev.* **2007,** *85* (7/8), 74–83.

Takeuchi, H. Osono, E.; Shimizu, N. The Contradictions That Drive Toyota's Success. *Harvard Bus. Rev.* **2008,** *86* (6), 96–105.

Toyota. *Production System*, 2020. https://www.toyotabharat.com/toyota-in-india/production-system/ (accessed February 26, 2020).

Trott, P.; Hartmann, D. A. P. Why 'Open Innovation' Is Old Wine in New Bottles. *Int. J. Innov. Manage.* **2009,** *13* (4), 715–736.

Tukker, A. Eight Types of Product–Service System: Eight Ways to Sustainability? Experiences from SusProNet. *Bus. Strat. Environ.* **2004,** *13* (4), 246–260.

Turrentine, T.; Kurani, K.; Heffner, R. Fuel Economy: What Drives Consumer Choice? *Access* **2007,** *31*, 14–19.

Tushman, M. L.; O'Reilly, C. A. *Winning through Innovation*; Harvard Business School Press: Boston, 1997.

Visnjic, I.; Neely, A. D. *From Processes to Promise: How Complex Service Providers Use Business Model Innovation to Deliver Sustainable Growth*; Cambridge Service Alliance, Cambridge, 2011.

Wang, H.; Choi, J.; Wan, G.; Dong, J. Q. Slack Resources and the Rent-Generating Potential of Firm-Specific Knowledge. *J. Manage.* **2013,** *42* (2), 500–523.

West, J.; Bogers, M. Leveraging External Sources of Innovation: A Review of Research on Open Innovation. *J. Prod. Innov. Manage.* **2013,** *31* (4), 814–831.

West, J.; Salter, A.; Vanhaverbeke, W.; Chesbrough, H. Open Innovation: The Next Decade. *Res. Pol.*; **2014,** *43* (5), 805–811.

Winter, S.; Lasch, R. Recommendations for Supplier Innovation Evaluation from Literature and Practice. *Int. J. Oper. Prod. Manage.* **2016,** *36* (6), 643–664.

Wong, C. W. Y.; Wong. C. Y.; Boon-itt, S. The Combined Effects of Internal & External Supply Chain Integration on Product Innovation. *Int. J. Prod. Econ.* **2013,** *146*, 566–574.

Zott, C.; Amit, R. Business Model Design: An Activity System Perspective. *Long Range Plann.* **2010,** *43* (2/3), 216–226.

CHAPTER 9

Integration Between the Indian and US Copper Markets

SWATY SHARMA

Mittal School of Business Lovely Professional University, Phagwara 110001, Punjab, India
E-mail: swaty.sharma@rediffmail.com

ABSTRACT

This chapter is an attempt to examine co-integration, causality, and volatility spillover among Indian copper and US copper market over 15 years from 2005 to 2019 by using Johansen co-integration, Granger causality and GARCH (1, 1) model. Result indicates long-term co-integration among these two markets. VECM indicates that US copper market has influence on Indian copper market. But Indian copper market has no influence on US copper market. Short-run connection among Indian copper market and US copper market is also found. GARCH result shows that Indian copper market grabs volatility from US copper market and same the United States as well. The US copper market shocks to Indian copper market. Granger causality result shows unidirectional causality from the US market to Indian market. Indian copper market is influenced by the United States copper market.

9.1 INTRODUCTION

Copper ranks third in global consumption behind aluminum as well as steel. Copper plays an important role for the contribution of national economies of all countries. Copper's global demand is continuously growing. Globally,

Constructive Discontent in Execution: Creative Approaches to Technology and Management.
Sanjeev Bansal, Anita Venaik, Swati Upveja, and Saritha S. (Eds.)

copper demand has increased by 350% during last 50 years, especially in sectors like construction, industrial machinery, electrical and electronic products, transportation equipment, as well as consumer and general products. The United States Geological Survey described that in 2014, globally copper reserves were 700 MMT. Indian copper prices reflect prevailing international spot market and the USD–INR exchange rates. India's production of refined copper in 2012 was around 4% of the total world production at 689,312 MT.

World-wide commodities demand as well as supply assume a noteworthy function for domestic commodity cost set up, as the world turns out to be more coordinated. Markets have seen major changes in trading volumes, market structures, and market participants during the last few decades. Global markets are changing, often in response to large public policy shocks, such as global trade diversion, US policy is appealing for commodities market analysis (Rapsomanikis et al., 2006; Irwin and Sanders, 2012; Beckman et al., 2017).

Many studies like (Adjemian et al., 2019; Ghosh et al., 1999; Harnandez, 2017) described that US financial market is the central role player in the world market as well as dominant in the flow of information among all countries.

Cross-country linkage in any class of financial assets has gained importance in the same pace as the world has moved toward becoming a global village. The formal introduction of liberalization, privatization, and globalization in India in the decade of 1990 helped the country a lot in its co-integration with the rest of world in terms of trade and investment. Worldwide commodities market has been growing rapidly (Hua and Chen, 2007; Fung et al., 2013; Xindan and Bing, 2008; Li and Zhang, 2013).

Co-integration test has been used by various researchers for spot and future market to know the relationship in order to arrive at a conclusion for efficiency of future market in price discovery (Chowdhury, 1991; Crowder and Hamed, 1993; Beck, 1994; Mananyi and Strutherrs, 1997; Kellard et al., 1999; Xin et al., 2006; Bekiros and Diks, 2008; Mckenzie and Holt, 2010; Sharma, 2017) in different market for various categories of commodities across the world. According to Yadav and Arora (2020), investors want to optimize the amount of their investments. Present chapter analyzes connection among Indian copper market as well as the United States copper market via applying Johansen co-integration test. On the other side GARCH test is applied to know volatility spillover among these two countries and Granger causality test is applied to know lead lag connection among these two.

This chapter is organized as follows: the second part discusses about the studies done so far. The third part discusses about methodology applied to examine the relationship among price index of Indian copper and US copper. Results of various models applied are discussed in the fourth part. Fifth part represents the conclusion of the study.

9.1.1 HISTORICAL PERSPECTIVE

Garbade and Silber (1983) analyzed spot price and future price movement for storable commodities. It was suggested that market integration depends on the supply of services. For highlighting the importance of US futures trading in a world market, Fung et al. (2003) examined the flow of information and volatility spillover among US as well as China commodity market with three commodities: copper, soybean, and wheat. It was found that Chinese market follows the US market, however, in the case of wheat, it was not true and the reason has been attributed to protection policy of Chinese government as wheat being an essential commodity for mass consumption. The same reason accounts for the result of Wang and Ke (2013) as well as Hua and Chen (2007) who studied that wheat market is found efficient in China in the price discovery in spot market, whereas for soybean, a long-term equilibrium relationship was found among cash price and future price. Again, no co-integration was found in wheat market across DEC of China and CBOT in another study. However, all three commodities have volatility spillover effect from the US market showing there is flow of information from the US market to Chinese market. Same result was obtained for copper in the research done by Gea et al. (2010). Integration and volatility transmission of price from US market to China could not be rejected. Like the effect of US market on China, the UK market has also a dominating role. The results obtained by Yin and Han (2013) are that after the global turmoil, intensity of spillover of UK exchange has increased. However, the direction of spillover is time-variant. It is noteworthy here that the model used by Yin and Han (2013) was BI-vitiate E GARCH. Pavabutr and Chaihetphon (2008) examined the efficiency of MCX India in the price discovery of gold by studying data from 2003 to 2007 using VECM. Kawamoto and Hamori (2011) examined in their study about the market efficiency and unbiased among futures market. It was found that WTI futures are efficient consistently as well as unbiased. Kumar and Pandey (2011) investigated cross-market connection of Indian commodity futures market with global market by using nine. For the copper market in London and UK, both markets influence each other for being informational link but if quantified. London metal exchange has greater influence on Shanghai exchange (Li and Zhang, 2009). Rutledge et al. (2013) examined international integration of Chinese copper future market via using co-integration and VECM. Long-run relationship was found among these markets. Li and Zhang (2014) analyzed international connection of Shanghai future market through SVAR model and found that CME and MCX of India has not much impact on the international market. On the other side, London metal exchange has lower impact on Shanghai exchange. Some researchers also empirically analyzed the price discovery in regional exchange (Gupta et al., 2018; Sahoo, 2009; Shiva and Sethi, 2015). Kanga et al. (2017) studied the non-ferrous metals in China and London markets, whereas Li and Zhang (2014) studied the causal relationship across future market of four countries (China, UK, US, and India) for a single metal copper using VAR model. It was found that Chicago Mercantile Exchange and MCX both have weaker impact on each other, on the other hand, China market was found influenced by LME from 2007, but later on the impact was found decreasing. Price of non-ferrous metals market in London leads the Chinese market in medium run. But in the case of aluminum and zinc in the long run, Shanghai market leads London market. This study was for the period 2008–2014 and revealed that global crisis has caused an increase in causality across the markets. Liu and Wang (2014), Wn and Hu (2016), and Yue et al. (2015) studied the cross-correlational properties for metal futures and found the following results. There exists a strong cross-correlation not only between the metal spot and future market but also among the metal futures (copper, aluminum and zinc) in China. Further, no significant effect on structural changes on the volatility correlation of copper, aluminum, and zinc has been found. Methodology used in this section is not much varied. DCC-GARCH and MF-DCCA models were used for correlation study.

9.2 DATA AND ECONOMETRIC METHODOLOGY

In this study, monthly dataset is used for the period 2005–2019. The purpose for choosing this time period is availability of data. Data for Indian copper are obtained from MCX official website and the US copper data are obtained from official website of US commodity market.

To study causal relation between Indian copper and US copper the Granger causality test was employed. This test is more reliable and efficient as compared with other methods used to study causal relation. Details of all these areas under:

For checking the stationary of data unit, root test is applied. Tests, such as DF, ADF, and PP test are to check unit root in time series. ADF is most popular among these entire tests.

9.2.1 AUGMENTED DICKEY-FULLER TEST

Mathematical equation can be written as:

$$\grave{E}_t = ¥_0 + ¥_1 t + \beta_{t-1} + \varepsilon_t$$

$\grave{E}_t$ is known as stochastic process. On the other side, $¥_{0,}¥_1$, and β all are known as parameters. Here, time period that is denoted by t and error term is denoted by ε_t. This test describes that first-order difference equation has unit root.

9.2.2 JOHANSEN CO-INTEGRATION TEST

To investigate the relationship between India's copper market as well as the United States copper market, Johansen test is applied. Theory of co-integration says that two same stochastic patterns nonstationary series can walk together in the long run (Engel and Granger, 1987). In any case, deviation from since a long time ago, equilibrium can happen in the short run. It must be performed among the arrangements having same level of combination (Johansen, 1991, 1999).

9.2.3 VECTOR ERROR CORRECTION MODEL

VECM is applied to examine short-run connection. If long-term connection is found between two variables, then VECM is applied to know short-run connection.

9.2.4 CAUSALITY TEST

Causality test is helpful to choose that one time series is useful to anticipate what's to happen to other time series.

9.3 RESULTS AND DISCUSSIONS

Start of examination of data is constantly done via analyzing stationary data. For investigation reason, ADF is utilized. Test results are represented with the help of Table 9.1. Here, results describe that data is nonstationary at level. On first difference, data test again now it is stationary.

TABLE 9.1 Stationary Test.

	Level	First Diff.
ADF test	0.1462	0.0000

Stationary of data is very important before applying any model. Lag selection is also important before running Johansen as well as Granger causality model. That is done by using VAR model. The result of VAR models describes 2 lags for running Johansen model.

TABLE 9.2 Co-integration Test.

Variables	Trace statistics	Maximum Eigenvalue	Critical values	P value
Copper	32.02846	0.110143	15.49471	0.0001
	11.95709	0.067157	3.841466	0.0005

Source: Author's calculation.

Johansen co-integration test was introduced by Johansen in 1988 that is based on maximum eigenvalue criteria. Table 9.2 shows the summary of test. Result indicates long-run co-integration among Indian copper market as well as US copper market at 5% confidence level. Even, it may very well be said that there is direct relationship among these two.

TABLE 9.3 VECM Result.

	Ind. coefficient	P value	US coefficient	P value
Z	−0.845835	0.0020	−0.226120	0.4304
Ind $copper_{t-1}$	1.004162	0.0001	1.179785	0.0000
Ind $copper_{t-2}$	0.281932	0.1703	0.346582	0.1133
US $copper_{t-1}$	−0.703173	0.0046	−0.879769	0.0009
US $copper_{t-2}$	−0.289684	0.1315	−0.359744	0.0786
Constant	0.013295	0.6713	0.016215	0.6265

Source: Author's calculation.

From Johansen co-integration test, it is found that there is long-term relationship among Indian copper market as well as US copper market. Due to this result, it is necessary to check whether there is short-term relation among these two. It will also support the above findings. To examine the short-term relationship among Indian copper market and US copper market, vector error correction has used. From Table 9.3 long-run causality is found among these two variables because *P* value is less than 5% and coefficient is negative. This means that the US copper market has influence on the Indian copper market. But Indian copper market has no influence on the US copper market. Short-run connection among Indian copper market and US copper market is also found.

TABLE 9.4 Result of Granger Causality.

	F value	*P* value
United States copper does not Granger cause India's copper	2.86450	0.0015
India's copper does not Granger cause United States copper	1.11169	0.6866

Source: Author's calculation.

Granger causality test is performed to know which the reason is and who the impact is. This test (Table 9.4) demonstrates that the United States copper market drives India's copper market, yet the India's copper market does not lead the United States copper market. It implies unidirectional causality among these two. It demonstrates how the United States copper market affected the India's copper market.

TABLE 9.5 Result of GARCH (1, 1).

	Coefficient	*Z* statistic	*P* value
United States copper	1.000854	1.707272	0.0000
RESID(-1)^2	−0.009434	−4.913722	0.0000
GARCH(-1)	0.910903	17.84335	0.0000

Source: Author's calculation.

Estimation of volatility among India and the United States copper market GARCH (1, 1) model is applied. Result in Table 9.5 shows that both ARCH and GARCH terms are significant. Result shows that Indian copper market grabs volatility from the US copper market and same the United States as well. The United States copper market shocks to Indian copper market. Both markets influence volatility to each other.

9.4 CONCLUSION

This chapter examines the integration, volatility spillover as well as causality among US copper market and Indian copper market. Results indicate long-term co-integration among these two markets. VECM indicates that US copper market has influence on Indian copper market. But Indian copper market has no influence on the US copper market. Short-run connection among Indian copper market and US copper market is also found. It can also be said that their prices move together. GARCH result shows that Indian copper market grabs volatility from the US copper market and the United States grabs volatility from the Indian market as well. The United States copper market shocks to Indian copper market. Granger causality result shows unidirectional causality from the US market to Indian market. Indian copper market is influenced by the United States copper market. It can be said that Indian copper market is led by the United States copper market. In concluding remarks, the present study empirically evidenced that the United States copper market contains sufficient information for forecasting Indian Copper market prices.

KEYWORDS

- **Johansen co-integration**
- **Granger causality**
- **volatility spillover**
- **copper**
- **Indian commodity market**
- **US commodity market**

REFERENCES

Adjemian, M. K.; Smith, A.; Arita, S.; He, W. Estimating the Market Effect of a Trade War: The Case of Soybean Tariffs. In *Paper Presented at the Agricultural and Applied Economics Association Annual Meeting*, Atlanta, GA, 2019; pp 21–23.

Beck, S. E. Co-integration and Market Efficiency in Commodities Futures Market. *J. Appl. Econ.* **1994,** *26*, 249–257.

Beckman, J.; Dyck, J.; Heerman, K. *The Global Landscape of Agricultural Trade, 1995–2014*. US Department of Agriculture, Economic Research Service: Washington, DC, 2017.

Bekiros, D. S.; Diks, C. G. H. The Relationship between Crude Oil Spot and Future Prices: Co-Integration, Linear and Nonlinear Causality. *Energy Econ.* **2008,** *30*, 2673–2685.

Bhar, R.; Nikolova, B. Analysis of Mean and Volatility Spillovers Using BRIC Countries, Regional and World Equity Index Returns. *J. Econ. Integr.* **2007,** *22* (2), 369–381.

Chowdhury, A. R. Future Market Efficiency: Evidence from Co-Integration Test. *J. Fut. Mark.* **1991,** *11* (5), 577–589.

Coccia, M. Varieties of Capitalism's Theory of Innovation and a Conceptual Integration with Leadership-Oriented Executives: The Relation between Typologies of Executive, Technological and Socioeconomic Performances. *Int. J. Publ. Sect. Perform. Manage.* **2017,** *3* (2), 148–168.

Crowder, W. J.; Hamed, A. A Cointegration Test for Oil Market Efficiency. *J. Fut. Mark.* **1993,** *13* (8), 933–941.

Engle, R. F.; Granger, C. W. J. Co-integration and Error Correction: Representation, Estimation and Testing," *Econometrica* **1987,** *55*, 251–276.

Fung, H. G.; Leung, W. K.; Xu, X. E. Information Role of US Futures Trading in Global Financial Market. *J. Fut. Mark.* **2003,** *21* (11), 1071–1090.

Fung, H. G.; Tse, Y.; Yau, J.; Zhao, L. A Leader of the World Commodity Future Market in the Making Case of China's Commodity Future. *Int. Rev. Finan. Anal.* **2013,** *27*, 103–114.

Garbade, K. D.; Silber, W. L. Price of Movements and Price Discovery in Futures and Cash Markets. *Rev. Econ. Stat.* **1983,** *65*, 289–297.

Gea, Y.; Wanga, H. H.; Ahnc, S. S. Implication of Cotton Price Behavior on Market Integration. *Agric. Econ.* **2010,** *41*, 443–451.

Gupta, S.; Choudhary, H.; Agarwal, D. R. An Empirical Analysis of Market Efficiency and Price Discovery in Indian Commodity Market. *Glob. Bus. Rev.* **2018,** *19* (3), 1–19.

Hernandez, M. A.; Ibarra, R.; Trupkin, D. R. How Far Do Shocks Move across Borders? Examining Volatility Transmission in Major Agricultural Futures Markets. *Eur. Rev. Agric. Econ.* **2013,** *41* (2), 301–325.

Hua, R.; Chen, B. International Linkage of Chinese Future Market. *Appl. Finan. Econ.* **2007,** *17* (16), 1275–1287.

Irwin, S. H.; Sandersm, D. R. Financialization and Structural Change in Commodity Futures Markets. *J. Agric. Appl. Econ.* **2012,** *44*, *3*, 371–396.

Johansen, S. Estimation and Hypothesis Testing of Co-Integration Vectors in Gaussian Vector Autoregressive Models. *Econometrica* **1991,** *59* (6), 1551–1580.

Johansen, S. Estimation and Hypothesis Testing of Co-Integration Vectors in Gaussian Vector Autoregressive Models. *Econometrica* **1999,** *59* (6), 1551–1580.

Kanga, S. H.; Tiwarib, A. K.; Albulescud, C. T.; Yoone, S. M. Time-Frequency Co-Movements between the Largest Nonferrous Metal Future Markets. *Resour. Policy* **2017,** *61*, 393–398.

Kawamoto, K.; Hamori, S. Market Efficiency among Futures with Different Maturities: Evidence from the Crude Oil Futures Market. *J. Fut. Mark.* **2011,** *31* (5), 487–501.

Kellard, N.; Newbold, P.; Rayner, T.; Ennew, C. The Relative Efficiency of Commodity Future Markets. *J. Fut. Mark.* **1999,** *19*, 4.

Kumar, B.; Pandey, A. International Linkages of the Indian Commodity Futures Markets. *Mod. Econ.* **2011,** *2*, 213–227.

Li, Z.; Zhang, L. H. An Empirical Study of International Linkages of the Shanghai Copper Futures Market. *Chin. Econ.* **2014,** *46* (3), 61–74.

Liu, L.; Wang, Y. Cross-Correlations between Spot and Futures Market of Non-Ferrous Metals. *Phys. A* **2014,** *400*, 20–30.

Mckenzie, A. M.; Holt, M. T. Market Efficiency in Agricultural Futures Market. *Appl. Econ.* **2010,** *34* (12), 1519–1532.

Pavabutr, P.; Chaihetphon, P. Price Discovery in the Indian Gold Futures Market. *J. Econ. Finan.* **2010,** *34* (4), 455–467.

Rapsomanikis, G.; Hallam, D.; Conforti, P. Market Integration and Price Transmission in Selected Food and Cash Crops Markets of Developing Countries: Review and Application. *Agriculture Commodity Market and Trade*; Edwar Elgar Publishing United Kingdom: Cheltenham, 2006.

Rutledge, R. W.; Karim, K.; Wang, R. International Copper Futures Market Price Linkage and Information Transmission: Empirical Evidence from the Primary World Copper Markets. *J. Int. Bus. Res.* **2013,** *12* (1), 113–129.

Sharma, S. Market Efficiency between Indian & US Crude Oil Future Market. *Proc. Comput. Sci.* **2017,** *122*, 1039–1046.

Sahoo, P. Efficiency and Futures Trading: Price Nexus in Indian Commodity Futures Markets. *Glob. Bus. Rev.* **2009,** *10* (2), 187–201.

Shiva, A.; Sethi, M. Understanding Dynamic Relationship among Gold Price, Exchange Rate and Stock Markets: Evidence in Indian Context. *Glob. Bus. Rev.* **2015,** *16* (5_suppl), 93S–111S.

Wang, H. H.; Ke, B. Efficiency Tests of Agricultural Commodity Futures Market in China. *Austr. J. Agric. Resour. Econ.* **2005,** *49*, 125–141.

Wu, D.; Hu, Z. H. Structural Changes and Volatility Correlation in Non-Ferrous Metal Markets. *Trans. Nonferrous Met. Soc. China* **2016,** *26*, 2784–2792.

Yadav, M. P.; Arora, M. Testing of Weak Market Efficiency in Indian Stock Exchange Employing Variance Ratio Test. *Int. J. Publ. Sect. Perform. Manage.* **2020,** *6* (5), 632–641.

Yin, L.; Han, L. Exogenous Shocks and Information Transmission in Global Copper Future Market. *J. Fut. Mark.* **2013,** *33* (8), 724–751.

Yue, Y. D. Liu, D. C.; Xu, S. Price Linkage between Chinese and International Non-Ferrous Metals Commodity Market based on VAR-DCC-GARCH Models. *Trans. Nonferrous Met. Soc. China* **2015,** *25*, 1020–1026.

CHAPTER 10

A Study on the Loyalty Market in E-Commerce Business

HIMANK BAJPAI[1*] and ANITA VENAIK[2]

[1]*Amity Business School, Amity University, Noida 201301, Uttar Pradesh, India*

[2]*Amity Business School, Amity University, Noida 201301, Uttar Pradesh, India*

[*]*Corresponding author. E-mail: bajpaihimank@gmail.com*

ABSTRACT

The study is an extension to my previous research paper on Customer Relationship Management and Loyalty Programs in Indian Business.

This report emphasizes the framework of E-commerce Business and the Loyalty Program in depth and how do these both combine to form an effective business strategy to win customers, increase the transaction value as well as the basket value for a customer.

It also talks about various components such as pillars of the E-commerce Business, how to drive repeat purchases using gift vouchers, coupons, point system.

Considering the current pandemic, the market has seen its rise and fall; businesses have seen a change management toward the customer purchases as well as repeat purchases. Most of the businesses have gone online and physical setup has been the least priority for majority of the businesses. Optimistically, most of the businesses have leveraged the opportunity to automate their offerings and make the most out of it by cutting their cost.

Constructive Discontent in Execution: Creative Approaches to Technology and Management.
Sanjeev Bansal, Anita Venaik, Swati Upveja, and Saritha S. (Eds.)

Hence, the paper would also talk about the COVID strategy opted by various brands to increase their return of investment into their line of businesses.

The competitive environment has forced the industries to expand the e-commerce business on larger scale and come up with various strategies to meet the supply and demand.

We will study the mix of e-commerce framework and the loyalty market framework as a unified solution to drive the change management in the system basis few loyalty strategies.

10.1 INTRODUCTION

10.1.1 LOYALTY PROGRAMS

Loyalty programs are a basic marketing strategy designed to create push among the customers toward the brand, product, or the offerings. Such programs cover business commerce enabling the rewards and features for the customers across industries. These strategies not only keep the 20% customers intact toward the brands but also help in pulling the 80% of the nonloyal customers to purchase.

These programs are widely used in building relationships with the customers and gaining their trust. The competition in the market has led to a provoked nature of an individual or an organization to build strong structures or programs so that they do not lose on their customers or clients.

Factors influencing Loyalty Programs:

- Satisfaction
- Community Outreach (Cause Marketing)
- Customer Expectations
- Communication
- Elasticity

How to Measure Customer Loyalty?

Source: Simon Spyer, May 25, 2016, Crmconduit, E-satisfaction website content.

It can be examined via measurable parameters such as customer behavior, referrals purchase trends, and historical trends.

- Customer Lifetime Value
- Churn Rate
- Visit Frequency

- Transaction Frequency
- Spend Per Transaction
- Net Promoter Score (NPS)

10.1.2 E-COMMERCE AND E-COMMERCE BUSINESS

E-commerce Business refers to all aspects of operating an online business and E-commerce refers specifically to the transaction that is carried out to make a purchase of any goods or services via internet commerce or electronic commerce. This was brought to eliminate brick and mortar system from the existing markets.
E-commerce makes product search easier over online platforms and enables small-scale businesses to go online and sell their products with the help of internet,
for example, online shopping, booking tickets, banking, networking, and hotel booking.

Source: Deepa Verma and Harita Mehla March 1, 2014 (Compiled by *International Journal of Engineering*)

The buying and selling conducted over internet over various technologies such as mobile/tablet/PC using electronic funds via apps such as Gpay, Paytm, PhonePay is termed E-commerce.

It can be between 2 business transmitting offerings in the form of funds, goods, services to complete the e-commerce business life cycle. A typical framework showcases how it works.

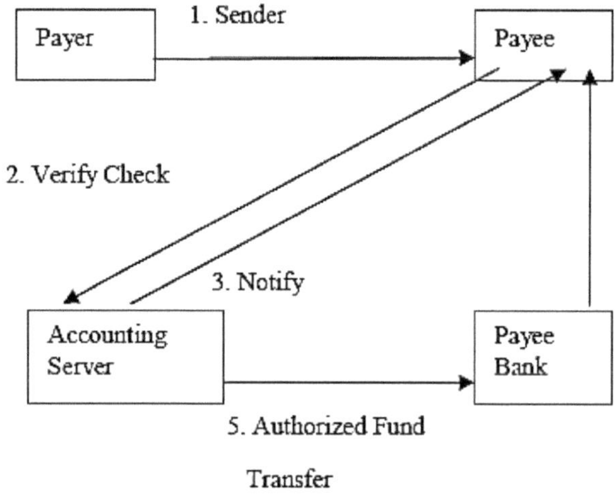

As per the above structure, the payer tries to transmit electronic check toward the payee and the payee submits the same to the concerned accounting server where the check is verified against the required assets digitally and the digital signature of the payer's account.

When the check is performed and authentication is completed the Accounting Server creates an order toward the bank's computers and authorizes the fund transfer to the payee's account.

Instructions and the confirmation are shared at both the ends once the transaction is successful.

The scope of E-commerce might be narrow but the E-business has a wider scope as e-commerce is a subset. Usually, e-commerce involves monetary transactions and might require a website to operate, however, monetary might not be involved and might require CRM, ERP, website, etc.

E-commerce might require internet to connect to the world but at other end the business might involve intranet, internet, or an extranet to operate functionally.

10.1.2.1 TYPES OF E-COMMERCE

Source: Shopify, E-commerce website content.

- **Business to Business**: Usually, it happens between manufacturers and the supplier of goods, e.g., a business might sell software-as-service to other business to ease out their work flow
- **Business to Consumer**: When a business sells goods or services to an individual, e.g., you buy shirt from a retailer
- **Consumer to Business**: Commercial transaction between the customer and the business firm, e.g., a photographer licenses the picture for a business to use it
- **Consumer to Consumer**: When a transaction happens between 2 customers, e.g., selling old products over OLX

E-commerce Advantages

1. **Large Market**: It has a better reach of market and connects a larger customer base to the business and vice versa. The customers can make purchases from across the world via gadgets.
2. **Customer Insights**: Customer journey can be tracked and mapped whether you are following any of the mechanisms, e.g., PPC Ads, SEO, or any other methodology. Customer insights such as their

punched keywords, experience, pricing strategy, and buying decisions can be tracked.

3. **Lower Cost:** As the e-commerce platforms have advanced, it is cheaper to manage inventories, lower down the cost on TV ads, etc.
4. **Opportunity to Sell:** Scope has widened as over the website the merchants can collect customer testimonials, reviews, demo videos, etc., which helps them in personalized selling, product recommendation that in turn helps customer registration and database management to understand the customer behavior and buying pattern, decisions.
5. **Instant Gratification:** E-commerce allows businesses to deliver within sometime of order placement. Customer satisfaction, reviews, feedback are uplifted using this mechanism and it helps businesses in their sales process especially for low cost or budgeted products that usually account to "impulsive buys."

E-commerce Disadvantages

1. **Lack of Personal Touch:** Usually issue for business selling high end or the expensive products as it requires a personal touch to pursue the customers to make the purchase sometimes. Most of the customers not only focus on the product but also on the customer service.
2. **Lack of Tactile Experience: Despite** all the advantages, customer cannot touch, experience, or feel the product physically before they make the purchase. The process can be tedious sometimes if the products are required to be returned by the customers. A 2-dimensional environment lacks the feel of touch, smell, taste, sound, hence, the brand experience might be lesser. Also, in the cases when a customer might want to try out the new products it becomes much difficult for them to trust the brands or the products which bring the market opportunity down.
3. **Competition:** Due to so much competition and accessibility, a lot of offline as well as online merchants had to cut down onto their margins as the customers can find the cheapest price available on the internet for any product.
4. **Internet Connection:** Customers need high-end broadband connection to support a lot of websites. The features, functionalities, and the way the market is advancing (try before you buy) the internet requirement and hardware requirement go high.

5. **Fraud:** A lot of customers who are not tech savvy are being cheated and looted upon fake schemes. Customer information had been stolen, they are misled to fill information that leads to legal and financial implications.
6. **Dependency:** The businesses and merchants are highly dependent on the e-commerce now; a slight lag, delay, or downtime can lead to huge revenue or business loss, e.g., stock markets

E-commerce Loyalty Programs

Source: Customer Insight Group Inc.

Organizations may award the customers in various ways in the form of diversified loyalty schemes; few of them are mentioned below:

1. **Points Based**: With this type of program, customer earns points for every transaction whether being online or physically at the store. These points can be converted into coupons or cash points for future purposes. The principle is "spend more to earn more."

Example:

Pros	Cons
• Price Integrity • Currency can be used at partner stores • Aspirational purchases to achieve rewards can provide business gains • Robust customer data and insights to drive business • Free membership facilitates to enroll maximum customers	• No instanat gratification to customers • Common program, special factor dissappears from the composition • Reward fulfilment can be expensive • Expiry of reward points may lead to dissatisfaction

2. **Tired Based**: To find a balance between attainable and desired reward values is to implement the tire-based program, which will automatically drive the customers' demand and supply into segments.

   Levels of loyalty are decided on the basis of customer purchases and points are awarded accordingly.

   Higher the purchase greater the points received leading to raise in loyalty segmentation of a customer. Every customer is ranked or leveled on the basis of their transactional history, which decides the measure of benefits. Reaching to a level may lead to gifts, coupons, discounts, etc.

Pros	Cons
• Customer segmentation is maintained easily • Higher value customer can be focused upon and revenue is generated • Customizable and engagement level is high • Aspirational purchases to achieve greater status can provide gains in overall wallet share • Customers less likely to cancel membership	• Not much of a benefit to low to moderately engaged customers • Negative impact if a customer is downgraded • Lower tier customer switches to points based system which is widely available hence customers can switch brands easily • Personalised communication be required at higher status level

3. **Association Based**: Collaborating with other companies' servers brings greater benefits to customers leading to building trust and retaining customers. This is also known as coalition program, which gives discounts and rewards redeemable across all the brands collaborated with and is a fine-tuned method to extend the loyalty benefits.

   Example: Barber shops collaborating with grooming products, dog food company collaborating with veterinary office for pet grooming, etc.

Pros	Cons
• Brands and business gets larger customer base and information • Rewards can be used with any partner anywhere • Funding is shared with partner to reduce operational cost	• Data is shared with coalition as well • Benefit program cannot be individually differentiated • Business runs with a risk of reward redemption with competitors

4. **Fee Based**: In this case the customer needs to pay a basic fee to get entitled to extensive discounts, products, sales benefit, or services. These are widely known as VIP or premium membership benefits and are being popular by credit card companies to spread awareness of credit cards as well as loyalty programs.

Example: Amazon Prime- 2-day free shipping delivery as complimentary service, Hotstar- Disney + as add on package, Lounge services and other benefits using credit cards, etc.

Pros	Cons
• An engaged customer sees the higher value of membership and encourages others as well • Easiest loyalty program to understand • Funds generated from onboarding members can be used to cover up the program cost	• Lower tier customers have entry barrier, hence, driving them away • Tedious task to manage the program • High in flow of queries compared to other programs

5. **Gamification Programs**: Turning your loyalty program into a game to repeat customers and shaping the brand image accordingly. You can involve the following elements to gamify your application or program even more:
   - Badges
   - Leaderboards
   - Weekly contestants

   Example: Uber rating customers and drivers-providing them badges, Spin the wheel contestant by Flipkart, Google pay keeps introducing game-based offers-discount coupons on festivals, etc.

Pros	Cons
• Vibrant and engaging program • Easily executable • Funds generated from onboarding members can be used to cover up the program cost	• Lower tier customers have entry barrier, hence, driving them away • Tedious task to manage the program • High in flow of queries as compared to other programs

10.2 LITERATURE REVIEW

Source: Deepa Verma and Harita Mehla March 1, 2014 (Compiled by *International Journal of Engineering*).

In recent years, Electronic Commerce has become popular due to its convenient services. Communication and technology have simplified the business to an extent that the rise in productivity has seen a drastic change management in the market.

With the rise in technology people have been tech savvy and 77% of people from developed economy are using internet, whereas 31% are from the developing nations. It is said that almost 24% of turnover is generated via online channel.

US had the majority of ecommerce business across the world followed by China and then India. Even Czech generates one of the largest contributions to the total revenue from this business.

China—The total revenue raised by China was around $36.6 billion in 2009 and the only reason to top the charts was the customer winning attitude and the customer satisfaction being driven by the country. The country has expanded in overseas countries as well, India being one of the biggest consumers of their products. The overall rise from 2009 to 2012 toward e-commerce business has seen a rise of 32% which sums up to 9.6% of their cross-border sales.

Russia—An overall evaluation of their business was charted out between 23 and 30 $ billion in 2015. The expected evaluation for 2020 was estimated to be around $50 billion, the major challenges the country faced was online payment methodologies, language barrier.

Brazil—This country is expected to progress with a double rate by 2016, i.e., $17 billion.

India—Considering a developing nation, the Indian markets are still trying to digitize its economy and enrol maximum potential to online market. The growth has been slow as the scope stands at 1.3 billion as customer base and 50 million customers access the internet via desktop mode and the consistent e-commerce base stands at 2–3 million. A single year from 2011 had seen a surge of 50%, i.e., 26.1–37.5 million bases.

Majority of which was via travel websites accounting to $14 billion. The businesses as of date are coming with various loyalty programs and redemption benefits to create a push and pull strategy because of which the population has noticed a greater benefit in online commerce than offline business. Mergers and acquisitions have led to greater benefits in various businesses by establishing manufacturing units across the country. This results in cost reduction, value for money, and instant customer satisfaction.

The businesses have realized the value of instant gratification as methodology due to which the chances of business commerce have increased to a huge customer base.

Every successful loyalty business is a composition of a capable mixture of E-commerce + Loyalty Program which makes the value proposition valuable and runs the business successfully. Below are the industry-specific E-commerce framework and loyalty business framework. Self-learning from the frameworks has been shown in a manner of conceptual framework by the end.

10.2.1 E-COMMERCE FRAMEWORK

Source: CCSU-BCOM January 9, 2019 (compiled by Intactone.com).

The E-commerce framework consists of software frameworks that drive the applications to support the E-businesses. An environment is created to support the supply chain or any other functionality to carry out the offerings via website or a software.

Components that are vital for framework are mentioned below:

1. **Quality Search Functionality**
   This plays a vital role in search functions and helps in increasing the sales rate. The search function is embedded and helps convert the search into desired results; it filters the keywords searched by the customers and displays the best possible results as per the availability.

2. **CMS (Content Management System)**
   It is a designed software system which manages the creation and modification of the digital content. WordPress, Joomla, Magento, Wix are some of the examples.

3. **Multi-Channel Functionality**
   The global spread of the business is highly important to implement a successful business. Managing products, listing, and orders plays a vital role in this.

4. **Mobile Support E-Commerce**
   Easy browsing and user-friendly interface are highly important; hence, multidevice capability is highly important to implement a successful ecommerce approach.

5. **Third-Party Systems and Plug-Ins**

   These help adaptability, customizations, and innovations that facilitate while developing the websites.

6. **Business Intelligence**
   Depth of transaction and browsing, taking advantage of opportunities that come up is highly important to pitch customers.

Types of E-commerce Business

- B2B: Between businesses, examples are tenders, supply of materials, etc.
- B2C: Between business and individuals, examples are Swiggy, Flipkart, Zomato, etc.

Pillars of E-commerce Business (Practices Amazon follows):
Source: Glenn Gabe August 24, 2009 (compiled by GSQI).

1. **Accessibility and Simplicity:** How easy it is to search and review the products and their information, check technical aspects and configuration, and see what other people have bought.
2. **Speed and Organization:** The speed at which the website loads, the arrangement of categories that are easy to access, and the search interface that allows you to quickly search within their key categories.
3. **Trust and Security:** In E-commerce, security is a major concern; a lack of security and confidence may be a significant obstacle to conversion.
4. **Communication and Customer Service:** Customers can conveniently locate whatever information they need on Amazon, from invoices to monitoring information to returns. Simply clicking on Your Account takes you to a self-help screen where you can perform a variety of customer service activities. Amazon allows users to perform a variety of account-related activities on their own. It is, by far, the quickest and most cost-effective way to handle Customer Service.

Computer Environments

- Internet: Global network environment
- Intranet: Government or corporate network that uses internet tools like browsers
- Extranet: Links multiple Intranets using Internet

Source: ICT technology, 2016 (compiled by Blogspot)
In e-commerce, infrastructure is the framework or backbone of the business. The types of technology included in each e-commerce infrastructure framework are depicted in the image below in three Level diagram:

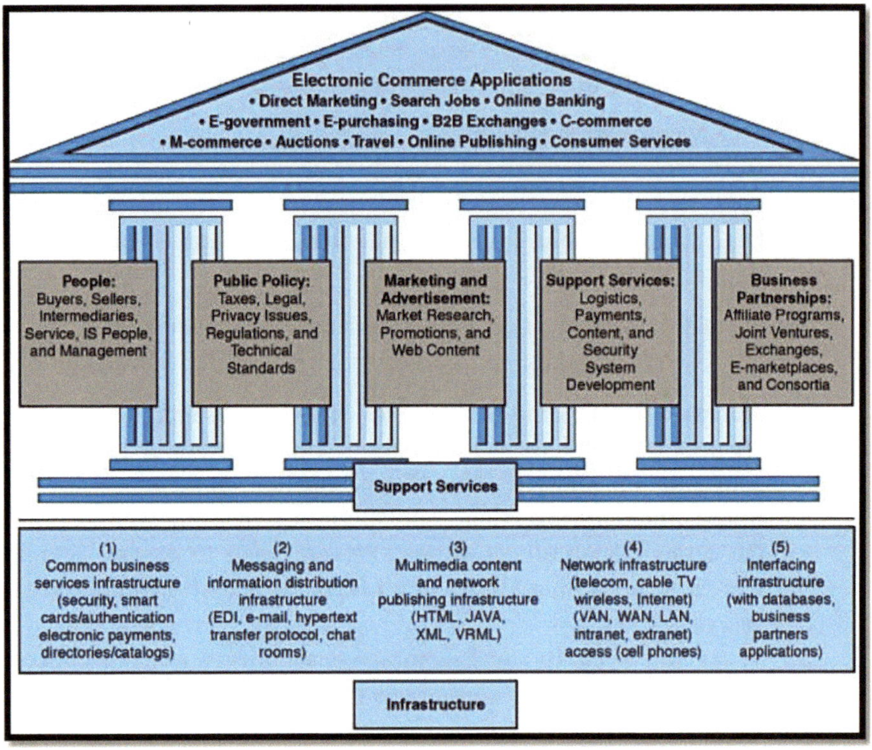

Bottom Level: Front technologies that include software or the hardware which together makes this level as one unit all together.

- Common Business Services Infrastructure: All the hardware required in the security system are placed here, for example, smart cards, authentications payment gateways. These help in maintaining the data integrity and avoid any security breach from or in the system.
- Messaging and Information Distribution Infrastructure: E-mail, HTTP, HTTPS, Chatrooms, etc., which helps distributing the information across platforms.
- Multimedia Content and Network Publishing Infrastructure: HTML, JAVA, XML, PHP, etc., which helps in CMS, i.e., Content Management Systems
- Network Infrastructure: Also known as highway that consists of LAN/VAN/WAN, Internet/Intranet/Extranet, Mobile phones, etc., which facilitates the business to be carried out.

- Interfacing Infrastructure: This combines various different modes like databases, ERP, applications together, to make system user friendly for the user.

1. **Middle Level**: Support Level services when bottom level comes together to reach out to the top level or the E-commerce applications for the end users.

   - People: Includes all the stakeholders like Buyers, Sellers, Channel Partners, Management
   - Public Policy: Policies that govern the E-commerce Businesses Ex. Taxes, legal environment, Regulations, Standards, etc.
   - Marketing and Advertisement: Marketing and Advertisement strategies adopted by the company to shape the content and the promotional offers it is giving to the customers.
   - Support Services: Includes the support services that facilitate and improve the business overall quality and brand value, for example, logistics, payment gateways, security.
   - Business Partnership: May include joint ventures, exchanges, or the marketplace coming together to sell the products. Example: Flipkart and Amazon come up with big billion sales they might tie up with certain banks to give extra discounts for the customers.

2. **Top Level**: Electronic Commerce Applications

   - Direct Marketing: Might sell products directly to customers via advertisement, promotional activities
   - Search Jobs: example Naukri.com, Indeed.com, etc.
   - Online Banking: Transactions being carried out using banking applications
   - E-Government Services: like E-Disha provides citizen services online
   - M-Commerce/E-Commerce—Interface to sell the products directly to customers via applications
   - Travel: examples like MMT provide the services
   - Online Publishing: Services from Edu-Tech companies like Unacademy, LinkedIn etc.
   - An E-commerce platform of your choice must support parameters mentioned below:
   - Robust Backend
   - Mobile-friendly or responsive E-commerce
   - E-commerce marketing (analytic tools)

An E-commerce website hosting platform must support parameters mentioned below:

- Speed: Server capacity
- Uptime: Any time, any place availability is checked by this factor
- Support: Support should not be limited to infrastructure but should support troubleshooting as well
- Scalability: Adaptive and work load balancing site that should not go down while peak hours or when overloaded
- Security: Payments and gateways should be standard compliant

10.2.2 LOYALTY PROGRAM LIFECYCLE

Every loyalty program would have a lifecycle process and if nurtured well the sustenance of the program will be on longer side. Loyalty programs are usually designed to collaborate with the customers on longer duration and they are not a, short-term plan. Various steps involved in this process are shared below:

1. Program Strategy Formulation

   This is one of the most important steps before a program is designed and formulation plays a vital role in success of the loyalty program.

   a) Formulation of Business Case: It should communicate the program benefits, highlight the objectives, and make recommendations and customer winning strategy.

      While it highlights the said benefits, it should also highlight the risk and pitfalls of the process and a change management strategy with the expected outcome from the program. Some other key points to be forecasted are mentioned below:

      - Cost of the loyalty program?
      - Implementation of manpower and time?
      - What is the risk involved?

   b) Roadmap Development: A better planning would facilitate the return on your investment, cost to company, and margin the sales budget; a good customer loyalty programme will produce large gains in recurring revenue for your company. A strategic blue print would help outlay the right picture to your team to have an effective productivity.

2. Program Design
   A program design would take care of all the aspects involved to deploy a running or a workable loyalty program. Below points would help in achieving the long-term goals.

   a) Initial Resource Allocation: Manpower required to have even work load distribution and getting the tasks done as per the agreed timeline with the customers.
   b) Features and Functionality: It should focus on what kind of technology, communication framework would be involved. The scope of the program should be exclusively called.

      - What kind of campaigns delivery is expected?
      - What are the channels and partners involved?
      - What kind of redemption benefits customer, incentives would have?

   c) Loyalty Process Preparation

      Designing and processing a program would involve the discussed resources and their productivity to close the targets and have a working model of the said loyalty design. It would also focus on customer experience procedure on the technical frontend as well as the benefits end.

      i. Technology Architecture: It focuses on the interface as well as communication channel for the customers to simplify the way around of the program and customer awareness.

         - Interface: E-commerce website, Member Portal, Mobile Application, Social Media, Customer Service, etc.
         - Communication: Designing of email, SMS, social media pages, mobile applications, surveys, forums, etc.
         - Reporting: Data modeling, CRM, data visualization, ETL (extract-transform-load) tools.

3. Program Implementation: Testing the program reporting, workarounds, and real-time environment successfulness. The program policies are formed and resources are aligned as per the tasks. Lastly the program is tested for due diligence and day-0 launch.

10.2.3 LOYALTY PROGRAM CONCEPTUAL FRAMEWORK

The below loyalty conceptual framework has been prepared based on my understanding of the actual workaround of loyalty framework in the said industry. The conceptual framework discusses how the point system is composed in the industry and the ROI (return of investment) is designed for any program.

ABC Lifestyle
Unleash Capabilities!

ABC Lifestyle is about unleashing the capabilities among target segment of various age groups. The company has four business units and a coalition loyalty program has been conceptualized for the Business ABC LifeStyle. The business will have 1 program named "ABC Rewards" under which different units would have different reward names.

Program Name: Every company/business unit has a loyalty program name that identifies the loyalty program uniquely. Program name will be different under coalition program; however, the currency used will be the same so that the customer can use the same currency across any business unit. This will help the business grow their business and improve the customer experience.

Currency Name: Every loyalty program would have its own currency name. In a coalition program the currency name would be the same but the program name would differ as the currency would be valid across the business to enhance business functionality and revenue generation.

Currency Value: Currency value might differ from business to business as per the market research and customer demand and supply. The ROI for every point might be more or less as per the market research and consumer ask.

Earn/Burn Rule: These rules define events or triggers when a customer would earn points in any organization and when and how can they use/burn these points. No segmentation is required in these points as it treats all the customers equally.

The company has four business units as mentioned below:

1. QSR (Quick Service Restaurant): Deals in Quick Burger delivery
    - Reward Name: QSR Rewards
    - Currency Name: ABC Rewards
    - Currency Value: 1 ABC Point = 1 Rupees
    - Earn Rule: 10 Spent = 2 ABC Points
    - Burn Rule: 2 ABC Points = 2 Rupees
2. ABC Fashions (Multi-Brand Outlet): It is a multi-brand fashion outlet that comprises various clothing brands
    - Reward Name: MBO Rewards
    - Currency Name: ABC Rewards
    - Currency Value: 1 ABC Point = 1 Rupees
    - Earn Rule: 10 Spent = 2 ABC Points
    - Burn Rule: 2 ABC Points = 2 Rupees
3. ABC Living (Multi-Speciality Hospitals): Has hospital with multiple speciality functionality.
    - Reward Name: MSH Rewards
    - Currency Name: ABC Rewards
    - Currency Value: 1 ABC Point = 1 Rupees
    - Earn Rule: 10 Spent = 2 ABC Points
    - Burn Rule: 2 ABC Points = 2 Rupees
4. ABC SPA (SPA Wellness Chain): Has various types of SPA's
    - Reward Name: SWC Rewards
    - Currency Name: ABC Rewards
    - Currency Value: 1 ABC Point = 1 Rupees
    - Earn Rule: 10 Spent = 2 ABC Points
    - Burn Rule: 2 ABC Points = 2 Rupees

- Tag Line: Unleash Capabilities

    Partnership and Offerings

    The company can partner with various channel partners to increase their customer acquisition and average transaction value or the basket value.

    1. Credit Card Companies: HDFC/ICICI can be linked with the organization and ABC Reward points can be used with CC company to encash the benefits at various platforms. Vice versa, partner bank's points can be redeemed in the ABC Lifestyle environment.

2. Airlines Partnership: ABC Lifestyle points can be redeemed in partner airline environment and vice versa can be implemented to enjoy the greater benefit in the coalition program.
    - Collaboration with OLA/Uber: ABC Lifestyle employees can be dependent upon the employee benefit program or the loyalty program company offers them, which in return would help them curb the attrition rate of the organization.

Communication Framework

Customer Engagement Platforms: Various platforms can be sought out so that customer analytics can be carried out and feedback mechanism to improve organizations reach be worked upon.

- Discussion Forums
- Social Media
- Live chat
- Automatic Call-back
- SMS Text Support
- Self Service Sites
- Mobile App
- Customer Portal
- Customer Satisfaction Surveys

10.2.4 LOYALTY COMMUNICATION TRIGGERS

Events that trigger to pitching loyalty schemes to customers.

- Joining Bonus: Customers can be awarded when they join the reward program of the company.
- Profile Update: When customers updated the profile in mobile application or the website, they can be awarded with the points so that customer acquisition can be improved.
- Transaction SMS: Loyalty benefits can be communicated when the customer makes the transaction and next bonus points can be communicated to increase the repeat purchases from the customers.
- Customer Activeness: If the customer is inactive from long time, "We miss you" messages can be sent or push notifications to bring them back to the platforms. Email/SMS can be way out used to outreach this.

Loyalty Notifications

The notifications mentioned below are multi-platform and can be segregated day-wise so that the customer is not bothered too much with similar type of notifications in single day.

The notifications can be held on platforms mentioned below:

- Push Notifications
- In-App
- SMS
- Email
- Campaigns

The said platforms can trigger notifications on the events mentioned below:

- **My Order**: Loyalty programs can be pitched in if the customer makes the purchases and cross selling can be proposed to increase the Average Transaction Value of a biller.
- **Reminders**:
  - **Items in cart**: We miss you messages to push the purchase from the customer and increase the Average basket Value of the customer.
  - **Subscriptions**: Update regarding the new products launched to create a pull strategy from the business.
  - **Restock**: Notification of restocking toward the customers Wishlist.
  - **Discounts**: Customers can be pitched for any kind of discounts, offers, schemes to drive sale.
- **Recommendations**: Can be made based on customer interest, offers can be driven or recommendations can be made based on customer's purchase history. This will keep the customer engaged and will increase the average transaction/basket value.
  - Offers based on interest
  - Offers to complete your purchases
  - Offers on products similar to past purchases
- **New Offers**: Creating customer acquisition techniques and pitching the offers, deals, discounts and the sales for the customer.
  - Welcome Offers
  - Deals, Discounts, and Sale

Customer Interaction Framework (SMS)

		Customer interaction templates
Day	**Activity**	**SMS**
0	Transacting SMS	Thank you for shopping with ABC Lifestyle. Hope you loved the purchased product and had an amazing time shopping with us. You have earned XX Pts. And your Total Point Bal is XX
1	Profile update	Dear Customer, update your profile and get discount voucher of Rs. XX valid at any ABC Lifestyle store on selected items.
3	Feedback	Dear Customer, Thank you for shopping with us. Please share your valuable feedback <Link>. This will help us in improving. Thank You
5	Referral program	Refer a friend and Get a coupon worth Rs. XX/-*. The coupon will be valid on minimum purchase of Rs. XXX. Click *link* to refer. T&C Apply
15	Profile completion (if not completed)	Dear Customer, update your profile and get discount voucher of Rs. XX valid at any ABC Lifestyle store on selected items.
30	Total points balance	Your ABC Loyalty points are XXX for the month of <Current Month> and redeemed points are XXX. Visit any of our stores or www.ABC Lifestyle.co, to shop more and earn points. T&C
45	We miss you message (if not active on app for long time)	We miss you at ABC Lifestyle! To get you shopping again, here's an exciting offer for you. Get XXXX bonus points on min. purchase of Rs. XXXX. Click <Link>. T&C
60	Repurchase message	Avail exciting benefits with ABC Lifestyle by investing Rs. 10,000 per month. Click <Link> to know more. T&C

Customer Interaction Framework (EMAIL)

		Customer interaction templates
Day	**Activity**	**EMAIL**
0	Transacting SMS	Hi <Customer Name>, We are pleased to inform you that your order has been placed. Thank you for shopping with us! Hope you loved the purchased product and had an amazing time shopping with us. You have earned XX Pts. And your Total Point Bal is XX How likely is it that you would recommend us to a friend or a colleague? Please rate us on a scale of 0–10 <SCALE 0–10> Mention the order details *For wrong quantity, damaged or missing items, please report the issue within 2 days of receiving the product. For returns, replacements, and other queries please visit FAQs or contact Customer Support.*

Customer interaction templates		
Day	**Activity**	**EMAIL**
2	Profile update	Dear Customer, Thank you for joining with us! Please Update your profile and get discount voucher of Rs. XX valid at any ABC Lifestyle store on selected items. *For any queries, please visit FAQs or contact Customer Support.*
0	Feedback	Feedback embedded in Transaction Email
6	Referral program	Dear Customer, Get coupon worth Rs. XXX when you refer a friend. The coupon will be valid on minimum purchase of Rs. XXX. Click *link* to refer. T&C Apply *For any queries please visit FAQs or contact Customer Support.*
10	Profile completion (If not completed)	Dear Customer, You are almost there! Update your profile and get discount voucher of Rs. XX valid at any ABC Lifestyle store on selected items. *For any queries, please visit FAQs or contact Customer Support.*
25	Total points balance	Dear Customer, Your ABC Loyalty points are XXX for the month of <Current Month> and redeemed points are XXX. You can also check your transaction history by visiting <Link>. You can use your ABC Rewards balance for subsequent purchases on <Link> till expiry. *If you have any questions please visit www.amazon.in/help to call or e-mail us*
40	We miss you message (If not active on app for long time)	Dear Customer, We miss you at ABC Lifestyle! To get you shopping again, here's an exciting offer for you. Get XXXX bonus points on minimum purchase of Rs. XXXX. Click <Link>. T&C *If you have any questions please visit www.amazon.in/help to call or e-mail us*
55	Repurchase message	Dear Customer, Avail exciting benefits with ABC Lifestyle by investing Rs. 10,000 per month. Click <Link> to know more. T&C *If you have any questions please visit www.amazon.in/help to call or e-mail us*

Loyalty + E-commerce Business Structure

<table>
<tr><th colspan="4">Customer experience management system</th></tr>
<tr><td>Interface</td><td colspan="2">Unified profile
Members | segments | registered | tiers</td><td>Communication</td></tr>
<tr><td>Member portal</td><td colspan="2">CRM
Masters | rules | policies</td><td>Email/SMS</td></tr>
<tr><td>Mobile app</td><td>Offers
Discounts | GV's | coupons</td><td>Points
Earn | burn | rewards</td><td>Social platforms</td></tr>
<tr><td>Social</td><td colspan="2">ROI modeling
Loyalty programs | offerings</td><td>Mobile app</td></tr>
<tr><td>Customer service</td><td colspan="2">Analytics
Transactions | events | basket value | notifications</td><td>Feedback/review/ surveys</td></tr>
</table>

10.2.5 CONCEPT RETURN OF INVESTMENT PLAN

ROI Plan Conditions

- From conceptual program presented above, a budget of 2.5% investment from margins is permissible by stakeholders to cover all the costs of the loyalty program.
- ROI—3–5X of 2.5% of the cost
- Quick Service Restaurant Chain—Quick Burger
  - Unit Price Ranges: 25–10 Rs.
  - Average Transaction Value (ATV)—150–300 Rs.
  - Sales—50 L per month
- Multi Brand Outlet Chain—ABC Fashions
  - Unit Price Ranges: 500–5000 Rs.
  - Average Transaction Value (ATV)—1300–5000 Rs.
  - Sales—20 CR per Month
- Multi-Speciality Hospitals—ABC living
  - Sales—50 K per month
- Wellness Chain—ABC SPA
  - Types of SPA—6
  - Types of Packages—4
  - SPA Cost: 5–7000 (Discount: 30–35%)
  - Packages: 15–25,000 (50% on rack rate)
  - Sales (Each SPA): 25 L per month

ROI Plan Assumptions

- Per spent—10
- Points—2
- Value (RS)—1
- On an average 30% of the Pts. are availed by the customers and 70% are not availed
- Cost to Company—Cost to company for each point is 15% and 85% is margin from the consumed points
- Conclusion—ROI calculated basis point or the value of the points, the business shall be able to meet the ROI between 3 and 5X

ROI Formula Used

- ROI = (Gain from Investment – Cost of Investment)/Cost of Investment

10.2.6 STRATEGIES ADOPTED IN LOYALTY MARKET FOR E-COMMERCE BUSINESS

Mufti (Post Lockdown Plan and Strategy)

Pre-COVID Customer Engagement goals that were designed based on push and pull strategy or the other strategies as per the market research were held obsolete and the new strategies were developed considering the business ramp-up post COVID and the strategies and the plan the organizations would need to increase the customer transactional value as well as create safe strategies to bring customers to the offline stores as well.

Onboarding—Strategy took a paradigm shift toward customer experiences and their gaining their trust. The communication strategy was to bring customer awareness toward safety measures and communication COVID-specific measures deployed by the company.

Earlier the brand used to focus on Transaction Value day +7 days target to create pull strategy via loyalty programs to facilitate the customer repeat visit.

"The Now Strategy"—The company changed their focus toward "the now" strategy, i.e., instant gratification of customers. The concentration shifted toward higher "Average Basket Value" while the customer was in the store or in the online shopping platform, i.e., E-commerce platform.

Pareto Rule—Budget constraint will force brands to nurture 20% of their customers to account for 80% of the sale or the conversions.

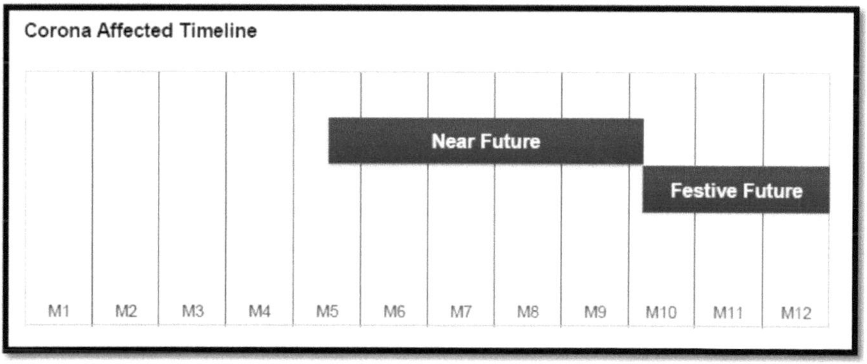

	A	B	C	D	E	F	G	H	I
1		Average Unit Price	ABV	Monthly Sales	Total Bills	2.5% of monthly sales (Max allowed pts. capacity)	Per Spent	Points	Value
2	Multi Brand Outlet	2750	3150	200000000	63492.063	5000000	100	2	1
3	Quick Service Restaurant	75	225	5000000	22222.222	125000	100	2	1
4	Multi Speciality Hospital			50000	NA	1250	100	2	1
5	Wellness SPA			15000000	NA	375000	100	2	1
6	Sum			220050000		5501250			
7									
8									
9			ABV	Monthly Sales	Total Bills	2.5% of monthly sales (Max allowed pts. capacity)	Per Spent	Points	Value
10			3150	200000000		5000000			
11			225	5000000		125000			
12			Unavailable	50000		1250			
13			Unavailable	15000000		375000			

Value	Total Redeemable Pts	Value of redeemable Pts.	Margin points	Assumption (30% will avail)	70% unavailed	15% cost of investment	85% Margin/Gain	ROI
1	2000000	2000000	3000000	600000	1400000	90000	510000	4.666667
1	50000	50000	75000	15000	35000	2250	12750	4.666667
1	500	500	750	150	350	22.5	127.5	4.666667
1	150000	150000	225000	45000	105000	6750	38250	4.666667
	2200500	2200500	3300750	660150	1540350			
				0.003	0.007			
	If total Redeemable is calculated basis value instead Points							
Value	Total Redeemable Pts	Value of redeemable Pts.	Margin points	Assumption (30% will avail)	70% unavailed	15% cost of investment	85% Margin/Gain	ROI
	63492.06349	63492.06349	4936507.937	19047.61905	44444.44444	2857.142857	16190.47619	4.666667
	22222.22222	22222.22222	102777.7778	6666.666667	15555.55556	1000	5666.666667	4.666667
	Cannot be calculated as ABV is not given							
	Cannot be calculated as ABV is not given							

Mufti planned: We will need quick win solutions for near future while gearing up for big customer engagement campaigns for the festive future.

Considering the lockdown till month 9, they hypothesized that the festive season would automatically create a pull strategy among the customers and the basket value will increase as well if market reopens.

Four key goals toward "the now" strategy:

1. Soft Goal:
   - Win Customer Trust
2. Business KPI's:
   - On-spot conversion with higher ABV (Average Basket Value)
   - Personalized offers
   - Brand-specific Goals

10.2.7 CUSTOMER ENGAGEMENT STRATEGIES

Education outreach on safety measures: Customer awareness plays a vital role in customer engagement strategies; hence, the brand focused on sending customized as well as safety measured messages, emails to the customer to create awareness toward them.

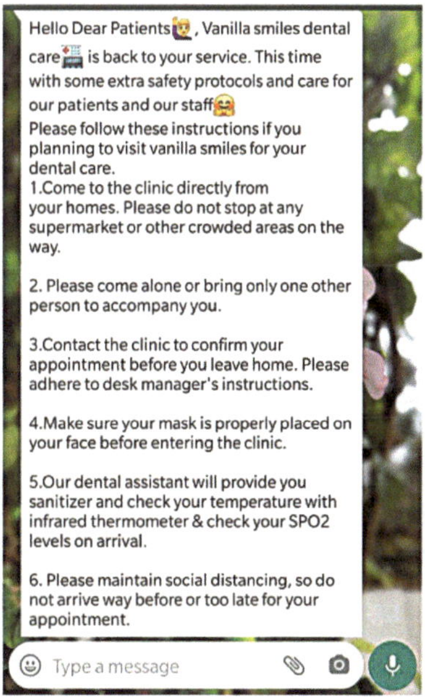

Instant Redemption Rewards: As a part of instant gratification methodology the brand focused on awarding their customer real time to increase the customers' purchase capacity as well as basket value. This would lead to winning customers real time and will improve the conversion rate of the business and the purchases.

- Utilize missed call to trigger same day rewards' when customers give a missed call by seeing an advertisement in the store or when they wait in the queue, trigger a coupon to motivate customers to make the purchase
- When the customer has made an appointment using WhatsApp, incentivize customer by giving discount coupon to ensure visit. This will facilitate repeat purchases and increased basket value as well as transaction value
- Use of gamification tools
    - Spin the wheel to get an instant coupon
- Scan an in-store QR code to play and win

Benefits for Higher Value Segments: Tier-based programs for their customers and tier-based gratification. This will lead to higher value for the loyal customers in the organization.

- Increasing points validity that might lapse
- Tier wise/spent benefits availing discount coupons

New business models to reach customers: New loyalty programs were introduced considering the market change and expected shift post COVID.

- Selling gift cards to the customers on discounted rate to generate revenue
- Spin the wheel and scratch card contest campaign for all the customers and give bonus points with validity
- Take feedback from customers post transaction on overall product/services
- Coalition Programs—giving program benefits beyond parent brand with the help of strategic alliance with other organizations to benefit the businesses
- Alliance with Flipkart Super-coin exchange program to channelize or improve the customer acquisition methodology.

BATA:

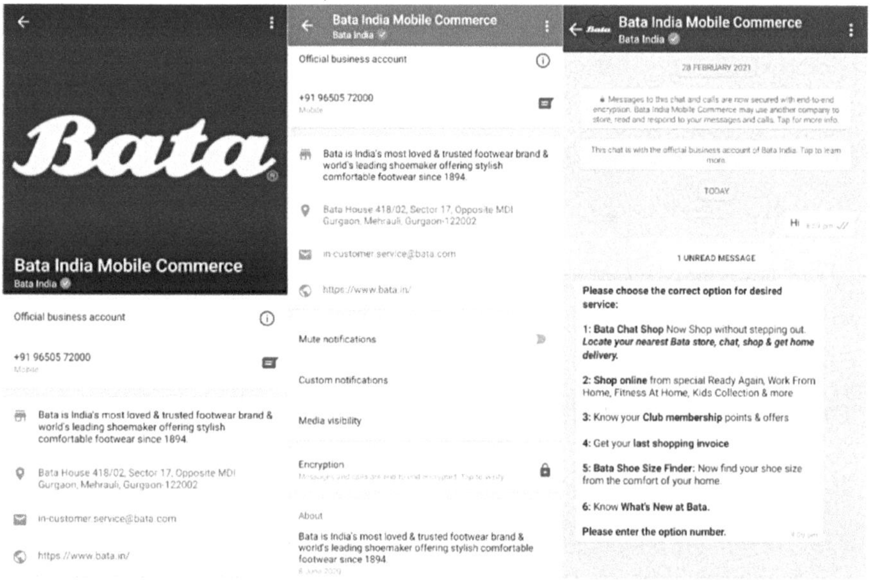

Spencer's

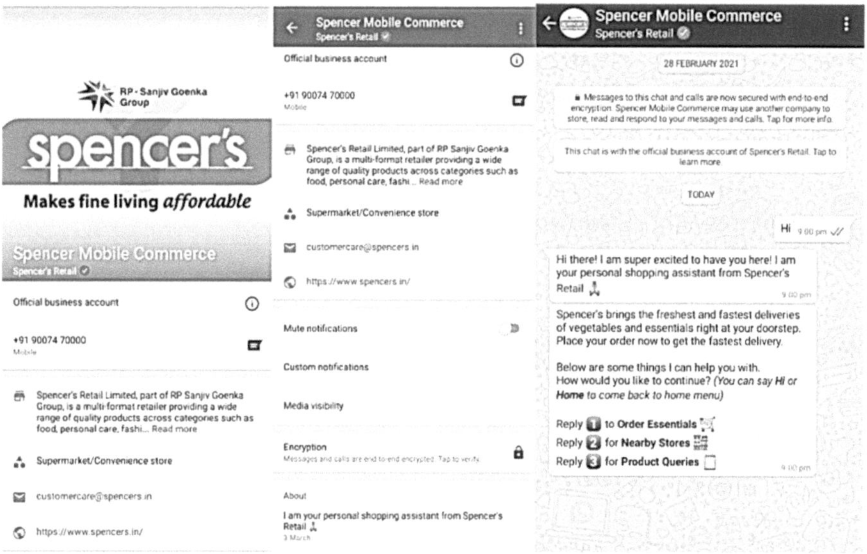

Both the brands BATA and SPENCER's have established Mobile commerce successfully and have innovatively brought e-commerce business to customer ease.

10.3 OBJECTIVES OF THE STUDY

To study the E-commerce and Loyalty Programs framework

To develop a conceptual framework of E-commerce Loyalty Framework

To study the strategies adopted in loyalty Programs for E-commerce Business

10.4 RESEARCH METHODOLOGY

10.4.1 SECONDARY DATA

The research is conducted based on the acquired secondary data or the strategies that were implemented real time in the organizations. Actual organization framework has been discussed with the examples.

A conceptual framework has been developed as to how industry works and has been showcased as learning.

10.4.2 DATA TYPE

Basis research papers, case studies, articles, and news articles have been showcased. Some of the concepts have been developed based on the learning and the real-time structure of the company.

10.5 FINDINGS AND SUGGESTIONS

10.5.1 FINDINGS

- **E-commerce Framework**
  - **Aggregation of the data:** Data is consolidated using various ETL tools
  - **Cleaning of data:** Outliers and irrelevant data are removed

- **Processing of the data:** A set of marketing tags are generated post data cleaning
- **Modeling:** Statistical models are created to study the consumer behavior
- **Reporting:** Data visualization, consumer insights, campaign ROI dashboards are prepared

• **Customer Lifecycle in Loyalty Program**

- **Enrol**: Customer acquisition is facilitated
- **Accrued with Brand**: Onboarding, customer engagement and marketing planning to associate customer with the brand is done
- **Accrued with Partner**: Campaign management, enrolment under partners
- **Redeem with the brand**: Program design, customer value management, redemption management
- **Redeem with the Partner**: Execute and track, reporting
- **Change Tier**: Customer activity is managed and basis purchase capacity tier is assigned
- **Share Experience**: Feedback mechanism, Change Management, Client Servicing

• **Mufti Post COVID Plan**

- Average Transaction value (ATV) saw rise from INR 2804 to 3875
- A jewellery brand saw rise of 114% in Average Transaction Value
- A footwear brand saw rise of 24% in Average Transaction value.

• **Customer Retention Strategies/Repeat Purchase Methodologies**:

- **Higher value segment customers**: Point validity is being increased for the 20% of the people who brings in 80% of the business

- **Lower Segment customers**: Decoy effect is being implemented and discount coupons are given to increase the customer spent capacity. This will help in tier upgradation of the customers from base tier to upgraded tier.
- **Instant Gratification Ideas**: On-spot conversions with Gamification tools such as spin the wheel, scratch the card, and instant rewarding ways like scan the QR code for discounts are being used to create pull strategy among the customers
- **Coalition Program**: Coalition program increases ROI for the businesses with the help of partnerships, unified point mechanism system in organizations.
- **Mobile/Electronic Commerce**: Businesses have used E-commerce as well as M-commerce as platform and strategy toward customer education against COVID as well as E-commerce business
- **Lead/Demand Generation**: Using Digital marketing platforms via E-commerce demand generation (SEO, SEM, SMM, SMO) is being worked upon, post COVID. Staying connected with the customer via emails, texts, calls, etc.

10.5.2 SUGGESTIONS

- **Mufti or any other brands-**
  - **In-Store Videos**: Can create In-Store videos of safety measures that should include store sanitization measures, product sanitization messages after trial by customers, thermal checking of store staff and customers entering the stores.
  - **Good to have**: No trial policy and no return policy
  - **Video links:** Links of said sanitization and other precautionary to be shared with customers which will motivate them to visit the stores.
  - **In Store Communication**: Poster/Standees of Do's and Don'ts for staff as well as for the customers
  - **Encourage:** Contactless payments/digital payments

- **Coalition Programs:** Companies to focus on concept framework or the coalition programs like Flipkart Exchange for unified customer gratification. Such programs will create pull strategies and will increase the purchase capacity as well as diversified business depth. Customers will be able to burn the earned points across businesses.
- **Augmented Shopping**: Try before you buy, applications to help customers visualize and try before they make the purchase. Same can be incorporated in the applications as well as stores to increase efficiency and reduce manpower for any business
- **Staff Free and Cashier Less Stores**: RFID tags, computer vision systems, machine learning, IoT devices, and facial recognitions can be used to increase productivity and efficiency of the business
- **Voice Commerce**: Customer can use voice commands to find products rather interface. Basket enabling option making the purchase and payments can be made easy
- **Robotics**: Delivery robots like Amazon Scout to deliver products, drone capabilities can be looked into

10.6 CONCLUSION

Loyalty market in India is still unexplored and customer awareness toward the programs is limited. Millennials are limitedly aware of the loyalty business in India despite they using some or the other programs or being enrolled in some or the other manner. E-commerce platforms have widely taken market from offline store shopping to online shopping. While it is important post COVID to consider safety first, it is equally important to gratify customers with a better loyalty program and to educate them toward the safety measures being followed by the brands.

Customer education is utmost important at the moment for any brand to grow and make the repeat customer visit to their stores. Average Transaction Value can be increased with the help of better redemption mechanisms; however, transaction value is observed to be widely increased by the loyal customers. The customers who are not so far loyal to the brand can be brought in by making offers that make them shop as well as change their tiers to trust the brands.

The future of E-commerce business in India is low; however, it can be improved with better strategies and customer awareness. Millennials can be targeted which would be new segment of customers to online shopping business.

10.7 LIMITATIONS OF THE STUDY

- The research study is restricted to E-commerce and Loyalty framework, further study can be done in E-commerce Automation
- Further research may also include change management in E-commerce Business due to COVID
- Statistical or primary data has not been curated in the report. Extensive analysis and in-depth analysis can be done
- ROI model can be further improvised considering various other factors and integrations considered in Loyalty Programs

KEYWORDS

- **COVID-19 impact on loyalty businesses globalization**
- **Covid-19 shock**
- **production**
- **e-commerce business strategies**
- **welfare affect**

REFERENCES

Apruve. E Commerce Advantages and Disadvantages. July 21, 2017. blog.apruve

CCSU. Ecommerce Framework, Intactone (Jan 9, 2019)

Cook, W. A. Strive for Loyal Brands, then Loyal Consumers. *J. Advertis. Res.* **1996,** *36*(6), 6–7.

Ganesh, J.; Reynolds, K. E.; Luckett, M.; Pomirleanu, N. Online Shopper Motivations, and e-Store Attributes: An Examination of Online Patronage Behavior and Shopper Typologies. *J. Retail.* **2010,** *86*(1), 106–115.

(Aug 24, 2009).

(2016)

Kooser, A. C. Online Loyalty Programs. *Restaurant Bus.* **2009,** *108*(11), 18.

Oliver, R. L. Whence Consumer Loyalty? *J. Market.* **1999,** *63*(4), 33–44. (April 2020)
Pilík M. On-Line Shopping on B2C Markets in the Czech Republic. *J. Competi.* **2012,** *4*(4), 36–49.
SaaSQuatch (-), Loyalty ROI: What do your acquisition rewards cost?, SaaSQuatch
Šipula, P. Jak nakupuje internetová populace v e-shopech. STRATEGIE.CZ. [Online] 2013. http://strategie.e15.cz/zurnal/ stem-mark-jak-nakupuje-internetova-populace-v-eshopech-980943 (accessed Mar 24, 2014).
StĜíteský, V. Internet jako globální marketingové médium. In: Baþuvþík, R., aj. Globální a lokální ,v marketingové komunikaci. Zlín, 2013.
Tomek, I.; StĜíteský, V.; Tahal, R. Segmentation of Czech Consumers Based on the Attitudes Towards Money. *Central Eur. Bus. Rev.* **2013,** *2*(2), 19–24.
Verma, D.; Mehla, H. A Study on E-Commerce – Conceptual Framework & Future Potential in India. *Int. J. Eng. Appl. Manage. Sci. Paradigms.* **2014,** *13*(01).

CHAPTER 11

Farm Trials as an Effective Extension Management Method for Faster Varietal Knowledge and Diffusion

SWATI NAYAK[1*] and RITESH DWIVEDI[2]

[1]*Amity Institute of Competitive Intelligence and Strategic Management, Faculty of Management Studies, Amity University, Noida 201301, Uttar Pradesh, India*

[2]*Amity Business School, Faculty of Management Studies, Amity University, Noida 201301, Uttar Pradesh, India*

[*]*Corresponding author. E-mail: swati.non@gmail.com*

ABSTRACT

This chapter discusses how on-farm trials conducted in agriculture research and development programmes can play a critical role in strengthening agriculture extension. This method by making the new technology validated in farmer field condition provides evidence around the realistic potential and impact of technology. This model can play a key role in ensuring knowledge and scaling of new technology through learning by doing. Since the time of green revolution, introduction and scaling of modern crop varieties remain as critical technological intervention in agriculture. However, if looked at most staple crop, rice, the varietal replacement rate that is essential for productivity gain remains very poor in entire South Asia including India. Despite new varieties being developed consistently, farmers continue to grow older germplasm. This calls for robust extension programmes that ensure the varietal knowledge and awareness reach

Constructive Discontent in Execution: Creative Approaches to Technology and Management.
Sanjeev Bansal, Anita Venaik, Swati Upveja, and Saritha S. (Eds.)

to farmers and the farmers are motivated for making adoption decisions. On-farm trials, serving as a comparative method to test the performance of a new variety against the older variety grown by farmers, can provide contextualized evidence for adoption decision. This chapter describes one such study (a randomized control experiment) conducted in India that evaluates the effectiveness of farm trials to popularize, spread, and adopt new climate-resilient rice varieties. Conducted across 128 villages in eastern Indian rice-growing ecology, this study establishes farm trials as a strong extension model apart from being a scientific platform for data generation.

11.1 INTRODUCTION

11.1.1 HISTORICAL AND CURRENT CONTEXT

11.1.1.1 VARIETAL REPLACEMENT SCENARIO

In the context of crop varietal development and advancement programmes of populous countries of South Asia, namely, India and Bangladesh, researchers have contributed in development of several hundreds of varieties. However, when we look at the number of products/varieties available in seed chain, constantly demanded, and used by the farmers, the results are very limited. This raises a big question on the effectiveness of extension and delivery of these products from lab to land, their dissemination and adoption. In India, for the major crops like wheat and rice, 60% of seed demand is distributed among only approximately two dozen varieties (Singh, 2015). This remains as global concern where the seed indenting trend shows dominance of only few and older varieties in seed chain (Singh et al., 2020). This is amid a scenario where scientists have developed around thousands of varieties and hundreds are reflected in seed chain. In South Asia, India has just above 40 varieties capturing more than 80% of seed demand (seednet.gov.in) and the other populous agrarian country Bangladesh has only around 30 varieties reflecting prominently in seed demand indents on a 3 years' average. Maximum of these varieties are 10 years and older and there are many varieties whose ages go up to 40 years. This indicates a very poor rate of product replacement and dissemination even though several hundreds of newer products have been developed for millions of farmers inhabiting diverse markets and ecologies.

11.1.1.2 THE IMPORTANCE OF VARIETAL PROGRAMMES IN AGRICULTURE

When we talk about specific agriculture technology, the development and use of high yielding varieties in agrarian nations have been established as the major critical factor for success in perspective of income and productivity gain for small holder farmers (Besley and Case, 1993) in developing nations. The South Asia's green revolution and its long-lasting impact is primarily entrusted on development, mass dissemination, and use of HYVs of rice and wheat, and hence, there remains a lot of thrust for the subject in the agriculture research arena. Apart from enhanced farm productivity and income, in many regions, the use of the HYVs has contributed toward strengthening non-farm economy and service sector as well (Hazell et al., 1993).

While varietal programmes have historical impact and contribution growth in agriculture and economy, over the last decade, scientists have invested in developing multiple climate resilient and high yielding varieties to mitigate the climate change risks associated with farming practices. Popularly known as STRVs (stress-tolerant rice varieties) these products have shown several evidence of ground impact. This has been studied, how climate change induced changes in the form of recurrent flood drought can make the farming systems fragile and how these recent developments of STRVs through breeding program are the potential solution forward (Dar et al., 2014). Several STRVs are developed from the most popular modern mega varieties through various gene incorporation and how there is increasing thrust of public system programmes on these products (Mackill et al., 2012).

While the diversity of products/varieties has expanded with several impact potentials ahead, the varietal replacement and adoption rate remains concern for all products across. This is reflected through stagnant productivity for major food crops. While analyzing pre and post green revolution scenarios, it has been reported around the stagnant yield rates in crops like wheat and rice in modern/post green revolution era (Ahmad and Haseen, 2012). Several studies raise this concern over slow varietal uptake and replacement in India despite HYV development being in a much accelerated manner (Janaiah et al., 2006). To bring the momentum of pre-green revolution era and accelerate varietal adoption, agriculture extension management/technology transfer systems are going to play a critical role for years ahead.

11.1.1.3 ROLE OF EXTENSION IN ACCELERATING VARIETAL ADOPTION

Agriculture extension management plays a critical role in ensuring spread of awareness, knowledge around product and technology use, its dissemination and scaling. The extension management practices establish the much-needed critical linkage between researchers and delivery of technology and impact at farmer field. It has been studied in detail that extension especially information access, participatory demonstrations, and trainings play critical role in popularization of varieties and subsequently their adoption (Ghimire et al., 2015). These become more important in the context of developing nations where most of the agriculture technology are yet to realize their envisaged impact goals (Faltermeier and Abdulai, 2009).

The current agriculture development programmes require redefined roles and capacity in extension and a more adaptive extension innovation system in the course of climate change and other complexities having arrived (Davis and Sulaiman, 2014). There are studies that establish adaptive and collaborative approaches in natural resource governance as very effective mean toward learning, knowledge production, stakeholder participation. This being equipped with institutional innovations are elements of successful extension innovation in developmental initiatives (McDougall et al., 2015).

While extension management has a key role to play for varietal adoption, varieties are critical products in agriculture input market that needs a robust product management system. This product management must include right strategy for product positioning and advancement as well as a life cycle management. The product positioning and advancement is only possible if the additional values from these products are identified and realized by the key stakeholders, especially the end user farmers. There lies a difference between the potential value of a product and the realized value of the product. While potential value depends on many idealistic contexts, the realized value is dependent on realistic and contexts that exist at farmer field/users. To create this learning, knowledge for a sustained adoption of product can be the core of new extension management strategy for spread of varietal knowledge and learning.

This paper studies the effect of such modern extension methods in accelerating knowledge and learning about a variety as compared to traditional programmes. This method is an improvised on farm trials called as comparative on farm trials or Head to Head Trial.

11.2 FARM TRIALS AND THE STUDY IN FOCUS

11.2.1 ON-FARM TRIAL, AS A KEY MODEL OF INTERVENTION

On-farm trialling of various agriculture technology, tool, products, and practices has been long considered one of the methods for scientific and reliable data generation. While in agricultural technology testing and advancement process, several researchers organize multi-staged research in research stations, the actual and realistic impact of a new technology can only be experienced and validated in farmer field. However, traditional and popular methods of varietal demonstrations are also carried out in farmers' field. However, these methods miss on contextual, comparative, participatory learning, and are mostly maintained in an idealistic condition. Neither these traditional methods generate reliable and scientific data and evidence for scientists to validate, nor farmers get enough opportunity for contextual learning and exposure. Therefore, comparative on farm trialling or popularly could act as a method for not only comparative performance evaluation of a new variety but also generate reliable evidence and learning at farmers' level for critical adoption decision and varietal choices.

A farm trial can vary in its lay-outs, while the basic principle is woven around comparative and experiential learning method, where a new variety is tested against old variety grown by farmers. The number of varieties tested at a site may vary. Based on the rate of inflow of new and promising products in a particular variety, extensionists can introduce multiple test varieties to farmers. A multi-strip farm trial can compare multiple new varieties against farmer variety. The simplest form of farm trialling is head to head trial (H2H) consisting of one new variety against one farmer variety. Farm trial is executed in an individual farmer field. In this comparative method (in the simplest form, head to head trials), two varieties are grown side by side in the same plot under same management practices. Out of these two varieties, one is a new variety and the other one is a locally popular, old variety already grown by the farmer. Apart from generating evidence around varietal performances, these trials can also act as a unique way of demonstrating varietal performance in farmer field and provide a comparative learning experience for farmers, neighbor, and more stakeholders visiting the plot. A season-long observation will help farmers to either select or reject a new variety against his/her own old variety.

11.3 A RANDOMIZED CONTROL EXPERIMENT TO EVALUATE THE EFFECTIVENESS OF FARM TRIAL AS EXTENSION METHOD

A randomized control experiment was conducted to evaluate the effectiveness of farm trials as a key extension method that could enhance knowledge, awareness about new varieties. This study was conducted in one of the predominant rice-rowing ecologies in Eastern India, i.e., the state of Odisha. The region being one of the most climatically vulnerable belts is in need of aggressive promotion, scaling, and adoption of newly developed climate-resilient rice varieties. These climate-resilient varieties are popularly known as stress-tolerant rice varieties (STRVs). To build system resilience against climate change-induced threats and make the farmers less vulnerable, several government initiatives in recent times emphasize on popularization of such varieties. This study considered climate-resilient variety as the technological intervention, farm trial as the method of extension that introduces the technology. The experiment was designed to measure the causal effects of various factors and interventions (popularly known as "treatments"). To keep the experiment free from any biases, under varietal introduction, only one STRV, namely, BINA Dhan 11 was kept as constant across the experiment.

Random selection of villages was carried out in one of the predominant rice-growing states of India. A detailed census survey was carried across the selected villages to collect information of all the households and identify the rice-growing men and women farmers. From the census data, the sample farmers were selected through randomization who received various treatments and who were in control groups. They were studied over a period of time. A total of three treatment groups and three control groups were part of the study and comparison through baseline and end line surveys was done. A total sample of 128 villages were studied with five farmers from each village participating in this experiment. To avoid spill over effect, one village comprised either of one control or treatment group alone, i.e., all the farmers in that village were from same treatment or control group.

This experiment also measured the gendered impact of extension by evaluating the response of men versus women farmers after receiving the treatment and who was more effective is dissemination or acquiring knowledge and learning of the new variety.

There are several evidence in last many decades in countries like India and Bangladesh, most of the public programmes have invested in women's network and social capital by leveraging the presence of thousands of millions women self-help groups (SHGs) which are collectives of individual and homogenous women mobilized for various income generation activities including farming. This study also studies the effect of working with such collectives for new extension methods.

11.3.1 THE EXPERIMENTAL DESIGN

The treatment and control groups under the experiments were, **T1** representing women farmers, who are member of women self-help group, growing new STRV in H2H trials; **T2** representing women farmers, who are not member of any women group, growing new STRV in H2H trials; **T3** representing men farmer growing introduced STRVs in head-to-head trials. The corresponding control groups for comparison and measuring differential effect were, **C1** representing women farmers, who are member of women self-help group, growing new STRVs in random fashion in any appropriate plot; **C2** representing women farmers, who are not member of any women group, growing new STRV in a random fashion in any appropriate plots; **C3** representing men farmer growing introduced STRVs in a random fashion in any appropriate plots. One village had only one type of group out of six groups (T1/T2/T3/C1/C2/C3).

11.3.2 OBJECTIVES AND SAMPLE FRAME

The key objectives of this experiment were primarily to evaluate the effect of innovative extension management method, i.e., head-to-head trials in farmer field on awareness, and diffusion of the new variety; also to find how the effects varied based on gender of farmer and to find how the effects varied based on farmers' socio-political affiliations.

The analyzed sample of this study consisted of six groups of respondents (T1, T2, T3, C1, C2, C3) as defined above in treatment and control group definition (Fig. 11.1). Originally the respondents/participant farmers were distributed across 128 villages (5 farmers per village): however, due to the weather-related challenges resulting failure of crop stand and other few unanticipated issues like migration or nonavailability of farmers in survey period, the studied respondents were 659. The 659 farmers' respondents were distributed as below (Table 11.1).

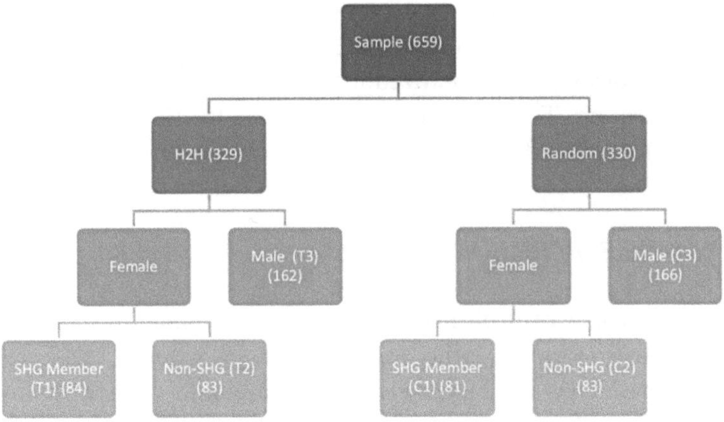

FIGURE 11.1 Sample distribution.

TABLE 11.1 Distribution of Sample Size Across Different Categories (District/Major Geographical or Ecological Unit Wise).

		District				
		Kalahandi	**Keonjhar**	**Koraput**	**Mayurbhanj**	**Total**
Treatment	C1	23	17	21	20	81
or control	C2	24	12	24	23	83
category	C3	41	27	54	44	166
	T1	24	18	18	24	84
	T2	24	12	24	23	83
	T3	41	32	47	42	162
Total		177	118	188	176	659

Respondents, in most cases, were the farmers themselves. However, in case of unavoidable absence of a farmer, a member of the household with next best knowledge of paddy cultivation by the family was chosen as a respondent. Caste-based profiling of respondents shows that majority belonged to scheduled tribes (ST—55.4%) followed by other backward castes (OBC—34.4%). Education wise, majority had primary education (45%) and those without any formal education constituted 35.5%.

11.4 KEY RESULTS AND FINDINGS

11.4.1 THE IMPACT OF FARM TRIAL ON VARIETAL DIFFUSION RATE

When new products are put into evaluation or test under on farm trial, there is time lag between the results/evidence generation and wide-scale promotion of the variety in the geography. While farmers realize the better performance of a product, to adopt the same, they need the access to quality seeds of same. Making a new product available in seed chain might take a few years. Through this time, one of the fastest and effective ways of varietal scaling and adoption is farmer-to-farmer diffusion. Varietal diffusion always happens through sharing of seeds at farmers' level. It is a common process when a new variety is adopted by neighbor or known farmers. Based on opinions, learnings acquired through personal observation, and discussion, other farmers wish to try new varieties. The extent of diffusion may differ based on factors like method of introduction of the variety, common observations by farmers, gender of the farmer who cultivated, and also if the farmers are linked to functional groups like community level institutions. The statistics presented below will help us understand the same.

According to the survey data, largely, 13% of farmers who grew new STRV, BINA Dhan 11, shared its seeds with other farmers. However, within the treatment group, 16.6% farmers disseminated the variety whereas in control group only 10% farmers did so (Fig. 11.2). The proportion of farmers who shared seeds of Bina 11 varied between the categories. It was relatively higher for female farmers who belonged to community institutions and followed H2H method of cultivation (24%). Hypothesis tests have been done to understand if differences between categories are significant.

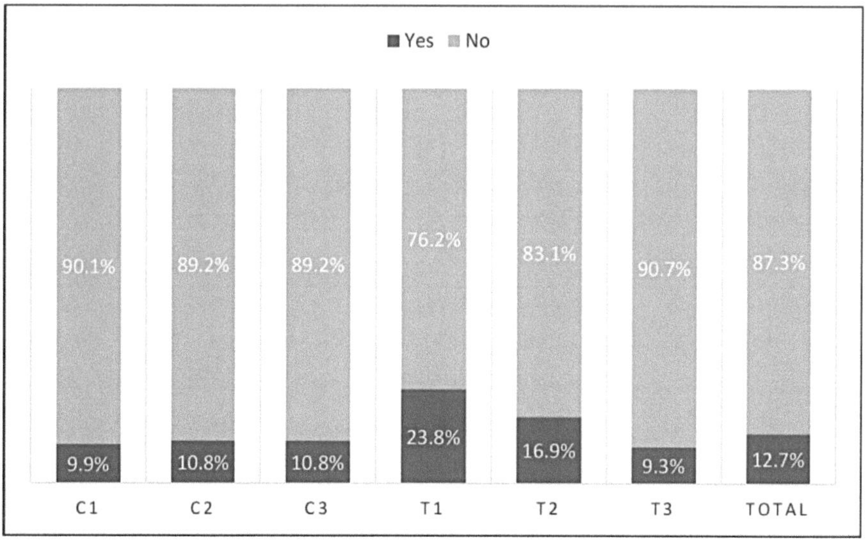

FIGURE 11.2 Percentage of farmers who shared new STRV seeds with other farmers.

BINA Dhan 11(STRV) growing farmers mostly shared seeds with neighbor household farmers (66%) followed by farmers of neighboring plots or other farmers (20–30%). Most of the receiver farmers were from the same village (87%). Nearly 24% cultivators shared seeds with farmers from nearby villages within the same block (Fig. 11.3 and Table 11.2).

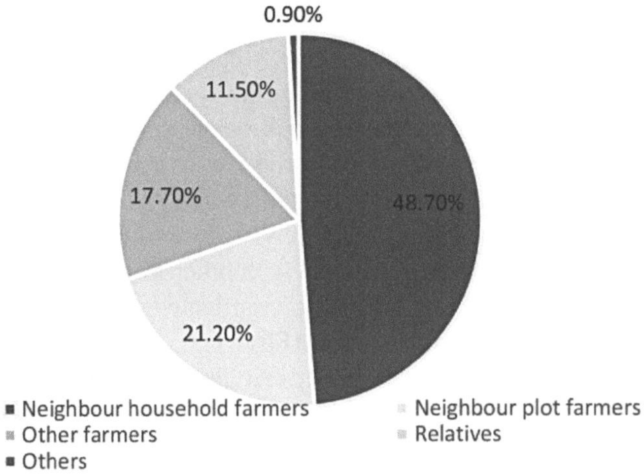

FIGURE 11.3 Stakeholders with whom new STRV seeds were shared.

When looked into geographical diffusion of the variety, though 75.3% of seed sharing happened within the village, a very promising 20.6% inter-village sharing showed the very high diffusion potential of the technology.

TABLE 11.2 Location of Stakeholders with Whom New STRV Seeds Were Shared.

		Responses	
		N	**Percent**
Location of people with whom shared[a]	Farmers from same village	73	75.3%
	Farmers from nearby village in same block	20	20.6%
	Farmers from different block	4	4.1%
Total		97	100.0%

Typically, each farmer growing STRV had shared the seeds with two other farmers. The quantity of seeds shared varied from as low as 1 kg to 120 kg. The average quantity of Bina 11 seeds shared by any cultivator was 15 kg.

TABLE 11.3 The Varietal Diffusion Across Treatment Versus Control Group

Treatment groups * If Bina 11 seeds shared from 2018 harvest (farm saved seeds)—cross tabulation				
		If Bina 11 seeds shared from 2018 harvest		
		Yes	**No**	**Total**
Treatment groups	H2H	49	280	329
	Random	35	295	330
Total		84	575	659

$|Z_{cal}|$ = sqrt (Pearson Chi-Square) = 1.650, Z....= 1.645, p value = ½ * (asymptotic significance (two-sided)) = ½ * 0.099 = 0.0495 (<0.05). Significant

The study established the varietal diffusion/scaling for the farmer who followed the H2H method were significantly higher (p value <0.05, Chi square test) than those farmers who received random seed kits for demonstration/introduction. This showed the effectiveness of innovative on farm trails/H2H on creating an overall trigger or influence among neighbor farmers (from both neighbor households and neighbor plots) leading to their interest or request for farm saved seeds from the host farmers who cultivated the STRV for the first time in their village. This indicated toward both visual/observation-based learning. Nearly 20% of farmers who received seeds from host farmers were neighbor plot farmers, who mostly learned about the performance of the varieties through visual observation in comparative trials and assessed the potential trait performance of new variety against their local popular variety throughout the season for various parameters. However, 60% of seed dissemination was across farmers from neighbor household which also includes strong contribution of farmer-led information and communication or dissemination of know-how through word of mouth, structured or unstructured knowledge dissemination within the village (Fig. 11.3 and Table 11.2). This was also observed to be spreading to nearby village within the same block. The findings strongly indicate the effectiveness of H2H trial as a medium of varietal knowledge, awareness, faster seed diffusion for the community.

11.4.2 GENDERED DIFFERENCE IN SEED DIFFUSION

The proportion of farmers who shared seeds of Bina 11 varied between the categories based on gender of farmers intervened (Table 11.4). It was relatively higher for female farmers who belonged to community institutions and followed the H2H method of cultivation (24%). It was also found 61% of total quantity of seeds shared came from female farmers and 81% of the receivers were males. Out of all female cultivators who shared seeds, 73% gave it to males only and 16% to females only and 94% of male cultivators, who shared seeds, gave it to males only. This indicates male farmers barely shared seeds with any female. The effectiveness of H2H method for wider/ faster dissemination of the new product was more pronounced in case of female H2H host (treatment group) farmers compared to male (Table 11.3). This also establishes that female farmers have proven to be more effective agents to disseminate the new products, or related information across male and female both. There could be also possibility of female farmers discussing the varietal performance at household level, with their husbands or other male members who in turn could have disseminated related information/ knowledge to other male farmers. The wider information, knowledge, and seed disseminations were seen to be from female farmers. Hypothesis tests have been done to understand if differences between categories are significant. The results were significant and established that the diffusion of the variety is more and wider in case of female respondents than the men respondents.

TABLE 11.4 The Gendered Impact Across Treatment Versus Control Group

Treatment groups * If shared Bina 11 seeds from harvest of 2018 crop—cross tabulation				
		If shared Bina 11 seeds from harvest of 2018 crop		
		No	**Yes**	**Total**
Treatment groups	Female–(H2H + random)	280	51	331
	Male–(H2H + random)	295	33	328
Total		575	84	659

$|Z_{cal}|$ = sqrt (Pearson Chi-Square) = 2.058, Z...... = 1.96, p value = asymptotic significance (two-sided) = 0.040 <0.05. Significant

11.4.3 EFFECT OF SOCIO-POLITICAL OR INSTITUTIONAL AFFILIATIONS ON EFFECTIVENESS OF FARM TRIALS

Overall, 81% of female receivers of the seeds of new variety (in subsequent year of 2019) were from SHGs, and they almost entirely received those from female farmers. For female cultivator who belonged to SHGs, nearly 90% of seed receivers from them were female from SHGs. In case of non-SHG female cultivator as well, majority (80%) of receivers were from SHG. Members of SHGs shared seeds mostly with members of the same SHG (62%).

While it was established that female farmers led to wider diffusion of varieties through seed sharing, there was observed significant difference in the dissemination pattern between the women farmers who were part of SHG or who were not part of SHGs (Table 11.5). This in turn established the socio-political affiliation of women farmers to a critical and popular community institution like SHG (self-help group) had no or little effect in augmenting the effectiveness of the extension method or varietal knowledge or dissemination.

TABLE 11.5 The Effect Through Institutional Affiliations Across Treatment Versus Control Group.

Treatment Groups * If shared Bina 11 seeds from harvest of 2018 crop—cross tabulation				
		If shared Bina 11 seeds from harvest of 2018 crop		
		No	**Yes**	**Total**
Treatment groups	Non-SHG female–(H2H + random)	143	23	166
	SHG female–(H2H + random)	137	28	165
Total		280	51	331

$|Z_{cal}|$ = sqrt (Pearson Chi-Square) = 0.785, Z....= 1.645, p value = ½ * (asymptotic significance (two-sided)) = ½ * 0.433 = 0.216 >0.05 (non-significant)

11.5 CONCLUSIONS

It was found that head-to-head trials (a popular comparative on farm trial method) were the more effective way for introduction, popularization, and diffusion of new climate-resilient variety, BINA Dhan 11, compared to the introduction through just provisioning seed mini kits. The diffusion and scaling of the variety through farmer to farmer shared seeds were higher for the villages and farmers who hosted H2H on farm trials. The dissemination happened not only between the host farmers and the neighboring plot farmers but also the neighbor household farmers indicating a wider discussion, word of mouth along with observation-based learnings. The knowledge dissemination of the variety was seen to be faster than what could be normally anticipated and nearly 23% of diffusion/exchange comprised farmers of not only host/treatment village but also neighboring villages in the same geographical block. The effect of H2H on farm trial came out more pronounced when these were hosted by the woman farmers. The woman host farmers had received same variety and same orientation training to cultivate the new test variety on farm trial. However, when it came to dissemination of knowledge/awareness about the variety and subsequently seed exchange, woman farmers were seen to be more effective. Therefore, the gender of host farmers was seen to have affected considerably the impact of treatment and the diffusion was faster and wider. This also established an interesting finding that the diffusion from women to men was more clearly visible, whereas the men to women diffusion was very less. This established a very strong potential of women as critical grass-root agents to disseminate technology and know-how in a much faster, inclusive, and wider manner. Interestingly, the sociopolitical/institutional affiliation of farmers, especially woman farmers studied, were seen to have no influence or impact on triggering higher dissemination of knowledge and variety in this particular study area and sample group. The diffusion rate was almost similar between the woman host farmers who were part of SHGs and who were not part of SHGs. This could be possibly due to several reasons. It could be due to the fact that the SHG formation in the studied geography is a relatively newer phenomenon or the SHGs are not fully functional and hence having lesser impact on members' activity and behavior. It could be also due to the fact that as the SHGs are very strong institutions and widely present in each village due to strong social mobilization exercises done by several public programmes in past and hence irrespective of whether any women are member or non-member are influenced equally by these collectives as a strong spill-over effect. As there were strong gendered differences seen in diffusion of variety there is high potential of later being true. This could be more strongly debated with similar or detailed gender-focused studies in wider geography. To summarize the findings of the study, it can be clearly concluded that experiential and comparative on-farm trials have a great potential to best widely used for varietal/product positioning in different markets by showing the performance against the predominant/popular products of farmers. The OFTs that are mostly seen as reliable method for scientific data and evidence generation have lot more to offer as a key extension approach for the agriculture programmes.

11.6 MANAGERIAL, SOCIAL, POLICY IMPLICATIONS

The findings of this study give several useful insights for the public or private agriculture extension management systems and extension functionaries on ground. It establishes that modern and inclusive extension methods driven by the concept of contextual and comparative learning can influence farmers for behavior change. Comparative on-farm trials can be used as one of the most potential ways of introducing new varieties. However, it also paves the way for potential use of this method for several agriculture technologies, e.g., introduction of new package of practice, new machinery, new knowledge materials, and also different combinations of different technology. All this possible technology or combination of technology can be put into a rigorous/season-long comparison against the farmer popular technology to see and experience the realistic competitive advantage in the given market or ecology. The concept of experiential learning is woven around comparisons that are carried out through observation, discussions, and doing by self. These methods were observed to trigger the scaling of new variety and scope for potential adoption indicating behavior change in the form of farmers learning from other farmers in a much faster manner.

Apart from the effectiveness of the new extension management here, the study also establishes understanding that woman farmers can be critical agents for dissemination of new varieties and know-how in a much faster manner. This is potentially due to a large social network, or keenness to learn and disseminate that exists among them. Though it might vary across geography and cultural setups, but it can be more effective where women are traditionally engaged with farming (e.g., the geography of study in focus, Odisha). Most of traditional programmes around agriculture technology dissemination consider the land owners, i.e., mostly/largely men as the lead farmers to be included in their training, extension or awareness creation initiatives. This study gives enough evidence for them to rethink and make those initiatives more gender inclusive for a better impact.

KEYWORDS

- **agriculture**
- **variety**
- **trials**
- **adoption**
- **knowledge**
- **extension**

REFERENCES

Ahmad, F.; Haseen, S. The Performance of India's Food Grain Production: A Pre and Post Reform Assessment. *Int. J. Sci. Res. Publ.* **2012,** *2*(3), ISSN 2250-3153. www.ijsrp.org

Dar, H. M.; Singh, S.; Singh, S. U.; Zaidi, W. N.; Ismail, M. A. Stress Tolerant Rice Varieties - Making Headway in India. SATSA Mukhapatra - Annual Technical Issue. **2014,** *18*, 1–14.

Faltermeier, L.; Abdulai, A. The Impact of Water Conservation and Intensification Technologies: Empirical Evidence for Rice Farmers in Ghana. *Agric. Econ.* **2009,** *40*(3), 365–379.

Kristin, D.; Sulaiman, R. The New Extensionist: Roles and Capacities to Strengthen Extension and Advisory Services. *J. Int. Agric. Ext. Educ.* **2014,** *21*(3), 6–18.

Raju, G.; Wen-chi, H.; Shrestha, R. B. Factors Affecting Adoption of Improved Rice Varieties Among Rural Farm Households in Central Nepal. *Rice Sci.* **2015,** *22*(1), 35–43.

Hazell, B. R. P.; Ramasamy, C.; Aiyasamy, P. K. *The Green Revolution Reconsidered: The Impact of High-Yielding Rice Varieties in South India*; Published for the International Food Policy Research Institute (IFPRI) by Johns Hopkins University Press:
Baltimore, MD, 1991.

Janaiah, A.; Hossain, M.; Otsuka, K. Productivity Impact of the Modern Varieties of Tice in India. *Develop. Econ.* **2006,** *44*(2), 190–207.

Mackill, D. J.; Ismail, M. A.; Singh, U. S.; Labios, R. V.; Paris, T. R. Development and Rapid Adoption of Submergence-Tolerant (Sub1) Rice Varieties. *Adv. Agron.* **2012,** *115*, 299–352.

McDougall, C.; Ojha, H.; Hall, A.; Sulaiman, R. Critical Policy Studies. In *Adaptive Collaborative Approaches in Natural Resource Governance: Rethinking Participation, Learning and Innovation*; Ojha, H. R., Hall, A., Sulaiman V., R., Eds.; Routledge: England, 2015; 9(3), pp 383–385.

Singh, R. Varietal Replacement Rates Among Field Crops: Current Status, Constraints, Impact, Challenges and Opportunities for the Indian Seed Industry. *Seed Times.* **2015,** *7*, 71–90.

Singh, R. P.; Chintagunta, A. D.; Agarwal, D. K.; Kureel, R. S.; Kumar, S. P. J. Varietal Replacement Rate: Prospects and Challenges for Global Food Security. *Glob. Food Sec.* **2020,** *25*(100324), 100324.

Timothy, B.; Case, A. Modelling Technology Adoption in Developing Countries. *Am. Econ. Rev.* **1993,** *83*(2), 396–402.

CHAPTER 12

Advancement of Nonlife Insurance in Both Public and Private Sectors in Bangladesh

MD. IBRAHIM* and SUNIL KUMAR ROY

School of Management Science, Apeejay Stya University, Sohna, Gurgaon, Haryana 122103, India

**Corresponding author. E-mail: ibrahim.sbc123@gmail*

ABSTRACT

Bangladesh has seen unprecedented advancements in the growth on private and public nonlife insurance sectors. The study is based on 14 years (2004–2017) whose information belongs to statistics related to GDP, population, and net direct premium in the nonlife insurance sector. Four indicators have been taken like "Growth Rate," "Market share," "Penetration Rate," and "Density Rate" for evaluating the advancement of nonlife insurance. The study reveals that the penetration rate, density rate, growth rate, and market share of public sector are lower as compared to those of private sector. The main reason is that the private sector is getting a portion of 50% of public sector business as per Insurance Corporation (Amendment—Act 1990), which has further amendment as Insurance Corporation Act—2019 and the private sector can provide commission to the insured, but which is not possible for the public sector. The average penetration rate of the public sector was .06% and it was .15% for the private sector. The average density rate of the public sector was Tk.40.83 and it was Tk. 98.55 for the private sector. The average growth rate of the public sector was 8.58% and it was 16.43% for the private sector. The average market share

Constructive Discontent in Execution: Creative Approaches to Technology and Management.
Sanjeev Bansal, Anita Venaik, Swati Upveja, and Saritha S. (Eds.)

of the public sector was 29.90%, whereas 70.09% was captured by private sector business. Reach of private and public sector nonlife insurance in the country is 0.17% in 2008, 0.18% in 2014, and 0.15% in 2017. The nonlife insurance density rate (both public and private) of Bangladesh was $ 1.40 in 2008 and it was $ 2.10 in 2017. To improve the advancement of nonlife insurance, both sectors should take necessary steps to cover the untapped and under development areas of Bangladesh.

12.1 INTRODUCTION

Mirsha (2009) has reported that insurance is to cover the risk associated with loss due to uncertainty associated with those people who are exposed to risk and they agree to get themselves ensured against that risk with financial uncertainties. A financial institution that delivers insurance services is called insurer, insurance company, or insurance carrier. A person or institution who receives insurance service is called insured or policy holder (Al-amin, 2016). Insurance Sector is an arm of financial sector which significantly contributes to managing risk and economic growth of the nation (Mall, 2018).

The idea of insurance becomes apparent or prominent as humans are automatically susceptible to many risks associated with their life which includes various risks from nonfinancial to financial arenas (Alli, 2011). Insurance sector comprises both nonlife and life insurance category (Mall, 2018).

Life insurance generates funds for long term, whereas nonlife insurance area generates funds for short term. Olayungbo (2016) studied that insurance acts as acclaim to economic growth rather than replacement.

Insurance as a sector guards individual household and organizations against a wide rage of risks at their individual level. At country level the insurance sector substantially reduces the government's burden of finance and leads to economic stability and success for business organizations. A healthy economy will always have a well-managed and matured insurance sector in their country as studied by Vayanos and Hammound (2006). Along with life insurance another sector that provides insurance coverage to nonlife sector is considered general insurance. The areas covered under general insurance are fire, marine, automobile, accidents at business premises, like retail stores, coffee houses etc. (Kumar, 2010).

The section likewise comprises individual line items like cars, mortgage holders (family), and others. Last, nonlife insurance gives assets to fix or make up for the genuine worth and cost of harms, mishap, and different misfortunes in all fields of material exercises. It gives a security net to the two endeavors and people. The insurance business likewise gives urgent monetary intermediation administrations, moving assets from the guaranteed to capital speculation, which is basic for proceeding with financial advancement and development all the while producing long haul assets for infrastructural improvement (Sarkar, 2013). Bangladesh's fast development rate throughout the decade has been possible due to the main advancements in local coactivity and furthermore worldwide economy (Mamun, 2011). The administration area has contributed fundamentally to Bangladesh's development story in the New Years. Gross domestic product starting from the administration area recorded 49.33% in 2016 (Trading economics.com Bangladesh). The shapes of insurance business have been changing across the worldwide and undulating impact of the equivalent can be seen in Bangladeshi market too. Insurance industry is a development-situated industry. In Bangladesh as well, the business has begun to uncover the potential after progression and privatization of the area. Ali (2018) studied that image and contribution of insurance sector is not respected as the contribution of banking sector is considered. The level of risk is very high in Bangladesh, but the insurance market is not prudential as compared to the level of risk. Most of the people or institution does not take the insurance policy willingly rather for meeting compulsory legal bindings (Khan and Uddin, 2008).

Bangladesh is geologically little and has the world's ninth biggest populace, yet it likewise has one of the least infiltration rates for nonlife insurance in Asia regarding premium as a level of GDP. Current insurance penetration rate is 0.55% (IDRA, 2019). The present circumstance mirrors the way that Bangladesh's insurance market is as yet in its outset meaning great development potential. Solid financial development of Bangladesh in the most recent decade joined with a populace of more than 15 crore makes it one of the possibly biggest protection markets later on. The expanded monetary movement combined with changes in nonextra security market would absolutely assist with growing the market in the years to come. The changes and opening up of the insurance area welcomed numerous private firms to fire up their business. It has been assessed that insurance area development is multiple points in financial aspects of Bangladesh. The explanation is 45 nonlife private insurance firms are putting resources into insurance area in Bangladesh. Islam (2019) in their study found that 73.5% share of life insurance sector and 26.5% share of nonlife insurance sector is inclusive of Islamic and microinsurance sectors.

Insurance sector has seen unprecedented growth after the alteration of Insurance Corporation Act in 1984. To satisfy with the needs of business network and exchange bodies, the public authority in force around then permitted setting up private insurance agency in 1984. The cycle was expressed for setting up insurance agency in private area with the goal of making a more effective and serious monetary framework reasonable for the Bangladesh economy (Law Ministry, 1984). Around then the government felt that to improve the client administrations and increment the extension of the insurance in Bangladesh, the market of the overall industry of public area has been tested as of late by an assortment of powers from web disintermediation to forceful promoting by another passageway, monetary assistance, rivalry from other speculation vehicles, and obviously client strengthening.

Islam (2019) studied that premium earned by nonlife insurance companies is Tk 2,908.1 Cr. As compared to life insurance that is Tk 8,203.1 Cr., this kind of premium generated by insurance firms shows their caliber in the country and how they can be considered a strong indicator of the economy.

The changing insurance industry advancement present may open doors for insurance an all-around characterized and favorable to activity business reaction. The backup plan must rethink how they handle client collaborations and adjust their contribution to clients such as buying rules, better agreement, and follow-up on the jumpers of consumer loyalty, dedication, and deserting. Simultaneously, they can upgrade the merchant technique by supportive of effectively trying to hold and draw in quality wholesalers. As per the PwC report, in 2019, insurance premium may grow from $1.58 billion in 2015 to $ 2.2 billion in 2020.

The business has a great deal of rivalry among the 45 privately owned businesses. A large number of these organizations have been set apart for in-proficiency and untrustworthy practices that have brought about issues with respect to customer certainty on the business (Mamun, 2011). If it is possible to rise 1% penetration of insurance industry, it can reduce uninsured losses and increase GDP growth. Ultimately, a radical change will come in the economy of Bangladesh (Rashid, 2019).

12.2 A PEN PICTURE OF INSURANCE INDUSTRY IN BANGLADESH

Insurance is certifiably not another idea to the individuals of Bangladesh (Chowdhury, 1981). Around 75 years back, during the British standard in the-then India, few insurance organizations started offering insurance, especially life, in this piece of the world. Since 1947 until 1971 insurance business acquired energy in this land considered east Pakistan. There were around 49 organizations executing both nonlife and life coverage business.

With the rise of the individuals' Republic of Bangladesh, the public authority, to make accessible the product of freedom to general mass, nationalized the insurance business in 1972 (Presidential request no-95). By the prudence of this request, all organizations and associations executing all kinds of insurance business in this nation went under this nationalization aside from postal and foreign life insurance organizations. Five Insurance Corporations were essentially settled, namely, Rupsa Jibon Bima Corporation, Jatiya Bima Corporation, Teesta Bima Corporation, Surma Jiban Bima Corporation, and Karnaphuli Bima Corporation. The Jatiya Bima Corporation was a controlling organization of other four corporations. According to this Teesta and Karnaphuli were made liable for nonlife insurance business and Surma and Rupsa were made liable for life coverage business. All the current 49 organizations were converged with these four Corporations. Finally, an underlying plan was changed under nationalization vide (Act VI, 1973) on fourteenth May 1973. The past five Corporations were annulled, and two Corporations were set up, namely, Sadharan Bima Corporation, for executing nonlife insurance business as it were, and Jibon Bima Corporation, for executing life insurance business. To fulfill with the needs of business network and exchange bodies, the public authority in force around then permitted arrangement insurance agency in 1984 in the private area with the vital correction of Insurance Corporation Act—1973, which has further alteration as Insurance Corporation Act—2019. Since 1985, the private insurance firm has begun executing insurance business.

12.3 REVIEW OF RELATED LITERATURE

The order of insurance headway through nonlife insurance has been an intriguing hold of exploration for some researchers. An unassuming endeavor has been embraced to look for related writing and investigations of nonlife insurance survey. After a consistent inquiry a concise outline of the significant examinations that are especially applicable to the nonlife insurance is introduced here.

Ahmed (1977) uncovered that protection industry in Bangladesh is as yet in a fundamental stage. With the freedom and with the nationalization of insurance business various issues sprung up and the business must be revamped through the experimentation techniques. Habibullah and Ghosh (1989) stated that public authority nationalized the insurance business which in one of the significant portions of administration industry of a nation with distinct targets. The public additionally has its own assumption out of the complete insurance sector. Azad (1999) told that insurance can assume an essential part in the economy by giving shield to properties, limiting danger that is the crucial to the development and advancement of business and industry. Other than Cooperative protection has a social component where case investors, who are more vulnerable segment of the individuals or have gathered together to defend their premium, can have procuring advantage. Islam (1999) found that the insurance business in Bangladesh is confronting intense lack of expert. Insurance work force and uncommonly the showcasing experts. The development of the insurance business relies much upon the informed and prepared experts. As an initial step, advertising staff calling needs to be normalized and controlled. Mamun et al. (2000) depicted that the nationalized general insurance area of Bangladesh is going through a urgent stage. On one side there are whines of administration, failure, dormancy, and decline in productivity. Then again, there are woman supporting the requirement for the advancement of the nationalized area highlighting its commitment to make sure about capital development, venture, and work notwithstanding giving monetary help to the insurance network. Shirazi et al. (2004) uncovered that nongovernment general insurance responds quickly to market demand, item interest, and changes of by and large social and business climate. Moreover, taking the upsides of ongoing change in reinsurance strategy nongovernment back-up plans have obtained a mentionable authority over expense procuring. Likewise, because of organization and failures of the SBC, private back-up plans are progressively procuring trust of the business networks and viably belittling the advancement cycle of business and exchange. Azam (2005) said that the development of insurance industry and the monetary improvement is associated. Financial advancement of a nation is halfway relied upon the improvement of insurance industry. As of now, insurance has gotten extremely nearer to people groups of very strolls. Rao (2007), in his article, uncovered that nonlife insurance industry performed magnificently in FY 2006–2007 as far as rising premium volumes, recording its most noteworthy development rate ever of 23 per penny, with an accumulation of Rs. 4626 crores. The superior volume crossed Rs. 25,003 crores. The growth rate during FY 2005–2006 was 16 per penny and during 2004–2005 it was 12 per penny. The private players whose excellent offer in FY 2000–2001 was Rs. 500 crores had taken it to Rs. 8700 crores, with their market share up from 4 per penny to 35 per penny. Rao (2007) in his article said that the credit for the expansion of the insurance market penetration and density ought to really go to the private area and legitimate guideline. The prolonged financial act associated with changes when all is said in done insurance market would positively assist with extending the market in the years to come. The opening up has forecasted well for the shoppers, who currently approach wide scope of new items especially unit connected items that have pulled in the consideration of the safeguarded. Haiss and Sümegi (2008) studied the progress of insurance business in economically sound nations and relatively less developed countries like Estonia, Romania, and Bulgaria.

Ali (2008) stated that the present legitimate position is that half of public area insurance business has been saved for nationalized company (SBC) and the organizations in the private area are qualified for composing the leftover half business of this area. It is apparent that the normal development of public area premium was around 9.36% throughout the years under audit while the pace of private area was 14.00% as it were. Haq (2008) depicted that the pattern of globalization may make new element of difficulties for insurance industry. The structure of venture arrangement of these insurance agencies was not talked about under those investigations. This paper fundamentally centers on this region of venture portfolio structure of general insurance agencies in Bangladesh.

Vadlamannati (2008) discussed that insurance business has positive influence on economic expansion for the longer period in Indian economy. Haq (2009) said that insurance genuinely assumes an indispensable job in the general public and the nation. Perhaps no nation can achieve financial advancement without improvement of insurance associations on sound premise. Ahmed et al. (2011) led an examination on the determinants of execution, size, danger, and influence are significant determinants of execution of disaster protection organizations of Pakistan. As indicated by their investigation Return on Asset (ROA) has measurably immaterial relationship with development, productivity, age, and liquidity. Mamun (2011) published an article on the subject of performance assessment of general (nonlife coverage) organizations in Bangladesh' and expressed that because of globalization, liberation, and psychological militant dangers, the insurance business has undergone a colossal change over the previous decade. Around the world insurance business was expanding at a low rate till 2007 and enlisted a growth of 3.3%. Lee et al. (2013) identified that global insurance industry has been growing since 1950 and there is a long-run equilibrium relationship between real GDP and real-life insurance premiums. Verma and Bala (2013) identified that life insurance has significant influences on the economic growth of India during 1990–1991 to 2010–2011. Kamrul and Khanam (2013) have directed an article on the subject of execution assessment of public sector nonlife insurance agencies in Bangladesh, where they presented the scenario of Shadaran Bima Corporation (SBC). They recommend that for additional constant development and improvement, SBC should take some important initiatives incorporating with appropriate techniques for the execution of resources, improvement of promotional activities, campaigning advancement programs, arrange human resource program, loosening up valuing principles. Cristea et al. (2014) found that insurance sector is a foremost component which significantly contributes to the GDP of certain European countries.

12.4 OBJECTIVES OF STUDY

The goals of the investigation are as given below:

- To look at the growth rate of nonlife insurance both public and private areas in Bangladesh.
- To think about the market share of the overall industry of nonlife coverage both public and private areas in Bangladesh.
- To think about the penetration rate of nonlife insurance both public and private areas in Bangladesh.
- To analyze the density of nonlife coverage both public and private areas in Bangladesh.
- To suggest for raising progression of nonlife insurance area in Bangladesh.

12.5 METHODOLOGY

The examination is chiefly founded on the secondary information. The information was gathered for the years 2004–2017 (14 years). The well-springs of this information incorporate yearly reports of SBC, IDRA, and other insurance firms. The financial data collected has analyzed using formulas relating to growth rate, market share, penetration rate, density level, etc. The statistical tools such as mean, standard deviation, and Mann–Whitney test have been used for investigating the comparative penetration rate, density rate, growth rate, and market share of public and private area nonlife insurance in Bangladesh. The Mann–Whitney test has been used for the result of hypothesis. The test is used when data is ordinal and unpaired. For data analysis IBM SPSS software (version 20) has been used.

12.6 STUDY BASIS HYPHOTHESIS

To accomplish the particular destinations of the investigation, the fundamental speculations detailed for the current examination are as per the following:

Ho: There is no huge gap of penetration rate between public and private nonlife insurance areas in Bangladesh.
H1: There is a huge gap of penetration rate between public and private nonlife insurance areas in Bangladesh.
Ho: There is no huge gap of density rate between public and private nonlife insurance area in Bangladesh.
H1: There is a huge gap of density rate between public and private nonlife insurance area in Bangladesh.
Ho: There is no huge distinction of growth rate between public and private nonlife insurance areas in Bangladesh.
H1: There is a huge distinction of growth rate between public and private nonlife insurance areas in Bangladesh.
Ho: There is no huge gap of market share between public and private nonlife insurance areas in Bangladesh.
H1: There is a huge gap of market share between public and private nonlife insurance areas in Bangladesh.

12.7 COMPARATIVE ANALYSIS OF ADVANCEMENT OF NONLIFE INSURANCE FOR BOTH PUBLIC AND PRIVATE SECTORS IN BANGLADESH

The advancement of nonlife insurance is estimated as far as insurance entrance and proportion of density. To see the development and openings in the insurance area in any nation, insurance infiltration (penetration), insurance thickness (density), piece of the pie (market share), and development (growth rate) in premium ought to be estimated. Bangladesh is geologically enormous and has the world's ninth biggest populace, for example 159.9 million of every 2016 (World populace Review.com—2017). Despite a particularly huge and colossal populace, the insurance infiltration (penetration) and thickness (density) levels are very immaterial.

The insurance Penetration, thickness, piece (market share) of the overall industry and development (growth) rate are closely related to GDP, population, and net premium. The following table is showing these factors:

12.7.1 TREND IN GDP, POPULATION, AND GROSS DIRECT PREMIUM (NONLIFE) IN BANGLADESH

For determining the penetration rate, density rate, growth rate, and market share of insurance business, GDP, population, and direct premium are correlated to each other. These components have been presented in Table 12.1 for the period from 2004 to 2017

TABLE 12.1 GDP, Population, and Gross Direct Premium (Nonlife) in Bangladesh.

Year	GDP Tk.	Populations	G. premium (public)Tk.	G. premium (pvt)Tk.	Total premium.
		Crore			
2004	581470.42	13.20	309.90	600.40	9103
2005	601222.96	13.40	356.20	709.50	1065.7
2006	642338.74	14.06	395.80	797.60	1193.40
2007	725672.37	14.26	455.70	741.70	1397.40
2008	822824.31	14.47	501.30	1116.40	1617.74
2009	705071.80	15.05	540.60	1228.40	1769.02
2010	797538.70	15.21	574.50	1488.90	2063.4
2011	915828.80	15.39	601.70	1727.40	2329.15
2012	1055204.04	15.57	800.50	2394.10	3194.62
2013	1198923.17	15.76	796.00	1903.20	2699.23
2014	1343674.40	15.94	800.80	2229.52	3030.41
2015	1515802.30	16.12	835.00	2390.83	3225.83
2016	1732863.90	16.30	872.80	1900.00	2772.88
2017	1975815.20	16.47	932.40	2049.00	2981.41
Mean	1043875.07	15.08	626.66	1519.78	2745.94

Source: Annual reports of SBC and Insurance Development and Regulatory Authority (2004–2017).

Table 12.1 shows the trend of GDP, population, and gross direct premium during the time of this examination. There is an upward pattern in gross direct charge pay of both public and private areas nonlife insurance firms. For assessing the advancement of nonlife insurance in Bangladesh, the following four indicators are considered:

To evaluate the advancement of nonlife insurance in both public and private sectors, it is needed to calculate the penetration rate, density rate, growth rate, and market share of nonlife insurance of both sectors.

DIAGRAM: Indicators of Measuring Nonlife Advancement.

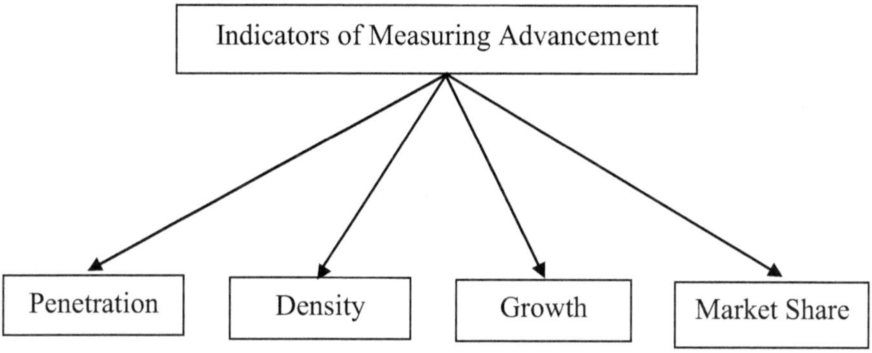

Source: Author's own.

12.7.2 PENETRATION RATE

Nonlife Insurance Penetration can be calculated by Gross premium to Gross Domestic Product (GDP). Table 12.2 has shown the penetration rate of nonlife insurance in Bangladesh.

TABLE 12.2 Penetration Rate of Nonlife Insurance Both Public and Private Sector in Bangladesh.

Year	Public sector	Private sector	Total
		Percent (%)	
2004	.05	.10	.15
2005	.06	.12	.18
2006	.06	.12	.18
2007	.06	.10	.16
2008	.06	.14	.20
2009	.08	.17	.25
2010	.07	.19	.26
2011	.07	.19	.26
2012	.08	.23	.31
2013	.07	.16	.23
2014	.06	.17	.23
2015	.06	.16	.22
2016	.05	.11	.16
2017	.05	.10	.15
Mean	**.06**	**.15**	**.21**
St.D (σ)	**.009**	**.040**	.049

Source: Annual Reports of SBC and Insurance Development and Regulatory Authority (2004–2017).

In Table 12.2, an upward trend in infiltration rate of nonlife insurance in both public and private sectors has been seen from 2004 to 2012, but from 2013 there has been a decreasing trend in both sectors. In case of public sector, the infiltration rate was .05% in 2004 and .08% in 2012 but .07%, .06%, .05%, and .05% in 2013, 2014, 2015, 2016, and 2017, respectively. In case of private sector, the penetration rate was .10% in 2004 and .23% in 2012 but .16%, .17%, .16%, .11%, .10%, and .15% in 2013, 2014, 2015, 2016, and respectively. On the other hand, the public sector showed a maximum average infiltration rate of .06% and .15% in the private sector. The standard deviation value of the public sector is .009 and that of the private sector is .040.

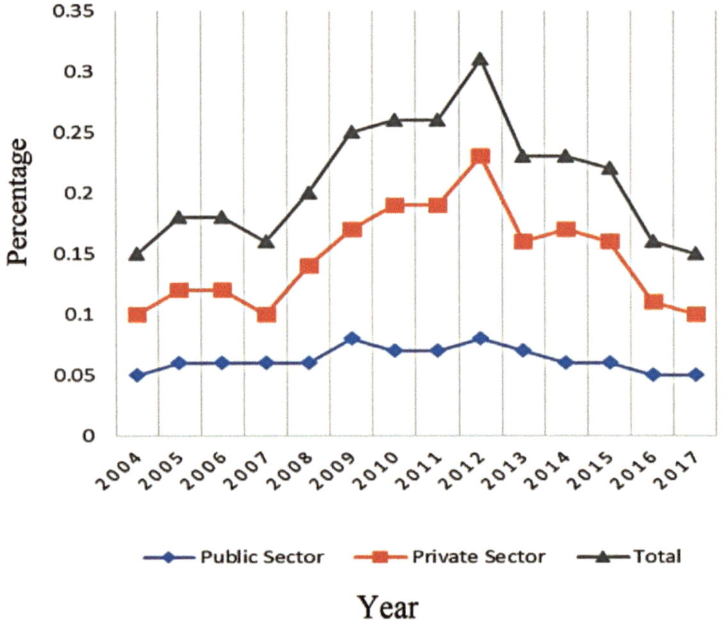

FIGURE 12.1 An impression of entrance rate among public and private area nonlife protection.

Source: Author's own.

12.7.3 DENSITY RATE

The nonlife insurance density can be ascertained by gross premium to total population. Table 12.3 shows the density rate of nonlife insurance in Bangladesh.

TABLE 12.3 Density Rate of Nonlife Insurance Both Public and Private Sector in Bangladesh.

Year	Public sector	Private sector	Total
		Tk.	
2004	23.48	45.48	68.96
2005	26.58	52.95	79.53
2006	28.15	56.73	84.88
2007	31.95	52.01	83.96
2008	34.64	77.15	111.79
2009	35.92	81.62	117.54
2010	37.77	97.89	135.66
2011	39.09	112.24	151.33
2012	51.41	153.76	205.17
2013	50.50	120.76	171.26
2014	50.24	139.87	190.11
2015	51.80	148.31	200.11
2016	53.54	116.56	170.10
2017	56.61	124.41	181.02
Mean	**40.83**	**98.55**	**139.38**
St.D (σ)	**11.24**	**37.68**	48.24

Source: Annual reports of SBC and Insurance Development and Regulatory Authority (2004–2017).

In Table 12.3, an increasing trend in density rate of nonlife insurance in both public and private sectors is observed. In case of public sector, the density rate was Tk. 23.48 in 2004, Tk. 37.77 in 2010, and Tk. 56.61 in 2017, whereas the private sector contains Tk. 45.48 in 2004, Taka 97.89 in 2010, and Tk. 124.41 in 2017. In case of total density rate of nonlife insurance is Tk. 68.96 in 2004, Tk. 35.66 in 2010, and 181.02 in 2017. The mean value of the public sector is Tk. 40.83 and 98.55 BDT showed as private sector. The standard deviation value of the public sector is 11.24 and that is 37.68 for the private sector. Here notice that 11.24 is closer to mean than 37.68. So, the public sector is more consistent than private sector. A reflection of density rate has been shown in Figure 12.2.

12.7.4 GROWTH RATE

Growth rate can be calculated by a formula, i.e., present year minus previous year, divided by previous year, multiplied by 100. Table 12.4 shows the growth rate of nonlife insurance in both govt. and private areas.

TABLE 12.4 Growth Rate in Gross Direct Premium of Nonlife Insurance Sector Both Govt. and Private Sectors.

Year	Public sector	Private sector	Total
		Percent (%)	
2004	1.37	17.40	18.77
2005	14.96	18.20	33.16
2006	11.10	12.40	23.50
2007	15.28	18.10	33.38
2008	10.00	18.60	28.60
2009	7.83	10.00	17.83
2010	6.27	21.20	27.47
2011	4.73	16.10	20.83
2012	33.00	38.60	71.60
2013	–.56	20.50	19.94
2014	.61	17.15	17.76
2015	4.26	7.23	11.49
2016	4.53	6.64	11.17
2017	6.82	7.84	14.66
Mean	**8.58**	16.43	25.01
St.D (σ)	8.54	8.11	15.18

Source: Annual reports of SBC and Insurance Development and Regulatory Authority (2004–2017).

$$\text{Note: 1. Growth rate} + \frac{\text{Present Year} - \text{Previous Year}}{\text{Previous Year}} \times 100$$

In Table 12.4, it is shown fluctuating upper level trends rate of nonlife insurance net premium in both public and private sectors in Bangladesh. In case of public sector, the growth rate was 14.96%, 11.10%, 15.28%, 10.00%, and 7.83% from 2005 to 2009, –.56% in 2013, 6.82% in 2017. This fluctuating scenery is also seen in case of private sector, where 18.20%, 12.40%, 18.10%, 18.60%, and 10.00% from 2005 to 2009. Again, it is 38.60% in 2012 and 7.84% in 2017. In case of total growth rate of nonlife insurance, the same fluctuating picture has been shown. The average growth rate of the public sector is 8.58%, whereas it is 16.43% for the private sector. The standard deviation value of the public sector is 8.54 and it is 8.11 for the private sector.

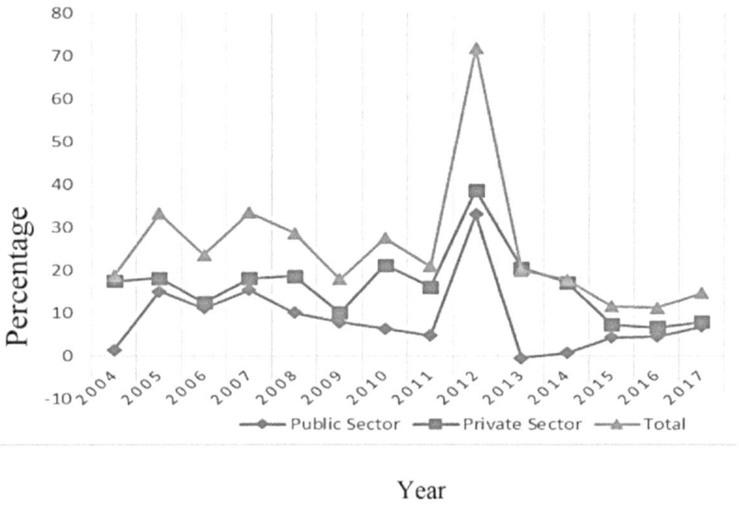

FIGURE 12.3 A reflection of growth rate between public and private sector nonlife insurance.
Source: Author's own.

12.7.5 MARKET SHARE

The market share of the public and private areas in the gross direct premium during the time of study has been introduced in Table 12.5. The headway of public and private non-extra security (nonlife insurance) areas can be analyzed further by taking a gander at the pattern in their piece (market share) of the overall industry during the examination time frame.

TABLE 12.5 Market Share in Gross Direct Premium of Public and Private Non-Life Insurance Areas in Bangladesh

Year	Public sector	Private sector	Total
		Percent (%)	
2004	34.04	65.96	100.00
2005	33.42	66.58	100.00
2006	33.17	66.83	100.00
2007	32.61	67.39	100.00
2008	30.99	69.01	100.00
2009	30.56	69.44	100.00
2010	27.84	72.16	100.00
2011	25.83	74.17	100.00

TABLE 12.5 *(Continued)*

Year	Public sector	Private sector	Total
		Percent (%)	
2012	25.06	74.94	100.00
2013	29.48	70.52	100.00
2014	26.42	73.58	100.00
2015	26.48	73.52	100.00
2016	31.48	68.52	100.00
2017	31.27	68.73	100.00
Mean	**29.90**	**70.09**	**100.00**
St.D (σ)	**3.06**	**3.06**	000.00

Source: Annual reports of public and private firms from 2004 to 2017 and IDRA.

In Table 12.5, it is revealed a downward trend of market share of public sector nonlife insurance in Bangladesh. On the other hand, an increasing trend of market share is occupied by private sector nonlife insurance. All things considered, it has been seen that 34.04% piece of the pie was acquired by open area in 2004, though 65.96% by private sector. And 27.84% was acquired by open area and 72.16% by private sector in 2010. Similarly, 26.42% acquired by open area and 73.52% by private area in 2015. But, in the time of 2016 and 2017, piece of the pie of public area has somewhat expanded and marginally diminished for private area. The normal piece of the overall industry of public area was 29.90% and 70.09% for private area during the investigation time frame. The standard deviation estimation of the two areas is 3.06%, which shows that private area is more reliable than that of public area. A reflection of market share has been shown in Figure 12.4.

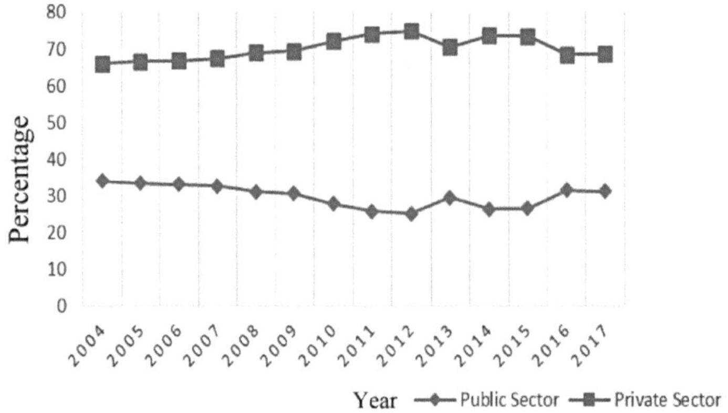

FIGURE 12.4 A reflection of market share between public and private sector nonlife insurance.

12.8 TEST OF HYPOTHESIS

TABLE 12.6 Test of Significance.

Test	Indicators	Z-values	Asymp. sig (2 tailed)
Mann–Whitney test	Penetration rate	–4.330	0.000
	Density rate	–4.043	0.000
	Growth rate	–2.964	0.003
	Market share	–4.503	0.000

Source: Author's own.

The Mann–Whitney test has been calculated based on the table relating to penetration rate, density rate, growth rate, and market share (Tables 12.2, 12.3, 12.4, and 12.5). The P-value for all indicators is 0.000, 0.000, 0.003, and 0.000, respectively, those are <.05 and it demonstrates that there is a serious dissimilarity among penetration rate, density rate, growth rate, and present market portion of the private at the same time public and nonlife insurance sector. Therefore, the study has rejected all null hypothesis and accepted alternative hypothesis. We can say that penetration, density, growth rate, and market share of public portion nonlife insurance is lower than that of personal sector.

12.9 FINDING OF THE STUDY

- The investigation presents that nonlife protection in both public and private areas has roistered an entrance (penetration), thickness (density), development (growth), and piece of the pie (market share) to the economy of Bangladesh.
- The study found that the nonlife protection infiltration pace (Insurance Penetration rate) of the public area is lesser than that of the private area. Be that as it may, both are an upward pattern till 2012. It has been again a diminishing pattern. The normal entrance pace of the public area was .06% and it was .15% for the private area. Here, the private area is conveying (.15 – .06) = .09% higher than that of the public area. The Mann–Whitney test demonstrated that there is a critical contrast between the entrance pace of public and private area nonlife protection in Bangladesh. Since P-esteem was 0.000 which is <0.05 along these lines, the invalid theory has been dismissed and elective speculation has acknowledged.

- The study draws out that the nonlife protection thickness pace (density rate) of the private area is higher than that of the public area. In any case, both are an expanding pattern during the investigation time frame. The normal thickness pace of the public area was 40.83 (TK) and it was 98.55(TK) for the private area. Here, the private area is conveying Tk. (98.55 – 40.83) = 57.72 higher than that of the public area. The Mann–Whitney test indicated that there is a huge distinction between the thickness pace of public and private area nonlife protection in Bangladesh. Since P-esteem was 0.000 which is <0.05 along these lines, invalid speculation has been dismissed and the elective theory has acknowledged.

The study uncovered that the development pace (growth rate) of nonlife protection of public area is lower than that of private area. There was a vacillated pattern of development rate during the investigation time frame. The normal development pace of the public area was 8.58% and it was 16.43% for the private area. Here, private area is involving (16.43 – 8.58) = 7.85% higher than that of public area. The Mann–Whitney test indicated that there is a huge contrast between the development pace of public and private area nonlife protection in Bangladesh. Since P-esteem was 0.003 which is <0.05 in this way, the invalid theory has been dismissed and elective speculation has acknowledged.

The study indicated that piece of the pie (market share) of private area is higher than that of public area. Be that as it may, both are an expanding pattern during the investigation time frame. The normal piece of the overall industry of public area was 29.90% and it was 70.09% for private area. Here, private area is conveying (70.09 – 29.90) = 40.19% higher than that of public area. The Mann–Whitney test indicated that there is a critical distinction between the piece of the pie of public and private area nonlife protection in Bangladesh. Since P-esteem was 0.000 which is <0.05 along these lines, the invalid theory has been dismissed and elective speculation has acknowledged.

12.10 CONCLUSION AND RECOMMENDATIONS

The protection (insurance) business of Bangladesh has opened up in 1984. The view of the individuals of our nation with respect to protection has changed from simply an act of "hazard decrease" to a technique for present moment "benefit-situated" venture. The penetration rate of nonlife protection in both public and private areas is a variable pattern. Infiltration pace of private area is higher than that of public area. The thickness pace of public area is lesser than that of private area. The development pace of private area is additionally higher than that of public area. The private area has caught the higher piece of the pie than that of public area. The public area needs to use its qualities to give an extreme battle to the private area. Yet, the public area could not battle with the private area, until and except if government does not change the arrangements of Corporation Act—2019, identifying with commission and half open related business. If a correction comes to the Insurance Corporation Act – 2019 relating to distribution of public related business disseminate half open related business to private firms, infiltration rate, thickness rate, development rate and piece of the pie of public area will twofold.

We may infer about the circumstances of nonlife protection that public nonlife and other private firms have primarily concentrated on the improvement of metropolitan market of Bangladesh and not the lower pay bunch individuals living in provincial zones. Along these lines, to get the genuine advantage of globalization, it is essential for all non-extra security (Nonlife Insurance Firms) firms to cover the undiscovered and a work-in-progress territory of Bangladesh. It may not be a savvy activity, yet it is required for more noteworthy interest of the protection business. Subsequently, to cover the rustic area, some imaginative measures ought to be taken like banc assurance, cooperation of co-usable society in towns, joint effort with nearby government, and so on. For instance, Green Delta insurance agency has taken a plan for strength of country individuals dressed in Tangail Zillah, SBC has taken a venture named WIBCI (climate Index Based Crops Insurance) in Raj Shahi, Sirajganj, and Noakhali Zillah in Bangladesh. Another region that could be covered is farming, which has remained to a great extent uninsured despite being the main control of the rustic individuals in Bangladesh. The individuals of provincial network consistently face a few issues like: denied from genuine cost of the farming item, decimate their yields by common catastrophe, absence of credit offices, and so on These issues can be settled by covering them with crops protection, steers protection which inlets their dangers. Last, they will feel great, which will at long last bring best of luck and prosperity for their locale.

12.11 FUTURE AREA OF THE STUDY

In the existing investigation, a stage has been taken to the progression of nonlife insurance in both public and private areas in Bangladesh. In any case, there is a plausible extension for future exploration.

1. The existing examination has decided the "penetration" rate, "density" rate, "growth" rate, and "market share" of nonlife insurance

in both public and private areas in Bangladesh. Exploration can be continuing in the future to discover administration nature of nonlife insurance in Bangladesh.

2. The present investigation has zeroed in just on the progression of nonlife insurance in both public and private areas in Bangladesh. Future investigation can be hold to examine the progression of both life and nonlife protection in Bangladesh.
3. This research has called attention to just on the progression of nonlife insurance in both public and private areas in Bangladesh. Future investigation can be made to look at productivity examination of nonlife insurance in both public and private areas in Bangladesh.

KEYWORDS

- **advancement**
- **nonlife insurance**
- **growth rate**
- **market share**
- **penetration rate**
- **density rate**
- **GDP**
- **population**
- **gross premium**

REFERENCES

Ahmed, N.; Zulfiqar, A.; Ahmad, U. Determinants of Performance: A Case of Life Insurance Sector of Pakistan. *Int. Res. J. Finance Econ.* **2011,** *61*, 123–28.

Ahmed, S. U. Insurance Business in Bangladesh. Bureau of Business Research, University of Dhaka, Bangladesh, 1977.

Alamin, M. Role of Insurance Company in Bangladesh Economy. *BBA Programm, PatuaKhali, Science and Technology University Dumkhali, Patuakhali.* 2016, 8602.

Alhassan, A. L.; Biekpe, N. Insurance Market Development and Economic Growth: Exploring Causality in 8 Selected African Countries. *Int. J. Social Econ.* **2016,** *43*(3), 321–339.

Ali, K. M. Prospects & Problems of Life Insurance in Bangladesh: Challenges Ahead. *Fair Rev.* **2018,** 1569.

Ali, M. H. Present Scenario of General Insurance in Bangladesh. *Ins. Bank. Dhaka Declarat.* **2008,** *1/11*(22), 1–4.
Alli, B. C. The Reforms of Insurance Companies and Its Transformation of Nigeria's Financial Sector. *The Magazine for African Layers,* 2011.
Azad M. A. K. Nature and Significance of General Insurance in Bangladesh: A Case study of Cooperative Bangladesh Insurance Limited. *Insurance J.* **1999,** *50*, 79–88.
Azam, M. S. Consumers' Attitude of General Insurance Service: Contrasting the Public and Private Sectors in Bangladesh. *Ins. J.* **2005**, *56*, 91–110.
Babbuli, I. M.; Bello, S. The Impact of Insurance Companies Towards the Development of Business Enterprises: Case Study of National Deposit Insurance Corporation (NDIC). *Int. J. Res. Bus. Manage. Account.* **2018,** *4*(2), 09–26.
Chowdhury, A. H. *Elements Insurance*. Bangladesh Insurance Academy, Bangladesh, 1981.
Cristea, M.; Marcu, N.; Cârstina, S. The Relationship Between Insurance and Economic Growth in Romania Compared to the Main Results in Europe–A Theoretical and Empirical Analysis. *Procedia Econ. Finance*. **2014,** *8*, 226– 235.
Dash, S.; Pradhan, R. P.; Maradana, R. P.; Gaurav, K.; Jayakumar, M. Impact of Banking Sector Development on Insurance Market-Growth Nexus: The Study of Eurozone Countries. *Empirica.* **2018**, *47*, 205–243.
Gupta, R.; Shastri, M.; Pandey, A. K.; Bhandwal, M. Pandemic 2020, Challenges, and Measures for Post Revival. In *Advances in Interdisciplinary Engineering. Lecture Notes in Mechanical Engineering*; Kumar, N., Tibor, S., Sindhwani, R., Lee, J., Srivastava, P., Eds.; Springer: Singapore, 2021. https://doi.org/10.1007/978-981-15-9956-9_52
Habibullah, M.; Ghosh, S. N. *General Insurance Business in Bangladesh: An Appraisal of SBC*. Bureau of Business Research, University of Dhaka: Dhaka, 1990.
Haiss, P.; Sümegi, K. The Relationship Between Insurance and Economic Growth in Europe: A Theoretical and Empirical Analysis. *Empirica.* **2008,** *35*(4), 405–431.
Haq, A. B. *Thoughts on Insurance: Bangladesh Perspective*. Adorn Publication: Bangladesh, 2008.
Hassan, K.; Khanam, F. A. Performance Evaluation of Public Sector General Insurance Company in Bangladesh – A Case Study on SBC. *Euro. J. Bus. Manage.* **2013,** *5*(25), 118–123.
Insurance Development and Regulatory Authority (IDRA). *Annual Reports***.** Bangladesh, 2019.
Islam, S. Insurance Laws of Bangladesh: How it Plays a Role in the Development of Economic Growth. Doctoral Dissertation, East West University, Bangladesh, 2019.
Islam, S. M. Thoughts on Building an Effective Marketing Force. *Ins. J.* **1999,** *50*, 33–38.
Jahangir, S. M. Growth in Insurance Sector Premium Income. *The Financial Express,* Wednesday, Nov 24, 2004, *12*(1), p 1.
Khan, M. S.; Uddin, M. N. Insurance Industry in Bangladesh: Opportunities and Challenges. *Thoughts Econ.* **2009,** *23*(4), 57–78.
Kramer, B. An Ordered Logit Model for the Evaluation of Dutch Non-Life Insurance Industry. *De Economist*. **1996,** *144*, 79–91.
Kumar, R. Performance Evaluation of General Insurance Companies - A study of Post-Reform Period. Ph.D. Thesis, Punjab University, India, 2010.
Lee, H. Insurance Development and Economic Growth. *Financial Statis. J.* **2019,** *1*(4), 1–17.
Lee, C. C.; Chiu, Y. B. The Link Between Life Insurance Activities and Economic Growth: Some New Evidence. *J. Int. Money Finance*. **2013,** *32*, 405–427.

Mall, S. Contribution of Insurance on Economic Growth in India: An Econometric Approach. *J. Appl. Bus. Econ.* **2018,** *20*(1), 85–92.

Mamun, Z. Performance Evaluation of General Insurance Companies in Bangladesh. *Ins. J.* **2011,** *58*, 21–67.

Mamun, M. Z.; Barua, A.; Islam, N. Performance of the Nationalized General Insurance Company of Bangladesh. *BIBM J.* **2000,** *25*(4), 26–38.

Ministry of Law and Justice Notification. Extra Ordinary. *Bangladesh Gazet.* Aug. 11, 1984.

Mishra, M. N. *Insurance, Principles and Practices*; S. Chand and Company Ltd: India, 1993.

Olayungbo, D. O. Effects of Life and Non-Life Insurance on Economic Growth in Nigeria: An Autoregressive Distributed Lag (ARDL) Approach. *Glob. J. Manage. Bus. Res.***2016,** *XV*(XI), 32–40.

Pradhan, R. P.; Arvin, M. B.; Norman, N. R. Insurance Development and the Finance-Growth Nexus: Evidence From 34 OECD Countries. *J. Multinatl. Financial Manage.* **2015,** *31*, 1–22.

Rao, C. S. Rewarding Reforms. *Asia Ins. Post.* **2007,** Aug 19–21.

Rao, G. V. Premium Performance. *Asia Ins. Post.* **2007,** *7*(10), 30–34.

Rashid, M. Potential for Growth: Transforming Bangladesh's Insurance Sector. *Dhaka Tribune*, June 2019. https://www.dhakatribune.com/opinion/op-ed/2019/04/28/transformingour

Sadharan Bima Corporation. *Annual Reports*; Sadharan Bima Corporation: Bangladesh, 2004–2017.

Samina, Q. S. Investment Portfolio of Insurance Companies in Bangladesh. *World J. Soc. Sci.* **2012,** *2*, 37–47.

Sarkar, A. Performance of Assessment of General Insurance Business in India. *Bus. Spectr.* **2013,** *2*, 35–54.

Shirazi, H.; Mamun, M. Z.; Arefin, K. Performance of Some Selected Non-Government General Insurance Companies in Bangladesh Compared to Government Insurance Company. *J. Bus. Admin.* **2014,** *30*(1, 2), 2–18.

Solaiman, M.; Haque, A. Development of Insurance Industry in Bangladesh: An Innovative Approach. *Ins. J.* **1999,** *50*, 43–48.

Vadlamannati, K. C. Do Insurance Sector Growth and Reforms Affect Economic Development? Empirical Evidence From India. *J. Appl. Econ. Re.* **2008,** *2*(1), 43–86.

Vayanos, E. R.; Hammond, J. D. Determinants of Household Life Insurance Premium Expenditure: An Empirical Investigation. *J. Risk Insur.* **2006,** *34*, 397–401.

Verma, A.; Bala, R. The Relationship Between Life Insurance and Economic Growth: Evidence From India. *Glob. J. Manage. Bus. Stud.* **2013,** *3*(4), 413–422.

CHAPTER 13

Assessing the Predictive Capability of the Theory of Planned Behavior in the Nigerian Context: A Study of Intention to Founding New Business

LAWAN AMDAN LAWAN[1*] and SUNIL KUMAR ROY[2]

[1]*Department of Marketing, Ramat Polytechnic Maiduguri, Borno State 600251, Nigeria*

[2]*School of Management, Apeejay Stya University, Sohna, Gurgaon, Haryana 122103, India*

[*]*Corresponding author. E-mail: lawanamdan@gmail.com*

ABSTRACT

This chapter presents an analysis of the intention of young undergraduates for their mindset for entrepreneurship in the county. Behavioral Intention is believed to be a significant predictor of any planned behavior, especially if the behavior is not easily observable and infrequent, such as founding or establishing a new business. The focus of the study is to test the predictive capability of the theory of planned behavior (TPB), which is the dominant intention model in extant literature in the context of Nigerian undergraduates. A total of 968 samples of various demographic characteristics from 18 universities, colleges, and polytechnics in the country, were drawn using a multistage sampling procedure. The study showed that the model proposed by the TPB is a worthy framework that can be used to foresee the intent to begin a business in the Nigerian context. Regression analysis specifically revealed that attitude is the strongest predictor of entrepreneurship intention,

Constructive Discontent in Execution: Creative Approaches to Technology and Management.
Sanjeev Bansal, Anita Venaik, Swati Upveja, and Saritha S. (Eds.)

followed by young entrepreneurs' control over behavior and subjective norm. The study recommends that youth entrepreneurship can be encouraged by targeting attitude change, confidence building, and a positive social outlook toward entrepreneurial behavior.

13.1 INTRODUCTION

A consensus on the definition of entrepreneurship is lacking in extant literature since virtually every study in the entrepreneurship-related field presented a divergent understanding. However, one definition we found interesting, particularly in the context of this study was published in OECD Economic Survey in 1997, the definition of entrepreneurship says, "it is a dynamic procedure of recognizing economic prospects and act upon them by emerging, creating and retailing services and goods."

This definition suggests that entrepreneurship cannot simply be a response to a given stimulus but requires some level of preparation. Kruegar et al. (2000) pointed out that it is difficult to divulge being an entrepreneur from career decisions as literature supports the idea that career choices are planned in nature. Approached from this perspective, past researchers believed that entrepreneurship is planned and intentional behavior.

Factors responsible for establishing the intention toward entrepreneurship started over four decades ago with Shapero's (1975) work "The Displaced, Uncomfortable Entrepreneur." Since then, several researchers in the field of social psychology targeted to unscramble the intention of entrepreneurs for its creation. Some of these scholars tried to understand the factors influencing entrepreneurial intention by studying graduates' demographic profiles and some personal features. However, Gartner (1989) cautioned that attributes related to personality, opinions, and insolences are continuously changing, they get redefined as students become exposed to real-world events and they are trained for their entrepreneur skills in a classroom setting. This approach comes with some drawbacks as studied by Gartner (1989) who found that researchers gathered entrepreneurial data after their exposure to the events which guides them for entrepreneurship with an assumption that their attitude and trait does not get altered.

In a related view, Robinson et al. (1991) studied that the traits related to personality for entrepreneurial studies have been fully stretched; therefore, additional efforts to study entrepreneurial intention based on these factors could only lead to less significant results. Similarly, Krueger et al. (2000)

observed that studying entrepreneurial behavior based on personal attributes and demographic factors leads to weak results because of their low predictive capabilities and poor explanatory power.

Other scholars explored the process underlying entrepreneurship intention using intention models. Krueger et al. (2000) observed intention models offered a comprehensive framework capable of explaining intention for getting entrepreneurs with their precise demographic characteristics.

One of such intention models identified in the extant literature, which have been more and more used in contemporary behavioral studies with great success particularly the TPB as studied by Ajzen's (1991).

Section 13.2 will briefly explain the TPB; later, the discussion focuses on the integration of the fourth construct (entrepreneurial knowledge received in a formal class setting) into the TPB. Subsequently, the methodology, analysis, findings, conclusion, and implications of the study, with future scope and limitations, will be discussed.

13.2 THE THEORY OF PLANNED BEHAVIOR

The TPB is an improvement on Ajzen and Fishbein's (1980) "Theory of reasoned action (TRA)," which was developed to evaluate the attitude–behavior relationship. They showed that the TRA was an effective model in explaining the attitude–behavior relationship, especially, if the behavior is mainly executed at will. However, Ajzen and Fishbein's TRA was not very effective when the undertaking cannot completely be executed by the individual. In this regard, Ajzen observed generally a person's behavior can hardly be completely voluntary or completely regulated. He stated that in most cases, an individual's behavior for his desires is measured from full control to uncontrol behavior.

Ajzen added on one hand that a person has total control over a given behavior when there are no real restrictions to the execution of the behavior. On the other hand, a person lacks complete control over behavior if the execution of the behavior involves funds or talents that the individual does not have (Ajzen, 1991).

Taking the above perceived or real scenario into cognizance, a new element was added to TRA as "Perceived behavioral control (PBC)" by Ajzen (1991). The PBC as a new component can equally impact intention, just as the attitudinal and normative elements. It is the addition of the third component—PBC—that transformed the TRA into what Ajzen described as TPB.

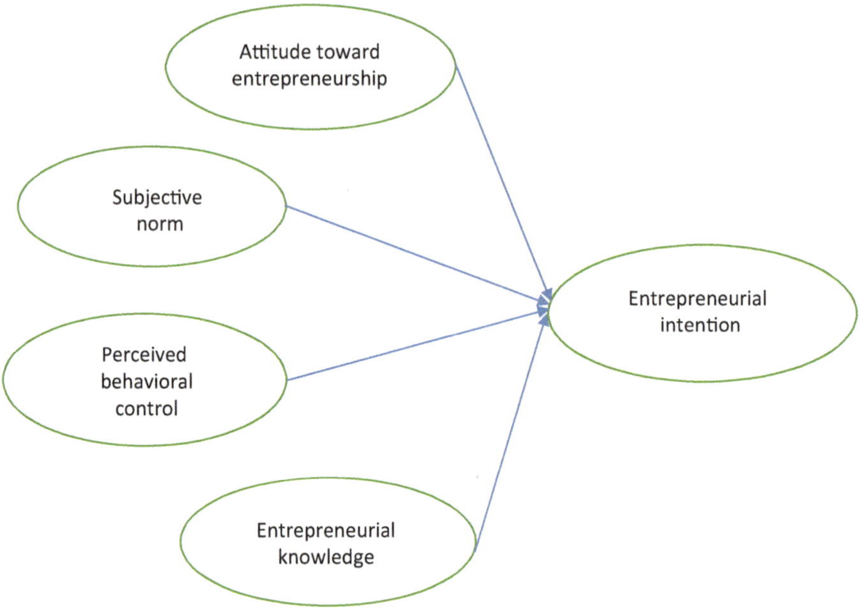

FIGURE 13.1 Conceptual model (extended model of TPB).
Source: Adapted from Ajzen, 1991.

Theory of planned behavior adopts that performing any particular action is a function of the individual's views about the expected outcomes of the action, which Ajzen referred to as behavioral beliefs, beliefs about what others normatively expect, which he referred to as the normative beliefs, and person's understandings about the existence of issues, which could ease or hamper the execution of the action, also called control beliefs. These factors collectively, create the intent toward the action (Ajzen, 2012).

A person's attitude concerning conduct reflects the level to which the person favors or disfavors the conduct. Subjective norm indicates the person's opinion of societal expectation regarding the execution or non-execution of a given behavior, and perceived behavioral control indicates the party's judgment of his/her capability and other issues, which could simplify or obstruct the action (Ajzen, 1991). In other words, the PBC reflects beliefs concerning the availability or non-availability of both internal and external resources required for the execution of a given activity.

Scholars in behavioral sciences, especially in the field of social psychology and marketing, have recorded a huge success in adapting the TPB to understanding the intention to behave in certain ways, particularly in such practical situations as career choices (Kim and Hunter 1993). The TPB has become the most dominant and widespread model used in predicting people's behavior, particularly the intent to involve in actions. It has been well validated in social psychology and increasingly endorsed as a robust research model for practically all planned and/or intentional behaviors in different context (Ajzen, 2001; Kolvereid, 1996), following hypotheses are proposed for the study.

H1: Intentions are significantly affected by attitude for business among undergraduates in Nigeria.

H2: Subjective norm significantly affects intention to found new business among undergraduates in Nigeria.

H3: Perceived behavioral control significantly intention to found new business among undergraduates in Nigeria.

13.2.1 THE TPB AND ENTREPRENEURIAL KNOWLEDGE

Following Kanothi's (2009) assertion that entrepreneurial training provides people with an ability to distinguish business openings and the skill, acquaintance, and attitudes to work upon, we refer to entrepreneurship education offered by the Nigerian higher education institutions as knowledge or training formally designed to equip undergraduates with capabilities and a positive mindset toward becoming self-employed after graduation. This definition indirectly expresses the fact that entrepreneurship knowledge is a prerequisite to an entrepreneurship career. Entrepreneurship is believed to be a planned undertaking, which is preceded by intention (Krueger, 2000). Hence, it is well suited for prediction by the TPB.

Although the TPB was built on the premise that individual's behavior is a kind of attitude for the performance, idiosyncratic norm, and control for perceived behavior. Ajzen studied that the TPB remains open and can accommodate a wide range of background and other exogenous factors that can be used to explain different behavioral process. Several scholars have advocated the modification of the original TPB model include different constructs as predictors of behavioral intentions in different fields, which they believe would improve the model's predictive capability (Yazdanpanah and Forouzani, 2015; Perugini and Bagozzi, 2001).

For instance, Karimy et al. (2015) extended the TPB by adding a smoking refusal technique to predict smoking behavior among Iranian students. Many other authors have extended the TPB by adding one or more variables to explain variance in behavioral intentions across different empirical settings in different domains (e.g., Muzaffar, 2015, purchase behavior; Hsu, 2012, tourism behavior; Cooke et al., 2006, drinking behavior; Rhodes and Courneya, 2003; Taylor and Todd, 1995, technology usage) among others.

In the entrepreneurship literature, research scholars have in the recent years used the TPB as a theoretical context for investigating intention toward taking self-employment as a career. Integrating entrepreneurial knowledge into the TPB model has offered a rational and largely appropriate framework for predicting the intent for entrepreneurial engagement by considering both attitudinal and societal issues (Krueger et al., 2000). For example, TPB is thoroughly used to predict the intention for starting new businesses among students in Scandinavia, the USA, Europe (Kuttim et al., 2014), Spain (Linan, 2005), The Netherlands (Karali, 2013), and Germany (Tegtmeier, 2012). It was also used with a great deal of success in Sri Lanka (Lin et al., 2013) and in Egypt by Hattab (2014).

The findings of these studies have provided support that prolonged kind of the TPB can be a useful process for envisaging entrepreneurial determination. Therefore, our objective to extend the TPB model to include entrepreneurial skill as an interpreter of meaning to for business skills for undergraduates in the Nigerian context is supported in extant literature. Following hypothesis is formed

H4: entrepreneurial knowledge offered in the Nigerian tertiary institutions will significantly influence the participants' intention toward founding new businesses.

13.3 METHODOLOGY

13.3.1 MEASURES

Instrument offered by Krosnick and Presser (2010) is used in the present investigation with full compliance and recommendations for survey instrument design along with Azjen's (2002) working portrayal of the constructs of TPB. Table 13.1 shows the complete details.

TABLE 13.1 Scaling and Measurement.

S. No.	Section	What is measured?	Number of items	Scale (5-point Likert scale)
1	Section A	Student's entrepreneurial intention (EI)	5	(SD–SA)
2	Section B	Students' perception of studied entrepreneurship courses in the class (ATE)	17	(SD–SA)
3	Section C	Students' attitude toward entrepreneurship related issues	16	(SD–SA)
4	Section D	Students' perceived social pressure/ expectations toward entrepreneurship and the drive to conform to the perceived pressure (SN)	17	(SD–SA)
5	Section E	Students' perception of their capacity to start and run new businesses (PBC)	16	(SD–SA)
		Total	71	

13.3.2 VALIDITY AND RELIABILITY OF RESEARCH INSTRUMENTS

To determine the inclusiveness of the characters underneath investigation in this study, the questionnaire was assessed firstly, examined by three professors (expert) in the domain of entrepreneurship. They offered useful suggestions on clarity and misconceptions, and result in deleting some obstruse statements, and questions which are of no relevance.

We also complied with Likert's (1932) initial work, which expected that a measurement instrument would be subjected to a pilot test to confirm its reliability. Hence, the instrument was pilot tested on final year students (n = 120), randomly drawn from the three types of institutions. The Cronbach's α coefficients as shown in Table 13.5 range from 0.725–0.840 for the pilot and 0.735–0.798 for the final study.

TABLE 13.2 Reliability Statistics for Pilot and Final Study.

	Pre-test (n = 120)		Final test (n = 968)	
Variables	Number of items	α	Number of items	α
Attitude toward entrepreneurship	16	0.725	16	0.745
Subjective norm	20	0.809	20	0.736
Perceived behavioral control	16	0.840	16	0.798
Entrepreneurship knowledge	28	0.793	28	0.782

13.3.3 POPULATION

As suggested by Carter et al. (2003), where stress was on important to study entrepreneurship by asking questions with target segment, and the people who are unexposed to the entrepreneurial skills they may come up with biased information, so target was colleges, polytechnics, and university students, having or not having any interest in business. A sample of 968 participants was drawn among final year students who may be prospective businessman in the future. As per Krueger et al. (2000), these kinds of samples are comprising of good intentions and acumen for business.

13.3.4 SAMPLE SIZE

The sample size for this study was based on Saunders et al.'s (2000) sampling table. The table provides absolute sample sizes at different margins of error. We adopt a multistage sampling procedure with the existing geopolitical structure in Nigeria, types of institution and schools in the institutions were used as parameters for stratification. The choice of this technique follows the study by Philip (2015) that multistage sampling is an appropriate sampling procedure for collecting primary data, especially where the population is geographically dispersed, and personal contact is required as it is highly flexible and effective in terms of cost, time, and generalizability.

13.4 ANALYSIS AND FINDINGS

Following a comprehensive review of the controversies surrounding the application of parametric tests in analyzing Likert scale data, we found enough convincing evidence that not only would the Likert scale be analyzed using such parametric tools but results in robust inferences (Jamieson, 2004; Carifio and Perla, 2008; Norman, 2010; Boone Jr., and Boone, 2012). Regression analysis was performed to understand the impact of predictor variables on intention toward entrepreneurship.

Correlation analysis was first conducted to assess the nature of the relationship among the explanatory variables. The result of correlation analysis indicates that the attitude toward entrepreneurship correlates significantly with the intent for business creation ($r = 0.524$, $p = 0.000$). Likewise, the perceived behavior ($r = 0.404$, p = 0.000), subjective norm ($r = 0.344$, $p = 0.000$), entrepreneurship education ($r = 0.332$, $p = 0.000$), also correlate significantly with the outcome variable. The correlation between the independent variables is significant at the 0.01 level and not more than 0.7, which further confirms the absence of multicollinearity.

TABLE 13.3 Independent and Outcome Variables Correlation Matrix.

Variables	Mean	SD	Y	X_1	X_2	X_3	X_4
Y (Entrepreneurial intention)	**3.70**	**0.41**	1				
X_1 (Attitude toward entrepreneurship)	3.66	0.42	0.524**	1			
X_2 (Subjective norms)	**3.75**	**0.42**	0.344**	0.411**	1		
X_3 (Perceived behavioral control)	**3.67**	**0.37**	0.404**	0.362**	0.416**	1	
X_4 (Entrepreneurship training)	3.57	**0.41**	0.332**	.0344**	0.248**	0.402**	1

**Correlation is significant at the 0.01 level (two-tailed).

*Correlation is significant at the 0.05 level (two-tailed).

The variables used in regression equation as the as predictors of intent to find a new startup is the intention for perceived behavioral control, entrepreneurship, subjective norm, and compulsory education for entrepreneurship. Therefore, the regression model of entrepreneurial intention ($\hat{Y}$) consists of four predicting variables namely, attitude toward entrepreneurship (X_1), subjective norm (X_2), perceived behavioral control (X_3), and entrepreneurship education (X_4); regression equation is given as

$$\hat{Y} = b_0 + b_1X_1 + b_2X_2 + b_3X_3 + b_4X_4 + e_i \tag{1}$$

where

$\hat{Y}$ = *entrepreneurial intention*
X_1 = *attitude toward entrepreneurship*
X_2 = *subjective norms*
X_3 = *perceived behavioral control*
X_4 = *entrepreneurial knowledge*
e_i = *random error.*

Hypotheses, to measure the strength of the entrepreneurial intent through regression model, is given as follows:

$HO\!: Y = \beta_0 + e_i$
$HA\!: Y = b_0 + b_1X_1 + b_2X_2 + b_3X_3 + b4x4 + e_i$

Based on the unstandardized coefficients listed in Table 13.3, the regression equation is given by: $\hat{Y} = 0.890 + (0.378)\,X_1 + (0.078)\,X_2 + (0.210)\,X_3 + (0.103)\,X_4 + \text{Error}$

TABLE 13.4 Summary of ANOVA.

Model		Sum of squares	Df	Mean square	*F*	*p*
1	Regression	54.979	4	13.745	124.800	.000
	Residual	106.058	963	0.110		
	Total	161.037	967			

Dependent variable: Entrepreneurial intention; Significant when $p < 0.05$

The ANOVA summary (Table 13.1) indicated that the model that contains all the four predictor variables is statistically significant: $F(4, 963) = 124.800$, $p = 0.000$. The result suggests that there will be more than zero variance in the outcome resultant upon the alteration in the predictor variable. Moreover, the model summary indicated significant multiple correlations between all the explanatory and the outcome variables ($R = 0.584$). This suggests that the explanatory variables are significantly influencing the outcome. As predicted, the R^2-value of 0.341 confirms the significance of the effect. Hence, about 34% of the variation in the intent of undergraduate students is described by the variables in the model.

TABLE 13.5 Model Summary.

Model	*R*	R^2	Adjusted R^2	Standard error of the estimate
1	0.584	0.341	0.339	0.332

Predictors: (constant), ET, ATE, SN, and PBC

Dependent variable: EI

13.4.1 DETERMINATION OF THE CONTRIBUTIONS OF EACH OF THE INDEPENDENT VARIABLES

The regression analysis presented in Table 13.3 indicated that attitude significantly influence the intent for entrepreneurship ($\beta = 0.387$, $t\ (963) = 12.835$, $p = < 0.01$, $pr = 0.336$) has studied. The standardized coefficient (β) proposes that when a change in attitude for entrepreneurial attitude leads to about a 39% change in the intent among students for their entrepreneurial attitude in the country. The semi-partial or part correlation 0.3362 which is 0.1128 indicates that attitude toward entrepreneurship uniquely accounts for an additional 11.3% of the variance in students' interest in business activities; this data is not supporting rest of the predictors in model. Hence, hypothesis H1 is supported.

The analysis further revealed that subjective norm is also a significant and positive predictor of entrepreneurship intent ($\beta = 0.080$, $t = 2.648$, $p =$

0.008, *pr* = 069). The standardized coefficient (*β* weight) indicates that a unit increase in subjective norm toward entrepreneurship results in 8.0% increase in intent for entrepreneurship among Nigerian undergraduates.

Similarly, the part correlation (0.0692), which is 0.0048, indicates that the subjective norm uniquely explained an additional 0.48% of the change in students' entrepreneurial intent, which cannot be accounted for, by the other predictors in the model. Hence, hypothesis H2 is supported.

The regression model also showed that students' perception of control for business startups has a significant influence on their intent of starting new organizations. The consistent regression constant and its related (*p* and *t*) values indicated that perception of entrepreneurship abilities is relatively a significant contributor to the intent for founding new firm [$\beta = 0.190$, $t\,(963) = 6.126$, $p = < 0.01$, $pr = 0.160$]. The standardized coefficient (*β* weight) showed that one unit change in perceived behavioral control leads to a 19% change in entrepreneurial intention of students. Further, the part correlation (0.1602), which is 0.0256, indicates the control for behavior exclusively responsible for an extra 2.56% of the modification in students' interest for entrepreneurship; this is not because of the presence of the rest of the predictors in the model. There is, therefore, enough evidence that hypothesis H3 holds true.

Finally, the analysis revealed that entrepreneurship skills learned in the class is a significant contributor to the intention for business venture creation among undergraduates in Nigeria ($\beta = 0.103$, $t\,(963) = 3.499$, $p = < 0.01$, pr = 091). Here, *β* indicates that 10.3% of the change in the entrepreneurship

TABLE 13.6 Multiple Regression Analysis of Variables Predicting Entrepreneurial Intention.

		B	SE	β	t	Significant value	Partial	Part	Tolerance	VIF
1	Constant	0.890	0.135		6.589	0.000				
	Attitude toward entrepreneurship	0.378	0.029	0.387	12.835	0.000	0.382	0.336	0.751	1.332
	Subjective norm	0.078	0.029	0.080	2.648	0.008	0.085	0.069	0.748	1.337
	Perceived behavioral control	0.210	0.034	0.190	6.126	0.000	0.194	0.160	0.715	1.399
	Entrepreneurial knowledge	0.103	0.030	0.103	3.499	0.000	0.112	0.091	0.793	1.262

Note: $R^2 = .341$; adjusted $R^2 = 0.339$; [$F\,(4{,}963) = 124.800$, $p = 0.000$)]

Dependent variable: Entrepreneurial intention

B, unstandardized coefficients; SE, standard error; *β*, standardized coefficients; *t* = *t*-value; *p*: *p*-value intent of the Nigerian undergraduate is due to a unit change in entrepreneurship education. Moreover, the part correlation (0.0912), which is 0.0083, indicates that the perceived behavioral control uniquely accounts for an additional 0.83% of the adjustment in students' entrepreneurship intent, which is not due to the presence of rest of the autonomous variables in model. Thus, hypothesis H4 is also supported.

The regression analysis showed that attitude toward business acumen responsible for the maximum change in intent for business acumen in the students. So, it is strongly predicted, upon comparing with other variables in model. The behavioral control is another strong predictor, followed by entrepreneurship education, and subjective norm. Collectively though, the regression model that is consisting of all the four independent variables (i.e., three constructs of the TPB plus entrepreneurial knowledge) explained only about 34% of the variation in the intent for new firm creation among the Nigerian undergraduates. It means that unidentified aspects beyond the scope of our study account for 66% of the intention to founding new businesses among the Nigerian youth.

13.5 DISCUSSION AND CONCLUSION

Present study tests the predictive capabilities of TPB in the Nigerian. We integrated entrepreneurial knowledge offered to undergraduates as a predictor variable acting alongside the three antecedents of intention postulated in TPB. The stretched model of the TPB provided the platform to assess the combined and individual effects of entrepreneurial knowledge, attitude, perceived social pressure, and perceived behavioral control toward entrepreneurship on intention to founding new business among the Nigerian undergraduates.

The results support the hypotheses that attitude toward entrepreneurship, societal pressure, perceived control over entrepreneurial behavior, and entrepreneurial knowledge are significant predictors of intention to start business among the students.

In line with findings of Roy et al. (2017); Marques et al. (2012); and Liman and Chen (2009), the result of this study specifically showed that attitude is relatively the strongest predictor of intention, as it accounts for the highest variation in the intention to initiate businesses among the students. Their perception of control over business behavior is the second-highest influence on the intent for business. Other studies such as Boissin et al. (2009) and Kreugar (2000) also demonstrated a similar result. Our study also found that

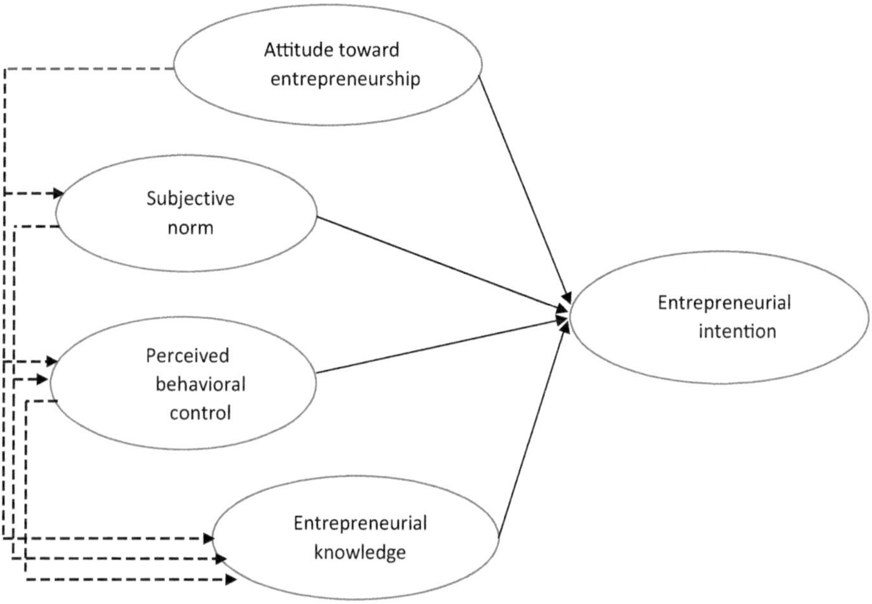

FIGURE 13.2 Final model *$p < 0.05$, ** $p < 0.01$, ***$p < 0.001$. Doted arrows represent the significantly positive correlation among the predictor variables.

Source: Adapted from Ajzen, 1991.

the perception of significant others toward entrepreneurship had the weakest, but statistically substantial consequence to start business. This concurs with the findings of Malebana (2014) and Autio et al. (2001), but incongruent with the results of Aloulou (2016), Linan and Chen (2009), Kruegar (2000), who did not find any indication that perceived societal reactions significantly influence intention toward business venture creation.

On measuring the relative contribution of the extended construct (entrepreneurship knowledge receive informal class setting), our result follows the findings of Oguntimehin and Olaniran (2017) and Adegboye et al. (2016) whose studies in the Southern Nigerian context demonstrated that entrepreneurship education had a significant influence for business acumen. Similar studies outside the context of Nigeria (Niţu-Niţu-Antonie and Feder, 2017; Bhuyan and Pathak, 2017; Choitung et al., 2017; Zhang, Wang and Owen, 2015) also found that the entrepreneurship education significantly influences the intention toward an entrepreneurial behavior.

The findings of the present study prove that the TPB is a worthy framework that can be used to predict intention to founding or establishing a business. Further, the present study validates the insertion of a fourth construct in the original Ajzens' TPB. Study in the same context by Gujrati et al. (2019b) found that a regression model, which consisted of only the three original TPB's antecedents of intention accounted for about 20% of the intention to founding new business among undergraduates in Nigerian students. This suggests that extending the model (inclusion of entrepreneurial knowledge as an independent variable acting alongside original TPB components) improved its predictive capability by 14%.

Our study strongly implies that apart from entrepreneurial attitude, perception of societal reactions to entrepreneurship, perception of control factors, and entrepreneurial knowledge received in the classroom; other factors beyond the scope of our study may account for about 66% variance in the intent for the creation of new firms among the Nigerian undergraduates.

In our view, the most compelling explanation for this is the numerous initiatives introduced by the current government aimed at supporting young people in Nigeria to embrace entrepreneurship as a career option, which saw the country rise 15 places (from 146 in 2019–131 in 2020) in the World Bank Doing Business Index. Some of these programs include Youth Entrepreneur Support Program (YES-P), Youth Initiative for Sustainable Agriculture in Nigeria (YISA), and N-Power; free 250,000 FGN business names registration for MSMEs, among others. These initiatives, which fell outside the scope of the present study may well explain the 66% variation in intention to founding new business among youth in Nigeria.

13.5.1 IMPLICATIONS OF THE STUDY

Our findings have a significant influence in practice and theory to both theory and practice. Theoretically, the investigation provided empirical backing for the TPB in predicting intent for entrepreneurship in a collectivistic African society. Further, the present study adds to the theory by affirming that the TPB does not only accommodate external factors but also adding the external factors such as entrepreneurship knowledge to act alongside "attitude, subjective, and perceived behavioral control" in predicting students' entrepreneurial intentions improves the predictive capability of the model.

In practice, government, policymakers, or institutions' administrators may use the acquaintance studied by study, which revealed the degree of effectiveness of the compulsory entrepreneurial knowledge offered in the Nigerian tertiary institutions in achieving its objective to evaluate and justify resource allocation for program and future involvements. The findings of the current study do not only expose the impediments in achieving the Government's desire to having business-oriented youths but also suggest ways of overcoming the challenges toward entrepreneurial career among undergraduates.

For entrepreneurship educators, the results of the present study serve as feedback, which will aid the designing of well-structured entrepreneurship courses that takes cognizance of students' attitude, subjective norm, and control factors toward entrepreneurship. Finally, students and future researchers can take the findings of the current study as a worthy reference point.

13.5.2 LIMITATIONS AND DIRECTION FOR FUTURE STUDIES

While the cross-sectional design adopted in the present study provided a meaningful insight into the relationship between attitude, subjective norm, control of behavioral, business acumen, and intent to founding new business among undergraduates, it could not account for the development of the changes in the students' intent from non-existence to existence, and/or from weak to strong intent, which can only be revealed through pre and post-test or longitudinal study designs. Therefore, more studies based on the longitudinal data and pre- and post-test designs are required to track students' entrepreneurial intention development before, during, and after completing their graduation.

Although the present study provided a piece of valuable information on the relationship between the TPB's antecedents of intention including entrepreneurial knowledge, it was not able to account for the intention to behavior relationship. It will be useful to extend the findings of this study by examining the intention to actual entrepreneurial behavior relationship in the future.

KEYWORDS

- **predictive capability**
- **entrepreneurship**
- **planned behavior**
- **Correlation analysis**
- **Nigeria**

REFERENCES

Abina, M. B.; Oyeniran, I. W.; Onikosi-Alliyu, S. O. Determinants of Entrepreneurial Intention Among Nigerian Students. *Ethiopian J. Environm. Stud. Manage.* **2015,** *8*(1), 107–112. DOI: http://dx.doi.org/10.4314/ejesm.v8i1.10

Ajzen, I. The Theory of Planned Behaviour. *Org. Behav. Human Decision Process.* **1991,** *50*(2), 79–211. http://dx.doi.org/10.1016/0749- 5978(91)90020-T

Ajzen, I. Constructing a Theory of Planned Behavior Questionnaire: Conceptual and Methodological Considerations. 2002, revised 2006. https://pdfs.semanticscholar.org/0574/b20bd58130dd5a961f1a2db10fd1fcbae95d.

Aloulou, W. J. Predicting Entrepreneurial Intentions of Final Year Saudi University Business Students by Applying the Theory of Planned Behavior. *J. Small Bus. Enterp. Dev.* **2016,** *23*(4), 1142–1164. DOI: org/10.1108/JSBED -02-2016-0028

Autio, E.; Keeley, R. H.; Klofsten, M.; Parker, G. G. C.; Hay, M. Entrepreneurial Intent Among Students in Scandinavia and in the USA. *Enterp. Innov. Manage Stud.* **2001,** *2*(2), 145–160.

Bhuyan, M.; Pathak, P. Understanding Entrepreneurial Intention of University Students in Uttarakhand: An Empirical Study. *Indian J. Comm. Manage. Stud.* **2017,** *8*(2), 93–100. DOI: http://dx.doi.org/10.18843/ijcms/v8i2/13

Boissin, J. J.; Branchet, B.; Emin, S.; Herbert, J. I. Students and Entrepreneurship: A Comparative Study of France and the United States. *J. Small Bus. Entrepreneurship* **2009,** *22*(2), 101–12.

Boone, H. N. Jr.; Boone, D. A. Analyzing Likert Data. *J. Ext.* **2012,** *50*(2). https://eric.ed.gov/?id=EJ1042448.

Carifio, J.; Perla, R. Resolving the 50-Year Debate Around Using and Misusing Likert Scales. *Med. Educ.* **2008,** *42*, 1150–1152. DOI: http://dx.doi.org/10.1111/j.1365-2923.2008.03172.x.

Cooke, R.; Sheeran, P. Moderation of Cognition-Intention and Cognition-Behaviour Relations: A Meta-Analysis of Properties of Variables From the Theory of Planned Behaviour. *Br. J. Soc. Psychol.* **2004,** *43*, 159–186.

Gartner, W. B. Who is an Entrepreneur? Is the Wrong Question. *Entrepreneurship Theory Pract.* **1989,** *13*(4), 47–68. DOI: org/10.1177/104225878901300406.

Godin, G.; Kok, G. The Theory of Planned Behavior: A Review of its Applications to Health-Related Behaviors. Am. J. *Health Promot.* **1996,** *11*(2), 87–98.

Gujrati, R.; Tyagi, V.; Lawan, A. L. Higher Education Students Perception Towards Entrepreneurship Education: Evidence From Northern Nigeria. *Int. J. Res. Eng. Appl. Manage.* **2019,** *5*(1). DOI: 10.18231/2454-9150.2019.0336

Gupta, R.; Shastri, M.; Pandey, A. K.; Bhandwal, M. Pandemic 2020, Challenges, and Measures for Post Revival. In *Advances in Interdisciplinary Engineering. Lecture Notes in Mechanical Engineering*; Kumar, N., Tibor, S., Sindhwani, R., Lee, J., Srivastava, P., Eds.; Springer: Singapore, 2021. https://doi.org/10.1007/978-981-15-9956-9_52,

Hattab, H. W. Impact of Entrepreneurship Education on Entrepreneurial Intentions of University Students in Egypt. *J. Entrepreneurship* **2014,** *23*(1), 1–18. DOI: 10.1177/0971355713513346

Hsu, C. H. C.; Huang, S. An Extension of the Theory of Planned Behavior Model for Tourist. *J. Hosp. Tour. Res.* **2012,** *36*(3), 390–417. DOI: 10.1177/1096348010390817.

Jamieson, S. Likert Scales: How to (ab) Use Them. *Med. Educ.* **2004,** *38*, 1217–1218. DOI: org/10.1111/j.1365-2929.2004.02012.x.

Kanothi, R. N. *The Dynamics of Entrepreneurship in ICT: Case of Mobile Phones Downstream Services in Kenya*; ISS Working Paper Series/General Series 466, Erasmus University Rotterdam: Netherlands, 2009; pp 1–76. http://hdl.handle.net/1765/18727

Karali, S. The Impact of Entrepreneurship Education Programs on Entrepreneurial Intentions: An Application of the Theory of Planned Behavior. Master's Thesis, Erasmus University of Rotterdam, Netherlands, 2013.

Karimy, M.; Zareban, I.; Araban, M.; Montazeri A. An Extended Theory of Planned Behavior (TPB) Used to Predict Smoking Behavior Among a Sample of Iranian Medical Students. *Int. J. High Risk Behav. Addict.* **2015,** *4*(3), e241715. DOI: 10.5812/ijhrba.24715

Kolvereid, L. Prediction of Employment Status Choice Intentions. *Entrepreneurship Theory Prac.* **1996,** *21*(1), 47–57. https://doi.org/10.1177/104225879602100104

Krueger, N. F.; Reilly, M. D.; Carsrud, A. L. Competing Models of Entrepreneurial Intentions. *J. Bus. Ventur.* **2014,** *15*(6), 411–432. DOI: org/10.1016/S0883-9026(98)00033-0

Kuttim, M.; Kallaste, M.; Aino Kiis, U. V. Entrepreneurship Education at University Level and Students' Entrepreneurial Intentions. *Social Behav. Sci.* **2014,** *110*, 658–668. www.sciencedirect.com

Likert, R. A Technique for the Measurement of Attitudes. *Arch. Psychol.* **1932,** *22*(140), 1–55. https://www.researchgate.net/publication/262011454_Likert

Lin, X.; Carsrud, A.; Jagoda, K.; Shen, W. Determinants of Entrepreneurial Intentions: Applying Western Model to the Sri Lankan Context. *J. Enterprising Culture* **2013,** *21*(2), 153–174. DOI: 10.1142/S0218495813500076

Linan, F. Intention-Based Models of Entrepreneurship Education Small Business. [Online], 2004, p 11–35. https://www.researchgate.net/publication/235937886_Intention-Based_Models_of_Entrepreneurship_Education

Linan, F.; Chen, Y. Testing the Entrepreneurial Intention Model on a Two Country Sample, 2006 https://dialnet.unirioja.es/servlet/articulo;jsessionid= 0CCB58BDD51E325 B9669 F56910BA0010.dialnet02?codigo=2046970

Linan, F.; Chen, Y. W. Development and Cross-Cultural Application of a Specific Instrument to Measure Entrepreneurial Intentions. Entrepreneurship Theory Pract. **2009,** *33*(3), 593–617.

Marques, C. S.; Ferreira, J. J.; Gomes, D. N.; Gouveia Rodrigues, R. Entrepreneurship Education: How Psychological, Demographic and Behavioural Factors Predict the Entrepreneurial Intention. *Educ. Train.* **2012,** *54*(8/9), 657–672.

Muzaffar, N. Developing an Extended Model of Theory of Planned Behavior to Explore Green Purchase Behavior of Pakistani Consumers. *Am. J. Bus. Manage.* **2015,** *4*(2), 85–101. DOI: 10.11634/216796061504654

Niţu-Antonie, R. D.; Feder, E. Exploratory Study on Student's Entrepreneurial Intentions in Developed and Emerging Countries. *Rev. Int. Manage.* **2017,** *18*(1), 31–43. https://search.proquest.com/ docview/1912934718?accountid=187781

Norman, G. Likert Scales, Levels of Measurement and the Laws of Statistics. Advanced Health Science. *Educ. Theory Pract.* **2010,** *15*(5), 625–32. DOI: 10.1007/s10459-010-9222-y

Oguntimehin, Y. A.; Olaniran, O. O. The Relationship Between Entrepreneurship Education and Students' Entrepreneurial Intentions in Ogun State-Owned University, Nigeria. *British J. Educ.* **2017,** *5(*3), 9–20. http://www.eajournals.org/wp-content/uploads

Perugini, M.; Bagozzi, R. P. The Role of Desires and Anticipated Emotions in Goal-Directed Behaviours: Broadening and Deepening the Theory of Planned Behaviour. *Br. J. Soc. Psychol.* **2001,** *40*(1), 79–98.

Philip, S. Multistage sampling, 2015. DOI: org/10.1136/bmj.h4155

Rhodes, R. E.; Courneya, K. S. Modelling the Theory of Planned Behaviour and Past Behaviour. *Psychol. Health Med.* **2003,** *8*(1), 57–69.

Robinson, P. B.; Stimpson, D. V.; Huefner, J. C.; Hunt, H. K. An Attitude Approach to the Prediction of Entrepreneurship. *Entrepreneurship Theory Pract.* **1991,** *15*(4), 13–32. https://doi.org/10.1177/104225879101500405

Roy, R.; Akhtar, F.; Das, N. Entrepreneurial Intention Among Science & Technology Students in India: Extending the Theory of Planned Behavior. *Int. Entrepreneurship Manage. J.* **2017,** *13,* 1013–1041. DOI: 10.1007/s11365-017-0434-y

Saunders, M.; Lewis, P.; Thornhill, A. In *Research Methods for Business Students,* 5th ed., Pearson Education: Harlow Gate, England, 2009.

Shapero, A. The Displaced, Uncomfortable Entrepreneur. *Psychol. Today* **1975,** *9*(6), 83–88.

Taylor, S.; Todd, P. A. Understanding Information Technology Usage: A Test of Competing Models. *Inform. Syst. Res.* **1995,** *6*, 144–176. DOI: 10.1287/isre.6.2.144

Tegtmeier, S. Empirical Implications for Promoting Students' Entrepreneurial Intentions. *J. Enterprising Culture* **2012,** *20*(2), 15–169. DOI: 10.1142/S0218495812500070

Yazdanpanah, M.; Forouzani, M. Application of the Theory of Planned Behaviour to Predict Iranian Students' Intention to Purchase Organic Food. *J. Cleaner Product.* **2015,** *107*, 342–352.

Zhang, P.; Wang, D. D.; Owen, C. L. A Study of Entrepreneurial Intention of University Students [Online], 2015. https://ideas.repec.org/a/bpj/erjour/v5y2015i1p22n2.html

CHAPTER 14

Contribution of IT: Future of Work in the Post-COVID-19 Pandemic

VIDHUSHI SHRIVASTAVA[1*] and SHIKHA KAPOOR[2]

[1]*Student MBA (IB&HR), Amity International Business School, Amity University, Noida 201313, India*

[2]*Professor HR&OB, Amity International Business School, Amity University, Noida 201313, India*

[*]*Corresponding author. E-mail: vidushishrivastava2@gmail.com*

ABSTRACT

The term "future of work" has taken on a whole new meaning in the aftermath of the coronavirus disease 2019 (COVID-19) pandemic. While businesses strive to ensure their employees' wellbeing during these challenging circumstances, productivity through remote working and employee engagement have become top priorities. When COVID-19 first began to spread in India, the Government of India imposed a nationwide lockdown to prevent the virus from spreading further. This lockdown presented a challenge to organizations because they needed to change their conventional working styles to ensure smooth operations and "working from home" provided an immediate solution.

As the concept of virtual working gained momentum, human resource (HR) managers began to ensure that brick-and-mortar workplaces were properly transformed into virtual environments. Work from home (WFH) was not a new concept; it had been used in the IT industry before itself. While the world became more technologically advanced, surviving in this new world was not an easy task. Organizational HR managers have been

Constructive Discontent in Execution: Creative Approaches to Technology and Management.
Sanjeev Bansal, Anita Venaik, Swati Upveja, and Saritha S. (Eds.)

seen remapping policies and frameworks to help them survive in this new normal. Our research focuses on how the future of work will be affected by COVID-19 pandemic. This study is primarily for those interested in learning more about how the future of work will change because of COVID-19 pandemic.

14.1 INTRODUCTION

Coronavirus disease arrived and blew mankind apart, causing havoc in almost every aspect of human life. Whether it is a demand loss in one sector or a demand gain in another, we have seen a slew of unpredictable paradigm shifts since the start of 2020. The impact of the pandemic on healthcare, the environment, and the economy is varied, but one thing that can be measured is the shift in workplace dynamics. When it comes to these changes, the world's response to the pandemic is the primary cause of this dynamic shift in workplaces. When the entire world was in lockdown, businesses had to ensure that their operations ran smoothly while adhering to the rules set forth by the organizations. To ensure business continuity, the HR team has been on the front lines, quickly informing employees about the organization's response to the pandemic. Human resource teams can be seen managing with efficiency and maintaining high employee morale in a variety of situations. Work from home became the go-to solution for business continuity.

By using technology, we can reduce the spread of coronavirus while maintaining operations and businesses. The role of technology is becoming increasingly important, as it is and will continue to assist in keeping society functional during lockdowns and quarantines. There have been some noticeable changes because of the pandemic.

- **Online shopping and delivery by robots:** Following the SARS outbreak in late 2002, the online market saw an increase in both business-to-business and business-to-customer transactions. Various Chinese e-commerce behemoths are accelerating the development of robots that will deliver packages to people following the COVID-19 pandemic to ensure the public's health and hygiene.
- **Digital and contactless payments:** Because cash may carry the virus, central banks in various countries have implemented a variety of measures to ensure that e-wallets are operated with ease of access. Paytm, Google Pay, and a slew of other online platforms are

introducing policies that are simple to understand and implement, thereby reducing the spread of the coronavirus.

- **Remote work:** Employees in almost every service sector have been asked to WFH. Virtual private networks, virtual meetings, cloud technology, and even technologies that allow a person to appear in front of a virtual background to protect their privacy at home enable remote work. Apps such as Zoom, Microsoft Teams, Google Meets, and WebEx are some examples of platforms that make remote work simple while also protecting sensitive data.
- **Distance learning:** Beginning in March 2020, nearly 191 countries closed schools and universities, affecting nearly 1.57 billion students. To ensure that education was not disrupted by the lockdown, many educational institutions offered online classes and courses. The technologies used in distance learning are such as those used in remote work and virtual reality, augmented reality, and other similar applications.

This pandemic and its crises force us to develop a wide range of skills and abilities, including the ability to take risks while remaining agile and consistent. We should improve our agility, resilience, flexibility, and digitalization skills. This is the stage where people believe that increasing automation and technological advancements will force them out of work, which is not the case; rather, progress in these areas will help them return to normal in these difficult times, so an organization or individual must train and develop themselves to become competent enough to survive. Continuous earning is also critical, as everyone in this situation needs to be up to date on current trends and competencies to stay aligned with the industry. To ensure the safety of employees, organizations have developed contactless or remote working in industries such as manufacturing. Proper safety measures have been provided, such as PPE kits, masks, sanitizers, weekly testing, and a group of 10–20 people can work in a single shift. If we talk about the pharmaceutical industry, sales managers who meet with doctors are given proper training and kits, and if a senior executive over the age of 50 works in sales, their organizations provide them with benefits such as WFH, online meetings, and sabbaticals.

Organizations are becoming more supportive and flexible to provide employees with the proper help they require to ensure proper work–life balance. Employee stress is being reduced through a variety of online events, as well as a no-work-after-5-pm policy, in which employees are not allowed to do any work after 5 pm. The ability of future leaders to respond, recover, and thrive in the COVID-19 pandemic will determine their success. How an organization handles the current situation, how quickly it recovers and emerges stronger, and how it prepares for the new normal will all help them become successful leaders in the future. Adapting to the current work environment can be difficult, but it is not impossible. In the post-pandemic stage, a new mankind will emerge, with different behavior and thinking compared to that before the outbreak.

14.2 LITERATURE REVIEW

New prospects can be generated by recognizing the shift and embracing technological advancement (Kumar, 2020). The future of work is being redefined by technology in the automotive sector and other sectors. A combination of digital skills with specific human experience and advanced technology is what is needed to build a correct work atmosphere and better productivity in the current times and after COVID-19. Fresh possibilities can be generated by recognizing the shift and embracing technical advances (Walsh and Resch, 2020). Organizations that prioritize their human capital will be able to mitigate risk and support value creation as compared to others. Mankind is going through a humanitarian revolution, that is, revolution 4.0. The emergence of a new mankind, whose everyday actions and thoughts will differ from what it was before the COVID-19 outbreak, will see the post-epidemic era. There is a great need for these to be incorporated into holistic post-pandemic thinking, considering the time value of the latest security initiatives being put into effect worldwide. We will be faced with a generation that thinks differently from the generation before the pandemic (El Omari, 2020; Mitra, 2020). The speed of transition, with businesses pushing for digitalization, has been exponential. However, no one would have expected that one of the biggest workplace improvements of our time will be intensified by a single global occurrence, the COVID-19 outbreak. Digitalization is critical, as it will help businesses allow their internal operations with employee communication and productivity software and maximize operational performance with agile business continuity plans. With industries struggling to thrive in the face of what is expected to be one of the hardest recessions to date, it is important to consider the changes that the global COVID-19 pandemic will bring about. New technologies such as artificial intelligence (AI), the internet of things (IoT), and automation can promote these improvements and push businesses to rethink their current systems and guidelines (Bahsoun et al., 2020). The pandemic and its inherent effects on industries have illustrated the need for adaptability and flexibility in today's workforce, intensified the transition to a modern, digital economy, and accentuated the value of HR in the new normal. Because of the pandemic's impact on the economy, to survive, companies were rapidly forced to change and adjust to the new standards. Pant (2020), in her study, talks about how leaders will now have to concentrate on developing a healthy working atmosphere that gives people the confidence to return to work premises and to adapt to the current virtual/physical integrated way of working, according to the five priorities of the company, Accenture, to help reopen and reinvent the company study. "There are three broad areas that businesses should urgently consider helping employees: allowing remote collaboration solutions for remote/WFH and ensuring safe connectivity; operating virtual events; and disseminating vital information to address frequently asked questions via omnichannel communication, including via chatbots." Therefore, businesses can redesign themselves, their practices, consumer interactions, employee, and social contracts, and do so in ways that can better stage the transition to the virtual/physical hybrid workplace, the new normal of employment, to further their purposes. Volini et al. (2020), in their article, on returning to work in the future of work talks about how organizations encountered a burst of growth during the COVID-19 pandemic, quick-forwarding into the future of work in ways that stress-tested their ability to combine people and technology in the most complex market climate that many of us have ever seen. However, while moments of crisis can lead to courageous and unprecedented acts, where the true road to recovery can begin is the durability of those acts. The road must be paved not only with good intentions but also with real progress. Intention, opportunity, insight, and possibility are no longer future-focused expectations in a post-COVID-19 world, but the truth of the here and now. Organizations face a choice between returning to a post-COVID-19 environment that is essentially yesterday's improved version or creating one that is tomorrow's sustainable version. The danger is more than falling behind it, which is the chance to never catch up at all. Work trends post-COVID-19 (Baker, 2020) states that the pandemic of the coronavirus will have a lasting influence on the future of work. The imperative for HR leaders is to assess the effect each trend would have on the operations and strategic objectives of their company, to determine which require immediate action, and to assess to what extent these trends alter strategic goals and plans for pre-COVID-19 are remote work, data collection, contiguous worker experience, and employee huminatirazation.

14.3 CONCEPTUAL FRAMEWORK

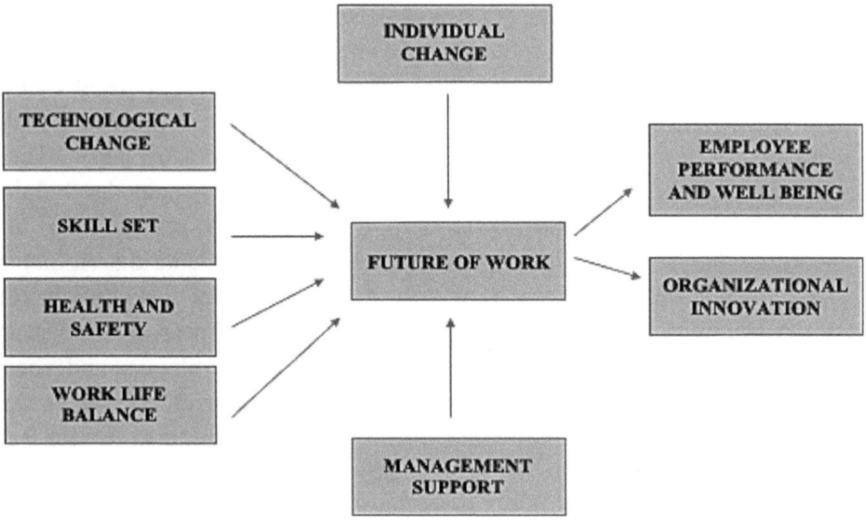

FIGURE 14.1 Conceptual framework.

14.4 NEED FOR THE STUDY

This research is essential because the COVID-19 pandemic has resulted in numerous technological changes that are evident. To gain a better understanding of how organizations are dealing with technological changes and how people are adapting to these changes, this research is carried out for businesses to adapt and change to advance and grow in the future.

14.5 RESEARCH METHODOLOGY

14.5.1 RESEARCH DESIGN

This research uses an exploratory design. Employees from private, public, and governmental organizations, who work in the Delhi National Capital Region (NCR), and whose age group was in the range 25–55 years were the primary target audience for the study.

14.5.2 *RESEARCH METHODOLOGY*

1. **Primary Source:** The survey that was conducted to gather responses and interviews with executives to learn how they are preparing their organizations for the post-COVID era were the primary sources of data collection in the research. A survey was conducted with the primary goal of gaining an understanding of what the future of work will entail. This research perspective was appropriate for achieving our study's goals.
2. **Secondary Source:** To explain the basic definition of the research subject, "Contribution of IT: Future of Work Post-COVID-19 Pandemic," a variety of academic papers were consulted.

14.5.3 *SAMPLE SIZE*

A total of 109 people were included in the study. It was decided to use a convenient sampling method.

14.5.4 *RESEARCH TOOL*

The instrument that was used in the research was a questionnaire. The questionnaire was created using a conceptual framework, and the data was then visualized using various infographics, with SPSS software being used to investigate the relationship between the scales.

14.5.5 *QUESTIONNAIRE DESIGN*

The questionnaire was created in perfect accordance with the study's goals and hypotheses. A questionnaire was created with each variable in mind, along with a set of descriptive questions on the following topics:

1. Technological change
2. Skillset
3. Health and safety
4. Work–life balance
5. Employee wellbeing and performance
6. Organization's innovation

On a 5-point scale, each variable was evaluated.

14.6 RESEARCH OBJECTIVES

- Researching the impact of technological change on business innovation.
- To investigate the impact of a person's skillset on their ability to perform.
- To investigate the impact of workplace safety and health on employee's satisfaction.
- To investigate the impact of work–life balance on employee's productivity and happiness.

14.7 HYPOTHESES

- H0: Technological change does not affect an organization's ability to innovate.
- H1: Technological change has a significant impact on organizational innovation.
- H0: A person's skillset does not affect their performance.
- H1: A person's skillset has a significant impact on their performance.
- H0: Employee wellbeing is unaffected by safety and health.
- H1: Safety and health have a significant impact on employee's wellbeing.
- H0: Work–life balance does not affect an employee's performance or wellbeing.
- H1: Work–life balance has a significant impact on employee's performance and wellbeing.

14.8 DATA ANALYSIS

The data analysis for hypotheses:

H0: There is no impact of technological change on organization's innovation.
H1: There is a significant impact of technological change on organization's innovation.

Skillset			**Employee Performance**
Technological Change			**Organizational Innovation**
Technological change	Pearson correlation	1	0.580**
	Significant value (two-tailed)		0.000
	N	109	109
Innovation	Pearson correlation	0.580**	1
	Significant value (two-tailed)	0.000	
	N	109	109

FIGURE 14.2 Correlation between technological change and organizational innovation.
**Correlation is significant at the 0.01 level (two-tailed).

There is a strong and positive correlation between technological change and organizational innovation in the future of work; $p = 0.00$ which is lower than the significant value; therefore, we reject the null hypothesis and there is sufficient evidence to conclude that there is a significant impact or correlation between technological change and organization's innovation.

The data analysis for the hypotheses:

H0: There is no impact of skillset on employee's performance.
H1: There is a significant impact of skillset on employee's performance.

Skillset			**Employee Performance**
Skillset	Pearson correlation	1	0.874**
	Significant value (two-tailed)		0.000
	N	109	109
Employee performance	Pearson correlation	0.874**	1
	Significant value (two-tailed)	0.000	
	N	109	109

FIGURE 14.3 Correlation between skillset and employee performance.
**Correlation is significant at the 0.01 level (two-tailed).

There is a strong and positive correlation between skillset and employee performance in future of work; $p = 0.00$ which is lower than the significant value; therefore, we reject the null hypothesis and there is sufficient evidence to conclude that there is a significant impact or correlation between skillsets and employee performance.

The data analysis for the hypotheses:

H0: There is no impact of safety and health on employee's wellbeing.
H1: There is a significant impact of safety and health on employee's wellbeing.

Health and Safety			**Employee Wellbeing**
Health and safety	Pearson correlation	1	0.185
	Significant value (two-tailed)		0.054
	N	109	109
Employee wellbeing	Pearson correlation	0.185	1
	Significant value (two-tailed)	0.054	
	N	109	109

FIGURE 14.4 Correlation between health and safety and employee wellbeing impacting future of work.

There is a weak and positive correlation between health and safety and employee wellbeing in future of work; $p = 0.54$ which is lower than the significant value (0.5); therefore, we reject the null hypothesis and there is sufficient evidence to conclude that there is a significant impact or correlation between health and safety and employee wellbeing.

The data analysis for hypotheses:

H0: There is no impact of work–life balance on employee's performance and well-being.
H1: There is a significant impact of work–life balance on employee's performance and wellbeing.

Work–life Balance			**Employee Performance and Wellbeing**
Work–life balance	Pearson correlation	1	0.198*
	Significant value two-tailed)		0.02
	N	109	109
Employee performance and wellbeing	Pearson Correlation	0.198*	1
	Significant value (two-tailed)	0.02	
	N	109	109

FIGURE 14.5 Significant impact between work–life balance and employee performance and wellbeing.
*Correlation is significant at the 0.05 level (two-tailed).

There is a weak and positive correlation between work–life balance and employee performance and wellbeing in future of work; $p = 0.02$ which is low than significant value (0.05); therefore, we reject the null hypothesis and there is sufficient evidence to conclude that there is a significant impact or correlation between work–life balance and employee performance and wellbeing.

14.9 DISCUSSION

This current situation has altered our working style by requiring us to work remotely. As a result, many organizations have changed their policies and provided adequate resources to their employees, such as software that allows organizations to track employee performance and productivity. The most serious threat to an organization is data. Hackers and employers can now easily access data and use it for their benefits thanks to remote access. Excellent cybersecurity is a requirement of the day. The E-HR summit discussed how an organization and its employees can survive in such a situation:

1. Adaptability
2. Innovation
3. Resilience
4. Reskilling and upskilling
5. Agility
6. Trust

If a company wants to stay intact, it needs to make sure that these factors are considered. The ability of an organization to adapt to these uncertain events will help it thrive, and nothing beats up having a sense of purpose. The other aspect is a necessity, which is known as the mother of all innovation. If an organization is open to innovation, there will be no setbacks. In the pre-COVID-19 era, the most important term was resilience, and employers should make sure that their employees are building resilience in themselves. Upskilling and reskilling are important aspects of an individual's life because they enable them to be competent enough to hold space for themselves. Companies should maintain their focus on increased workforce and workplace agility. Finally, when it comes to trust, it is the past time for businesses to recognize that this is the movement that will foster a sense of belonging and confidence among employees.

14.10 CONCLUSION

In just 10 months, the novel coronavirus has completely displaced the traditional way of working and replaced it with technology-driven work. As we begin to adjust to our new normal, we can see the long- and short-term changes in the workplace that are the cause of coronavirus. We do not know how long or how severe the economic impact of this pandemic will be. When the government imposed a nationwide curfew, the term "WFH" drew a lot of attention. A term that was previously only associated with the IT sector has now become synonymous with the ability to work efficiently. Furthermore, COVID-19 has also accelerated the advancement of technology and made it necessary for people to use it. These technological advancements will bring new features to our work that will make it more efficient, healthy, and productive. The security aspect of remote working is a major disadvantage. As a result of the sudden increase in cybercrime following the release of COVID-19, businesses should ensure that their data is secure. Remote working has completely removed the previously existed "blurred line" between work and personal life, so balancing the work–life of employees has become a major concern. Employees who are unable to achieve proper balance are becoming less productive at work.

14.11 SUGGESTION

1. In these difficult times, the HR department of an organization is the one that brings stability to the organization.
2. A compassionate, collaborative, and contact-free economy is on its way, and everyone should be ready.
3. The company should establish a set of working hours and no work after those hours.
4. Employees should be supported by their employers by assisting them in achieving a work–life balance.
5. There should be defined policies in place, as well as sessions or seminars to assist employees in reducing their stress and workload.
6. Employee safety should be prioritized, as people over the age of 50 are more vulnerable and susceptible to these diseases.
6. A shift in leadership style may also be beneficial. Empathy-based leadership will make employees feel safe and connected to their organizations.

KEYWORDS

- **remote working**
- **COVID-19**
- **challenges of organizations**
- **employee safety**
- **leadership style**

REFERENCES

Cai, L. The Critical Importance of Learning and Development in a Post-Pandemic Digital Age. *Training Magazine* [Online] May 21, 2020. Training. https://trainingmag.com/critical-importance-learning-and-development-post- pandemic-digital-age/

Cityairnews. E-HR Conclave 2020: Startup Innovation Spirit of New India Organized by Amity University [Online] Sept 10, 2020. https://www.cityairnews.com/content/e-hr-conclave-2020-startup- innovation-spirit-of-new-india-organized-by-amity-university

Deloitte. Addressing the Impact of COVID How the Future of Work is Transforming Our Work, Workforce and Workplace [Online] 2020. https://www2.deloitte.com/content/dam/Deloitte/global/Documents/About-Deloitte/gx-recover-dig-cap-design-digitally-enabled-flex-work.pdf

Kumar, A. The Future of Work—Technology Transforming HR Practices. *SME Futures* [Online] June 7, 2020. https://smefutures.com/the-future-of-work-technology-transforming-hr-practices/

Kang, M. COVID 19 has been both Good and Bad for Work Life Balance. *Peoples Matter* [Online] n.d.. https://www.peoplemattersglobal.com/article/employee-relations/covid-19-has-been-both-good-and-bad-for-work–life-balance-26159

McKinsey and Company. How Covid 19 has Pushed Company Over the Technology Tipping Point and Transforming Business Forever [Online] Oct 5, 2020. https://www.mckinsey.com/business-functions/strategy-and-corporate-finance/our-insights/how-covid-19-has-pushed-companies-over-the-technology-tipping-point-and-transformed-business-forever

United Nations. The World of Work and Covid 19 [Online] June 2020. https://www.ilo.org/wcmsp5/groups/public/@dgreports/@dcomm/documents/genericdocument/wcms_748428.pdf

Xiao, Y.; Fan, Z. COVID-19: 10 Tech Trends Getting us Through the Pandemic. World Economic Forum [Online] April 27, 2020. https://www.weforum.org/agenda/2020/04/10-technology-trends-coronavirus-covid19-pandemic-robotics-telehealth

CHAPTER 15

Ranking of Indian Ice Cream Brands from Perspective of Cold Chain Supply Management Using QFD and AHP

SWATI UPVEJA, ASWIN SAMBHU PR, SATHIYA PRIYA A.* and SUNMATHI B.

Amity Business School, Amity University Noida 201301, Uttar Pradesh, India

**Corresponding author. E-mail: upveja.swati@gmail.com*

ABSTRACT

This study was undertaken to explore the impact of the cold chain on effective food supply chain management (SCM). An interactive approach was followed with an ice cream-consuming sample of people to better understand their perception of ice cream as a product and analyze how the existing brands can effectively handle the ever-increasing consumer requirements in this sector and what they can offer from within their capacities, using quality function deployment (QFD). Also, an attempt was made to find the best brand of ice cream, based on the consumer inputs, from three brands of ice cream which are available in India, using the analytical hierarchy process (AHP). This study is driven by "Voice of customer (VoC)" collected from ice cream consumers, using opinion polls. The data inputs were also extensively collected from the executives of three Indian ice cream brands through separate focus group sessions and expert opinion surveys. The study was undertaken in five stages, with ice cream as a product with the first two stages involving extensive data collection and the next two stages involving data analyses using QFD as well as AHP, and the final stage was getting

Constructive Discontent in Execution: Creative Approaches to Technology and Management.
Sanjeev Bansal, Anita Venaik, Swati Upveja, and Saritha S. (Eds.)

insights. This study carefully evaluated the correlation between the average consumer's inputs and the associated technical requirements of the processes related to ice cream as a product through the QFD model and figured out the best candidate which satisfies the needs of the consumers to a larger extent among the three brands of ice cream which were investigated using AHP model. The outcomes of this study can be useful to companies and people associated with the cold supply chain of ice cream as it is a direct depiction of the consumers' mindset and a comparison of it with the existing infrastructure of the cold chain. Hence, this would give them a clear indication about the direction in which their efforts need to be more directed toward gaining more customer satisfaction and greater receptibility and acceptability of their product among the highly potent ice cream craving consumer market segment in India. Future studies shall take more criteria in AHP that may influence decision making in real-life situations. Also, the levels of the VoC and the technical requirements may extend to tertiary or in a few cases up to quaternary levels in the actual scenarios. This study is the first attempt to explore the impact of the ice cream cold chain on effective food SCM in India. Also, this study has used tools, namely, QFD and AHP to analyze increasing consumer requirements in this sector also to explore the best brand of ice cream, based on the consumer inputs from three brands that are available in India.

15.1 INTRODUCTION

Cold chain is a special mode of the otherwise normal supply chain, with a vast number of products—both raw materials and finished goods—handled day to day, on a large scale right from sourcing to final distribution and delivery of the product to the customer. There are differences in the requirement of each of the product category which depends on cold chain infrastructure, in terms of the physical conditions of the cold chain. Therefore, to better understand the cold chain, a particular product category was chosen. Hence, ice cream as a product category was chosen, majorly due to its heavy dependence on the cold chain and its nature of high perishability. Another reason for selecting ice cream as a product category of focus was due to the increasing slope of its market growth. At the same time, even after being a prospective business unit, there are hardly any major national brands in India. Sparing a few such as Amul, there is absolutely no prominent national-level market leader who can boast of a widespread supply chain of ice cream in India. Hence, it was necessary to understand how the brands can better satisfy consumer needs. Also, it was necessary to evaluate the performance of the brands based on the inputs from the consumers to understand which brand was best in meeting the consumer requirements.

Globally, ice cream is one of the most popular and liked desserts. Since the ice cream industry is marginally capital intensive, with a large population of people from almost all age groups expressing interest in the products, it is very competitive. In 2014, China took over the United States as the largest ice cream market globally.

The ice cream industry in India is one of the fastest booming sectors of the dairy/food processing industry. Even though India has a relatively lower per capita consumption of ice cream, standing at around 400 mL as compared to the USA and China with their respective per capita ice cream consumption clocking at 22,000 and 3000 mL, respectively. India still has a huge potential to explore the depths of the Indian ice cream market segments. With the ever-increasing rate of cold chain infrastructure in the country and an improvement in terms of disposable income that is coupled with the consistently changing lifestyle, the sector has a bright potential for growth and establishment.

In 2016 alone, the ice cream sector in India garnered a revenue of over USD 1.5 billion and since then it has been projected to accumulate a scale of revenue close to USD 3.4 billion by 2021 and USD 5.82 billion by 2025. Lately, alternatives to original ice creams, such as frozen desserts based on vegetable oils, have been denting the market share of ice cream in India. Key players in the Indian market offering frozen desserts are Kwality Walls, Cream Bell, Vadilal, etc.

In India, even with a multitude of brands throughout the length and breadth of the subcontinent, there is still a lack of a prominent market leader on a national front. This can be attributed to the fact that the ice cream industry in India is largely regional and the vast majority of brands present in the country are largely concerned about smaller markets spanning up to a couple of states only, if not districts. There are very few national brands of ice cream such as Amul and the most prominent reason associated with this is the mentality toward nationalization may be attributed to the high perishability issue of ice cream-based products and the requirement of prolonged cold chain infrastructure (1). This may also explain why there is not a sudden boom in the ice cream industry and no sudden emergence of a profitable market leader.

The outcomes of this study can be useful to companies and people associated with the cold supply chain of ice cream as it is a direct depiction of the consumers' mindset and a comparison of it with the existing infrastructure of the cold chain. Hence, this would give them a clear indication about the direction in which their efforts need to be more directed toward gaining more customer satisfaction and greater receptibility and acceptability of their product among the highly potent ice cream craving consumer market segment in India.

15.2 LITERATURE REVIEW

15.2.1 COLD SUPPLY CHAIN

Grobler and Yadavalli (2008) discuss the findings of a case study from Greater Gauteng area on the supply chain management (SCM) practices at Centurion Ice Cream and Sweets CC, a significant manufacturer of ice cream in that area. First, the levels of the current SCM environment were evaluated ahead of identifying the distribution function as a prime candidate for further analysis. As a result, the Monte Carlo simulation was carried out to investigate the impact of different scenarios associated with distribution. The paper concludes with a study and evaluation of information technology as the enabler for better performance in the supply chain.

15.2.2 QUALITY FUNCTION DEPLOYMENT (QFD)

Holmen and Kristensen (1998) presented a case study to showcase how QFD can be implemented in the pre-interactive stage associated with a single product development project. It also investigated on the possibility of using the detected correlations and non-correlations among the characteristics of the prospective product by customers as a realistic tool for distinguishing between the suppliers.

Prasad et al. (2014) aimed to define and model a supply chain to attain a strategic fit between competitive strategies as well as the strategies associated with the supply chain. The normal boundary intersection (NBI) method was applied and a weighted additive model was prepared to undertake multi-objective optimization. The QFD-based optimization methodology was utilized for designing a supply chain. Then the corresponding SCP index was calculated using QFD and utility-based optimization. The objective of computing the SCP index was to provide a concise means for aiding the managers in making decisions associated with choosing the optimum set of objectives related to supply chain design to fufill the competitive strategy.

Suryaningrat (2016) studied the processed foods based on the local Casava fruit which has a high potential in the Indonesian markets. It has been in use in numerous small- and big-scale industries in the form of raw materials to produce goods that have economic value. This can be attributed to the high business competition in this sector. Quality function deployment as a methodology was implemented in this study to help the business clients in understand customer requirements and then strategically prepare and implement their business models with a view of accommodating the technical requirements to attain those needs and finally provide customer satisfaction. As a result, the customer requirements focused in this study were taste, texture, smell, and color associated with the processed cassava food product. These qualitative requirements were later correlated to the technical requirements to achieve best results in the form of QFD.

Akdag et al. (2013) focused on the use of QFD to transform the needs of the customers into quality characteristics of private hospitals. Quality function deployment implemented in this study found that the attitude and behavior of the hospital staff got the highest priority among the parameters evaluated and also shed light on the strong inter-relationship between the factors such as skills of the physician, availability of enough modern equipment, and also the behavior and attitude of the hospital staff.

Khorshidi et al. (2016) investigated the implementation of QFD and SERVQUAL methodologies with the objective of understanding service quality in the case of train services. As a result, the SERVQUAL questionnaire was developed in congruence with the internal services of the sector associated with trains, and based on the responses obtained, QFD was initiated to correlate the responses to the technical requirements. Moreover, SERVQUAL aided in evaluating the quality of the train's services and implementation of QFD helped in the overall process improvement based on the results of SERVQUAL.

15.2.3 ANALYTICAL HIERARCHY PROCESS(AHP)

Al Harbi (2001) applied AHP in the stream of project management to identify the best contractor. Five project contractors were evaluated in the case study. The criteria for evaluation were their experience, stability at the financial end, performance levels, level of manpower, facilitation of equipment, and load of work they possessed at the time. Pair-wise comparison of the contractors was carried out and priority level-based rankings were established. Using this overall priority value, the best contractor out of the five investigated contractors was selected.

Korpela and Tuominen (1996) showcased an integrated approach for the objective of site finalization for the warehouse using qualitative as well as quantitative governing factors. The main objective of making optimum use of the available resources and find a site for warehouse operations. The study implemented AHP to analyze the qualitative criteria associated with the site selection and also made use of cost analyses to quantify the logistic cost crater associated with each of the decision alternatives. Hence, with proper consultation from the AHP and the cost analysis, the resulting benefit-to-cost ratios were made on the basis of decision making.

Ortiz-Barrios et al. (2020) combinedly used AHP with other preferential decision-making models like DEMATEL and TOPSIS to assess and study the overall performance of the suppliers of pork in the supply chain associated with the pork business to better understand the prevalence of the bullwhip effect in this sector. Categorization and further subcategorization of selected criteria and associated relative weight calculation were undertaken using AHP. Domain experts were tasked to undertake the pair-wise comparisons and then further steps of AHP were initiated.

Harsudiyono et al. (2019) investigated on the selection of food programs offered by Jakarta provincial government using AHP. The implemented AHP model focused on freshness, taste, naturality, and goodness of the product with three decision alternatives in the form of grades as good, average, and less to undertake pair-wise comparisons and found that the criteria followed the order their priority as freshness, naturality, taste and then the goodness of the product with their associated weights in the order as 0.409, 0.264, 0.187, and 0.187, respectively.

15.3 RESEARCH METHODOLOGY

15.3.1 RESEARCH OBJECTIVES

- The first objective of the research is to attain valuable insights from the consumers of ice cream, as VoC, about their expectations, needs, and requirements with respect to ice cream as a product.
- The next objective was to attain valuable and critical details about the technical requirements from domain/industry experts from 3 brands of ice cream.

- To examine how the existing players can effectively handle the ever-increasing consumer requirements in this sector, using QFD.
- To find the best brand of ice cream, based on the consumer inputs, from 3 brands of ice cream which are available in India, using the AHP.

15.3.2 RESEARCH METHODOLOGY

The study was driven by primary data collected from people of 3 different age groups, namely 17–24 years, 25–32 years, and 33–40 years, using opinion polls, to account for the likes and dislikes and opinion independence of the target population and to avoid age-based preferential biases. The data inputs were also extensively collected from the executives of three companies that were directly associated with three different brands of ice cream by separate focus group sessions and expert opinion surveys. The study was undertaken in four stages, with ice cream as a product with the first two stages involving extensive data collection and the next two stages involving data analysis using QFD and well as AHP, and the final stage was compiling the results.

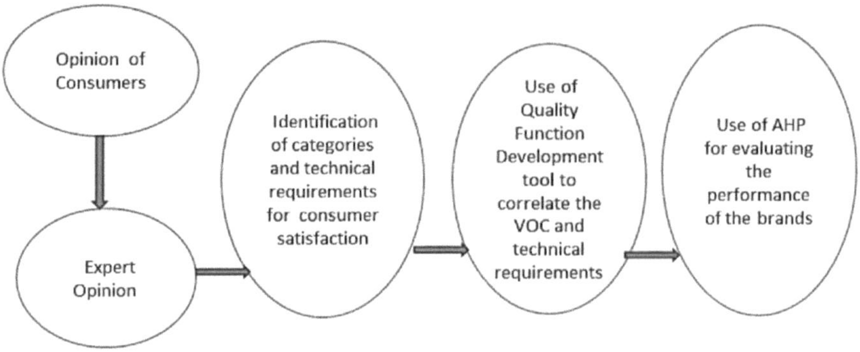

FIGURE 15.1 Research methodology used in this study.

15.3.3 DATA COLLECTION FROM CONSUMERS

First stage of the study consisted of collecting primary data from people who consumed ice creams and were actually interested in ice cream as a product. Data was collected from opinion polls as voices of the consumers about ice cream as a product which they usually consumed. They were asked to give their requirements, preferences, interests in how they want their product to be. Then the collected information was sorted and rearranged to form primary VoC with a secondary subcategorization to each of the primary needs and wants of the target population. Hence, the voice of consumers (VoCs) was rearranged into well-structured primary and their corresponding secondary needs and wants respectively, as shown in Table 15.1.

TABLE 15.1 Voice of the Consumers for Constructing the House of Quality.

S.No.	Primary VoC	Secondary VoC	Code	Weight
1	Product improvement	Improve the quality of lower cost variants	Va1	2
		Need for low-fat variants	Va2	2
		Need for low sugar/diabetic-friendly variants	Va3	2
		Need for blend/combination of flavors	Va4	3
2	Packaging	Not easily damageable packaging	Vb1	3
		Need for eco-friendly packing	Vb2	1
3	Safety	Trustworthiness of brand	Vc1	4
		Should be germ free and safe to use	Vc2	4
		Clearer ingredients details and lifetime indicators	Vc3	2
4	Healthiness	Natural chemical-free additives	Vd1	3
		No artificial sweeteners	Vd2	3
		Need more nutrition in the products	Vd3	2
		Need more real extracts than food essence	Vd4	2
5	Durability	More shelf life	Ve1	5
		Should not melt easily	Ve2	5
		The cream should not break into parts	Ve3	4
		Should not form larger crystals upon freezing	Ve4	3
6	Product form	Should be thicker with a smooth texture	Vf1	4
		Need for some edible part at the bottom of ice cream bars to collect the melted portion	Vf2	1
7	Freshness	More natural taste according to advertized flavor	Vg1	5
		Fruits and nuts should be crispy and remain whole	Vg2	5
8	Miscellaneous	Improve quantity according to the charged price	Vh1	4
		More flavor variety for lower cost variants	Vh2	2

15.3.3.1 DATA COLLECTION FROM THE COMPANIES

The second stage of the study consisted of separate focus group sessions and expert opinion surveys with executives from the three different brands B1, B2, and B3. The purpose was to collect information about the technical requirements that are to be considered to meet the VoCs which were recorded during stage 1 of the study. The opinions collected from the executives were then compiled and then sorted and rearranged to form a comprehensive set of primary and their associated secondary technical requirements, as shown in Table 15.2.

TABLE 15.2 Technical Requirements for Constructing the House of Quality.

S. No	Technical requirements		Code
1	Blending	Formulation and ingredients selection	TA1
		Creation of the recipe/mix	TA2
2	Pasteurization	Temperature cycles control	TB1
		Monitoring microbial activity	TB2
3	Homogenization	Multi stage homogenization	TC1
		Ensuring superior quality of resulting emulsion	TC2
4	Aging of mix	Regulate the temperature with the time of aging	TD1
		Addition of liquid flavors and food color	TD2
5	Freezing	Overrun calculation	TE1
		Whipping and air incorporation	TE2
6	Solid matter addition	Selection of fruits, nuts, and other materials	TF1
		Freshness of toping material	TF2
7	Packaging	Packaging material innovation	TG1
		Labeling innovation and quality markings	TG2
8	Hardening	Tighter temperature control of the freezer	TH1
		Rate of cooling/freezing	TH2
9	Supply chain	Setting ideal storage temperature at all points	TI1
		Decrease in lead time	TI2
		Minimizing the change in temperature of the product	TI3

15.4 DATA ANALYSIS AND INTERPRETATION

15.4.1 QUALITY FUNCTION DEPLOYMENT

Stage 3 of the study consisted of organizing the VoCs and the technical requirements to meet their demands into a QFD or house of quality. The VoCs formed the rows and the technical requirements formed the columns of the main body of the house of quality. Then based on the inputs from the company executives of B1, B2, and B3 brands the VOCs were mapped to the technical requirements using a 3-point scale with 1 being least correlation,

3 being moderate correlation, and 9 being strong correlation, all represented using blue, yellow, and red color codes. Also, the technical requirements were mapped according to their level of correlation on a 2-point scale, coded in red and green codes to depict negative and positive correlation respectively, as shown in Figure 15.2.

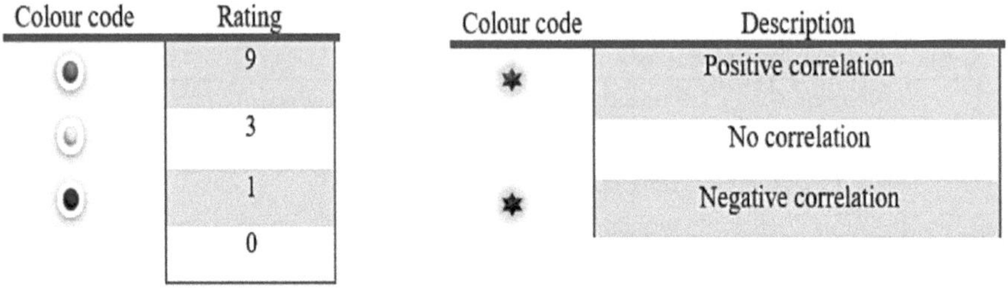

FIGURE 15.2 Description of color coding used in the main body and top part of the house of quality.

After completing the main body of the QFD matrix, the relative importance values of the technical requirements were drawn out based on the assigned weights to each of the VoCs. Then based on the relative importance values, the level of significance of the technical requirements was drawn and as a result, the technical requirements were ranked according to their significance levels. After that, based on the weights assigned to the VoCs the 3 ice cream brands are evaluated on a scale of 1 to 5, with 1 being the lowest and 5 being the highest conformance of a brand to the particular VoC.

15.4.2 QFD—HOUSE OF QUALITY MODEL

The house of quality model of QFD, using the color coding scheme as given in Figure 15.2 was made, based on the VoCs and the relevant technical requirements associated with satisfying the VoCs. The complete house of quality representation is shown in Figure 15.3.

15.4.3 ANALYTICAL HIERARCHY PROCESS

Stage 4 of the study was aimed at finding out which among the 3 brands of ice cream was best to be chosen as a representative that best satisfies the VoCs. So, it was done to identify the best brand that satisfies the conditions of the

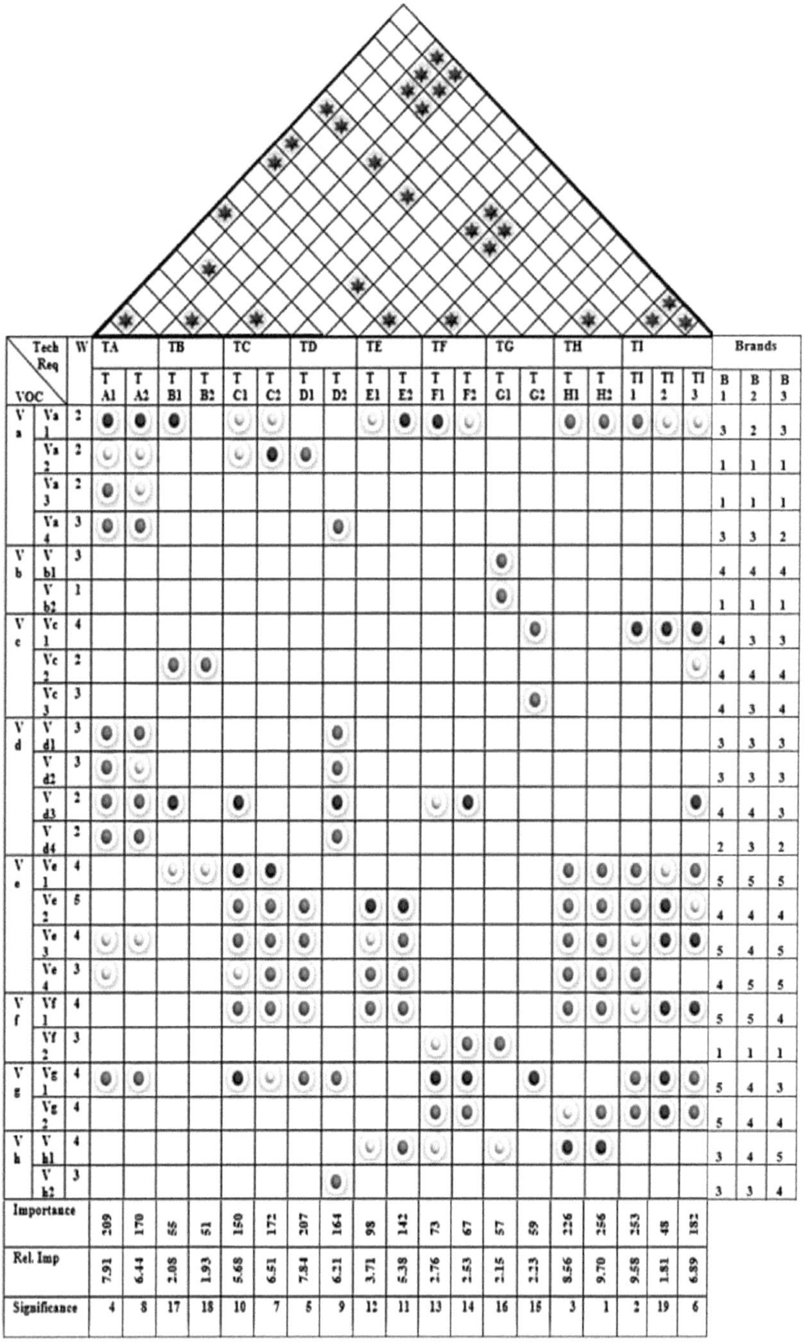

FIGURE 15.3 Quality function deployment house of quality representation.

VoCs. This task was accomplished using AHP. For the sake of decreasing the complexity of calculations, only four major primary requirements from the VoC were considered in AHP. The four primary requirements were selected based on the inputs from the consumers as well as from the weights assigned to them. As a result, the four highly weighted primary VoCs were chosen to initiate the AHP. Each brand was pair-wise compared with all the four primary VoCs separately and found that the consistency levels of all the calculations fell within the 10% mark, hence, validating the procedure. Finally, the brand with maximum value for money weight was identified, based on the calculations of pair-wise comparison in AHP. Hence, stage 4 ended with identifying the best brand to go for from among the three brands, namely, B1, B2, and B3, based on the VoCs.

15.4.3.1 PAIR-WISE COMPARISON OF CRITERIA

The four criteria used in AHP were durability, freshness, cost, and safety. These criteria were particularly selected from the weights assigned to them along with other VoCs during stage 1 of the study. Then a matrix of the relative importance of these criteria was made. A scale of the relative importance of the criteria was established. This scale was used to decide the relative importance of one criterion or how one criterion is preferred over another among the four selected criteria. The rating scale is as shown in Table 15.3:

TABLE 15.3 Rating Scale used in AHP.

Importance number	Importance level	Detailed explanation
1	Equal	Both criteria are equally important
3	Moderate	One criterion is slightly more important than the other
5	Strong	One criterion is strongly important than the other
7	Very strong	One criterion is very strongly important than the other
9	Extreme	One criterion is important to the highest possible level than the other
2, 4, 6, 8	In between the earlier mentioned values	Can be used as a compromise between the respective values if above distinct odd numbers of importance cannot be ascertained

Thus, based on this rating scale, the relative importance of all four criteria was investigated and depicted in the form of a matrix, as shown in Table 15.4.

TABLE 15.4 Pair-wise Comparison Matrix of the Selected Criteria.

	Durability	Freshness	Cost	Safety
Durability	1.000	3.000	5.000	0.333
Freshness	0.333	1.000	3.000	0.333
Cost	0.200	0.333	1.000	0.143
Safety	3.000	3.000	7.000	1.000

In this matrix of the relative importance of criteria, the criteria listed in the first cell of each row are preferred over the criteria listed in the first cell of each of the subsequent columns by the number present in their corresponding common cells. Hence, the diagonal elements in all the matrices in AHP are unity.

15.4.3.1.1 Normalization of Pair-wise Comparison Matrix and Determination of Priority Vector

From the matrix of the relative importance of the criteria, the column sums of each of the criteria are found. Then the relative importance values of each of the four criteria in the above pair-wise comparison matrix are normalized to get each of the column sum equal to unity. This is done by dividing each element into the columns with their corresponding column sums. Hence, the normalized weights for the relative importance matrix are as listed in Table 15.5.

TABLE 15.5 Normalized Weights of the Pair-wise Comparison Matrix of Criteria.

	Durability	Freshness	Cost	Safety
Durability	0.220588	0.409091	0.3125	0.184211
Freshness	0.073529	0.136364	0.1875	0.184211
Cost	0.044118	0.045455	0.0625	0.078947
Safety	0.661765	0.409091	0.4375	0.552632
Sum	1	1	1	1

After the matrix was homogenized, the eigenvector or the priority vector was calculated for each of the criteria and finally, the values in the priority vector were ranked according to the increasing order of their value. The priority value for each criterion in a row is the row average value of the elements in their respective rows. The priority vector, also known as the real-value vector (RVV), of the four selected criteria is shown in Table 15.6.

TABLE 15.6 Normalized Weights and Priority Vector of the Pair-wise Comparison Matrix of Criteria.

	Durability	Freshness	Cost	Safety	Priority	Rank
Durability	0.220588	0.409091	0.3125	0.184211	0.281597	2
Freshness	0.073529	0.136364	0.1875	0.184211	0.145401	3
Cost	0.044118	0.045455	0.0625	0.078947	0.057755	4
Safety	0.661765	0.409091	0.4375	0.552632	0.515247	1
Sum	1	1	1	1	1	

Hence, according to rank from the priority vector, the order of importance of the selected criteria, in decreasing order, was found to be safety, durability, freshness, and cost.

15.4.3.1.2 Consistency Check for the Values in the Priority Eigenvector of the Criteria

The consistency of the priority vector values is extremely important as it gives the level of agreement of the result to the actual scenario. The consistency levels of less than 10% is acceptable in AHP and is considered as a valid result. The consistency of the priority eigenvector is found by first finding the principal eigenvalue, λ_{max}.

The principal eigenvalue, λ_{max}, of the selected criteria can be found by first multiplying the total of the relative importance value of each criterion to its corresponding value in the priority vector and adding up the multiplied values of all the criteria. Hence, λ_{max} can be calculated as follows.

$$\lambda_{max} = \sum_{k=1}^{n} (T)_k (PV)_k$$

where

n = total number of criteria used in the AHP,

T_k = total of the relative importance value of the *k*th criteria, column-wise,

PV_k = the corresponding priority vector value or the priority index of the *k*th criteria, row-wise.

Hence, the principal eigenvalue, λ_{max}, of the selected criteria can be calculated. From the principal eigenvalue, λ_{max}, the consistency index (CI) can be calculated as follows.

$$CI = \frac{\lambda_{max} - n}{n-1}$$

Also, the random consistency index (RI) can be found from a pre-defined table, as shown in Table 15.7.

TABLE 15.7 Random Consistency Index Values.

N	**1**	**2**	**3**	**4**	**5**	**6**	**7**	**8**	**9**	**10**
RI	0.00	0.00	0.58	0.90	1.12	1.24	1.32	1.41	1.45	1.49

Now, the consistency ratio (CR) can be found from the calculated CI and RI values, as shown below.

$$CR = \frac{CI}{RI}$$

Principal eigenvalue, λ_{max}	4.199278
CI	0.066426
RI ($n = 4$)	0.9
CR = (CI/RI)	0.073807

From the calculations, the CR was found to be 7.38% which is well within the permissible level of 10%. Hence, the data are consistent and correctly represent the criteria taken in the calculation and the eigenvector of priority can be accepted.

15.4.3.2 HIERARCHY OF BRAND DECISION MAKING BASED ON CRITERIA

Since the priority vector shows acceptable level of consistency, the next step is to step into deciding which brand of ice cream among B1, B2, and B3 is the best in satisfying the criteria which have been derived from the consumer requirements or the VoCs. For this purpose, a layout of the decision hierarchy is made, as given in Figure 15.4, to understand the flow of decision making through the further steps of AHP.

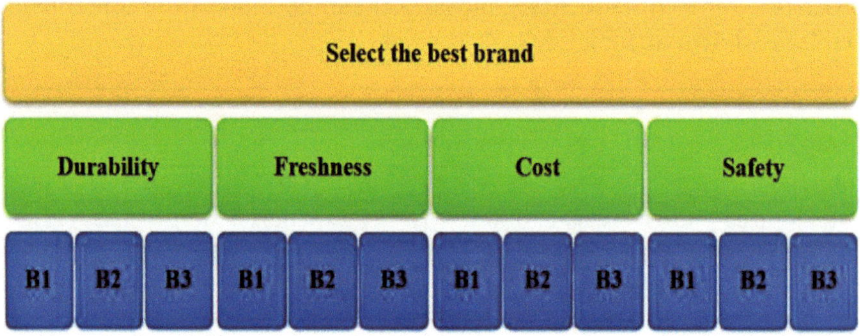

FIGURE 15.4 Decision hierarchy for choosing the best brand based on the four criteria.

15.4.3.3 PAIR-WISE COMPARISON OF BRANDS WITH RESPECT TO THE CRITERIA

15.4.3.3.1 Based on Durability Criterion

15.4.3.3.1.1 Pair-wise Comparison of Brands

The three brands of ice creams are pair-wise compared based on their durability using the same scale which have been in use throughout the AHP above. The resultant matrix is as shown in Table 15.8.

TABLE 15.8 Pair-wise Comparison of Brands with Respect to Durability.

	B1	B2	B3
B1	1.000	0.333	0.200
B2	3.000	1.000	0.333
B3	5.000	3.000	1.000
Sum	9.000	4.333	1.533

15.4.3.3.1.2 Normalization and Priority Vector Determination

The normalized matrix of pair-wise comparison of brand is shown in Table 15.9. Priority vector was calculated for all the following matrices as per the steps discussed earlier.

TABLE 15.9 Normalized Matrix of Pair-wise Comparison of Brands with Respect to Durability.

	B1	B2	B3	Priority	Rank
B1	0.111111	0.076923	0.130435	0.106156	3
B2	0.333333	0.230769	0.217391	0.260498	2
B3	0.555556	0.692308	0.652174	0.633346	1
Sum	1	1	1	1	

15.4.3.3.1.3 Consistency Check for the Values in the Priority Eigenvector of the Brands

Consistency of the values of the eigenvector of priority of brands were also evaluated using the same technic discussed in the earlier sections.

Principal eigenvalue, λ_{max}	3.055361
CI	0.027681
RI ($n = 3$)	0.58
CR =(CI/RI)	0.047725

From the calculations, the CR was found to be 4.77% which is well within the permissible level of 10%. So, the data are consistent and correctly represents the priority of the brands, and hence the eigenvector of priority can be accepted.

15.4.3.3.2 Based on Freshness Criterion

15.4.3.3.2.1 Pair-wise Comparison of the Brands

TABLE 15.10 Pair-wise Comparison of Brands with Respect to Freshness.

	B1	B2	B3
B1	1.000	3.000	7.000
B2	0.333	1.000	5.000
B3	0.143	0.200	1.000
Sum	1.476	4.200	13.000

15.4.3.3.2.2 Normalization and Priority Vector Determination

TABLE 15.11 Normalized Matrix of Pair-wise Comparison of Brands with Respect to Freshness.

	B1	B2	B3	Priority	Rank
B1	0.677419	0.714286	0.538462	0.643389	1
B2	0.225806	0.238095	0.384615	0.282839	2
B3	0.096774	0.047619	0.076923	0.073772	3
Sum	1	1	1	1	

15.4.3.3.2.3 Consistency Check for the Values in the Priority Eigenvector of the Brands

Principal eigenvalue, λ_{max}	3.096726
CI	0.048363
RI ($n = 3$)	0.58
CR = (CI/RI)	0.083384

From the calculations, the CR was found to be 8.33% which is well within the permissible level of 10%. Hence, the data are consistent and correctly represents the priority of the brands, and hence the eigenvector of priority can be accepted.

15.4.3.3.3 Based on Cost Criteria

15.4.3.3.3.1 Pair-wise Comparison of the Brands

TABLE 15.12 Pair-wise Comparison of Brands with Respect to Cost.

	B1	B2	B3
B1	1.000	0.333	3.000
B2	3.000	1.000	5.000
B3	0.333	0.200	1.000
Sum	4.333	1.533	9.000

15.4.3.3.3.2 Normalization and Priority Vector Determination

TABLE 15.13 Normalized Matrix of Pair-wise Comparison of Brands with Respect to Cost.

	B1	**B2**	**B3**	**Priority**	**Rank**
B1	0.230769	0.217391	0.333333	0.260498	2
B2	0.692308	0.652174	0.555556	0.633346	1
B3	0.076923	0.130435	0.111111	0.106156	3
Sum	1	1	1	1	

15.4.3.3.3.3 Consistency Check for the Values in the Priority Eigenvector of the Brands

Principal eigenvalue, λ_{max}	3.055361
CI	0.027681
RI ($n = 3$)	0.58
CR = (CI/RI)	0.047725

From the calculations, the CR was found to be 4.77% which is well within the permissible level of 10%. Hence, the data are consistent and correctly represents the priority of the brands, and hence the eigenvector of priority can be accepted.

15.4.3.3.4 Based on Safety Criterion

15.4.3.3.4.1 Pair-wise Comparison of the Brands

TABLE 15.14 Pair-wise Comparison of Brands with Respect to Safety.

	B1	**B2**	**B3**
B1	1.000	5.000	3.000
B2	0.200	1.000	0.333
B3	0.333	3.000	1.000
Sum	1.533	9.000	4.333

15.4.3.3.4.2 Normalization and Priority Vector Determination

TABLE 15.15 Normalized Matrix of Pair-wise Comparison of Brands with Respect to Safety.

	B1	B2	B3	Priority	Rank
B1	0.652174	0.555556	0.692308	0.633346	1
B2	0.130435	0.111111	0.076923	0.106156	3
B3	0.217391	0.333333	0.230769	0.260498	2
Sum	1	1	1	1	

15.4.3.3.4.3 Consistency Check for the Values in the Priority Eigenvector of the Brands

Principal eigenvalue, λ_{max}	3.055361
CI	0.027681
RI ($n = 3$)	0.58
CR = (CI/RI)	0.047725

From the calculations, the CR was found to be 4.77% which is well within the permissible level of 10%. Hence, the data are consistent and correctly represents the priority of the brands, and hence, the eigenvector of priority can be accepted.

15.4.3.4 CALCULATIONS OF THE VALUE FOR MONEY (VFM) VECTOR

Value for money vector (VFM) or the overall weight matrix is the final matrix that shows which among the three brands are best, with respect to the selected criteria. The VFM can be found in this case as all the matrices involved so far were found to have CR levels well under than 10%. Hence, the priority vectors obtained so far in the matrices of pair-wise comparison of criteria as well as brands were found to be consistent and acceptable.

In order to find the VFM matrix first the option performance matrix (OPM) needs to be made. The OPM is a matrix that contains the three priority eigenvectors of the brands which were separately found during the pair-wise comparison of the brands with the four selected criteria, namely, durability, freshness, cost, and safety. The OPM represents the merit index values or the priority vector values of the four criteria used, namely, durability, freshness, cost and safety, relative to the three brands, namely, B1, B2, and B3, respectively. The OPM matrix is as shown in Table 15.16.

TABLE 15.16 Option Performance Matrix.

$$OPM = \begin{vmatrix} 0.106156 & 0.643389 & 0.260498 & 0.6333457 \\ 0.260498 & 0.282839 & 0.633346 & 0.1061563 \\ 0.633346 & 0.073772 & 0.106156 & 0.260498 \end{vmatrix}$$

The eigenvector or the priority vector found in Table 15.5, during the pair-wise comparison of criteria, known as the RVV is also used in the calculation of the VFM matrix. The RVV is as shown in table 15.17.

TABLE 15.17 Real-Value Vector.

$$RVV = \begin{vmatrix} 0.281597 \\ 0.145401 \\ 0.057755 \\ 0.515247 \end{vmatrix}$$

The value for money vector (VFM) is the product of the two matrices, OPM and RVV. So, the VFM vector can be found in the following way.

TABLE 15.18 Calculations for VFM Vector.

$$VFM = [OPM][RVV]$$

$$\begin{vmatrix} 0.515247 \end{vmatrix}$$

TABLE 15.19 The VFM Vector.

$$VFM = \begin{vmatrix} 0.106156 & 0.643389 & 0.260498 & 0.633346 \\ 0.260498 & 0.282839 & 0.633346 & 0.106156 \\ 0.633346 & 0.073772 & 0.106156 & 0.260498 \end{vmatrix} * \begin{vmatrix} 0.281597 \\ 0.145401 \\ 0.057755 \end{vmatrix}$$

Hence, the VFM vector was found out to be as shown in Table 15.19.

$$VFM = \begin{vmatrix} 0.464817 \\ 0.205756 \\ 0.329427 \end{vmatrix}$$

The maximum value in the overall weights matrix or the value for money vector is 0.464817 and is associated with brand B1. Hence, B1 is the best brand in satisfying the consumers' requirements, with respect to the selected criteria.

15.5 RESULTS AND DISCUSSION

Through the four stages of this study, care was taken in ensuring proper consumer requirement data that were gathered, sorted and organized them from the sample of people who took part in this study. Also, proper care was given in ensuring that all the essential and prominent technical requirements of the ice cream supply chain processes were addressed, which had a strong and direct implication on the partial or complete fulfilment of the consumers' requirements. In order to carefully depict and analyze the relationship between the VoCs and the technical requirements, they were studied using QFD tool. Then AHP was used to compare the selected shortlisted criteria on the basis of which the best brand, among the three brands, were found which had the highest possibility of satisfying the given consumers' requirements.

The results from each stage of the project are discussed in the following subsections.

15.5.1 STAGE I: DATA COLLECTION FROM CONSUMERS

From the wide variety of needs, wants and requirements pointed out by the sample of people who took part in this study, the whole volume of their requirements was arranged, sorted and combined to form 8 major primary needs and 23 corresponding secondary level needs. The 8 major primary needs which were identified are, product improvement, packaging, safety, healthiness, durability, product form, freshness and some other miscellaneous needs. Based on the comparative evaluation of the three ice cream brands using the views of the consumers, the graph, as shown in Figure 15.4, was made from the inputs of QFD and the following results were drawn.

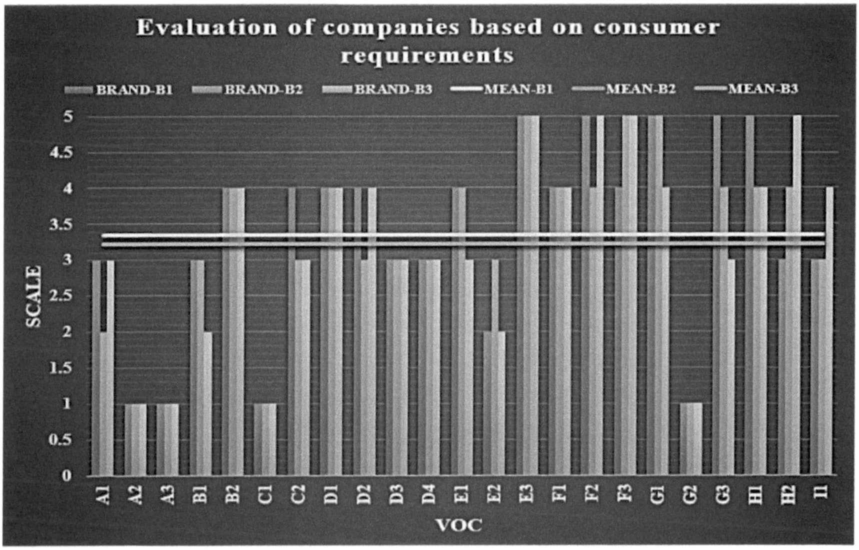

FIGURE 15.5 Evaluation of the three ice cream companies based on the VoCs.

i. Brand B1 was found to have a higher average performance among the three brands, based on the VoCs.
ii. Both brands B2 and B3 was found to have equal average performance; hence, the mean lines of both B2 and B3 are coinciding in the graph shown in Figure 15.5. This suggests the tight competition in this sector.
iii. The average performance of all the three brands, as rated by the consumers, are found to be very close to each other suggesting a closer competitive nature of the players in the ice cream market.

15.5.2 STAGE II: DATA COLLECTION FROM INDUSTRY EXPERTS FROM THREE COMPANIES

Valuable information collected from the three domain experts included prospective technical requirements that could be used to satisfy the requirements of the consumers which were obtained in stage 1. Based on their inputs, nine primary technical requirements were identified which were further subcategorized to obtain 19 associated secondary technical requirements. The nine primary technical requirements which were identified were activities related to blending, pasteurization, homogenization, aging of the mix, freezing, solid matter addition, packaging, hardening, and the supply chain.

15.5.3 *STAGE III: QFD*

Based on the inputs from the sample of people who took part in the study and from the inputs obtained after consulting with the domain experts, all the identified and requirements from both the sides where rearranged to form the body of the QFD matrix. The rows in the main body of QFD represented the VoC and the columns represented the technical requirements. The VoCs and technical requirements were correlated in the body of the QFD matrix and depicted using distinct color codes.

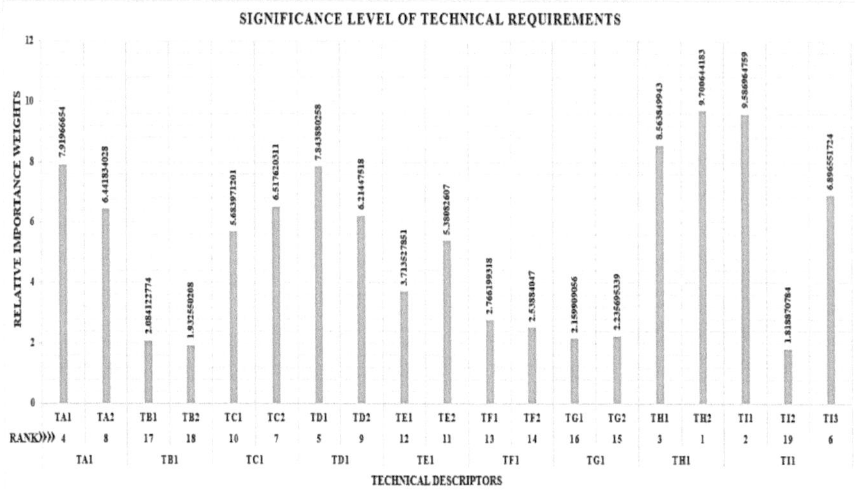

FIGURE 15.6 Significance level of the technical requirements that were investigated.

Calculations were carried out on the basis of the correlation values and the following observations were made.

i. Based on the level of significance of the technical requirements, it was found that four out of the five top priority technical requirements were about temperature regulation.
ii. The technical requirement with the highest level of significance was the rate of cooling/ freezing in the hardening process.

iii. Altogether in the top five technical requirements with the highest significant levels the requirements associated with the hardening process topped the chart with two out of top five technical requirements. Hence, it validates the importance of the fact that the hardening process gives ice cream the final hard non-melted shape it has when it moves out of the production facility or indirectly it implies into the quality of the ice cream at its source before departing to the distribution channel.
iv. It was also found that maintenance of ideal storage temperature at all the points acquired second position in terms of relative importance level or the significance level of the technical requirements, citing the implication it has in maintaining the proper product form and controlling the deformation and loss of quality of the ice cream with respect to its melting.
v. Consumers also had a higher level of association and a greater emphasis on the flavor and ingredients selection of the ice creams which they consumed. During the data collection in stage 1, it was observed that most of consumers who participated in the study were very particular about the flavor, ingredients, quality of the materials used and the make of the ice cream as a whole. This is very evident from the high level of significance of formulation and ingredient selection step, as observed in the QFD.
vi. Blending process, with formulation, ingredient selection, and creation of recipe was also found to have higher significance with 1 out of 5 and 2 out of 10 top priority technical requirements. This may be attributed to the fact that ingredients and recipe may be a direct influencing medium on the likeness of the consumers as they can directly experience these properties of the ice cream while they consume it. Also, apart from the ingredients and the formula, all other processes of manufacture, maintenance and distribution of ice creams are almost the same. So, being the only major distinguishing features that differentiates different varieties of ice cream are their flavor and ingredients or recipe may be the reason on these technical requirements getting a higher level of significance.
vii. Aging of the mix and homogenization also acquired higher levels of significance with in the top 10 highly significant technical requirements. This may be due the fact that the consumers had put a greater emphasis on the texture and the form of the ice cream. Homogenization and then aging process is mainly responsible for

providing proper fat dispersion and partial crystallization of the milk fat thereby enhancing the whipping qualities of the mix and improving its texture.

viii. Supply chain attributes such as maintaining proper storage temperature throughout the supply chain and minimizing the change in temperature of the product while moving through the supply chain also had high levels of significance. This may be attributed to the fact that temperature maintenance is one critical component when it comes to preserving the form, shape, and other physical condition of ice creams once they are out of the production process.

ix. Even though there is an outcry in the public to ban plastics and an urge to develop environment friendly packaging materials, the technical attributes associated with packaging received very low significance from the calculations. It shows that the consumers are more inclined toward the quality of the actual ice creams and its features rather than the containers or packaging materials and their associated quality grades in which they are stored.

x. On the other hand, even though the consumers were bothered about the need for germ freeness of the ice creams which they consumed, understood from the higher weights they associated to the safety aspect of ice creams in the VoC, the significance level indicator showed the lowest significance for the pasteurization step from the calculation which were based on the consumer inputs. It may be understood that the consumers have a greater trust on the brand of ice creams which they consume and also entrust the brands with the responsibility of providing germ free products to them. It may also be assumed that the consumers are not well aware of the possible contamination from the microorganisms or pathogens that could survive in cold ice creams if not pasteurized well.

15.5.4 STAGE IV—AHP

After the evaluation of the results from QFD, the next phase was to find the best brand among the three investigated brands B1, B2, and B3, on the basis of some criteria. For the purpose of avoiding the large volume of calculations from large number of matrices associated with the number of criteria, four major criteria from the VoC were chosen to perform AHP.

The selection of the four major criteria to evaluate the performance of the brands and find the best one was done on the basis of the inputs from the sample of people who participated in the study and also from the importance weights which the consumers associated to their requirements during stage 1 of the study. Hence, the chosen criteria for AHP were durability, freshness, cost, and safety. The results from this stage of the study are as follows. Based on the calculations from the pair-wise comparison of the criteria, the ranking of the criteria was obtained in the order as safety, durability, freshness, and finally cost.

i. Based on the calculations from the pair-wise comparison of the brands with respect to the individual criteria, brand B3 dominated in the criterion of durability, brand B1 dominated in the criteria of freshness as well as safety, and finally brand B2 dominated in the criterion of cost.
ii. The CRs of the pair-wise comparison of the criteria was found to be 0.073866 or 7.38%. Similarly, the CRs of the pair-wise comparison of brands with respect to individual criterion in the order of the criteria as durability, freshness, cost and safety was found to be 0.0477254 or 4.77%, 0.0833843 or 8.33%, 0.0477254 or 4.77%, and 0.0477254 or 4.77%, respectively.
iii. The calculations from all the pair-wise comparisons and their associated priority vectors had a CR less than 8.5%, where the acceptance limit for the CR is 10%. Hence, the priority vector associated with all the pair-wise comparisons are acceptable and withing the consistency levels. This validates the obtained results.
iv. The maximum value in the overall weights matrix or the value for money vector is 0.464817 and is associated with brand B1. Hence, B1 is the best brand in satisfying the consumers' requirements, with respect to the selected criteria.

15.6 CONCLUSIONS AND RECOMMENDATIONS

15.6.1 OUTCOME OF THE STUDY

This study used opinion polls to collect the inputs from the consumers related to their needs and wants associated with ice cream as a product and then consulted domain experts from three companies which dealt independently in production and selling of ice creams. The collected data from the consumers as well as the executives from the three companies were sorted, organized and arranged as the rows and columns, respectively, of a QFD matrix. The views and opinions from both the consumers as well as the domain experts were collected only up to the secondary level, as any further subclassification increased the overlapping of the inputs in one category with others to a significant level and also increased the complexity of the data representation and analyses in QFD as well as AHP. Hence, this study carefully evaluated the correlation between the average consumer's inputs and the associated technical requirements of the processes related to ice cream as a product through the QFD model and figured out the best candidate which satisfies the needs of the consumers to a larger extent among the three brands of ice cream which were investigated using AHP model. Hence, brand, B1 was found to be the best brand out of the three selected brands, from the context of this study. Also, as a relevant secondary result, it was observed from the significance level indicators of the technical requirements taken in this study that temperature regulation at all stages of the supply chain, including the different steps in the production process, played a vital role in ensuring the creation and upkeep of those product characteristics which were desirable to the consumers and indirectly helped in creating overall consumer satisfaction. Also, from the pair-wise comparison of the criteria in AHP it was found that safety factor was the highest ranked and cost was the lowest ranked. This sheds light of the need to improve the safety aspects of the products like brand image, germ freeness of the products, and more transparency in the declaration and depiction of ingredients and additives and also the life time indicators. The lowest priority rank-to-cost criteria means that the consumers are not too much bothered about the cost of the product, provided they receive a higher quality or properly maintained product of sufficient quality. So, it can be said that the consumers positively support the quality aspect in the cost to quality trade-off. Hence, it may be broadly said that any company or brand dealing with products which require an efficient cold chain infrastructure, may give proper importance and priority to the upkeep of temperature maintenance and regulation throughout the entire cold supply chain, rather than selectively focusing on certain aspects of the cold chain. This would help them ensure greater shelf life of their products, germ freeness and also preserves the actual form and physical attributes of their products to a significant level thereby enabling them to satisfy their customers, gather more revenue through increased sales, and an increase in the acceptance of their product within the customers.

15.6.2 LIMITATIONS OF THE STUDY

Following are the limitations of this study.

i. For the sake of minimizing the complexities associated with the volume of calculations involved, the study considers primary data inputs from the consumers as well as the domain experts only up to primary and secondary levels. Levels of VoC and also the technical requirements may extend to a tertiary or in few cases up to quaternary levels in the actual scenarios.
ii. The number of criteria taken in AHP is less compared to the actual number of criteria that may influence decision making in real life situations.
iii. Cost of setting up and maintaining the cold chain infrastructure by the companies dealing with ice creams were not taken into account in this study.
iv. Voice of the consumers was limited to the inputs from people of age groups of 17–40 years only. Hence, the results of the study may not involve the influence of any distinct consumer requirements from consumers of age outside of 17–40 years in real life.
v. The evaluation of the three ice cream brands in this study was done without taking into account the differences in their ways of doing business as well as the availability of cold chain facilities and infrastructure with them.

KEYWORDS

- **quality function deployment (QFD)**
- **analytical hierarchy process (AHP)**
- **the voice of consumer (VoC)**
- **ice cream**
- **cold supply chain**

REFERENCES

Al-Harbi, K. M. A. S. Application of the AHP in project management. *Int. J. Proj. Manag.* **2001**, *19* (1), 19–27.

Chan, L. K.; Wu, M. L. Quality Function Deployment: A Literature Review. *Eur. J. Oper. Res.* **2002**, *143* (3), 463–497.

Deros, B. M.; Rahman, N.; Rahman, M. N. A.; Ismail, A. R.; Said, A. H. Application of Quality Function Deployment to Study Critical Service Quality Characteristics and Performance Measures. *Eur. J. Sci. Res.* **2009,** *21* (4) 319–333.

Ghosh, D.; Roy, S. A Decision-Making Framework for Process Plant Maintenance. *Eur. J. Ind. Eng.* **2010,** *4* (1), 78–98.

Göransson, M.; Nilsson, F.; Jevinger, A. Temperature Performance and Food Shelf-Life Accuracy in Cold Food Supply Chains—Insights from Multiple Field Studies. *Food Control.* **2018,** *86*, 332–341.

Grobler, J.; Yadavalli, V. S. S. Managing the Cold Chain: A Case Study at a South African Ice Cream Company. *S. Afr. J. Ind. Eng.* **2008,** *19* (2),

Harker, P. T. The Art and Science of Decision Making: The Analytic Hierarchy Process. In *The Analytic Hierarchy Process*; Springer-Verlag, 1989; pp. 3–36.

Harsudiyono, I.; Ranggadara, I.; Kurnianda, N. R.; Suhendra. Selection Government Food Programs using Analytical Hierarchy Process. *Int. J. Recent. Technol. Eng.* **2019**, *8* (3),

Holmen, E.; Kristensen, P. S. Supplier Roles in Product Development: Interaction versus Task Partitioning. *Eur. J. Purch. Supply Manag.* **1998,** *4*, 185–193.

Jato-Espino, D.; Castillo-Lopez, E.; Rodriguez-Hernandez, J.; Canteras-Jordana, J. C. A Review of Application of Multi-Criteria Decision making Methods in Construction. Autom. Constr. **2014**, *45*, 151–162.

Khaira, A.; Dwivedi, R. K. A State of the Art Review of Analytical Hierarchy Process. *Mater. Today: Proc.* **2018,** *5* (2), 4029–4035.

Khorshidi, H. A.; Nikfalazar, S.; Gunawan, I. Statistical Process Control Application on Service Quality using SERVQUAL and QFD with a Sase Study in Trains' Services. *TQM J.* **2016,** *28* (2), 195–215.

Korpela, J., Tuominen, M. A. Decision Aid in Warehouse Site Selection. *Int. J. Prod. Econ.* **1996,** *45*, 169–180.

Meddaoui, A.; Bouami, D. Decision Making in Maintenance using Analytical Hierarchy Process and Time-Driven Activity Based Costing. *Int. J. Product. Qual. Manag.* **2014**, *13* (4), 450–470.

Ortiz-Barrios, M; Miranda-De la Hoz, C; López-Meza, P; Petrillo, A; De Felice, F. A Case of Food Supply Chain Management with AHP, DEMATEL, and TOPSIS. *J. Multi Criteria Decis. Anal.* **2020,** *27*, 104–128.

Prasad, K. G. D.; Subbaiah, K. V.; Rao, K. N. Supply Chain Design through QFD-Based Optimization. *J. Manuf. Technol. Manag.* **2014**, *25* (5),

Saaty, T. L. Decision Making with the Analytic Hierarchy Process. *Int. J. Serv. Sci.* **2008**, *1* (1), 83–98.

Sinha, M.; Camgöz Akdağ, H.; Tarım, M.; Lonial, S.; Yatkın, A. QFD Application using SERVQUAL for Private Hospitals: A Case Study. *Leadersh. Heal. Serv.* **2013,** *26* (3), 175–183.

Subbaiah, K. V.; Prasad, K. G. D.; Rao, K. N. Customer-Driven Product Planning using Conjoint Analysis and QFD-ANP Methodology. *Int. J. Product. Qual. Manag.* **2011**, *7* (3), 374–394.

Suryaningrat, I. B. Implementation of QFD in Food Supply Chain Management: A Case of Processed Cassava Product in Indonesia. *Int. J. Adv. Sci. Eng. Inf. Technol.* **2016**, *6* (3)

Toloie-Eshlaghy, A.; Homayonfar, M. MCDM Methodologies and Applications: A Literature Review from 1999 to 2009. *Res. J. Int. Stud.* **2011**,

Vaidya, O. S.; Kumar, S. Analytic Hierarchy Process: An Overview of Applications. *Eur. J. Oper. Res.* **2006**, *169* (1), 1–29.

CHAPTER 16

Regional Comprehensive Economic Partnership and the Indian Dairy Sector: A Case Using SAP–LAP Approach

SWATI UPVEJA

Amity Business School, Amity University Noida, 201301, Uttar Pradesh, India, E-mail: upveja.swati@gmail.com

ABSTRACT

Regional Comprehensive Economic Partnership (RCEP) is a proposed Free Trade Agreement in the Asia Pacific region among the 10 member states of the Association of Southeast Asian Nations [Brunei, Cambodia, Indonesia, Laos, Malaysia, Myanmar, Philippines, Singapore, Thailand, and Vietnam and 5 FTA partners Australia, China, Japan, New Zealand, and South Korea]. The goal of the present research paper is to identify the challenges and issues in RCEP from an Indian Dairy perspective. In the present research, the authors have used the Situation Actors and Processes–Learning Action and Performance (SAP–LAP) approach to carry out the research. The present study has illustrated the identified challenges and issues in RCEP from the Indian Dairy perspective using the SAP–LAP technique. The research is exploratory in nature and may be useful for the policymakers and the dairy sector globally.

16.1 BACKGROUND

To boost the economic growth, India opted for free trade policy since it sought various ways to foster its trade with other nations. It is evident from the various bilateral and multilateral trade pacts signed by India in recent years.

Constructive Discontent in Execution: Creative Approaches to Technology and Management.
Sanjeev Bansal, Anita Venaik, Swati Upveja, and Saritha S. (Eds.)

Although multiple bilateral deals lead to so-called "noodle bowl" problem where multiple deals overlap each other and sometimes become inconsistent too. In order to comply, the country has to incur very high transaction cost. Thus, multilateralism is inevitable. In the past, India has not extracted ideal outcomes out of multilateral trade deals. India has started viewing future agreements with suspicion. It is currently negotiating over various regional or multilateral trade deals, namely, the Comprehensive and Progressive Agreement for Trans-Pacific Partnership, Asia Pacific Trade Agreement, and Regional Comprehensive Economic Partnership (RCEP), which is one of the most debated trade deals among all.

16.2 INTRODUCTION

Regional Comprehensive Economic Partnership was a proposed Free Trade Agreement (FTA) among 16 countries. These countries include 10-member States of the Association of South East Asian Nations (ASEAN), namely, Brunei, Cambodia, Indonesia, Lao PDR, Malaysia, Myanmar, The Philippines, Singapore, Thailand, and Vietnam; and the 6 States with which ASEAN has existing FTA, namely, Australia, China, India, Japan, South Korea, and New Zealand." The RCEP negotiations, if finalized, would have brought the biggest economies in the region into a regional trading agreement in the biggest trade pact in the world accounting for almost half of the global population, contributing about 30% of the combined GDP of all countries. Australia, RCEP (2019). Thus, RCEP would be the largest trading bloc in the world not only in terms of gross domestic product but also in terms of population.

16.2.1 IMPACT OF RCEP ISSUES ON INDIA

India was skeptical about the deal throughout all the negotiations of RCEP trade deal as China was the major trade partner among all the countries hence the low-priced imports of China were the biggest threat to Indian domestic industry. Already India runs a large trade deficit from China (53 billion $) along with 10 other RCEP countries. Also, taking all the countries under consideration situation was even worse as India had 21% of its entire exports from these countries in the year 2018–2019 whereas imports mounted to 34%. Furthermore, the unmet demand for exemption from the Ratchet mechanism created another disagreement for India as it would not be able to protect the interest of its traders under the obligation of Ratchet. The tariffs and quotas relaxations were irreversible for the countries under the trade deal thus making it impossible for the country to take any protective measures.

Another reason for India's disagreement was the calculation of the base year for tariff exemption to all RCEP countries. One of the key areas of negotiation under RCEP was "tariff modalities" on goods which leads to the removal of all types of bounties on its exports. The negotiations were based on thresholds which were computed both in terms of the number of tariff lines as well as the percentage of imports from the other 15 RCEP countries. The imports were computed as the average imports during the period 2012 and 2013 while the base rate for commencing tariff reductions was the Most Forward Nation (MFN) rate as of 1 January 2014. This Mechanism by default would have caused a surge in imports which was the concern. RCEP Report GOI (2019).

16.2.2 RCEP CHALLENGE: INDIAN DAIRY SECTOR

Trade agreements do not always lead to the welfare of all the countries involved and the simple fact is that negotiating countries may have conflicts of interest on certain issues. Several times, the deal is not conducive to the growth of a few domestic enterprises and India also faced the same in terms of RCEP membership as it would have made India part of the largest trade pact but at the same time, domestic industries would have been under threat. However, a number of sectors were concerned that they have much to lose out of this deal and one such sector was dairy sector. Dairy provides marginal and landless farmers with 25% of their household expenses as income from crops is seasonal. These figures would get badly affected and unemployment can overshadow the growing GDP of the country if dairy persists in the negotiations of RCEP. The agonizing stalemate in the dairy sector was that tariffs clauses for agriculture in RCEP were much lower than compared to the existing WTO agreement. R. Rama Kumar, Chair Professor at the Tata Institute of Social Sciences has said that "While the WTO allows a country to fix tariffs up to a certain maximum, or bound tariff, for a given commodity line, the RCEP binds countries to reduce that level to zero within the next 15 years. Currently, India's the average bound tariff for dairy products is about 63.8% while its average applied tariff is 34.8%. Therefore, it could unveil the dairy sector by removing tariff protections, for which dairy sector was not prepared. Most of the countries in RCEP are the largest contributors to the global milk trade (Table 16.1).

Accepting the RCEP deal as it is by the Indian government would mean inviting Australia and New Zealand to capture the Indian dairy industry. Both the countries were trying hard to get the access of Indian dairy market which is the largest in the entire world, hence this deal was a big opportunity for them. However, the deal was not less than suicide for Indian dairy farmers as the two countries' low-priced imports of milk powder, butter, and cheese would have pressurized the price of milk by the farmers too. Moreover, the price per liter of milk received by an average Indian (30/L) must have fallen by approximately ₹19/L because against the Indian price of 300/kg, New Zealand's export price of skimmed milk powder (SMP) is 150/kg (as per the estimations made by Amul) This would have made dairying unprofitable for the Indian farmers also it would have put India's food security at stake.

TABLE 16.1 Share of Global Trade in Milk and Related Products from RCEP Countries.

Products	Share of RCEP in global trade (%)
Milk	51
SMP	45
Butter oil	38
Cheese	35
Butter	31

Source: A victory for the dairy sector, The Hindu (6 November 2019).

After the government promoted multinational companies to enter the domestic dairy sector, few multi-national companies (MNCs) entered, thus creating demand from domestic farmers as the applied tariffs on dairy products being 35%. As per the recommendations made by RCEP it was supposed to fall to zero for all member countries, so making it profitable for the MNCs to purchase low priced imported milk from countries such as Australia and New Zealand further it would push the domestic prices of milk too and making it difficult for the domestic dairy sector to compete. However, in reality, the fact is that India is the world's largest producer and consumer of dairy. Therefore, as per the estimations of Niti Aayog India's milk production will reach 330 MT in 2033 while the demand will reach the level of 292 MT which confirms the excess of milk supply. Further projections made by international organizations have assured the surplus supply of milk, milk products, livestock, and fisheries so there would been no need of imports even in future. This report has ensured the sufficient availability of roughages and fodder in 2033 Ramakumar, R (2019) The last argument of dairy sector against RCEP agreement was based on the socio-economic cost as it would have affected 70 million households dependent on dairy in India whereas in New Zealand it is just 10,000 and in Australia it is only 6,300. Thus, the livelihood of 70 million farmers at stake made the deal even difficult to go ahead with.

TABLE 16.2 Trade in Dairy Products: Principal Exporting Countries

Whole milk powder thousand tons (product weight)	**Average (2013–2015)**	**2016**	**2017**
World	2,538	2,465	2,408
New Zealand	1,365	1,344	1,357
European Union	385	380	371
Uruguay	76	126	108
Argentina	155	110	78
SMP	**Average (2013–2015)**	**2016**	**2017**
World	2083	2187	2333
New Zealand	581	574	697
European Union[a]	581	574	697
United States	556	593	643
New Zealand	395	444	408
Australia	161	164	165
Butter	**Average (2013–2015)**	**2016**	**2017**
World	947	963	929
New Zealand	490	503	514
European Union	151	208	166
Belarus	74	84	88
Australia	65	29	29
United States	42	31	23
Cheese	**Average (2013–2015)**	**2016**	**2017**
World	2376	2478	2573
European Union	742	800	848
New Zealand	294	355	350
United States	336	289	342
Belarus	161	204	199
Australia	162	167	170
Saudi Arabia	118	131	129

Source: Report of Food and Agriculture Organization (FAO) November 2017.

As per the report of FAO, New Zealand and Australia are among those countries which contribute maximum in trade of dairy products specifically the whole milk powder, skimmed milk, cheese and butter. Till now as per the import policy of India, it has put a ban on the import of all dairy products. However, as per the guiding principle of RCEP it would have to remove all the barriers on all the products so dairy was no exception. Thus, New

Zealand and Australia getting access to the Indian market which in turn make livelihood of Indian farmers difficult who do dairying at a small level by keeping 2–3 milking cows or buffalos.

16.2.3 SAP-LAP ANALYSIS

The SAP-LAP paradigm is depicted in Figure 16.1 and the proposed framework of SAP-LAP paradigm is shown in Figure 16.2. It is on the basis of flexible systems management (Sushil, 1997).

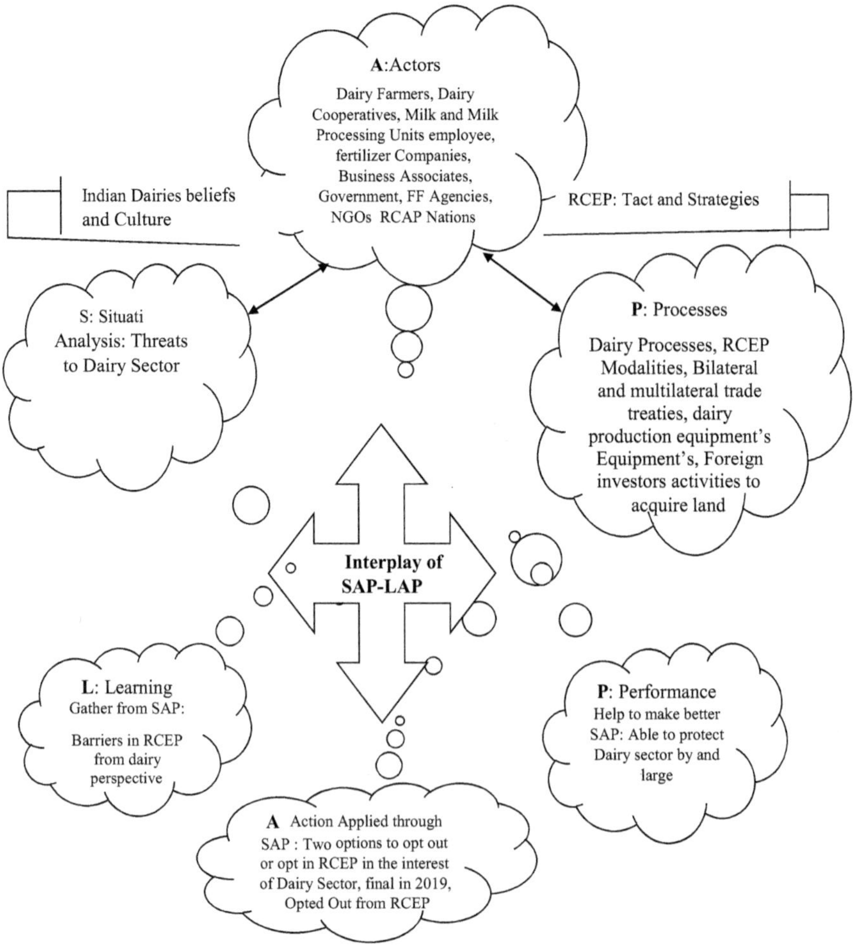

FIGURE 16.1 The SAP-LAP paradigm.

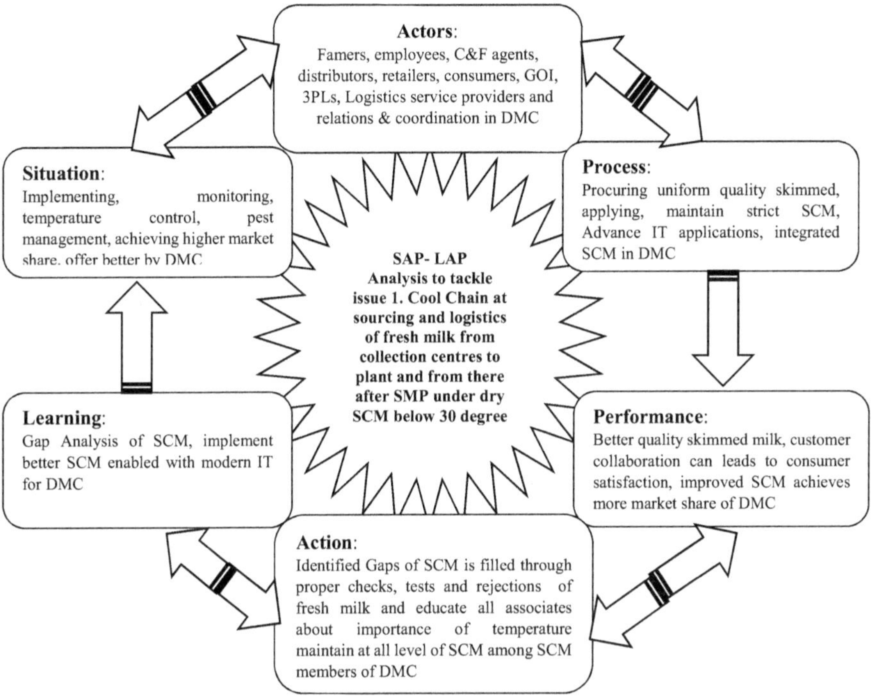

FIGURE 16.2 Proposed framework of SAP-LAP paradigm in DMC.

16.3 THREATS TO DAIRY SECTOR

16.3.1 SITUATION

- Indian is one of the largest manufacturers and processors of milk and milk products: 176 million tonnes/year produced 150 million dairy farmers, average milk production per animal is 3 L/day and 375 gm/day per capita availability.
- As it is evident from land holding data of Indian farmers, the average farm size is 0.1 ha (Department of Animal Husbandry and Dairying, 2019), 100 million Indian dairy farmers are the backbone of the dairy sector, due to RCEP implementation in India, there will be the surge in the production costs of milk and milk products and downward trends in earning of dairy farmers in turn bring dairy farmers into dire straits, that is, current realization of dairy farmers is INR 30/L where due to RCEP implantation this will drastically fall at INR 19/L (Report)

- Ratchet mechanism of RCEP states that once the trade relief in tariff and quotas on export and import offered to trade nations cannot be withdrawn (Reported by Grain, 2019)
- The biggest fall in RCEP will be a severe threat to our Indian Food Security.
- The dairy supply chain of India is complex in nature and unique one.
- Cutting-edge rivalry is expected in Indian milk market if the global firms such as Lacetacis, Dodla Dairy, Hutson, Nestle, Danone, etc. enter.
- There is a sharp hike in demand for the dairy products by the households specifically in metro cities as a result of the upsurge in the income of households.

16.3.2 ACTOR

- Board of dairy firms, top management, managing director, chief executive officer, general manager sales and marketing, logistics head, and the supply chain department.
- Dairy farmers, dairy cooperatives, milk and milk processing units' employees, fertilizer companies, business associates, government, freight forwarding agencies, NGOs, RCEP nations, foreign investors.
- All the suppliers or business associates.
- State governments, Government of India, foreign governments, World Trade Organization

16.3.3 PROCESS

- Indigenous dairy practices
- Applying traditional equipment, whereas high cost of modern dairy equipment
- Bilateral and multilateral trade treaties
- RCEP members such as Japan and Australia demonstrate high food safety standards, but they are incompatible with the small-scale food productions and processing system with respect to India
- RCEP offers an alternative entry route to the India dairy market: The big dairy firms such as Fonterra from New Zealand
- Genetically modified products
- Main raw material is to be standardized fresh milk

- To avoid adulteration in fresh milk, proper milk testing is prescribed before the collection of milk
- Existing SCM requires upgradation
- Manufacturing depends upon the availability of fresh milk around the year, sales, and marketing department's yearly sales projections

16.3.4 LEARNING

- DMC's production planning is based on the availability of the right kind of fresh milk and sales and marketing sales projections on yearly basis and sales projects
- Use of proper cool chain and dry chain, and space available for storage at retail can boost sales
- Proper SCM creates wonders for DMC
- Channel partner's awareness, education, and training on the SCM are required
- Creation for phasing out an old set of processing and replacing with modern systems
- The crucial challenge is to streamline connectivity among distributors and their central distribution hub, C&F agents to encourage the right communication at right time and at the right place

16.4 CONCLUSION AND DISCUSSION

The present research paper identifies challenges and issues in RCEP from the Indian Dairy perspective using the SAP–LAP technique. India is a leading manufacturer and processor of milk and milk products. The most important observation highlighted from this case is that due to RCEP implementation in India, there would been a surge in the cost of production of milk and milk products which will further reduce the earnings of dairy farmers in turn bring dairy farmers into dire straits, that is, current realization of dairy farmers is INR 30/L where due to RCEP implementation this would have drastically fallen at INR 19/L. The major challenges were the provision of irreversibility of trade reliefs under RCEP by member countries, non-competitiveness of Indian dairy sector along with the complexity of Indian dairy supply chain. This agreement would have severely impacted dairy farmers, dairy cooperatives, milk and milk processing units' employees, fertilizer companies, business associates, government, freight forwarding agencies, NGOs, RCEP nations, foreign investors. Therefore, one can conclude that the Indian diary sector was not prepared for this level of international competition. As a major part of earning of small farmers comes from dairy which helps them to bear their household expenses as their earnings from crops are seasonal. This situation would further deteriorate in terms of income and employment loss as the inclusion of the dairy sector in the RCEP deal would cause mass unemployment among farmers. Also, this study focuses on the gravity of a better supply chain to provide better quality skimmed milk, customer collaboration can lead to consumer satisfaction, and improved SCM achieves more market share of DMC.

KEYWORDS

- **Regional Comprehensive Economic Partnership (RCEP)**
- **trading block**
- **free trade areas (FTA)**
- **Situation Actors and Processes–Learning Action and Performance (SAP–LAP)**
- **individual entrepreneurial orientation**
- **entrepreneurial orientation**
- **management students**

REFERENCES

ASEAN. Guiding Principles and Objectives for Negotiating the Regional Comprehensive Economic Partnership, 2012.

ASEAN Joint Declaration by Leaders on the Launch of the Regional Comprehensive Economic Partnership, 2016.

Australia RECP. *Regional Comprehensive Economic Partnership*; Department of Foreign Affairs and Trade, Australian Government, 2019.

Business Line. RCEP would Hurt Dairy Sector Heavily, Cautions SJM [Online] Oct 2, 2019. https://www.thehindubusinessline.com/economy/sjm-urges-modi-government-to-oppose-dairy-sector-inclusion-in-rcep/article29575133.ece#

Business Standard. India Opts Out of RCEP: Industry and Farmer Group Hails Govt's Move [Online] Nov 5, 2019. https://www.business-standard.com/article/pti-stories/industry-traders-farmers-welcome-india-s-decision-to-not-sign-rcep-119110401629_1.html

Chaudhary, D. R. RCEP Member Countries Split Over Deal for India, *Economic Times* [Online] Nov 4, 2019. https://economictimes.indiatimes.com/news/politics-and-nation/rcep-member-countries-split-over-deal-for-india/articleshow/71884653.cms (accessed Nov 13, 2019).

Curran, E. What's the RCEP and What Does India's Exit Mean for the Trade Deal? *Bloomberg* [Online] Nov 6, 2019. https://www.business-standard.com/article/current-affairs/what-s-the-rcep-and-what-does-india-s-exit-mean-for-the-trade-deal-119110500186_1.html (accessed Nov, 6th 2019).

Israni, H. What's in It for India. *Vivekananda International Foundation* [Online] 2018. https://www.vifindia.org/article/2018/november/28/rcep-what-s-in-it-for-india

Kher, R. Opinion. The RCEP is a must for India [Online] 2018. https://www.livemint.com/Opinion/8d0oL0au6FRutsrgJ4IoPK/Opinion--The-RCEP-is-a-must-for-India.html (accessed 17 Nov 2018).

Mahajan, A. RCEP. A Death Knell for Dairy Sector [Online] 2019. https://ashwanimahajan.wordpress.com/2019/10/01/rcep-death-knell-for-dairy-in-india/

Narayan, B.; Mathur, S. Why India's Decision to Pull Out of RCEP has both Pros and Cons. *Economic Times* [Online] 2019. https://prime.economictimes.indiatimes.com/news/72214498/economy-and-policy/why-indias-decision-to-pull-out-of-rcep-has-both-pros-and-cons

Ramakumar, R. A Victory for the Dairy Sector. *The Hindu* [Online] Nov 6, 2019. https://www.thehindu.com/opinion/op-ed/a-victory-for-the-dairy-sector/article29891203.ece

RCEP Report, GOI. *Regional Comprehensive Economic Partnership*; Members' Reference Service Larrdis Lok Sabha Secretariat. Government of India: New Delhi, 2017.

Seymour, H.; Jeffery, W. RCEP: An Economic Architecture for the Indo-Pacific? [Online] 2019. https://www.orfonline.org/expert-speak/rcep-an-economic-architecture-for-the-indo-pacific-57242/ (accessed 10 Dec).

The Economic Times. Is India Ready for RCEP Embrace. [Online] 2019. https://economictimes.indiatimes.com/news/economy/policy/is-india-ready-for-rcep-embrace/articleshow/71802490.cms?from=mdr

Vijayakumar, V. K. India's RCEP Walkout Shows Its Industry is Still Incompetent. *Quartz India* [Online] 2018. https://qz.com/india/1753077/modis-rcep-walkout-shows-indias-incompetence-in-global-trade/ (accessed Dec 2, 2019).

Wilson, J. Mega-Regional Trade Deals in the Asia-Pacific: Choosing between the TPP and RCEP? *J. Contemp. Asia* 2015, *45* (2), 345–353.

Wilson, J. Investing in the Economic Architecture of the Indo-Pacific. *Indo-Pacific Insights Series*; Perth US Asia Centre, 2017.

CHAPTER 17

From Discovery to Design: Technological Innovation of Surgical Devices

BHAWNA SHARMA[1*] and SUDIR PADROO[2]

[1]*Amity Business School, Amity University Maharashtra*

[2]*Meril Endo-Surgery Pvt. Ltd. Mumbai*

[*]*Corresponding author. E-mail: bhawnasharma22@gmail.com*

ABSTRACT

The Global medical device market is growing at the rate of 5% per year and will reach around US $800bn by 2030 (KPMG Report, 2018). High rise in demand of medical devices and services is expected as the lifestyle diseases have become more prevalent and this economic development unleashes the market growth avenues for medical device companies. It was the early years of the 20th century when the experts were exploring newer avenues for creating anastomosis and thus innovate devices which could offer better wound healing without compromising the hemostasis and sterility. Surgical stapling devices have provided options for creating better clinical outcomes with optimum tissue transaction and anastomosis. In this work, an attempt is made to explore technological advances of surgical devices. In this study, we have given a glimpse of conventional and modern and briefed on their amendments and modifications over time. This study has elaborated and provided insights for understanding new surgical stapling advancements. The major focus of all the corporates involved in manufacturing these devices revolves around five basics which are very well particularized in the chapter as the surgical stapler design continues to evolve while still maintaining the basic principles. This study provides the better insights for these advancements.

Constructive Discontent in Execution: Creative Approaches to Technology and Management.
Sanjeev Bansal, Anita Venaik, Swati Upveja, and Saritha S. (Eds.)

17.1 INTRODUCTION

The global medical device industry has set an objective to design and develop novel, clinically relevant, state-of-the-art surgical devices and is thus expanding its product portfolios. The need of developing products through innovation, advance technology, and collaboration with medical professionals and healthcare organizations are poised to bring in solutions for better patient outcomes.

The mechanical and electronic advances across varied scientific disciplines have produced distinguished surgical devices that are used during the different basic and advance surgeries. Introduction of new medical devices and continuing technical improvements in the existing devices are changing the ways surgeons perform the traditional tasks and enable them to develop the new techniques with the aim of improving patients' outcomes. In today's time, how they are carried forward has led the think tanks to develop devices based on new surgical techniques. Every innovation in instrument has its own benefits and limitations in tissue reintegration. These differences, if managed and understood properly, allow its accurate and optimal usage.

In this piece, we are focused on drawing out attention toward the continuous development of surgical stapler also known as mechanical closure devices.

The shape, stability, and integrity of the titanium staples in a surgical stapler depends upon the tissue compression which eventually supports in creating stable anastomosis. It is important to know how tissue interacts with stapling devices, which helps in appropriate selection of devices for a particular tissue type. A known fact is that every tissue behaves differently due to its intrinsic characteristics. Tissue compressibility is subject to its biochemical properties that help us establish the adequate compression force desired before firing and after firing. The surgical staplers are an example of the device that has evolved through the ongoing innovation and is currently being used in several surgical procedures.

17.2 HISTORICAL BACKGROUND OF SURGICAL STAPLING

It was the early years of the 20th century when the experts were exploring newer avenues for creating anastomosis and thus innovating devices which could offer better wound healing without compromising the hemostasis and sterility. In 1826, French surgeon F. N. Denans and a Belgian Surgeon

J. H. F. Henroz from Liege published the results of their experiments of using a mechanical device for the first time in dogs to perform an intestinal anastomosis. In further advancements, surgical stapling devices were introduced in the year 1908 by Prof. Humer Hultl along with a Hungarian businessman Victor Fischer, who helped him design the device. Like any other start-up they had a tough time commercializing the product as it was an expensive affair to manufacture it and moreover the device developed was bulky and unwieldy to use. However, in the year 1920 Dr. Hultl's student Aladar Peltz integrated two innovations to the existing design which helped him in reducing the weight of the device, had silver staples, and was later known as Petz Clamp. The device could be fired only once in a surgery, as it was required to be unassembled, cleaned, reloaded, and sterilized before reusing it. In 1934, the innovations were still going on and Dr. H. Friedich of Ulm Germany came up with the replaceable reload/cartridge, which made the reusability possible in a surgery. This innovation introduced newer ways of making anastomosis. In 1952, the concept was further polished in Soviet Union and thus first commercially produced reusable stapling device was developed by Alexander Shalinov from Ukraine. In 1964, an American surgeon, Dr. Mark Ravitch brought samples of stapling devices after attending conference in Russia. He introduced them to an entrepreneur Leon C Hirsch, who then founded the United States Surgical Corporation (USSC) and started manufacturing the stapler under its Auto Suture Brand. The first product they sold was in 1967. In 1977, Ethicon and Johnson & Johnson entered the stapling device market and are now being used across the globe. In 1998, the electrosurgical device maker Valleylab was acquired by USSC and USSC got acquired by Tyco Healthcare. In 2007, Tyco Surgical devices were marketed by Covidien which was an Ireland-based company. In 2015, Covidien merged with Medtronic.

17.3 CAUSE OF EVOLUTION OF SURGICAL DEVICES

Every tissue behaves differently as thickness of each tissue varies and so are the intrinsic biomechanical properties of tissue. The choice of stapler and staple size will depend on the characteristics of each tissue and the disease condition. It will also play a major role in deciding the compression force and time required before and after firing the stapler. It completely depends upon the experience of a surgeon and his skill level to assess the tissue type and its characteristics and thus make a choice.

Surgical staplers are an example of the device that has evolved through the ongoing innovation and is currently being used in several surgical procedures. Choice of surgical device is primarily based on the tissue characteristics as listed below. These diverse tissue characteristics have fuelled the evolution of surgical devices.

Tissue Creep: Flowing away of tissue from the point of applied force.

Tissue Hysteresis: Lagging effect behind the cause. Time is necessary to achieve a balance between the elastic forces and pressure applied.

Biphasic Nature: Tissue is composed of both fluid and solid material.

Tissue Viscoelasticity: Properties of both viscous fluid and elasticity of a solid such as the ability to store the energy of deformation.

Tissue Thickness: Tissue thickness varies from organ to organ, person to person, gender to gender.

17.4 TECHNOLOGICAL INNOVATION OF MEDICAL SURGICAL DEVICES

17.4.1 PRIMITIVE AGE—THE PIONEERS OF SURGICAL INTERVENTIONS

While the world has moved from simple suturing needles to robotic surgery, surgeons have witnessed a major paradigm shift in the way surgeries are being performed.

As per Indian history, Sushruta "the father of surgery" had performed the very first surgery in 600 B.C. He pioneered the use of suturing material and surgical instruments. He developed the devices for performing various plastic surgeries and also wrote a book called Sushruta Samhita which had all the major surgical text.

17.4.2 SUTURES—NEXT GENERATION SURGICAL TOOL

India was a huge market for surgical sutures of natural origin. However, over a period of time with consistent innovation the surgical suturing material is now synthetically designed and modified as per use. Theses surgical sutures are available in two major categories:

- **Absorbable:** The absorption of such sutures occurs by natural enzymatic degradation in case of sutures from the natural origin (gut) and the synthetic sutures get absorbed by hydrolysis. Like—gut, polydioxanone (PDS), polyglecaprone, polyglactin, etc.
- **Nonabsorbable:** Nonabsorbable sutures are of chemical origin and retained in the body till any further surgical intervention. Like—nylon, polypropylene, silk, polyester.

Nowadays, there are sutures which have antibacterial coating to avoid postoperative surgical site infections. Also, the needles used in these surgeries have evolved from time to time. These are several types of suture needles which have been designed for different surgical interventions. The tip or the needle point are of the following types: Round bodied, taper point, conventional cutting, reverse cutting, reverse cutting prime, ultra-point reverse cutting, spatula, etc.

17.4.3 MECHANICAL STAPLERS

The mechanical stapler products are mainly used for transection, resection, and creating anastomosis in alimentary tract. However, some of them are also used in certain thoracic surgeries like wedge resection, lobectomy, pneumonectomy, bullectomy, etc. These devices are divided in two categories based on the mode of access.

a) **OPEN** and **b. LAPAROSCOPIC**

   The open surgical stapling products are those instruments which are used in the open surgeries wherein the incisions made are big enough to introduce entire device into the body. The laparoscopic instruments or devices are those which gain access into abdominal cavity through a small hole/port via another device called trocar sleeve/cannula.

   The open devices are linear cutter, linear staplers, circular stapler, etc and the laparoscopic devices are endoscopic linear cutter (ELC), circular stapler with long length, etc.

   Here, we will discuss how the medical device industry innovated and improvised their products for better clinical outcomes and offered ease of use to the operating surgeon.

Linear Cutter

Linear cutter is a reloadable surgical stapler which is mainly indicated for transection and resection and can also be used to create anastomosis. The cartridges are having titanium staples for various tissue thicknesses and have different color codes for ease of identification. White cartridge is used for vascular tissues, blue for medium thick tissues, and green for thicker tissues. However, some companies have launched other color cartridges as well with certain specifications which are unique to them only. A major medical device company came up with gold cartridge which offers an optimal thickness between the two conventional sizes. Also, they have launched an innovative device which offers multiple staple heights within one black colored cartridge.

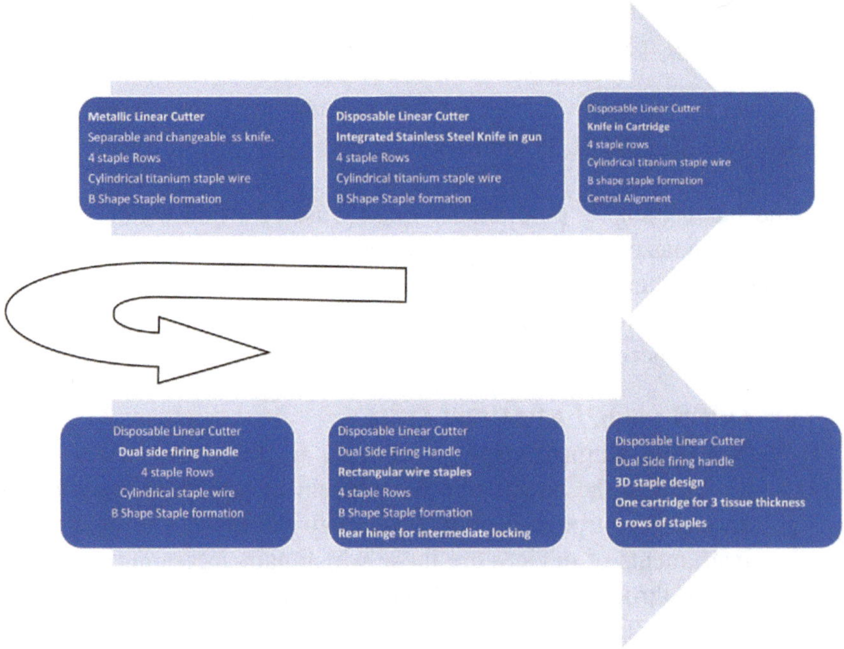

FIGURE 17.1 Technological innovations and improvisation in linear cutter.

Circular Stapler

The circular staplers place circular rows of titanium staples which may be 1 row, 2 rows, or 3 rows which is achieved after squeezing the firing handle. While the staples are being placed, the circular knife within the housing resects the excess tissue in circumferential manner. It is indicated for creating anastomosis between two tubular structures. These anastomoses are usually end to end and end to side. The medical device companies have been working on creating newer devices to achieve a secure anostomosis with superior hemostasis. Some of the circular staplers offer varied range of staple height to accommodate various tissue thicknesses while some have fixed stapler heights like that of linear cutter cartridges. Also, there are some firms which have fixed anvil and some are having the anvil top which tilts while extracting out the device. The very recent advancement in this product category is the 3 row staplers, 3 rows with stepped staple technology, and the powered circular stapler.

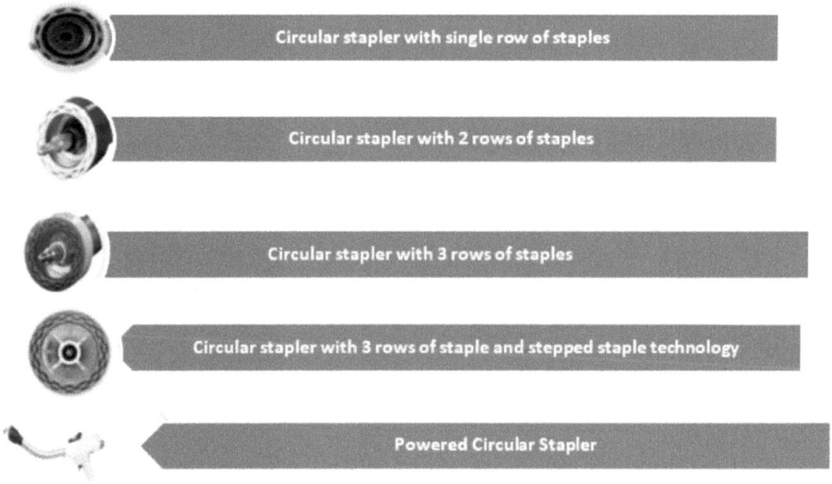

FIGURE 17.2 Technological advancement in circular staplers.

Endoscopic Linear Cutters (ELCs)

Presently, there are many types of ELCs in the market. However, the most used ones are from two medical devices giants. Performing a surgery using laparoscopic technique is in itself a growth area for many of the developing surgeons and nations. There is definitely a longer learning curve for getting trained of laparoscopic techniques. Use of ELCs certainly needs assistance if in case the surgeon is new to the device and has not performed many surgeries using it. While some companies have a full length gun with a small plastic reload/cartridge, some are having cartridges which have half of the shaft within it.

Since these devices are used in laparoscopic procedures, so the articulation of the distal end is a very important aspect. To achieve that some companies have knobs at the proximal end of the gun while some need assistance of other device or abdominal wall to make it articulate.

Initially, all the ELCs were having straight shaft, which later changed to articulating ones. And instead of having two rows in the conventional linear cutter, the ELC came with a three row design for better wound security. Also one firm introduced the stepped staple technology wherein the three rows of staples are of three different heights. One firm launched the cartridge in which they claim that their cartridge surface has better tissue grasping compared to the conventional staple surface.

In the recent years, the powered version of ELCs has also been accepted by the surgeons. These powered devices offer ease of use and better precision compared to the manual ones.

17.5 RECENT ADVANCES IN SURGICAL STAPLING DEVICES

Medical device market is all set for its concurrent growth. It is estimated that global sales revenue will witness poised growth of 5% a year and would reach dollar 8 hundred billion by the year 2030. This prognoses is due to higher demand of technological advancements, increasing demand, new adaptive technology, the increasing number of chronic illness, and subsequent surgeries are driving the surgical stapler market as lifestyle diseases have become the most prevalent these days. This has lead to the introduction and unleashing of technological advancements in medical devise segment.

As per recent KPMG market assessment report on medical devises, it has been acknowledged that "The major focus of all the corporates involved in manufacturing these devices revolves around five basic characteristics of tissue and the 'Tenets of William Halstead' also known as Halstead Principle."

17.6 CONCLUSION

Innovation in surgical device industry may not be a cake walk as its entry in market is scrutinized and regulated by several authorities. Each medical device has to undergo in vitro, animal and human trials before they can be commercially launched in healthcare market. It is evident in this study that a simple device like a **Linear Stapler** took more than 200 years to be what we see now. Companies have worked on two aspects in case of all the device categories from surgical sutures to modern day laparoscopic instruments: (1) Ease of use for the surgeons and (2) Safer for patients.

The latest advancement in medical device technology has changed the way surgeries were being perceived in initial 90s. What we all know today as a simple gall bladder removal surgery aka Lapchole or Lap Cholecystectomy used to be an invasive procedure wherein patient really had to spend days in hospital for the postoperative care and consume pain killer/analgesics and a lot more. The laparoscopic devices and technique has made such procedures like day care ones. In this chapter, we have explained only one type of medical device while a lot must be done and discussed at such platforms to emphasize the innovations required and to enhance the pace at which they are being introduced for commercial use.

KEYWORDS

- **stapling devices**
- **medical devices**
- **surgical staplers**
- **mechanical staplers**
- **surgical advancements**
- **tissue strength**
- **would healing**

REFERENCES

AD G, L T, D N, RC I. The History of Surgical Staplers: A Combination of Hungarian, Russian, and American Innovation [Internet]. PubMed. 2021. https://pubmed.ncbi.nlm.nih.gov/31267894/ (accessed July 31, 2021).

A Novel Powered Circular Stapler Designed for Creating Secure Anastomoses [Internet]. Oatext.com. 2021. https://www.oatext.com/a-novel-powered-circular-stapler-designed-for-creating-secure-anastomoses.php (accessed July 31, 2021).

Covidien - Wikipedia [Internet]. En.wikipedia.org. 2021. https://en.wikipedia.org/wiki/Covidien (accessed July 31, 2021).

[Internet]. Bmedesign.engr.wisc.edu. 2021. https://bmedesign.engr.wisc.edu/projects/f16/surgical_stapler/file/view/1221a327-4a20-4154-b863-34fc331f67bd/FinalPoster-surgical_stapler.pdf (accessed July 31, 2021).

[Internet]. Scribd.com. 2021. https://www.scribd.com/document/400093855/ACB-DefiniefArtikel-Schiappaetal (accessed July 31, 2021).

Micro-Surgery Selected Robotic: Topics by Science.gov [Internet]. Science.gov. 2021. https://www.science.gov/topicpages/m/micro-surgery+selected+robotic.html (accessed July 31, 2021).

Surgical Stapling Devices Market Size, Trends | Growth Dynamics, 2026 [Internet]. Fortunebusinessinsights.com. 2021. https://www.fortunebusinessinsights.com/industry-reports/surgical-stapling-devices-market-101593 (accessed July 31, 2021).

CHAPTER 18

Augmented Reality (AR) and Virtual Reality (VR) as a Sales and Marketing Strategy

ABHISHEKH NEGI

Amity Business School, Amity University Noida 201301, Uttar Pradesh, India, E-mail: abhishek.negi24@gmail.com

ABSTRACT

As marketing is being driven by the needs and demand of the customers, they expect brands to provide experiences that make use of new technology as it becomes available. The study is an effort to see and evaluate how augmented reality (AR) and virtual reality (VR) can boost marketing and develop strategy to make it better. AR and VR have the potential to be used as a retail marketing strategy across multiple channels, if the goal of implementing the technology is to enhance consumer shopping experiences rather than to solve problems. The use of the qualitative approach method is one aspect that should be done in future. AR and VR experts will provide more information about the technology and how marketers can use it as a sales and marketing strategy.

18.1 INTRODUCTION

18.1.1 BACKGROUND

Marketing is to fullfill many wants and needs of the customers to make them brand loyal, who expect brands to provide experiences that make use of new technology as it becomes available. This means that marketers must keep up

Constructive Discontent in Execution: Creative Approaches to Technology and Management.
Sanjeev Bansal, Anita Venaik, Swati Upveja, and Saritha S. (Eds.)

with new developments in order to meet customer expectations and provide the best possible experiences. Undoubtedly, technologies have shown tremendous potential and are already disrupting the market. Industries use latest technologies which help them to gain customer loyalty and at the same time beat their competitors.

Augmented reality (AR) and virtual reality (VR) are interactive technologies that have the potential to improve the customers' shopping experience. AR is a type of human–computer interaction in which computer-generated information, images, and sounds are superimposed. We need not confuse AR with VR. VR is a computer-generated, artificial simulation or recreation of a real-life environment or situation. It makes its users to interact with simulated reality through vision and hearing clearly. It immerses users in a 360 degree environment in which they can move around at their own pace to investigate whatever piques their interest.

AR is used in a large scale for marketing by big corporate giants like Disney, Coca-Cola, and National Geographic for campaigns, as well as in various places were footfall is more in public spaces such as children parks, big shopping malls as well as in Times Square in New York. In fact Volkswagen in the past used AR for service manuals to provide step-by-step repair assistance to its customers and also allowing their service engineers to investigate repair process.

In 2016, Nintendo used AR technology for the first time in a mobile game, Pokémon GO, which drew a huge attention and became one of the most popular searches on social media. It used various animated creatures who were superimposed on real-world locations. They made humans so passionate and on real basis people started searching out and catch these creatures in the wild by exploring the real human world.

Realtors use VR to create virtual tours that provide a 360 degree walk-through of the property, allow them to experiment with different paint colors on the walls, or simply add furniture to see how the property will actually look.

Retailers can use VR to help customers make purchasing decisions even when they are unable to physically interact with the products. The world's first virtual department store was launched by eBay Australia. Shoptical, a Google Cardboard headset, allowed customers to view 3D images of products and examine different features, colors, and materials, simulating the familiar physical shopping experience. It enabled users to browse, sort, and interact with items of interest simply by looking at them. It generated invaluable data for eBay to analyze what draws shoppers' attention and how they browse in a VR environment.

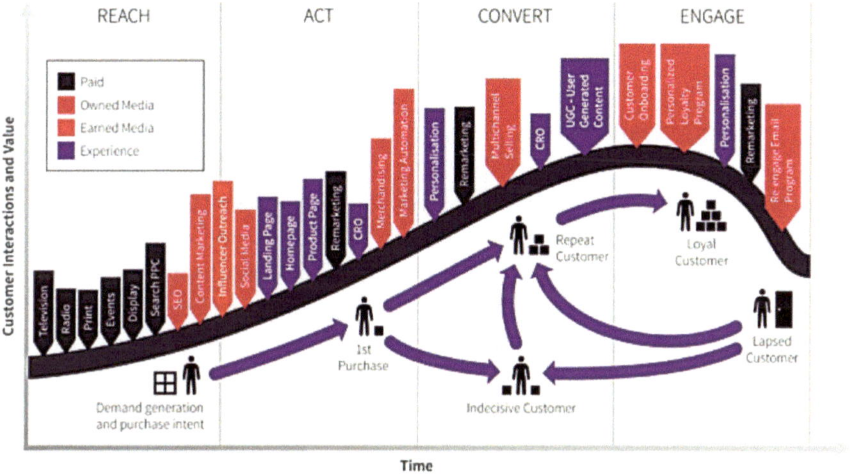

FIGURE 18.1 Lifecycle marketing model.

Source: Reprinted from Hall, 2021. Image courtesy of Smart Insights. https://www.smartinsights.com/paid-search-marketing-ppc/paid-search-strategy/how-to-optimize-your-google-ads-conversion-journey/

18.1.2 BENEFITS OF AR AND VR

18.1.2.1 CUSTOMER ENGAGEMENT

AR and VR are an excellent combination of technologies for engaging customers. What would you do if you entered a mall and needed to visit a well-known fashion outlet? First, look for a signboard. Simply open an app on your phone, type in the name of the store, and follow. Isn't that interesting? App like Snapchat, with filters representing the items you want to buy. From try-on features to a chatbot to connect with a sales representative, you have it all on your phone.

18.1.2.2 CUSTOMER SATISFACTION

This is one of the most critical aspects of running a successful retail business. A memorable happy experience frequently results in a satisfied customer. These technologies are likely to provide a more enriching experience for the customer, increasing the likelihood of customer satisfaction significantly. Because this technology is designed to make it easier and more memorable for customers, it is likely to give businesses an advantage in terms of satisfied customers.

18.1.2.3 CUSTOMER AWARENESS

Customer engagement and interactivity are important not only after the customer has been onboarded, but also to inform and attract. These AR/VR technologies can be effectively used as marketing tools to raise product awareness. If you can interact with a virtual product and see all of its features and benefits, to attract customers, resulting in increased sales numbers.

18.1.2.4 CUSTOMER RETENTION

As important as it is to attract a customer to buy a product, it is also critical to retain an existing customer. A satisfied customer is likely to return. These technologies serve the purpose of customer engagement and interactivity, providing them with a memorable experience, bidding a happy sale farewell, and increasing the likelihood of customers returning. As a result, the company's profits will increase.

18.1.3 USES OF AR AND VR

18.1.3.1 BEAUTY AND MAKEUP

With the popularity of AR and VR technology, this industry has begun to give it traction and leverage in order to provide better service to their customers. We can site a customer visits a beauty showroom; it will be far easier to try a virtual try instead of being in trouble with removing existing make-up products. How's it going to assist? It is easier and faster to make choice without putting and removing fuss. It would save a company a significant amount of testing costs for each product.

18.1.3.2 FASHION

VR and latest in fashion can go hand in hand as navigation in the AR application or a virtual tour of the store. Similarly, one of the amazing features of

VR is that it will make a customer or a designer to wear product where a customer wears a head-mounted device (easy-to-use device) and selects the best fit in for his model , which will save time and cost and is feasible to a great extent too.

18.1.3.3 DEPARTMENTAL STORES

What if you went to a department store and saw an item in front of you and wanted to see its features and benefits? Would you wait for someone to come and assist you? Or if you have an application that allows you to rotate a product, see its features, and use it as well as mantle and dismantle it after scanning it. That is what this AR/VR does. It creates a wonderful experience.

18.1.3.4 E-COMMERCE

With features such as 3D virtual try-ons—Lenskart is giving 3D virtual try-on options on models, where a user gives his/her dimension and sees a model either in VR headset if physically present or on an application.

18.1.3.5 AUTOMOBILES

This industry is severely constrained by a lack of available space. For example, there are numerous variants to a specific model of a car, but all of them cannot be displayed in a single showroom due to obvious space constraints. However, if there is a solution in which a user scans one model of a car and virtually sees other variants appear in front of him/her. That would be fantastic. It would simplify the customer's decision-making process while saving the company money on rental costs.

18.1.3.6 FURNITURE AND HARDWARE

AR/VR configurators are a well-known technology in this market segment. It has also been shown to be highly effective for customers. Where a customer can virtually plan his or her room with virtual furniture and hardware, as well as scan the environment in real time to see how a piece of furniture would look before purchasing it.

18.1.3.7 TRAVEL AND TOURISM

Customers are frequently pleased and make their travel decisions on 2D images. However, having a 360 degree view of a location before visiting it or a fully immersive interactive tour of a location in VR will be an entirely different experience for a customer. These technologies can be found on the websites of all travel and tourism companies, and they will significantly improve customer engagement, decision-making, and, as a result, sales numbers. Another excellent way to make use of these technologies is to use an advanced AR-enabled navigation solution, in which you scan a location and identify eating hubs, bars, and shopping malls while standing in one place.

18.1.3.8 ELECTRONICS

How many times have you purchased a particular technology only to discover that after installing it, you are unable to use it effectively? Then there are the user manuals but VR is going to solve all for us in a dramatic way.

18.1.4 AR AND VR IN INDIA

AR had been widely adopted in India, most notably in Myntra, where AR was used to provide customers with a 360 degree experience. Because shopping is no longer a need-based activity, but rather an experience; retailers must provide unique opportunities to customers. AR and VR technologies enable retailers to develop big strategies to flourish.

While other companies, such as Grohe, Europe's largest manufacturer of sanitary ware fittings showroom, in many different places, India has yet to see major breakthroughs in VR technology outside of the gaming industry. To increase consumer engagement and traffic, the company used VR to provide an immersive experience of their products, such as shower systems, which are otherwise difficult to explain verbally.

Research Reveals

- Brands could use AR and VR in their marketing activities to improve experience, which could then have a positive impact on sales due to higher engagement levels.

- If brands implement AR and VR, they will only be successful at influencing behavior if the following design requirements are met:
  1. Customers are made aware of the technology.
  2. AR and VR are simple to use.
  3. The technology is of high caliber.
- AR and VR can be integrated across multiple channels, and as previously stated, it is most effective when used to enhance experience, giving the technology a purpose within the retailing industry.

18.1.5 KEY DRIVERS OF AR AND VR IN INDIA

18.1.5.1 IKEA, HYDERABAD

IKEA has an AR application that allows users to check and see their IKEA products virtual time using the ARKit technology in Apple iOS 11. The free iPhone and iPad app, dubbed IKEA Place, features realistically rendered, true-to-scale 3D products. "The app automatically scales products based on room dimensions with 98% accuracy," the company stated in a press release.

18.1.5.2 SMARTIVITY, NEW DELHI

Creator of STEM-based educational content in the form of toys and DIY kits incorporate AR technology. Previously, the company claimed to have a presence in 500+ offline stores and e-commerce stores. In October 2015, it received a $200k seed funding from S Chand publications. S Chand led a $1.2 million funding round in May 2016, with participation from other institutional investors such as Tandem Capital and AdvantEdge.

18.1.5.3 SMARTVIZX, NOIDA

It helps its potential users in the real estate and design industries to explore virtual spaces such as buildings and workplaces. The technology aids in the facilitation of consumer purchasing behavior and decision-making. Clients include Rockworth, Quikr, PNB Metlife, and Developer Group, among others. In 2016, Indian Angel Network and Stanford Angels contributed $500k in seed funding.

18.1.5.4 EMPOWER LABS, HYDERABAD

DeltaT is the creator of a mobile-based AR game. There will be offensive and defensive weapons in the gameplay, and the player will have to unlock them by performing certain activities and progressing through levels. Currently, in-app purchases are the company's primary revenue generator. Because the game's features include real-world settings, the company believes that growing its user base will fuel the opportunity to form long-term partnerships with consumer brands and drive revenue through it. In June 2016, the start-up raised INR 3 crore from investors.

18.1.5.5 OOBEDU, MUMBAI

It integrates educational content with AR to provide students with interactive AR-based learning experiences. The learning kit, in conjunction with a smartphone application, aids in experiential learning. It currently offers a "World of Alphabet" product for children, with an app available on the Google Play Store and the iOS store.

18.1.5.6 VADR, GURGAON

Organization has created a VR analytics suite to help VR developers and businesses better understand their users. While users are immersed in the VR experience, it ensures that the massive amount of data generated is captured and presented using advanced visualization techniques. Its analytics features include business intelligence, device performance optimization, user behavior analytics, and the ability to view information as heat maps, charts, or graphs. Clients include those in the real estate, gaming, and industrial training industries.

18.1.5.7 INFURNIA, BENGALURU

They are the providers of in-store technology solutions for architectural design, interior design, and modular furniture. It enables interactive visualization, customization, and 3D walkthroughs of home interiors. Customers can use the software to create digital replicas of interiors and even customize the look and furniture in the room. It is used by retailers for in-store cataloguing. Idein Ventures has previously invested in the company.

18.1.6 OPPORTUNITIES AND CHALLENGES OF AR AND VR

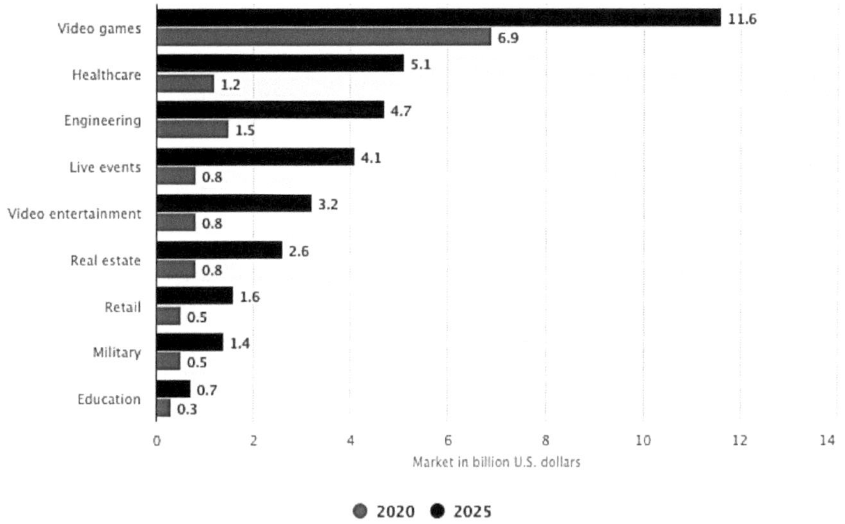

FIGURE 18.2 Future of forecast size of the augmented and virtual reality.

Source: Reprinted from Velev and Zlateva, 2019. Open access.

18.1.6.1 OPPORTUNITIES FOR AR

When compared to VR, AR has a higher growth potential. In contrast to VR's fully immersive experience, AR allows users to see their surroundings while wearing an AR headset or using an AR mobile app. The physical environment is enhanced with a digital overlay of information, allowing users to carry on with their daily activities.

Microsoft's HoloLens is a more advanced version of an AR enabler (also known as mixed reality), in which the technology places digital objects in the user's field of view that can be manipulated via haptics integration (control). A feature like this would completely transform industrial training in industries like manufacturing, automobile, health care, and education.

18.1.6.1.1 *Health Care*

- AR will revolutionize medical and surgical procedures for both patients and doctors. Monitors are currently required in operating rooms to display vital statistics during surgeries.

- Remote support of live medical procedures by expert doctors, guided annotations on a medical procedure for student education, augmentation of live pictures with notes and medical references to students during training phases are just a few of the implications AR is set to have in the health care industry.

18.1.6.1.2 Manufacturing

Manufacturers are eager to embrace AR technology in order to improve workplace efficiency. Workers in a plant operate machines on a daily basis with a high percentage of them receiving training on various aspects of machinery. AR technology is already making inroads on the factory floor and is expected to grow at an exponential rate in the coming years.

AR aims to reduce production time and quickly identify machine problems. The following are some of the potential advantages of AR in manufacturing:

- Faster workplace: Manufacturing jet and turbo engines is one of the most dangerous and intricate processes in the industry, necessitating the assistance of only highly experienced and trained personnel. Engineers can now see the renderings of bolts, cables, part numbers, and instructions on how to assemble a specific component with the help of AR glasses, cameras, and motion sensors that overlay all relevant digital information.
- Reduce maintenance time: With the help of AR firm Reflekt, automotive company Bosch is able to drastically reduce its maintenance procedures in order to stay competitive in the automotive industry. AR makes it possible for anyone to perform mechanical tasks by guiding them through 3D models, eliminating the need for maintenance manuals and displaying the machine's status in real time for timely maintenance.
- Training assistance: When it comes to assisting in industrial training scenarios, both AR and VR are demonstrating enormous potential. AR headsets aid in the tagging of specific objects and provide a digital overlay of information on the display medium that not only provides information on the procedure of a specific task, but also assists trainers in streamlining the training facilities on the manufacturing plant.

- Visual prototyping/device design improvement: With the help of AR, product design engineers can now study and test complex physics at a level of detail previously unattainable through physical testing. AR enhances the efficiency and usefulness of virtual prototyping by providing an operational visualization of the device under development. Aberdeen Group observed one example at the recent LiveWorx 2017 show: A case study that used an AR-based design tool to extract 30% more cooling capacity from a product.

18.1.6.1.3 Gaming and Entertainment

AR and VR dominated the Game Developers Conference in 2017. Mobile AR has become the new medium for game developers to focus on future consumer gaming entertainment, thanks to the success of PokemonGo in 2016. AR-enabled mobile applications work by analyzing the environment and superimposing digital information onto the actual landscape (due to dramatic improvements in processing power and mobile camera technology). Mobile technologies are improving in this area, particularly in the areas of motion sensing and depth sensing.

For example, the iOS game Piclings makes use of the iPhone camera to create level layouts. The game recognizes the images captured by the camera; digitally recreates them and incorporates them into the game world. Live camera feeds can be integrated into games such as Star Wars Arcade.

Unlike VR, which has a high risk of motion sickness/nausea, AR significantly reduces any such effects because the user's eyes are fixed on both real world and virtual objects in the same frame of view. AR is transforming today's gaming and is expected to expand rapidly in the following ways:

- Activity-driven games and enhanced interactivity: AR is proving to be a game changer in the way AR-enabled games are designed. Games are becoming more user interactive, requiring players to move around and incorporate their surroundings into their gameplay. This element of fun will enhance the gaming experience.
- Goldmine for brand advertiser partnerships: As AR is primarily about displaying digital content via the headset or mobile applications, brands can integrate their marketing campaigns into an AR-enabled gaming app to reach a larger audience, resulting in users purchasing from various brands (and thus unlocking discounts) from the app itself.

18.1.6.1.4 Education

Educational content combined with the interactive and immersive features of AR technology has the potential to transform the education industry. Based on our analysis of the educational landscape, we have identified a few functions where AR will add a different experience.

- Enhanced health education: Education in health-related fields necessitates an understanding of the structure and function of the human body, which cannot be accurately conveyed through two-dimensional images.
- Content creation: AR technology enables any school or training program to create 3D interactive/holographic instructional materials with the assistance of startups that provide content creation tools (without any prior coding knowledge). Students can receive animated, immersive, and three-dimensional instruction whether they are in a workplace, laboratory, or classroom setting. Augment is one such classroom educational tool that allows teachers to create scannable handouts and students to generate 3D models and relevant animations for the subject/topic under discussion.
- Portable, less-expensive, and evolution to BYOD culture in classrooms: Prototypes, printed materials, and physical models are all expensive, difficult to transport, and have fixed functions. Furthermore, the difficulties encountered due to logistics management for all supplemental material and inventory management are enormous. AR is digitizing all educational materials, removing the need for institutes to invest in physical materials. Students can browse the material using any compatible device and access the augmented content from any location.
- Higher retention and enhanced learning experience: Students can use AR to access augmented models of anything from a part of the human anatomy to a famous monument. For example, after scanning a photo associated with a 3D model of the Eiffel Tower and viewing the augmented image, students are directed to a web page containing additional information about the monument. A learning cycle is formed as a result of such an experience.

18.1.6.2 OPPORTUNITIES FOR VR

According to market research, VR will be worth more than $15 billion by 2020. The current market is being driven by hardware from companies such as Oculus, Samsung, and Sony, but software and applications will be required to sustain interest and market growth. In both the United States and Europe, business models such as VR hardware, both high-end and mobile-enabled devices, are experiencing rapid growth. Several VR content creation companies are emerging in the market, using Oculus, Sony, and other corporate VR devices for testing and development. Companies like Google, Samsung, Sony, and Microsoft are strategizing their devices for VR compatibility, which is expected to grow over the next 5 years.

VR technology is expected to disrupt the gaming and media industries, as well as make significant inroads into the consumer market as technology improves and prices fall. Getting more people to try VR technology and understand its potential remains a challenge but the emergence of low-cost mobile VR solutions will likely attract new users. Furthermore, expecting consumers to wear cumbersome head-mounted devices will be a limiting factor for the growth of VR headset sales, necessitating hardware innovation in this market.

18.1.6.2.1 Gaming and Entertainment

- Integrating and improvising social aspect in gaming: VR solutions have the potential to create a social experience in the gaming industry like never before. The virtualized elements and environment that the user sees while wearing the headset can not only aid in communication with other virtual world players, but with advancements in haptics technology (enabler of sense of touch), the dynamics of team play will be revolutionized. When compared to TV-screen-based gaming, this provides the gaming industry and its users with a greater number of tools. It will instill "asynchronous gameplay," in which different users have different types of information and must combine them to solve a problem in front of them.
- Revolutionize the user interface: With VR gaming taking off in the market, the industry will see the elimination of all unnecessary mouse/keyboard interfaces for control; VR makes the user feel as if they are inhabiting a different world, and completely works on haptic "button" control or hand-held motion controllers; camera viewpoint field of view of the user and voice commands will drive the majority of the user control.

18.1.6.2.2 Retail

In the retail industry, VR technology has enormous potential. Companies such as IKEA and Dwell use VR to immerse customers and readers in an interactive and highly personalized furniture shopping experience.

Here are a few examples of opportunities where retail needs and VR offerings intersect:

- The traditional method of purchasing furniture is to see and inspect it in person. Users can view objects in a virtual environment, customize their properties, and even see how they would appear in different environments using VR.
- Launching a virtual store: The VR app places the user in the center of a 360 degree environment, giving them a realistic sense of the space. The shopping experience becomes more realistic and tangible when immersed in this environment, ultimately assisting the user in evaluating a purchase. This could be the case of a futuristic shopping experience in which users can evaluate and shop for products from the comfort of their own home using a VR headset and have them delivered.
- Some retail stores, such as IKEA, may not be in a nearby neighborhood. VR transports people to inaccessible locations and saves time.
- Customization potential: In-store VR cataloguing experiences can aid in product viewing in detail and provide a great deal of customization. Complicated actions, such as selecting and customizing objects, are dependent on the available applications and hardware. Systems with intricate controllers, such as the HTC Vive and Rift, make it simple to interact with complex menus integrated into the environment. Users of Magix Home, for example, can manipulate furniture using task-specific controls that directly mimic real-world movement. Changing the color of a chair is accomplished with simple gestures that feel like a layer of functionality added to the user's hands.
- A location marker indicates areas within the virtual space to which you can teleport. Gaze-based interactions (using one's head and eye movement to aim) are used to control the reticle position, which tracks the user's eye movement. Hold the reticle over the location marker and wait for it to time out, or click the action button to move locations within a virtual environment immediately. When positional tracking technology becomes more widely available, simplified methods such as teleporting will be a viable and accessible option for exploring virtual worlds.

18.1.6.2.3 Marketing and Media Content

Several brands are embracing VR as a content marketing tool. With tech titans investing heavily in hardware they are widely adopted at both the business and consumer levels. Consumer demand for content on such platforms will skyrocket, making VR yet another channel for brands to reach out to their target customers. Let's look at a few examples of current VR-based brand campaigns and how they work:

- In 2016, official car of the Wimbledon Championships by Jaguar, the brand created a VR experience that allowed fans to "fly" into the center court and get a bird's-eye view of British Champion Andy Murray in action. At this year's Masters of Marketing 2016, this campaign received the Steve Wozniak Award for Tech Excellence.
- Volvo created virtual experience provided consumers with a cockpit view of the vehicle and the ability to take it for a virtual test drive. This virtual showcase showcased the car's features in an unprecedented way, resulting in the car's first run of orders being sold out in 2 days.
- Nat Geo has collaborated with Felix & Paul Studios and Oculus and provided a real-time life experience for their 100-year anniversary of National Park service.

2015 was the first year that an airline offered a virtual reality experience. Qantas has launched a pilot program to provide its customers with in-flight entertainment via Samsung Gear VR, which will display virtual 3D destinations, new Qantas products, and in-flight movies.

18.1.6.2.4 Health Care

The health industry is investigating VR for solutions to a variety of problems, as well as how the technology can improve a variety of medical treatment methods.

VR provides:

- Physicians: The ability to assess injuries
- Medical students: The opportunity to learn medical procedures firsthand.
- Patients: A method to hasten their recovery in novel ways.

18.1.6.3 CHALLENGES

18.1.6.3.1 Communication

The terminology used in AR and VR is frequently confused and misunderstood. For example, while AR and VR are not the same and share only a few characteristics, the industry generally lumps the two together.

18.1.6.3.2 Technical

- A lack of integration with existing tools makes scaling development difficult.
- Hardware product quality, resolution, and usability issues.
- Transition issues from existing mobile platforms to head mounted and other display mediums.
- Connectivity issues.

18.1.6.3.3 Social Challenges

Wearing an AR headset in public is not advised at this time due to the privacy implications of a head-mounted camera facing them. However, the use of such headsets in workplace scenarios allows the technology implications to avoid such social consequences, and AR technology can help improve collaborative synergies between various teams. The future of AR in the workplace appears bright—a new tool that augments workplace computing systems and replaces the use of tablets and smartphones. The theme that keeps coming up in the development of future AR headsets is changing the way future workplaces get work done, driving new ways of creating, discussing, and demonstrating ideas.

Currently, the most significant barriers to widespread adoption of AR in organizations are a lack of ROI, security concerns, insufficient budget allocation for these new technologies, and a lack of skills/knowledge for development and implementation.

18.1.6.3.4 *Technology-Based Barriers*

- Computing power: Because AR and VR technologies are still in their infancy, the main barriers are a lack of computing power to render the graphics of the created virtual environment and a lack of uniform cross-platform technical standards. Low levels of computing power (unless someone buys a high-end system to accompany the headset, which proves to be very expensive for an end-consumer with no definite use case currently for that cost) stymies market adoption on a larger scale.

- AR Hardware: There are currently no AR headsets available for purchase by consumers. HoloLens and MetaVision have both released developer versions, but have yet to make the leap to mass market release. Furthermore, AR headsets are now very expensive, making them an unappealing investment for an end user looking for gaming/entertainment purposes. Furthermore, the current device design is not sleek enough for comfortable end-user use, and there is still a long way to go in terms of achieving a streamlined design.
- Smartphone hardware development: Currently, 80% of smart-phones in the market lack AR-capable hardware (processors, phone cameras). The mobile devices do not have room mapping or depth sensing technology. With Apple and Google releasing high-end phones with these features, it is reasonable to expect that other smartphone manufacturers will follow suit in order to enable this hardware improvement in their future releases.
- Not-so-impressive content delivery: Watching a game in VR (football or basketball) has not satisfied end users, who believe that the sporting event cast in VR is nothing more than a TV broadcast stuffed into the headset. Consumers were dissatisfied with MLB games livestreamed by Intel, which had issues with both streaming resolution and viewpoints offered.
- VR pricing: The price of a VR headset does not justify an end user's use case for gaming or consuming VR content currently available in the market.
- Connectivity: VR and AR technologies, from collaborative enterprise to consumer entertainment, are already requiring more hardware development than ever before. However, the speed of data communication is another factor which will enhance flawless communication.
- Security: A big issue comes when data security is a consideration like the confidentiality of data, integrity of software, and availability issues.

KEYWORDS

- **augmented reality**
- **virtual reality**
- **retailing**
- **marketing**
- **experience**
- **interactivity**

REFERENCES

Bulearca, M.; Tamarjan, D. Augmented Reality: A Sustainable Marketing Tool? *Glob. Bus. Manag. Res. Int. J.* **2010,** *2*(2/3), 237–252.

Craig, A. *Understanding Augmented Reality*; Morgan Kaufmann: Amsterdam, 2013.

Hall, M.D. How to optimize your Google Ads conversion journey. Smart Insights. 21 Dec, 2021. https://www.smartinsights.com/paid-search-marketing-ppc/paid-search-strategy/how-to-optimize-your-google-ads-conversion-journey/

Huang, T.; Hsu Liu, F. Formation of Augmented-Reality Interactive Technology's Persuasive Effects from the Perspective of Experiential Value. *Internet Res.* **2014,** *24*(1), 82–109.

Huang, T.; Liao, S. A Model of Acceptance of Augmented-Reality Interactive Technology: The Moderating Role of Cognitive Innovativeness. *Electron. Commer. Res.* **2014,** No pagination.

Kipper, G.; Rampolla, J. *Augmented Reality*; Syngress: Waltham, MA, 2012.

Lysonski, S.; Durvasula, S. Consumer Decision Making Styles in Retailing: Evolution of Mindsets and Psychological Impacts. *J. Consumer Market.* **2013,** *30*(1), 75–87.

Olsson, T.; Lagerstam, E.; Kärkkäinen, T.; Väänänen-Vainio-Mattila, K. Expected User Experience of Mobile Augmented Reality Services: A User Study in the Context of Shopping Centres. *Pers. Ubiquitous Comput.* **2013,** *17*(2), 287–304.

Velev, D., and Zlateva, P. Analysis of v-Commerce as the New Online Sales Channel. International Journal of e-Education, e-Business, e-Management and e-Learning. Volume 9, Number 2, June 2019. http://www.ijeeee.org/vol9/483-BN039.pdf

Index

E

F

I

L

N

P

Q

R

S

T